D0206175

CRUSADE TEXTS IN TRANSLATION

About the volume:

This is a translation of the *Itinerarium Peregrinorum et Gesta Regis Ricardi*, 'The Itinerary of the pilgrims and the deeds of King Richard,' based on the edition produced in 1864 by William Stubbs as volume 1 of his *Chronicles and Memorials of the Reign of Richard I*. This chronicle is the most comprehensive and complete account of the Third Crusade, covering virtually all the events of the crusade in roughly chronological order, and adding priceless details such as descriptions of King Richard the Lionheart's personal appearance, shipping, French fashions and discussion of the international conventions of war. It is of great interest to medieval historians in general, not only historians of the crusade. The translation is accompanied by an introduction and exhaustive notes which explain the manuscript tradition and the sources of the text and which compare this chronicle with the works of other contemporary writers on the crusade, Christian and Muslim.

The translation has been produced specifically for university students taking courses on the Crusades, but it will appeal to anyone with an interest in the Third Crusade and the history of the Middle Ages.

About the author:

Helen Nicholson is Lecturer in Medieval History at the University of Wales, Cardiff, and writes on the history of the Military Orders in the Middle East and Europe.

Chronicle of the Third Crusade

Crusade Texts in Translation

Editorial Board

Titles in this series include:

The Conquest of Jerusalem
and the Third Crusade
Sources in Translation
Peter Edbury

The Song of the Cathar Wars
A History of the Albigensian Crusade
Janet Shirley

Chronicle of the Third Crusade

A Translation of the

Itinerarium Peregrinorum et Gesta Regis Ricardi

HELEN J. NICHOLSON

Ashgate

Published by
Ashgate Publishing Ltd.
Gower House
Croft Road
Aldershot
Hants GU11 3HR
England

Ashgate Publishing Company
Old Post Road
Brookfield
Vermont 05036
USA

ISBN 1 85928 154 0

British Library Cataloguing–in–Publication Data
Nicholson, Helen
Chronicle of the Third Crusade: A Translation of the Itinerarium peregrinorum et gesta Regis Ricardi
1. Crusades—Third, 1189-1192. I. Title.
940.1'8

US Library of Congress Cataloging–in–Publication Data
Ricardus, Canonicus Sanctae Trinitatis Londoniensis.
[Itinerarium peregrinorum et gesta Regis Ricardi. English]
Chronicle of the Third Crusade: A Translation of the Itinerarium peregrinorum et gesta Regis Ricardi / Helen J. Nicholson.
p. cm. Includes bibliographical references and index.
Translated from the version of the chronicle published by William Stubbs in 1864 as v. 1 of Chronicles and memorials of the reign of Richard I.
1. Crusades—Third, 1189-1192. I. Nicholson, Helen J. II. Stubbs, William, 1825-1901. III. Title.
D151.R52713 1997 97-19537
956'.014--dc21 CIP

Camera ready copy by N²productions
Printed and bound in Great Britain by Galliard (Printers) Ltd

Crusade Texts in Translation 3

Contents

Foreword

This is a translation of the *Itinerarium Peregrinorum et Gesta Regis Ricardi*, one of the most controversial chronicles of the Third Crusade. Despite its high level of accuracy and the wealth of detail it contains, historians have been cautious in using it; partly because of disputes over its authorship and dating, and partly because the chronicle is very long and its Latin is sometimes difficult. No complete translation has been produced since 1848, and this is now completely outdated in scholarship and language as well as being difficult to find.

I have translated the version of the chronicle published by William Stubbs in 1864 as volume 1 of his *Chronicles and Memorials of the Reign of Richard I*, because this gives the most comprehensive and detailed account of events. Stubbs' edition is also fairly widely available. There is no recent edition of the long version of the chronicle, and at present there seems to be no academic demand for one.

Everyone who studies the *Itinerarium Peregrinorum* owes an enormous debt to Hans Mayer for his ground-breaking edition of the oldest version of the chronicle, published in 1962 as *Das Itinerarium Peregrinorum: eine zeitgenössische englishe Chronik zum dritten Kreuzzug in ursprünglicher Gestalt.* The introduction and notes to this translation make frequent reference to his edition.

Many other scholars have lent their support to this translation, although I alone take responsibility for the final result. In particular, Malcolm Barber, Norman Housley and Jonathan Riley-Smith gave their encouragement and advice; John Ilsley gave me useful advice on medieval shipping; Benjamin Kedar supplied me with a copy of the unpublished chronicle of Guy of Bazoches; Bill Zajac drew my attention to the *Itinerarium*'s comments on the conventions of warfare. John France and Denys Pringle gave assistance with some difficult points. Particular thanks are due to my colleague Peter Edbury, for numerous discussions of problems and for reading the translation in the later stages and saving me from many errors. My greatest debt is to my husband, who not only checked the text but also prepared text and maps for the publisher.

Abbreviations

CFMA	Classiques français du moyen âge (1912–present), Paris: Champion.
E-B	*Chronique d'Ernoul et de Bernard le Trésorier* (1871), ed. L. de Mas Latrie, SHF, Paris: Jules Renouard.
EFMI	*Epistola de Morte Friderici Imperatoris,* in Chroust, A. (1928), *Quellen zur Geschichte des Kreuzzugs Kaiser Friedrichs I. Monumenta Germaniae Historica: Scriptores Rerum Germanicarum* nova series 5, Berlin: Weidmannsche Verlagsbuchhandlung.
HGM	*L'Histoire de Guillaume de Maréchal* (1891–1901), ed. P. Meyer, SHF, Paris: Librarie Renouard.
LFWT	*Das lateinische Fortsetzung Wilhelms von Tyrus* (1934), ed. M. Salloch, Leipzig: Kommission-Verlag Hermann Eichblatt ('the Latin Continuation of William of Tyre').
RHC	*Recueil des Historiens des Croisades* (1841–1906), Academie des Inscriptions et des Belles-Lettres, 16 vols., Paris: Imprimerie Nationale.
RHC Occ	*Recueil des Historiens des Croisades: Historiens Occidentaux* (1841–95), 5 vols.
RHC Or	*Recueil des Historiens des Croisades: Historiens Orientaux* (1872–1906), 5 vols.
RS	Rolls Series. Rerum Britannicarum Medii Aevi Scriptores (1858–96) 251 vols., London.
SHF	Société de l'histoire de France.

List of Maps

Introduction

The *Itinerarium Peregrinorum* and the Third Crusade.

The Third Crusade of 1187–92 was both a pilgrimage and a holy war. Those who 'took the cross', by sewing a cross on to their clothing, had made a solemn religious vow to go on a pilgrimage to the Holy Sepulchre in Jerusalem, supposedly the site of Christ's tomb which had been found empty on the first Easter morning. But it was understood that, unlike traditional pilgrims, they also formed an army that was fighting to recover the territory of Christ from the hands of the Muslims.

Until 1187 part of Syria and Palestine was controlled by the descendants of those European Christians who had settled there after the capture of Antioch and Jerusalem during the First Crusade, 1095–99. The largest 'Crusader State' was the kingdom of Jerusalem, which was then ruled by Queen Sybil, the daughter of King Amalric, and her husband, Guy de Lusignan, a nobleman from Poitou in France.

The *Itinerarium* opens as Saladin, sultan of Egypt and Damascus, launches an attack on the kingdom of Jerusalem. The military orders of the Temple and Hospital, who are responsible for defending the kingdom, are massacred; the king and the True Cross, the sacred talisman of the kingdom, are captured; and the holy city of Jerusalem falls to Saladin's forces. The chronicler then tells how European Christians set out from the West to recover the Holy Places. After a long siege, the important port of Acre is recaptured from the Muslims. Under King Richard 'the Lionheart' of England, the crusading army marches south to Jaffa and then moves inland to attack Jerusalem. However, due to quarrels in the crusading army and doubts over whether the city can be held after it has been recaptured, they do not besiege the city, and in the end King Richard makes a truce with Saladin and sails home to curb his ambitious brother, Count John. The chronicle ends on a note of sadness, mixed with praise for the courage and longsuffering of the crusaders and the courage of the hero, King Richard.

This is not the only account of the Third Crusade.[1] The most important Muslim histories of the period are by two of Saladin's officials, his secretary 'Imād al-Dīn al-Işfahānī and Bahā' al-Dīn ibn Shaddād, 'the Qāḍī'. Their accounts are as strongly prejudiced in favour of Saladin as the author of the *Itinerarium* is towards King Richard. Yet they usually endorse the *Itinerarium*'s account of events, as the reader will see from the notes to the translation. The other leading source, Ibn al-Athīr, was much more critical of Saladin; but most of what he wrote on the Third Crusade was based on the work of Bahā' al-Dīn and 'Imād al-Dīn.

In western Europe, the only source written from the point of view of the French king was that by Rigord, in his panegyric-cum-biography of King Philip II. The German sources are far more extensive, concentrating on the abortive expedition of Emperor Frederick I. A number were published in 1928 by A. Chroust as *Quellen zur Geschichte des Kreuzzuges Kaisar Friedrichs I*, and of these the best known is the *Historia de Expeditione Friderici Imperatoris*, which is anonymous but traditionally attributed to a certain Ansbert.

The English sources are extensive, but uneven. Roger of Howden, a royal clerk, accompanied King Richard's fleet to the Holy Land, but then returned in August 1191 with King Philip of France. His first work, the *Gesta*, has a rather confused account of the events of 1187; by the time he came to compose his *Chronica* he had tidied this up.[2] His writings are most valuable for his account of King Richard's voyage to the Holy Land, and his dating where the *Itinerarium* has no dates. Richard of Devizes, a monk at St Swithin's, Winchester, seems to have drawn on an eyewitness who had accompanied the crusade as far as Sicily and then returned with Queen Eleanor and the archbishop of Rouen. His account of the rest of the events of the crusade has large gaps, but he does provide details of Richard's arrival at Acre and the fall of the city in summer 1191 and the negotiations of August and September 1192. Ralph of Diceto, dean of London, did not go on crusade but his chaplain did and sent him information; Ralph also incorporated information from appeals for help sent to the West from the Holy Land. Likewise, Ralph of Coggeshall, a monk of Essex, tells us that he obtained information about the later events of the crusade from Hugh de Neville, and on King Richard's journey home from Anselm, the king's chaplain. William of Newburgh, an Augustinian canon of Yorkshire, seems to have had access to better

1. The works which follow are in the Bibliography under 'Primary sources'.
2. See Gillingham, J. (1982), 'Roger of Howden on Crusade'.

information on the events of 1187 than his compatriots, as his account is clear and chronological. Hans Mayer suggested that he had used the 'Latin Continuation of William of Tyre'.[3]

The 'Latin Continuation' of Archbishop William of Tyre's famous chronicle of the Holy Land was composed in England around 1220 according to its editor, Marianne Salloch, but she believed that it was based on an earlier chronicle written in England by 1194, and that it was used by the original writer of the *Itinerarium*. Mayer disagreed: he believed that the writer of the 'Latin Continuation' used the *Itinerarium*.[4] The problem was also discussed by Hannes Möhring, who concluded that the author of the 'Continuation' was a compiler who drew on the *Itinerarium*.[5] The problem is compounded because the version of the 'Latin Continuation' which survives includes extensive extracts from Roger of Howden's *Chronica*, so that at some points it actually contradicts itself: for instance, in its account of the battle of Hattin (p. 70) it first states, incorrectly, that the master of the Knights Templar escaped alive from the field of battle, as in Howden's *Chronica*, and then states, correctly, that the master was captured, as in the *Itinerarium*.

The key to the problem seems to lie in a comparison of the early chapters of the *Itinerarium*, Book 1 chapters 1–16, with the beginning of the 'Latin Continuation', Book 1 and Book 2 chapters 1–10. The *Itinerarium* begins breathlessly with a grand exordium: 'In the year of the Incarnation of the Word 1187...the Lord's hand was aroused against His people.' The 'Continuation', on the other hand, begins at a more sedate pace, referring back to the work of William of Tyre. The words 'In the year of the Incarnation of the Word 1187' appear half way through the prologue, so that rather than providing a stirring beginning to an epic work they are all but lost in the narrative.

The 'Latin Continuation' is a careful, ordered and chronological account, where the events which appear in hurried disorder in the *Itinerarium*'s opening chapters are set in context and explained. In the 'Continuation', the reader is guided gently through the history of the kingdom of Jerusalem from the point where William of Tyre's chronicle broke off. In the *Itinerarium*, the reader is dropped into the thick of events with hardly any explanation of what is going on. The *Itinerarium* begins as a jumble, almost as if it were a collection of notes hastily thrown together

3. Mayer, H. (1962), *Das Itinerarium Peregrinorum*, p. 181.
4. Mayer, H. (1962), *Das Itinerarium*, pp. 151–61, referring to *Die lateinische Fortsetzung Wilhelms von Tyrus* (1934), ed. M. Salloch.
5. Möhring, H. (1982), 'Eine Chronik aus der Zeit des dritten Kreuzzugs', 162–7.

as an introduction to the siege of Acre and the Third Crusade; or as if it were a rhetorical account of Saladin's conquests such as we might find in a contemporary papal letter urging the Christians of western Europe to join the Crusade, or a newsletter from the Military Orders. It is thin on facts and heavy on dramatic effect. It is easy to imagine that a writer composing a history of the Third Crusade could have used the opening chapters of the *Itinerarium* as a source and tidied up its account to make decent, sober, informative history. It does not seem very likely that a writer would have taken the tidy account of the 'Continuation' and deconstructed it to form the dramatic early chapters of the *Itinerarium*.

For example, after mentioning Saladin in chapter 1, we would expect the writer of the *Itinerarium* to go on to describe his origins and rise to power. But instead, the writer describes the events of 1 May 1187, and then goes back to describe Saladin's origins in chapters 3 and 4. The account in chapter 5 of the disputes in the kingdom of Jerusalem before Saladin's invasion would be better placed straight after the introduction of chapter 1, or at least before the battle of 1 May 1187. Instead they are jammed in between Saladin's rise to power and his invasion of Palestine, far too briefly to give the reader any clear understanding of what was going on. The 'Continuation', on the other hand, arranges events in a clear and logical order. The most obvious explanation seems to be that the *Itinerarium* came first and the 'Continuation' is based on it.

Other European works relating to the Third Crusade include accounts of the voyages of northern European crusading expeditions to the East, such as the *Narratio Itineris Navalis ad Terram Sanctam*, published by A. Chroust.

A number of sources originated in the Holy Land. The *Libellus de Expugnatione Terrae Sanctae per Saladinum* purports to have been written by a warrior who was actually involved in the defence of Jerusalem in October 1187. It gives a very detailed account of the events of 1187; it was later continued by a western European author using Book 1 of the long version of the *Itinerarium*. The French continuations of William of Tyre's history of the Holy Land (*Eracles*) start where his history ended in 1185 and seem to give an account of the events of the crusade from the point of view of the Palestinian nobility. The problem with these continuations is, as Peter Edbury has recently shown, that they appear to have been written a long time after the crusade. The only part of *Eracles* which could be based on a contemporary work is the narrative for 1187. Some manuscripts of the version of the French continuations known as 'the Chronicle of Ernoul and Bernard the Treasurer' (E-B) claim that the account of the events of 1187 was written by a certain Ernoul, then squire of the Palestinian noble Balian of Ibelin.

A Latin poem of the events of 1187–90 also survives, presumably written by a crusading priest. This was published by Hans Prutz in 1881 as 'Ein zeitgenössisches Gedicht auf die Belagerung Accons', but because it is in verse historians have found it difficult to use. Another Latin poem recounting events at the siege of Acre was composed by a certain 'Monachus', a Florentine and bishop of Acre in the early thirteenth century.[6] He seems to have accompanied the contingent of the bishop of Verona (lines 37–48), who arrived at the siege of Acre in October 1189 (see Book 1 chapter 31, below). In addition, a trouvère named Ambroise composed a verse chronicle in Norman-French, which is discussed below.

Some charter and letter evidence survives, published in summary form by R. Röhricht, in *Regesta regni Hierosolymitani*, pp. 175–89. A selection of these letters were translated by Peter Edbury as part of his *The Conquest of Jerusalem* (Scolar Press, 1996).

Manuscripts of the *Itinerarium*.

There are basically four different versions of the text surviving. When William Stubbs produced his edition of the *Itinerarium Peregrinorum et Gesta Regis Ricardi* for the Rolls Series in 1864 he labelled the four manuscripts he used 'A', 'B', 'C', and 'G'.[7] When Hans Mayer produced a new critical edition of the *Itinerarium Peregrinorum* in 1962, he listed fifteen known manuscripts, twelve of which survive, and he grouped them according to Stubbs' system.[8] The G group is the largest, with eight manuscripts identified. There are four known manuscripts of the A group and two of the B. C, the text which Stubbs used as his base manuscript, is unique. As Stubbs and Mayer have listed and described these manuscripts adequately for scholarly purposes, I will not give further details here.

6. Ed. Stubbs, W. (1870), in vol. 3 of Roger of Howden's *Chronica*, pp. cvi–cxxxvi. One Walter of Florence was bishop of Acre between 1208 and 1213: Hamilton, B. (1980), *The Latin Church*, p. 395. Possibly this is the author.
7. Stubbs, W. (1864), pp. lxxi–ii.
8. Mayer, H. (1962), pp. 7–45.

The authorship of the *Itinerarium Peregrinorum*.

Who wrote the *Itinerarium*, and when?

This question has proved difficult to answer; for, as modern scholarship has shown, the *Itinerarium* as published by Stubbs is in fact a compilation.

In the translation of the text published by H. Bohn in 1848 the chronicle was attributed to Geoffrey of Vinsauf, who wrote a book on poetry dedicated to Pope Innocent III (1198–1216).[9] One manuscript names a 'Guido Adduanensis'.[10] The writer who continued the *Libellus* in the early 1220s used the *Itinerarium* and wrote that it had been translated out of French by the prior of Holy Trinity in London.[11] In his edition of the text William Stubbs concluded that the whole chronicle was an original work composed in Latin by Richard de Templo, prior of Holy Trinity in London.[12] Yet problems remained. Book 1 seemed to have circulated separately from the rest: Gerald of Wales and William of Newburgh seem to have known Book 1 but not the rest of the chronicle, and the manuscript published by Bongars in the *Gesta Dei per Francos* in 1611 contained only part of Book 1. In 1897 Gaston Paris published the *Estoire de Guerre Sainte*, a French verse chronicle on the Third Crusade by one Ambroise, who claimed to be an eyewitness of the crusade. Books 2 to 6 of Stubbs' edition of the *Itinerarium* were so similar to Ambroise's work that Paris concluded that the *Itinerarium* was nothing more than a translation from Ambroise's work.

In 1962 Hans Mayer published an edition of what he argued was the original version of the *Itinerarium*. He demonstrated convincingly that the *Itinerarium* as published by William Stubbs was a compilation of a number of works on the Third Crusade. Mayer showed that Bongars' manuscript, which Stubbs had labelled 'G' and which contained only part of Book 1, was actually close to the original text. He called this 'IP1'.[13] He went on to argue that this text was later used by a second writer/compiler, who added to it a Latin translation of Ambroise's *Estoire de Guerre Sainte*. This writer also added additional material, some of which

9. Bohn, H. (1848), *Chronicles of the Crusades*, pp. iii–v.
10. Stubbs, W. (1864), pp. xli–ii.
11. *Libellus*, p. 257.
12. Stubbs, W. (1864), p. lxxix.
13. Möhring (1982) calls it 'Historia Hierosolymitana' or HH, but I have used Mayer's name for this part of the text as it is better known to English-speaking readers.

was taken from the work of Ralph of Diceto, some from Roger of Howden, and some of which has no identified source. This long version of the *Itinerarium* Mayer labelled 'IP2'. It is represented by Stubbs' manuscript groups A, B and C,[14] although in Book 1 A sometimes follows IP1 rather than IP2. The writer of C added additional material in the course of the chronicle to improve the continuity of the text and added an appendix on the character of King Richard I and his domestic reforms. Stubbs used manuscript C as his base text, and, while recognising its composite nature, it is the version translated here.

The author of IP2 is generally accepted to have been Richard de Templo, prior of the Augustinian priory of Holy Trinity in London from 16 July 1222 to 1248 or 1250. The reasons behind this deduction have been discussed by both Stubbs (pp. xl-lxix) and Mayer (pp. 89-106) and I will not repeat them here.

Stubbs (pp. xlvii-iii) and Mayer (pp. 94-6) argued that Richard was clearly an ex-Templar who had transferred to the Augustinian order. This may be so, and it may be additional evidence that he had been present on the Third Crusade (see below). However, he shows no special knowledge of the Templars, and does not correct IP1's errors on the date of the release of Master Gerard de Ridefort from captivity (see below), nor does he point out that Robert de Sabloel became master of the Temple (see Bk. 2 ch. 18, and note). I am therefore inclined to think that 'de Templo' was no more than a family surname, although we may only speculate as to its origins.

Other problems remain:
Who wrote IP1?
When was IP1 written?
When did Richard de Templo write?
Where did the additional unique material in IP2 come from?

Who wrote IP1?

Mayer suggested that the original *Itinerarium*, IP1, was written by an English Templar chaplain in Tyre. This conjecture reestablished the *Itinerarium* as a primary source for the early stages of the Third Crusade, but aroused considerable controversy among historians. The arguments have been summarised and the theory thoroughly refuted by

14. Mayer, H. (1962), *Das Itinerarium*, pp. 1-44.

Hannes Möhring.[15] However, Möhring's work remains little known to English-speaking readers.

The main bases for Mayer's theory were: (a) there is favourable material on the Templars in Book 1 chapters 2, 5 and 29; (b) the writer seems well-informed on events in the Holy Land; (c) the writer makes special mention of King Henry II of England in chapter 12.

However, (a) is not sufficient evidence of Templar authorship. Firstly, the writer's knowledge of the Templars is very limited. It is restricted to three martyrdoms. This material could have come from Templar appeals for aid sent to the West which have not survived; or, if the writer was present at the siege of Acre, he could have heard it from the Templars there.

Secondly, the writer does not mention the Templars when we would expect them to be mentioned. He says nothing about the Templars' involvement in the defence of Tyre in the winter of 1187-88, although this was particularly emphasised by Thierry, grand commander of the Temple, in his letter to Henry II of England.[16] He also omits to mention their successful defence of their tower at Tortosa in early summer 1188, when Saladin was forced to withdraw;[17] and he omits their long defence of their castle of Ṣafad - instead he tells us about the defence of the lord of Toron's castles![18]

Thirdly, he makes a significant error about the Templars, dating the release of their master, Brother Gerard de Ridefort, to May 1189.[19] In fact he was released in May 1188! It would be incredible if a Templar did not know the correct date of the master's release.

Finally, other authors, who were definitely not Templars, were actually more complimentary about the Templars than the *Itinerarium*. The *Libellus* and the Latin poem about the siege of Acre published by Hans Prutz say a great deal more in praise of the order than the *Itinerarium* does.

As for (b), the writer is not particularly well-informed about events in the Holy Land - his knowledge of events in 1187 is rather sparse, compared with *Eracles* or with the *Libellus*. If he were an eyewitness, we would expect far more detail. However, he does know a good deal about the siege of Acre.

---

15. Möhring, H. (1982), pp. 149-62.
16. *Conquest of Jerusalem* (1996), pp. 165-6.
17. See note 51 on Book 1 ch. 13, p. 43 below.
18. See note 55 on Book 1 ch. 15, p. 45 below.
19. See note 56 on Book 1 ch. 15, p. 45 below.

Point (c) is valid. The writer of IP1 does make a point of mentioning Henry II of England, and later of mentioning the archdeacon of Colchester, although he did not know his name (chapter 40).[20] The book ended with the death of the archbishop of Canterbury, which may reflect the writer's national interests.

The most likely solution is that IP1 was written by a crusader, possibly an Englishman.

When was IP1 written?

This is a knotty problem. Mayer decided that IP1 was begun after 1 August 1191 and completed before the final treaty which ended the crusade on 2 September 1192. The writer knew that the siege of Acre continued for two years;[21] but he did not know that the crusade was finally a failure.

However, the problem is more complex than this. Why does IP1 end with the death of the archbishop of Canterbury, in November 1190 - and not in the summer of 1191, or later? Why does the writer tell us during his account of Emperor Frederick's crusade that the duke of Swabia still has an eternal mark of honour in compensation for losing his teeth during a battle against the Turks,[22] when in fact the duke died in January 1191? Why is the writer so favourable towards the duke of Swabia during his account of the emperor's crusade, but so hostile to him later in the chronicle?[23]

In fact, using the chapter numbers of Stubbs' edition (as IP1 had no chapters - these were inserted by IP2) one would almost think that the writer of chapters 25 onwards had never read chapters 18 to 24; while chapters 2 to 17 are a rather sparse and confused account of the events of May 1187-May 1189 which sit oddly beside the ordered detail of the later chapters.

Mayer considered that the whole of IP1 was written in the same style, although he admitted that chapters 18-24 had been based on a German source.[24] In the course of translation I found variations in style which divide IP1 into three rough sections. These would be Book 1, chapters 1-17; chapters 18-24; chapters 25 to the end. Chapter 32 seems to fit bet-

20. See Book 1 ch. 40, p. 96 below.
21. See Book 1 ch. 26, p. 70 below.
22. See Book 1 ch. 23, pp. 61-2 below.
23. For example, Book 1 chs. 22, 23, 24; cf. chs. 44, 45.
24. Mayer, H. (1962), pp. 65-6, 71, 172-9.

ter with the style of the earlier chapters than the later ones, and may be an interpolation. The internal contradictions in the text and changes in style suggest that these three parts were originally written by at least three different people.

I am inclined to conclude that the writer of IP1 may well have been writing in the crusader army between 1 August 1191 and 2 September 1192, but he was a compiler rather than a wholly original author. He put together a rough account of events of 1187–89 from what oral information and reports he could glean from those present in the crusading army, including the stories of the deaths of two Templar martyrs, as reported by the Templars. He acquired a written account of the German crusade which he inserted into his chronicle. Thirdly, he finished off with a written account of the siege of Acre. This was largely eyewitness and written by a crusader. Possibly this crusader arrived in the Holy Land with the fleet from the north in early September 1189. In any case, the account broke off in November 1190.

The fact that this account shows an interest in the archbishop of Canterbury may mean that its writer was English. As the final version of IP1 added information about the money King Henry II of England had sent to the Holy Land, perhaps the compiler of IP1 was also English. This hints at the possibility that there was a connection between them. Perhaps the compiler of IP1 was the same as the original author of the third section of IP1, who started out writing an account of the siege but broke off when all seemed lost in the winter of 1190–91, and later went back and added material on 1187–89 and the Emperor Frederick's crusade.

In any case, IP1 was a successful work which circulated widely, as five manuscripts or manuscript fragments survive and another three are known to have existed. It was used by the author of the 'Latin continuation of William of Tyre' and by the compiler of IP2.

When did Richard de Templo write?

The history of a crusade was most likely to be written either while it was in progress, in its immediate aftermath or in preparation for the next one, to encourage recruitment and remind the leaders of what went wrong last time.[25] Clearly IP2 was written some time after the Third

25. For instance, the Lyon *Eracles* seems to have reached its present form shortly before 1250, which would coincide with the first crusade of Louis IX: see *Conquest of Jerusalem*, p. 7.

Crusade was completed, as it incorporated material from many other sources. It could have been written for the Fourth Crusade, circa 1202, or the Fifth Crusade, circa 1216–20. The Fifth Crusade appears more likely, as two other chronicles of the Third Crusade were completed in the early 1220s: the Latin continuation of William of Tyre and the *Libellus*. IP2 must have been written before 1222, the assumed date of the *Libellus*, because the author of the *Libellus* used IP2.

Another clue is Richard de Templo's attitude towards of the king of France, who is depicted as a powerful political figure. In Book 2 chapter 13 we are told 'The king of France is a man of such great name, whose edict is obeyed by so many princes and so many nations'; in Book 3 chapter 21 he is described as 'the most powerful and prestigious of Christian kings'. This was not the case in 1189–91, but was becoming true by 1202 when Philip invaded Normandy, and certainly was by the end of 1216, when he had conquered Normandy, Anjou, Brittany and Poitou, taken over Artois, defeated Flanders and the emperor and invaded England. For these reasons, Mayer's suggested date of 1217–22 seems likely, although he reaches this conclusion by way of a different line of argument.[26]

Clearly, then, IP2 must represent Richard I and the Third Crusade as they were seen by the next generation rather than by contemporaries. It could even be argued that the one of the intentions of Richard de Templo in writing this chronicle could have been to bolster the prestige of the English monarchy in a period of political crisis. In 1217–22 the king of England, Henry III, was a minor; in the reign of his father John, 1199–1216, territory had been lost to the king of France and relations between the king and his barons had deteriorated into civil war and French invasion. In contrast, IP2 described a king of England who was an effective and successful military leader and who knew how to ensure the loyalty of his forces by giving gifts and consulting them on strategy. However, despite the obvious relevance of Richard de Templo's work to the English political situation in 1217–22, his version of events was not in fact much different from that of contemporaries of the Third Crusade such as Roger of Howden or Ralph of Diceto. Although his work was more distant from actual events, comparison with the contemporary Muslim sources for the Third Crusade shows that its information is just as reliable as the more contemporary European sources.

The C manuscript used by Stubbs for his edition of 1864 and trans-

26. Mayer, H. (1962), pp. 105–6.

lated here contains additional material on the reign of Richard I, which was added still later. Stubbs dated this manuscript to the late thirteenth century (p. lxxii). The information C gives on the domestic reforms during Richard's reign appears reasonable and is corroborated by Roger of Howden's *Chronica*, although it has not been directly copied word-for-word from Howden. The material on Richard's return to England was copied directly from Diceto. C's description of Richard I's character reflects the growing legend of Richard I as a idealized monarch. In this respect, C has great value in itself as a record of how Richard I was viewed in England by the late thirteenth century.

What were the sources of IP2?

When Richard de Templo came to write a complete history of the crusade, he used IP1 as the best available starting point. He also used the work of Ambroise to fill out IP1's account of the siege of Acre, and for details of the rest of the crusade. However, he seems to have had more information than Ambroise now includes.

There are two sections in Book 1 which clearly come from a different sort of source. Chapters 47 to 57 are a collection of 'amazing stories', the legends of the siege. This section is independent of the rest of the work; it has no dates and does not relate to events before or after it in the text. Chapters 66 to 77 are a series of anecdotes about the famine of the winter of 1190–91. Each anecdote ends with a few lines of poetry, blaming the marquis of Montferrat for not sending the crusaders food. Again, this section does not fit in with the rest of the account; there are no names, and no dates. Both these sections could have been derived from material which circulated independently and orally before being written down.

Ambroise includes most of the 'amazing stories', and most of the anecdotes, but not all of them. Ambroise's amazing stories are not quite the same as those in IP2. Ambroise also ends each of the famine anecdotes with a refrain – but not the same refrain as in IP2.

Historians have assumed that Richard de Templo took this material from Ambroise, but that he had a longer manuscript of Ambroise's *Estoire* than the one which has survived, and that he translated these stories and anecdotes rather loosely. While the copy of Ambroise which we have does have obvious gaps, this assumes that the copyist of Ambroise's work managed to leave out odd complete stories from these two sections in particular. It also assumes that the author of the IP2 was no more than a compiler – that he never went on crusade and all his material was obtained second hand. Yet his work indicates that he was on the crusade himself.

In Book 2, chapter 10, Richard de Templo gives a detailed itinerary for the English crusading army, which is not in Ambroise (who appears to have been with the fleet: see lines 553–5). He writes here in the first person: 'We crossed through Viaria...' As Mayer points out (p. 151) this itinerary does not appear in any other work. Why should it not have been the route our writer took as a young man going on the crusade?

If it was Richard de Templo's own route, this would explain his detailed, heartfelt descriptions of crusaders parting from their families in Book 2 chapter 7 – such descriptions are commonplace in crusader literature, but this one is particularly convincing. He notes that family and friends accompanied crusaders as far as Vézelay, and then went home (chapter 9). Ambroise does not tell us this, as he was not there. Richard de Templo's description of King Richard's arrival at Messina (chapter 13) is vivid and detailed. He can also tell us exactly what Richard was wearing when he rode to meet the emperor of Cyprus on 11 May 1191 (chapter 34). His account is full of additions to Ambroise's version of events, adding a few events, or a vivid description; a few people here, showing more mature judgement there. I have noted these differences in the notes. He also exalted the image of Richard I into a giant figure of reckless courage and prowess. John Gillingham has noted: 'This was the image of the king which he himself was at pains to cultivate...since it was politically valuable and helped to maintain the morale of his troops.'[27]

But if Richard de Templo was on the crusade himself, why did he compile a history from other people's work? Why not write his own?

He followed the normal procedure for historical writing in his day. He followed the respected authorities, IP1 and Ambroise, tidying up and adding as he felt necessary. In the same way, when Peter of Tudebrode wrote his history of the First Crusade he followed the *Gesta Francorum*, even though he had been on the crusade himself. As Peter of Tudebrode was from northern France and the author of the *Gesta* was from southern Italy, their view of events must have differed considerably. Yet a later writer was expected to follow earlier authorities.

If Richard de Templo was on the Third Crusade himself, he would have had independent access to the 'amazing stories' and anecdotes of Book 1 chapters 47–57 and 66–77. He included them as Ambroise did,

27. Gillingham, J. (1984), p. 90.

but he added some which he remembered himself; and perhaps he did not remember the rest quite as Ambroise had done. If these amazing stories and anecdotes about the famine had an oral existence prior to insertion in Ambroise's history and IP2, then we have evidence here of how the crusaders themselves saw the crusade and how they developed the account of the crusade which they would have eventually retold in Europe.

The 'amazing stories' are religious; they include a story of a brave and faithful woman; they are earthy and sometimes rather distasteful to modern readers; they are amusing. It is tempting to think that they reflect the tastes of the crusaders as a whole.

The anecdotes about the famine of winter 1190–91 have one overriding purpose; to denounce the marquis of Montferrat for breaking his word to the besiegers. We probably have here the remains of a rude song of the sort Duke Hugh of Burgundy and King Richard I sang about each other (Book 6 chapter 8) or the sort the legendary hero Roland was determined would never be sung about him.[28]

Ambroise's own sources have not received much attention. As he claims repeatedly to be an eyewitness, he has been regarded as his own source. However, it is worth noting that the earl of Leicester receives particular attention; three of his great deeds of prowess are recounted (here Book 4 chapters 30 and 33, and Book 5 chapter 52). Probably either Ambroise, or his source, was close to the earl of Leicester and had an interest in extolling his deeds.

The value of IP2.

IP2 is a valuable historical source even though much of it is taken from other sources. Comparing it to other sources, we can see how the early thirteenth-century chronicler worked: combining material from various sources; translating word-for-word, but sometimes rather carelessly; adding his own analysis and inserting his own memories and experience as appropriate.

When IP2 is compared to Ambroise, the difference in approach between the chronicler writing in Latin and the poet composing in the vernacular becomes very marked. Ambroise wrote in a brisk, simple style with a relatively small vocabulary, suitable for recitation. IP2 is

28. *La chanson de Roland*, lines 1014, 1466, 1517.

written in a complex, rhetorical style using a wide vocabulary, and never uses one word where ten will do.[29] This work was clearly intended for a sophisticated audience, even for private reading. The authors of IP1 and IP2 were anxious to impress the reader with their classical knowledge - they frequently quote familiar lines from classical authors such as Horace and Virgil. IP1 assures us that the siege of Acre was as significant as the siege of Troy. IP2 shows off its author's skills as a poet. Both chroniclers were fond of alliteration. Their prologue demonstrates that they were writing for posterity.

Yet the work of the poet composing an historical epic was not so very different from the work of the chroniclers writing in the classical historical tradition. Ambroise pauses in the middle of his work to refer to the wars of Alexander the Great and the siege of Troy and assures us that the siege of Acre was more significant than these wars were. He was also writing for posterity, to immortalize the names of the heroes of the crusade. IP1 and IP2 take at least as much pleasure in the bloody details of battle as any epic poet would, and IP2 frequently reminds us that Richard I was a more heroic figure than the epic hero Roland. In fact, although the *Itinerarium* and Ambroise's *Estoire* sprang from different literary traditions, their approach to their subject was remarkably similar, and the same educated nobility who enjoyed hearing the *Itinerarium* read to them would also have enjoyed hearing Ambroise's work recited.

The translation.

As this translation has been prepared for student use I have tried to make it as accessible as possible, avoiding unnecessary technical terms and archaic language. Where there is no comparable modern term I have explained the word in the notes. My aim has been to produce readable modern English while staying close to the original Latin, in order to retain as much of the authors' own work as possible. I have translated word-for-word and tried to avoid paraphrasing and summarising, although those familiar with medieval Latin will know that sometimes paraphrasing is unavoidable.

In preparing this translation I have referred to the previous translations of the *Itinerarium*. The only previous full translation is the translation of manuscript A published by H. Bohn in 1848. Translations of selected

29. This was also the complaint of T. Archer (1889, 1978), p. 352.

parts of the text have been published by T. Archer (1889), J. Brundage (1962) and E. Hallam (1989). These are listed in the Bibliography by translator's name, under Primary Sources. If I have avoided their errors, no doubt I have made some more of my own! I have also compared the text to Gaston Paris' edition of Ambroise's *Estoire*, which has helped to clarify various points where the *Itinerarium* is unclear.

I have also included with the translation notes giving background information, correcting the occasional errors in the *Itinerarium*, and giving cross references to other evidence.

In translating a medieval chronicle the translator has to choose between substituting modern versions and spellings of personal names and place names for the medieval ones, or using the original ones and giving the modern versions separately. This is a particular problem in crusade sources, as the official versions of place names in the Middle East have changed frequently, and the names used by crusade historians are not necessarily those which appear on the map. I have tried to compromise by using the modern name when it is close to the medieval name (Acre, Jerusalem, Ascalon, Beirut) and using the medieval name where it is different from the modern one (Cayphas for Haifa, Joppa for Tel-Aviv Yafo, Babylonia for Egypt) with the modern name in square brackets. I hope that this will give the reader an appreciation of the crusaders' use of place names in the Holy Land. European place names have been translated into their modern form, except where I could not identify them.

For Muslim personal names I have used the *Itinerarium*'s version of the name or the form of the name most familiar to modern English-speaking readers, adding in square brackets the full, transliterated version of the name as given by Lyons and Jackson (1982). For European personal names I have used the modern European spelling where it is close to the version given by the *Itinerarium* and by Ambroise (such as Gerard, Guy, Geoffrey), but used their spelling where there is no consistent modern European spelling or where they made an error, as their errors are in themselves valuable historical evidence (such as Reinfrid for Humfrey of Toron, or Henry for Hugh of Burgundy). The correct name is added in square brackets.

Biblical and classical quotations are those identified by Stubbs in his edition of 1864. I have usually used the Revised English Bible for the biblical translations, but sometimes use a different version or a direct translation where this makes better sense in the context. Where Stubbs identified a line of our authors' own poetry, I have put this in inverted commas. Classical translations have been checked to the editions of the works published in the Loeb Classical Library, as this is the most accessible version of the text, although I have not usually followed the Loeb translation.

The maps.

The place names on the map are given in the form used in the text or, if they do not appear in the text, the footnotes. The only exception is Kerak, which the *Itinerarium* confuses with Crac de Montréal. Here the modern form of the name is used to prevent confusion.

Chronicle of the Third Crusade

The *Itinerarium Peregrinorum et Gesta Regis Ricardi*

Prologue to the deeds of King Richard of England, of the king of France, and of the emperor of Germany

It sometimes happens that with the passing of time even notable and extraordinary deeds fade from memory and pass into oblivion. In this way the glory of numerous kings has withered away, although their magnificent deeds were famous in their own time. When new, their exploits were held in high public esteem as an inspiration to the people; but now they have vanished with them into the grave.

The ancient Greeks were inspired to remedy this problem with the written word, and urged their writers - whom they called 'historiographers' - to record histories of events.[1] The happy result was that the written record spoke in place of the living voice so that the virtues of these mortals did not die with them.

The Romans emulated the Greeks: to ensure that virtue would live forever, they not only took up the work of the pen, but also erected statues. In this way, through visual representations of the ancients and challenging posterity in words they directed their message by various routes to the inner person - through both the eyes and the ears. So they firmly impressed on the minds of their would-be imitators a love of virtue.

Who would know of the journey of Jason, the labours of Hercules, the glory of Alexander or the victories of Caesar if we lacked the benefits of writing? Furthermore, if truth-conscious Antiquity had not left us histories to read no one would be inspired to imitate the deeds of the Holy Fathers, whom the Church frequently commends and commemorates. Indeed, when orators extolled the kings of ancient times, the kings' greatest desire was that they would come to the notice of posterity through being celebrated by their own contemporaries.

However, although innumerable writings exist about the deeds of the

1. *Rerum*, in manuscripts of groups G and A. B and C have *regum*, 'of kings'.

past, most were written from hearsay and few are eyewitness accounts. Dares of Phrygia's[2] account of the destruction of Troy is given more credence than others because he was present and saw for himself what others reported from hearsay. On the same basis this history of Jerusalem which we recount should not be unworthy of belief. We proclaim to you what we have seen [1 John ch. 1 v. 3]. Our pen recorded noteworthy events while the memory of them was still fresh.

Perhaps the discerning audience may demand a more cultured literary style; but they should realise that we wrote this while we were in the military camp, where the battle's roar does not allow leisure for peaceful thought. Truth is sufficient to please; and although undecorated with polished pomposity, it may still lure the audience into its mystery.

2. Dares of Phrygia, priest of Hephaestus at Troy (Homer's *Iliad* 5. 9) was reputed to be the author of a lost pre-Homeric account of the Trojan war. A supposed Latin prose translation survives, *Daretiis Phrygi de Excidio Trojae Historia*: 'Dares of Phrygia's History of the Destruction of Troy'. It was probably written in the fifth century AD.

Book 1

Chapter 1: The Lord exterminates the people of Syria because of the people's sins.

In the year of the Incarnation of the Word 1187, Urban III occupied the Apostolic See, Frederick [Barbarossa] was ruling in Germany, Isaac [Angelus] at Constantinople, Philip [II] was reigning in France, Henry [II] in England, and William [II] in Sicily. Then the Lord's hand was aroused against His people – if we can properly call them 'His', as their immoral behaviour, disgraceful lifestyle, and foul vices had made them strangers to Him. For shameful practices had broken out in the East, so that everywhere everyone threw off the veil of decency and openly turned aside to filthy things. It would take a long time to describe their murders, robberies and adulteries, and it is not part of our scheme, which is to describe events and not to write a moral tract. Suffice it to say that when the Ancient Enemy spread the spirit of corruption far and wide, he particularly seized on Syria. So the region from which other areas had received religion now became an example of all immorality.

The Lord saw that the land of His Nativity, the place of His Passion, had fallen into the filthy abyss. Therefore He spurned His Inheritance, permitting the rod of His fury, Saladin [al-Malik al-Nāṣir Ṣalāḥ al-Dīn Abu'l-Muẓaffar Yūsuf ibn Ayyūb], to rage and exterminate the obstinate people. Since they had no sense of honour to restrain them from illicit deeds, He preferred the Holy Land to serve the profane rites of Gentiles for a time than for His people to flourish any longer.

Various disasters foretold the approaching destruction: famine, earthquakes and frequent eclipses of both the moon and the sun. Even that strong wind which the astronomers had predicted from a planetary conjunction became another indication of these events. It certainly was a strong wind, for it shook the four corners of the earth and foretold that the whole globe would be shaken in uproar and battles.[1]

---

1. For this forecast of a strong wind which would cause death and destruction see also Rigord, pp. 72–7; Roger of Howden, *Gesta*, 1 p. 324; *Chronica*, 2 p. 290.

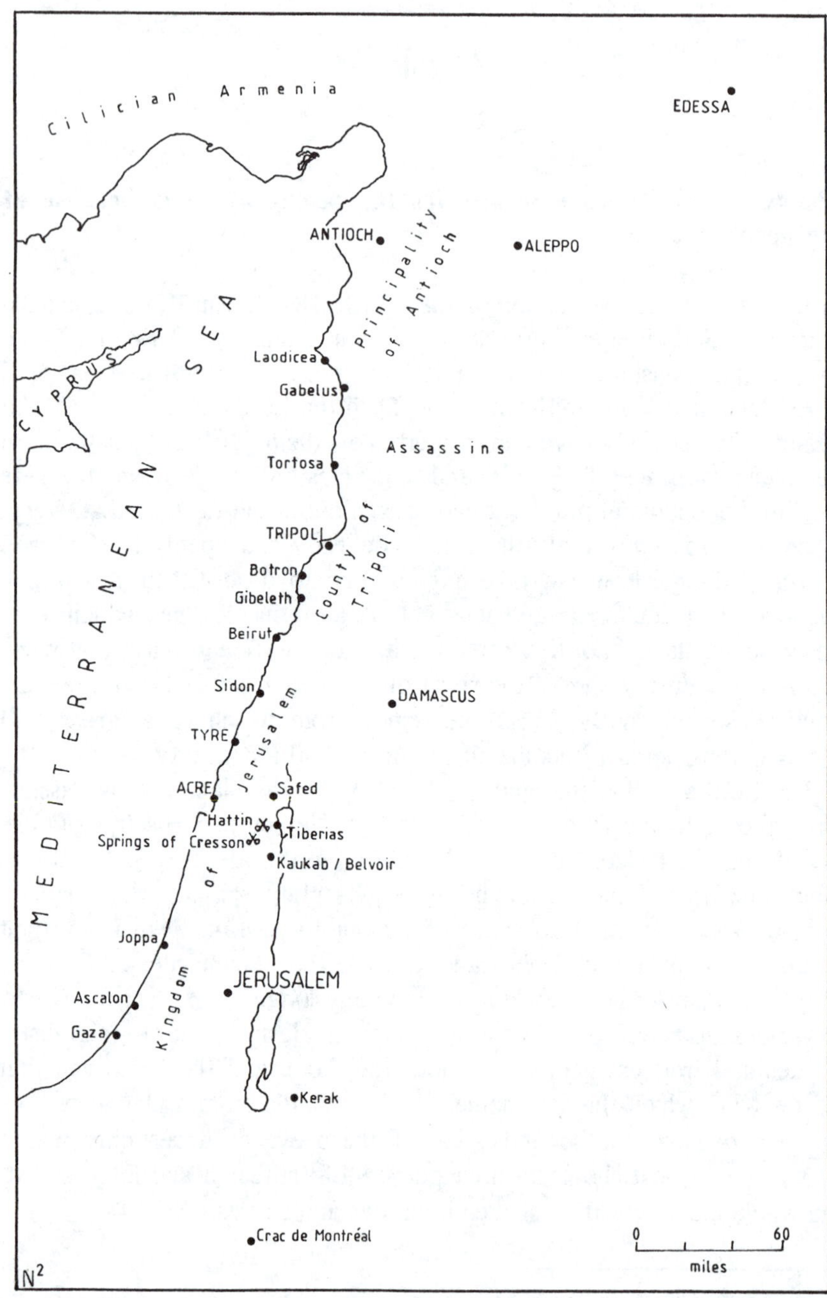

Map 1. Sites connected with the campaigns of Saladin in the Holy Land, 1187-89.

Chapter 2: Saladin routs the Master of the Temple and others [Battle of the Springs of Cresson, 1 May 1187].[2]

So Saladin assembled armed forces and marched violently on Palestine. He sent the emir of Edessa, Manafaradin [Muẓaffer al-Dīn ibn Zain al-Dīn 'Alī Kuchuk Keukburī, lord of Harrān and Edessa],[3] on ahead with 7000 Turks to ravage the Holy Land. Now, when this Manafaradin advanced into the Tiberias region, he happened to encounter the master of the Temple, Gerard de Ridefort, and the master of the Hospital, Roger des Moulins.[4] In the unexpected battle which followed, he put the former to flight and killed the latter.[5]

In this conflict, in which a handful of our people were surrounded by an immense army, a remarkable and memorable event occurred. A certain Templar - a knight by profession, of Touraine by nation, Jakelin de Mailly by name - brought all the enemy assault on himself through his outstanding courage. While the rest of his fellow knights (estimated to number 500) had either been captured or killed, he bore all the force of the battle alone and shone out as a glorious champion for the law of his God. He was surrounded by enemy troops and almost abandoned by human aid, but when he saw so many thousands running towards him from all directions he strengthened his resolve and courageously undertook the battle, one man against all.

2. This gives us very little idea of the background to the events which follow. There is a hint at the beginning of chapter 5. For more detail, but prejudiced against King Guy and the master of the Temple, see *The Conquest of Jerusalem*, pp. 11-32.
3. See 'Imād al-Dīn, p. 15.
4. The orders of the Temple and Hospital were religious orders based in Jerusalem, with military functions. The Hospital of St John had been founded in the late eleventh century to care for sick pilgrims to the Holy Land. The order of the Temple was founded c. 1119 on the initiative of the Catholic patriarch of Jerusalem specifically to defend Christian pilgrims. During the twelfth century both the orders took on the defence of the Christians' territory against Muslim attack. Because they combined the monastic and knightly functions they were very popular in the West and were widely endowed with property and privileges. For general information on the military orders see Forey, A. (1992), *The Military Orders: From the Twelfth to the Early Fourteenth Centuries.*
5. The most detailed account of the battle is in *Libellus*, pp. 210-6. Pope Urban III sent an account of the battle to the English clergy, translated in *Conquest of Jerusalem*, pp. 156-7. See also William of Newburgh, p. 256; Ralph of Diceto, 2 p. 50; Roger of Howden, *Gesta*, 2 p. 10, *Chronica*, 2 p. 319; 'Imād al-Dīn, pp. 15-16. Later accounts are in *Conquest of Jerusalem*, p. 32; E-B, pp. 146-7; *LFWT*, pp. 67-8.

His commendable courage won him his enemies' approval. Many were sorry for him and affectionately urged him to surrender, but he ignored their urgings, for he was not afraid to die for Christ. At long last, crushed rather than conquered by spears, stones and lances, he sank to the ground and joyfully passed to heaven with the martyr's crown, triumphant.

It was indeed a gentle death with no place for sorrow, when one man's sword had constructed such a great crown for himself from the crowd laid all around him. Death is sweet when the victor lies encircled by the impious people he has slain with his victorious right hand. And because it so happened that the warrior had been riding a white horse and had white armour and weapons, the Gentiles, who knew that St George had this appearance in battle, boasted that they had killed the Knight of Shining Armour, the protector of the Christians.

The place where he had fought was covered with the stubble which the reapers had left standing when they had cut the grain shortly before. Such a great number of Turks had rushed in to attack, and this one man had fought for so long against so many battalions, that the field in which they stood was completely reduced to dust and there was not a trace of the crop to be seen.

It is said that there were some who sprinkled the body of the dead man with dust and placed the dust on their heads, believing that they would draw courage from the contact. In fact, rumour has it that one person was moved with more fervour than the rest. He cut off the man's genitals, and kept them safely for begetting children so that even when dead the man's members - if such a thing were possible - would produce an heir with courage as great as his.

Saladin was greatly exhilarated by his troops' victory and his mind was kindled with the desire of seizing the kingdom of Jerusalem. And so he turned his mind to greater things.

Chapter 3: Saladin's descent and origins.

To inform eager Posterity more fully about this great persecutor of the Christian faith, we shall set down something about his origins, as far as brevity permits.

He was from the nation of *Mirmuraenus*.[6] His parents were not descen-

---

6. Mayer, H. (1962), *Itinerarium Peregrinorum*, p. 250 note 1, states that this is a

ded from the nobility, but neither were they common people of obscure birth. His father's given name was Job [Ayyūb], and his was Joseph [Yūsuf]. Giving Hebrew names of circumcision when their sons are circumcised is a rite which thrives among many of the Gentiles and follows Muslim tradition.

The princes take their names from the title of the law of Muḥammad, so that their names may remind them to be studious defenders of that law. Now, in the Gentile language the law is called the *Hadin*. From this he was called *Salahadin*, which translates as 'reformer of the law', or 'peacemaker'.[7] And just as our princes are called emperors or kings, so among them those who are preeminent are named *Soldans*, as if to mean 'sole dominion'.

His origins. Saladin received the first auspices of his future power under Nuradin [al-Malik al-Ṣāliḥ Nūr al-Dīn Maḥmūd ibn Zangī], sultan of Damascus [Dimashq]. Saladin collected illgotten gains for himself from a levy on the girls of Damascus: they were not allowed to practise as prostitutes unless they had obtained, at a price, a licence from him for carrying on the profession of lust. However, whatever he gained by pimping like this he paid back generously by funding plays. So through lavish giving to all their desires he won the mercenary favour of the common people.

He was given the hope of winning a kingdom by a Syrian soothsayer, who told him his future and that he would be sovereign over Damascus and Babylon [Cairo]. So he treasured ambitions in his heart, and although his influence was limited to a few possessions he began to hope for more than a kingdom. As time passed, he reached the age when his physical strength required that he take up the office of knighthood. He went as a candidate for knighthood to Enfrid of Turon [Humfrey II of Toron, or Tibnīn],[8] an illustrious prince of Palestine, and received the belt of knighthood from him in accordance with the rite of the Franks.

---

corruption of *Amīr al-Mu'minīn*, i.e. 'Leader of the Believers', which was a stock part of the caliph's title. Our writer apparently took the phrase from the titles at the end of Saladin's letter to Frederick I, below, Bk. 1 ch. 18. In fact Saladin was a Kurd. For his origins see Bahā' al-Dīn, p. 4.

7. MSS A and G omit 'or peacemaker'. In fact the name means 'Goodness of the Faith': Holt, P. M. (1986), *The Age of the Crusades*, p. xii.
8. Another tradition says Hugh of Tiberias, who appears in ch. 10, below. Humfrey II of Toron appears to be the original person involved in this legend: see Duparc-Quioc, S. (1955), *Le Cycle de la Croisade*, p. 131.

Chapter 4: Saladin seizes the kingdoms of Egypt, Damascus, India, and other lands.

At that time [1169] a certain Gentile, Shawar by name [Abu Shujā' ibn Mujir Shāwar], had obtained the whole of Egypt [as vizier], under the authority of the Molan [the Caliph: Abū Muḥammad 'Abd Allāh al-'Adid] which means 'Lord' in the language of that country. Amalric the victorious king of Jerusalem had forced him to pay an annual tribute. Now, the Molan used to make a public appearance three times a year to receive the Egyptians' adoration. Among his subjects he was believed to have such great power that the Nile was said to flood at his command. What is more, he respectfully fulfilled the statutes of the Gentiles' religion, having as many concubines as there are days in the year. So he lived a decadent life among his girls, having entrusted the affairs of the kingdom to Shawar.

At that time Saladin was fighting for the Egyptians with his uncle Saracun [Asad al-Dīn ibn Shādhī Shīrkūh]. He treacherously killed these unsuspecting men, and so won the lordship of all Egypt. Later, in fact not long afterwards, Nuradin came to the end of his life. Saladin married his widow, put Nuradin's heirs to flight, and seized the government of the kingdom of Damascus [1174].

It was the caprice of Fortune that wished for these rapid changes. She raises up a rich man from a pauper, the lofty from the humble, a ruler from a slave. If we measured the value of things by rational judgement and not by general opinion, we would reckon the power that comes from worldly success as worthless, since too often it is the most evil and unworthy people who obtain it! That pimp, who had a kingdom of brothels, an army in taverns, who studied dice and rice,[9] is suddenly raised up on high. He sits among princes, no, he is greater than princes! 'Holding the throne of glory' [1 Samuel ch. 2 v. 8] he rules the Egyptians, he subdues Damascus, he seizes the land of Roasia [al-Ruhā, or Edessa; now Urfa] and Gesira [al-Jazīra] and he penetrates and governs the most remote parts of India.

Saladin makes one monarchy out of all these kingdoms. Storming and seizing, now by a trick, now by arms, Saladin brings all these kingdoms under his control. Then he makes a single monarchy out of all these

9. The original *aleis et alliis* means literally 'dice and garlic', but in English this loses the rhythm and the sense of frivolous pastimes.

sceptres. He alone claims the governments of so many kings! Still the tyrant's greed is not content with this. The more he has, the more he wants, and he strives with all his strength to seize the Lord's Inheritance.

Then the opportunity arises for him to obtain his desire. Now he hopes to gain what he had never even dared to wish for.

Chapter 5: The quarrel which arose between the Christian leaders.

The populace were dangerously divided because of the struggle between Count Raymond [III] of Tripoli [Tarābulus] and Guy, eighth king of the Latins, over the kingdom of Jerusalem.[10] This opportunity violently kindled the sultan's greed, promising swift and certain success in his plans. Yet the sultan did have some pretext for declaring war. Reginald [de Châtillon], prince of Antioch [Antakya],[11] had broken a truce which our people and the Gentiles had sworn to observe.

How the prince of Antioch broke the truce by killing pagans who were travelling outside his frontier. On one occasion a very numerous and opulent company of Gentiles was crossing from Damascus to Egypt. They were not afraid to travel past the frontier with the Christians' lands because of the truce. Suddenly the aforesaid prince rushed down on them and carried them dishonourably away as captives with all their baggage.[12] So the sultan, burning with ambition and furious at the insult done

---

10. According to Roger of Howden, *Gesta*, 1 p. 359 (translated in *Conquest of Jerusalem*, pp. 154–5) and *Chronica*, 2 p. 316, Raymond of Tripoli became a traitor because he had wanted to marry the queen, Sybil, when she was forced to divorce Guy in order to inherit the crown. However, Sybil had remarried Guy. In fact the count was already married to Eschiva, lady of Tiberias. For different account of these tensions see *Conquest of Jerusalem*, pp. 12, 14, 17, 38–9, where they are blamed on a private quarrel between Gerard de Ridefort, master of the Temple, and the count of Tripoli.
11. Reynald de Châtillon was still being given the title of prince of Antioch in 1187, even though his stepson Bohemund had succeeded him as prince of Antioch in 1163, while Reynald was in a Muslim prison. In 1187 he was also lord of Transjordan through his marriage before November 1177 to Lady Stephanie de Milly, and lord of Hebron. For his career see Hamilton, B. (1978), 'The Elephant of Christ'.
12. See Bahā' al-Dīn, pp. 42, 114. For this incident see Hamilton, B. (1978), 'Elephant of Christ', pp. 106–7.

to him, roused the forces of his whole empire and invaded the kingdom of Jerusalem with violence and power.

His army contained such a number of people, such dissimilar races with such diverse religious observances that if we were to describe them as fully as the law of history demands the length of the description would defeat our intention of brevity.[13] However, although it was an innumerable multitude its size can be estimated to some extent if we name only the commanders.

The size of the army Saladin brought when he came to defeat the Christian army. There came Nuradin, emir of Amiza,[14] with all his company.

Jarafarahadin emir of Robis [Shīrkūh ibn Nāṣir al-Dīn Muḥammad, emir of al-Raḥba] came; the emir of Raechis [Raqqa]; and the emir of Faraquin [Mayyāfāriqīn: Ḥusām al-Dīn Sonqor al-Khilāṭī].

The emir of Mossetar [lord of Masyāf in N. Syria];[15] the emir of Nesebin [Niṣībīn],[16] bringing with him Duke Mezaedin [probably 'Izz al-Dīn Mas'ūd, lord of Mosul].

Also the emir of Byla [al-Bīra][17] came, and the emir of Torvesello [Tell Bāshir, or Turbessel: Badr al-Dīn Dildirim al-Yārūqī ibn Bahā' al-Daula]; the emir of Damascus, and the caliph of Baghdad; Emir Alirius; Emir Myrchalius; Emir Mestoch [Saif al-Dīn 'Alī ibn Aḥmad al-Mashṭūb].[18]

Duke Sanscous of Doada came [probably Shams al-Dīn Sonqor].

Bellegemin [Ḥusām al-Dīn 'Abū'l-Haijā' al-Samīn][19] came; Emir Megesimus [probably Mujāhid al-Dīn Yurun-Qush]; Emir Gwahadin Sanscous [see emir of Faraquin, above]; Duke Acalatin [probably Saif al-Dīn Bektimur, lord of Khilāṭ]; the emir of Rohequis [Edessa]; Emir Alexandrin.

---

13. MSS groups G and A omit the list of names which follows, and continue: 'Parthians, Bedouins, and Arabs...', as at the very end of the list here. The compiler of IP2 seems to have put this list together from an independent source of information and names of Muslim leaders who appear in the rest of the book. The copyist of MS A, although he used IP2, did not use it here. Some names are repeated, appearing under their title and their name. Mayer (1962), pp. 255-6 and index, tried to identify them all and I give his identifications.
14. Mayer (1962) points out that this appears to indicate Nūr al-Dīn Muḥammad ibn Qara-Arslān, lord of Āmid, but he had died in 1185.
15. Rashīd al-Dīn Sinān, the Old Man of the Mountain: Mayer (1962), p. 255.
16. 'Imād al-Dīn Zangī, from Sindjar.
17. Probably Shihab al-Dīn Mahmūd ibn Shihāb al-Dīn Ilyas, lord of al-Bīra.
18. See Bk. 3 ch. 15, below.
19. See Bk. 1 ch. 54, below.

Duke Haelicalin [same as Duke Mezaedin above?] came, bringing with him his brother Sanguin ['Imād al-Dīn ibn Maudūd ibn Zangī II of Sinjār].

The emir of Damietta also came; the emir of Maelis [Mārdīn]; Safahadin Berbensis; Sensedin of the Mountains [probably Shams al-Dīn ibn Munqid]; the emir of Babylonia [Egypt: al-Mālik al-Afdal Nūr al-Dīn Abū' l-Hasan 'Alī ibn Sālāḥ al-Dīn, commander of Saladin's Egyptian forces]; the sultan of Coimo [Iconium, now Konya: Qilij-Arslān II]; Baffadin Archadius;[20] Duke Ayas of Stoi [Ayāz al-Ṭawīl];[21] the emir of Carracois [Emir Bahā' al-Dīn al-Asadī Qara-Qūsh];[22] Sanscous of Halabi [probably Sonqor al-Ḥalabī]; Duke Dorderin Hedredin [lord of Tell Bashir, see above]; Duke Serbeth of Harengo [Surkhak of Ḥārim]; the emir of Souz; emir Bedredin [the lord of Tell Bashir again]; the emir of the Kurds; the emir of Boysseleth [Buṣrā? Baisān?]; the emir of Gibel [Jabala];[23] Emir Sassachius [Emir Mestoch?]; the emir of Crach [Kerak];[24] Emir Waradin, and Elias and Jebedin; Duke Altilaban[25] with 300 Turks and bringing with him ten emirs, each ready for war with a retinue well instructed in arms.

Besides these aforenamed, Saladin also had 500,000 Saracens, Parthians, Bedouins, and Arabs, Medes, Kurds and Egyptians. They were as divided in place of origin, rites and name as they were united in their determination to destroy the Holy Land.

The deceit of the count of Tripoli.[26] It is said that the count of Tripoli deceitfully put himself in command of leading the army against the enemy. He actually intended to betray his people, as he had agreed with Saladin.

---

20. This must be Saladin's brother al-'Ādil: see Bk. 6 ch. 22, p. 364 below.
21. See Bk. 4 ch. 14, p. 243 below.
22. See Bk. 3 ch. 15, below.
23. Mayer adds that Jabala was not captured by the Saracens until 1189.
24. Mayer states that this should be al-'Ādil, brother of Saladin and lord of Kerak; but Kerak did not fall to the Saracens until late 1188.
25. Mayer states that although this indicates Shihāb al-Dīn Maḥmūd al-Ḥarimī, Saladin's uncle, he had in fact died in 1177-78.
26. The details on the treachery of the count of Tripoli here and in chapter 5 are not in MSS G and A but were inserted by the compiler of IP2, apparently from Ambroise. Cf. Ambroise, lines 2447-9, 2512-21. The English sources agree on the count's treachery, as does Guy of Bazoches, 'Cronosgraphia', fol. 63v. The Palestinian Frankish sources depict him as a Christian patriot: *Conquest of Jerusalem*, pp. 36-8, 46-7.

The vision which appeared to King Guy's chamberlain. As our people were advancing to meet the sultan the day of calamity was approaching. A dreadful vision appeared to the king's chamberlain: he saw an eagle flying over the Christian army, carrying seven darts and a crossbow in its talons and crying out in a terrible voice: 'Woe to you, Jerusalem!'

To interpret the mystery of his vision, we believe it is sufficient to refer to the Scripture: 'The Lord has bent his bow, and made it ready; he has also prepared for him the instruments of death' [Psalm 7 vv. 12-13]. For what are the seven darts, if not an allegorical representation of the seven deadly sins, from which the unfortunate army was soon to perish? We may see in those seven things the whole of the punishments which threatened the Christians.

Not much later the outcome of events showed that this dire interpretation was all too accurate.

The Christians are crushed, and Christ's cross captured with King Guy and Acre, and the Land of the Promise conquered [Battle of Hattin, 4 July 1187].[27] The conflict had not yet begun, but just as the battle lines were advancing on each other at a place not far from Tiberias[28] called Mareschallia [Meskenah], right at the moment of engagement the aforesaid count of Tripoli fell back and feigned flight. It was rumoured that he did this in order to break up our formation and that he had agreed to abandon his own people, to strike fear into those whom he should have assisted while arousing the enemy's courage.[29]

So the Lord's people were left bewildered in the moment of crisis. Then the Lord 'gave His people to the sword' [Psalm 78 v. 62] and – as the sins of humanity demanded – He gave up His inheritance to slaughter and pillage.

What more can we say?

---

27. The most thorough account of this battle is *Libellus*, pp. 218-28; trans. by Brundage, J. (1962), *The Crusades*, pp. 153-63. See also Ambroise, lines 2522-75; *Historia Peregrinorum*, pp. 119-20; Roger of Howden, *Gesta*, pp. 10-15, 36-7, *Chronica*, 2 pp. 319-20, 340-2; Ralph of Coggeshall, p. 21; Bahā' al-Dīn, pp. 110-6; 'Imād al-Dīn, pp. 24-7; *Conquest of Jerusalem*, pp. 35-41, 45-8; E-B, pp. 158-60. For translations of contemporary letters written soon after the event see *Conquest of Jerusalem*, pp. 158-63 and Barber, M. (1993), *The New Knighthood*, pp. 115-6.
28. King Guy was leading the Christian forces to relieve Tiberias, which was under siege by Saladin and being defended by Lady Eschiva.
29. He died soon afterwards: Bahā' al-Dīn, p. 112; and see the account translated in *Conquest of Jerusalem*, pp. 164-5.

It is not part of our plan to enumerate the mournful details of the battle, and our immense sorrow does not permit us to say more. But to cut a long story short: our people were at the mercy of the enemy. So many were slaughtered there, so many wounded, so many thrown into chains that they were completely destroyed. Even the life-giving wood of the Cross of Salvation, on which our Lord and Redeemer hung, down whose trunk flowed the pious blood of Christ, whose image angels adore, humans venerate, demons dread, through whose help our people had always won the victory in war - alas! was now captured by the enemy. And the bearers of the Cross fell with it, the bishop of Acre and the precentor[30] of the Lord's Sepulchre: the first was killed and the other was captured. As the Cross fell to the ground, King Guy felt compassion for it and, indeed, placed his own hope in it. He rushed forward and embraced it, intending - if it pleased God - to recover it, but if not, to fall with it.[31]

It was on account of our wicked deeds that the Cross received this second affront - the first had been when Cosdroes [Chosroes], king of the Persians, captured it.[32] The Cross which had absolved us from the ancient yoke of captivity to sin was led a captive for us, and dishonoured by the hands of godless Gentiles. If you have understanding, see God's great anger! Yes, how wicked His servants must be, when He reckons Gentiles to be a less unworthy guard for the Cross than Christians!

Ancient times produced no events as sorrowful as this, because neither the capture of the Ark of the Lord nor the captivity of the kings of the Jews can compare with the disaster in our own time, when the king and the glorious Cross were led away captive together. There was a marvellous and mournful multitude of captives. The victor decided their fate. Part was kept unharmed, and part was sent to heaven with happy and hasty gain, slain by the sword.

---

30. *Libellus*, p. 219, and Ambroise state that the bishop of Lydda and the bishop of Acre were carrying the cross.
31. This sentence only appears in MS C and is from Ambroise, line 2575.
32. Chosroes II (590-628) captured Jerusalem and thus the cross in 614. Jerusalem had previously been ruled by the emperor of the Eastern part of the Roman Empire, from Constantinople.

Saladin cuts off the prince of Antioch's head, and commands that the Templars and the outstanding warriors be killed.[33] Among others, Reginald, prince of Antioch, was presented to the sultan. The tyrant, either because of his fury or deferring to the excellence of such a great man, cut off the distinguished and aged head with his own hand. He also ordered that all the Templars be beheaded, except the Master of the Knighthood. He decided to have them utterly exterminated because he knew that they surpassed all others in battle.

O zeal of faith! O fervour of soul! A considerable number took the Templars' tonsure and flocked together to the executioner. Under the pious fraud of their new profession they joyfully offered their neck to the smiter's sword. Among these knights of Christ a certain Templar named Nicholas had been so successful in persuading the rest to undergo death willingly that the others struggled to go in front of him and he only just succeeding in obtaining the glory of martyrdom first - which was an honour he very much strove for. Nor was the miraculous power of divine mercy missing. A ray of celestial light shone down clearly on the bodies of the holy martyrs during the three following nights, while they were still lying unburied.[34]

At last the battle's strife was stilled. Saladin had watched captives taken on this side, the slaughtered fall everywhere on that. He raised his eyes to heaven and gave thanks to God for the victory he had won - he used to do this whenever things went well for him.

Among other things, it is said that he often used to say that he got this victory not through his power but through our sin. The turn of events not infrequently gave confirmation of this. In other engagements our people's army, no matter how small it was, had always conquered with divine assistance; but now because we were not with the Lord nor the Lord with us, our people completely succumbed even before the conflict, although there are thought to have been more than 20,000 knights.

---

33. For the executions see *Libellus*, p. 228; Ralph of Coggeshall, p. 21; William of Newburgh, p. 259; Roger of Howden, *Gesta*, 2 p. 22, *Chronica*, 2 p. 320; Bahā' al-Dīn, pp. 43, 113-5; 'Imād al-Dīn, pp. 27-8, 30-1; E-B, p. 174. Most sources also mention that the captured Hospitallers were executed with the Templars.

34. This episode only appears in the *Itinerarium* and in *LFWT*, p. 70, which appears to have copied it from IP1. The story seems to have originated with the Templars, as the story of Jakelin de Mailly's death in ch. 2, above, probably did. It may have been written down and sent to the West in a Templar newsletter which does not otherwise survive; or it may have circulated orally. Elsewhere the *Itinerarium* does not show particular interest in the Templars.

What is more, because royal edict had summoned the forces of the whole kingdom to that disastrous battle, only those who could not bear arms because of disability of age or sex were left to guard the castles and towns.

This miserably fated battle was fought on the day of the Translation of St Martin [4 July]. In a single moment, it carried away and extinguished all the glory of the kingdom.

The sultan was sure that the fortresses of the country could be easily occupied, as their defenders had been slaughtered. The victor led the king as a captive around the castles of Syria, to be a laughing-stock and to display him to the towns he wanted to capture, to encourage the people to surrender. He came to Acre ['Akko] first and captured it at once without making an assault [9 July 1187].[35] He agreed to give the citizens their liberty, allowing them to take themselves and their possessions wherever they wished.

Chapter 6: The capture of Christians who unsuspectingly sailed into Acre.

Meanwhile, sailors were proceeding on their usual courses to Acre. Some carried merchandise and others pilgrims, people from all over the Christian world. Alas! Because they did not know what had happened, they sailed into the enemy port and were taken prisoner. What a pitiable disaster! When they first saw the coast from afar, they greeted it, but chains were waiting for them when they disembarked; they were glad to have avoided shipwreck, but they fell on to swords; exhausted from the journey, they expected to find peace, and they found pursuit. Many were kept as prisoners, a considerable number were subjected to mockery and abuse, a few were allowed to return. By allowing them to depart poor and naked, the enemy intended to make an example of them to terrify those who were to come.

35. Tiberias had already surrendered, 4 July. Lady Eschiva of Tiberias and her sons were allowed to go to Tyre: see p. 41, below. For the date of the fall of Acre see 'Imād al-Dīn, p. 33.

Chapter 7: The Marquis Conrad evades the aforesaid capture, and goes to defend Tyre.

Among others the marquis came from Constantinople.[36] As the sun was setting, his ship lowered sail and hove to. The stillness of the city seemed suspicious; at other times the arrival of a ship used to be the signal for rejoicing. When they noticed that Saladin's standards were erected throughout the city, greater fear struck them. The others were in despair at the sight of the Gentiles' galleys already coming towards them, but the marquis ordered everyone to be quiet, and placed himself at their head as their spokesman.

So when the messengers arrived and asked who they were, he asserted that the ship was a cargo ship and that he was the ship's master. He was not unaware of what had happened in Acre, he said, and he was a devoted subject of the sultan; and he gave a firm promise that at dawn the next day he would come into the city with his merchandise.

The nationality of the marquis, the defender of Tyre. That night, with a favourable wind, he slipped away to Tyre [Sūr] and took over its defence. His arrival was much to the advantage of the Christians who came later, and it would have brought glory to him as well if he had continued in the same way as he had begun.

That marquis – Conrad by name, Italian by nation – was an extraordinary man of action and hard working in all his endeavours. But no matter how well an enterprise begins, if it ends in disgrace it deserves abuse rather than praise.[37]

---

36. For the career of the Marquis Conrad of Montferrat in Constantinople see Brand, C. M. (1968), *Byzantium confronts the West*, pp. 80–4.
37. For the marquis' career in the Holy Land, see Jacoby, D. (1993), 'Conrad, marquis of Montferrat, and the kingdom of Jersalem (1187–92)'. The marquis was admired and feared by the Muslim chroniclers: Bahā' al-Dīn described him (p. 144): 'the marquis – a man accurst by God – was an important personage, distinguished by his good judgement, the energy and decision of his character and his religious zeal.' He depicts him as largely responsible for promoting the crusade. For a letter from Conrad to Archbishop Baldwin of Canterbury asking for his aid in encouraging kings and others to come to the aid of the Holy Land, see *Conquest of Jerusalem*, pp. 168–9.

Chapter 8: After Saladin has captured Beirut and Sidon he is forced to flee from Tyre. He captures Ascalon by deceit, with a false treaty.

After Acre had surrendered, the sultan attacked and captured Beirut [Bayrūt: 6 August] and Sidon [Sayda: 27 July]. He hoped to claim Tyre with the same ease but he was shamefully repulsed and forced to retreat.[38]

Then, taking King Guy with him, he reached Ascalon [Tell-Ashqelon], set up stonethrowers and attacked the city. As there were only a few, unarmed defenders its capture should have been easy, even though the multiple fortifications of the place gave an impression of invincible strength.

The insatiable plunderer pressed on with all his heart to force the city to surrender to him. But because he did not know what state the city was in and that it had no arms, fighting men or food, he did not believe it could be taken by storm. So he made an agreement with the citizens, by which they would be able to depart unconditionally with their property, and the king would also be freed immediately together with fifteen of the more elite captives.[39]

On the day when this treaty brought the surrender of the city, there was an eclipse: 'As if in sympathy, the sun took from the city and the globe' the benefit of light.[40] But then that perjured and perfidious tyrant broke part of the pact. He sent the king away to Damascus, and held him there in chains until the following May [1188]; and he refused to release him from captivity until he had sworn to renounce the kingdom.

38. More detailed accounts of Saladin's conquests of summer 1187 are in *Libellus*, pp. 228-36; Bahā' al-Dīn, pp. 116-7; 'Imād al-Dīn, pp. 39-43; *Conquest of Jerusalem*, pp. 52-4.
39. According to Roger of Howden, *Chronica* 2 p. 321, and Ralph of Coggeshall, p. 22, Queen Sybil was in Ascalon with her two daughters and was responsible for negotiating King Guy's release.
40. *Libellus*, p. 238, also mentions the eclipse.

Chapter 9: Jerusalem is captured, and those of the people who have been ransomed are expelled. But those who are not ransomed are taken captive.[41]

And so, urged on by the Fates, the hasty and hostile victor attacked Jerusalem [20 September 1187]. The sacrilegious man besieged the city, constructed siege machines, and irreverently invaded the holy places. There used to be a stone cross which our knights had once erected on the walls in memory of their victorious capture of this city after their capture of Antioch [during the First Crusade, 1099]. Those savages destroyed this with a missile from a catapult, and flattened no small part of the wall with it.

The citizens threw up what defences they could, but our people's efforts had no effect. They fired bows, crossbows, and stonethrowers in vain. So both weapons and machines clearly declared the Lord's anger and foretold the destruction of the city.

A very great number of people had gathered there from the neighbouring castles and everywhere about, trusting more in the sanctity of the place than its defences. But hardly twice seven knights could be found in all that multitude. Even the priests and the clergy too, whose profession does not require them to bear arms, took up the duty of fighting for the time being. They strove strenuously for the Lord's House, remembering that all laws and rights allow force to repel force. But the cowardly and fearful common people ran to the patriarch and the queen, who were then in command of the city [Patriarch Heraclius and Queen Sybil], complaining tearfully and begging insistently that they should come to an agreement with the sultan as soon as possible and surrender the city to him.

Yet, the treaty they made was more to be regretted than commended. Each person was to pay the price of their own head. A man paid ten bezants, a woman five and a child one.[42] Anyone who could not afford to pay was taken captive. So it happened that although many made the

41. The best account of the siege of Jerusalem is in *Libellus*, pp. 241–51; the writer took part in the defence. See also *The Conquest of Jerusalem*, pp. 55–67 and E-B, pp. 217–34. These were written much later but seem to be based on a contemporary account, perhaps the original chronicle of Ernoul: see Edbury, P. (1997), 'The Lyon *Eracles* and the Old French Continuations of William of Tyre', p. 143. See also Bahā' al-Dīn, pp. 118–20.

42. For the bezant see Spufford, P. (1986), *Handbook of Medieval Exchange*, p. 294. The Europeans in the Levant and North Africa used the term 'bezant' to refer to the gold dinar and other units of account which derived from it.

payment for their salvation, either from their own property or begged from elsewhere, 14,000 of the rest were left without a redeemer and went under the yoke of perpetual slavery.

Those who had bought their liberty were offered the option of either proceeding to Antioch or going down under escort to Alexandria in order to embark for Europe. On that day, that bitter day [2 October 1187], the exiled people parted from each other on different roads, and deserted the holy city. The lady of cities was reduced to servitude; the city who was the inheritance of her sons was subjected to an alien race, because of the evil of those who dwelt within her. Jerusalem, the glorious City of God, where the Lord suffered, where He was buried, where He revealed the glory of His Resurrection, was thrown to the filthy enemy to be dishonoured. There is no sorrow like this sorrow, when they possess the Holy Sepulchre but persecute the One who was buried there; and they hold the Cross but despise the Crucified.

Our people had held this most sacred city for around eighty-nine years. The victorious Christian force recovered it together with Antioch after the Gentiles had held it for forty years [400 years]. For in the year of Our Lord 1099 Bohemond, Raymond, Tancred, Duke Godfrey, Count [Duke] Robert of Normandy and the other Franks had captured it and expelled the Saracens. However Saladin expelled the Christians and captured it in the year of Our Lord 1188 [1187].

When the city had been surrendered, a crier of the law of Muḥammad ascended the height of the rock of Calvary and there loudly proclaimed their filthy law. The terrible enemy also undertook another unspeakable action. There was a cross fixed on top of the spire of the Hospitallers' church. They tied ropes around it and threw it down, spat contemptuously on it, hacked it into pieces, then dragged it through the city dung-pits, as an insult to our faith.

Chapter 10: Saladin besieges Tyre a second time by land and sea, and flees again.

Queen Sybil, the daughter of King Amalric, together with the Patriarch Heraclius, the Templars, the Hospitallers and an immense assembly of fellow-exiles, directed her steps towards Antioch. In the interests of brevity, we will pass over her sad meeting at Nablus with her captive husband the king, and how the marquis violently carried off to Tyre the ship in which she had arranged to set sail for Europe.

However, we judge that the following certainly ought to be recorded: Saladin, burning with the desire of seizing Tyre, marched again with all his forces to storm the city.[43] Not content with a land siege, as the city is surrounded by the sea he also besieged it with galleys, setting up an attack on all sides. Leaving no stone unturned, he also produced the marquis' father [William of Montferrat the elder], who was his prisoner, captured in an earlier battle [Hattin]. He was confident that the son, stirred by filial affection, would give up the city in return for his father's release. So first he offered to surrender him, then he threatened to destroy him; he tried various approaches. But he was completely mistaken: for the marquis could not be moved. He laughed at the offers, jeered at the threats, and whenever Saladin paraded his father in chains to arouse his compassion, the marquis at once snatched up a crossbow and fired at his father; letting his aim wander, but as if intending to shoot him.[44] When the sultan sent messengers with repeated threats that his father would be killed, the marquis retorted that he wholeheartedly desired this to happen, for then that wicked man would have a good end after all his shameful deeds and he would have been found worthy of having a martyr for his father.

So as the tyrant had been deluded in his confidence, he tried his luck at another approach. Because artifice got him nowhere, he set out to discover what he could achieve with arms.

About the origin of the defences of Tyre. Tyre is sited in the heart of the sea, ringed with fortifications on all sides. The small part which is not closed off by the depths of the sea is fortified by multiple walls. It was once famous for its kings: it produced the founders of Thebes and Carthage. When Solomon was reigning in Judaea, Tyre rejoiced in its own king. But although it then stood at the head of its own kingdom,

---

43. For the second siege of Tyre see Bahā' al-Dīn, p. 121; 'Imād al-Dīn, pp. 63–80; *The Conquest of Jerusalem*, pp. 67–70; E-B, pp. 236–8. Ambroise states firmly that he is not going to discuss this siege, but will concentrate on King Guy. Ibn al-Athīr, 1 pp. 707–11, blames Saladin's own policies for his failure to capture Tyre.
44. See also *Conquest of Jerusalem*, pp. 53–4, where this incident is assigned to the first siege of Tyre in August 1187. These and *LFWT*, p. 79 (which is copying IP1) are the only sources which say that Conrad actually shot at his father: see Edbury, 'The Lyon *Eracles*', p. 147. Similarly in the Colbert-Fontainebleu *Eracles* (*RHC Occ.* 2 p. 188), Saladin tries to persuade the garrison of Beaufort to surrender by producing their lord, Reynald of Sidon, whom he is holding prisoner; but the garrison only fire arrows at Reynald.

with the passing of time it became part of the kingdom of Jerusalem.

The greedy enemy attacked it by land and sea. It was afflicted by famine within and various incursions without.

On the day after Holy Innocents, i.e. the feast of the glorious martyr Thomas [29 December 1187], the citizens won a famous victory. When dawn was breaking, they came out with a few small boats, and broke up the sea blockade in a naval battle.[45]

They seemed to be coming out to escape rather than to do battle. But through divine power all the enemy fleet was so overcome by their first attack that they led part of it back into the city with its crews, while part was put to flight, only to be dashed to pieces and perish on the sands beyond.

When the Gentiles saw the naval battle, they thought that the city would be empty of defenders, and they attacked it eagerly, certain of victory. They had already brought up their scaling ladders to the walls and a great many were hurrying to climb up when the marquis ordered the gates to be thrown open, and Hugh of Tiberias with his brothers[46] and the rest of their companions threw down the attackers.

Saladin leaves Tyre in confusion. Saladin saw that fate was against him. His remaining stonethrowers and galleys were being burned up before his very eyes. He made an inglorious retreat, bitterly cursing Muḥammad [1 January 1188].

Not much later, around the beginning of May [1188], he released the king from his chains. Having broken the earlier treaty which he made with the citizens of Ascalon, he now made a new and harsh condition for the king's release, i.e. that he should swear to give up the kingdom, as we have already said.

---

45. According to Brother Thierry, grand commander of the order of the Temple, the Templars and Hospitallers also took part in this naval battle: his letter to King Henry II of England is translated in *Conquest of Jerusalem*, pp. 165–6.
46. Ralph, Otto and William. The four were the sons of Eschiva of Tiberias by her first husband the castellan of St Omer. Ralph was later famed as a jurist: see Riley-Smith, J. (1973) *Feudal Nobility*, esp. pp. 122–4, 156–9.

Chapter 11: The meeting of the king and queen at Tortosa.

There is an island called Arados, from which the city of Antarados, commonly known as Tortosa [Tartūs], takes its name. The queen proceeded here to meet the king. They exchanged kisses, they intertwined embraces, their joy elicited tears, and they rejoiced that they had escaped the disasters which had befallen them.[47]

At the request of the new prince of Antioch [Bohemond III][48] the king stayed for some time at Antioch and later at Tripoli, waiting for Christians to come from Europe to assist the Holy Land. At that time the king's brother, Geoffrey de Lusignan, suffered a repulse from the marquis, who would not allow him to enter Tyre. He then came to Tripoli to his brother the king.[49]

Chapter 12: King Henry's money.[50]

We are of the opinion that this and other things should in no way be passed over in silence. A long time before, Henry II king of the English had accumulated a great deal of money with the Templars and Hospitallers. This money was usefully employed in the defence of Tyre and the rest of the kingdom's business. With pious and necessary forethought the magnificent king had sent this money to Jerusalem over a period of many years for the support of the Holy Land. It is said that the sum amounted to 30,000 marks [£20,000].

---

47. The paragraph which follows is only found in MSS B and C and forms part of IP2. It seems to derive from Ambroise, lines 2697–700.
48. The author of IP2 is assuming that because Prince Reynald had just been killed, this must be a new prince of Antioch. In fact this was Reynald's stepson, who was prince 1163–1201. But there was a new count of Tripoli, Bohemond of Antioch's younger son Bohemond, later Bohemond IV of Antioch and Tripoli (see *Conquest of Jerusalem*, pp. 164–5).
49. At this point the story of King Guy's fortunes breaks off and resumes again in ch. 25, below. The account now follows Saladin's northern campaigns of 1188 and his capture of the castles of Transjordan, and then crosses to Europe.
50. For this see Mayer, H. (1982), 'Henry II of England and the Holy Land', and Tyerman, C. (1988), *England and the Crusades*, pp. 54–6. The money was originally paid in penance for Henry's role in the murder of Archbishop Thomas Becket, and was intended as a war chest for when Henry should come on crusade.

Chapter 13: Saladin captures a great many towns in both Palestine and the principality of Antioch.[51]

So Saladin left Tyre [1 January 1188]. He captured a great many castles in Palestine, and then withdrew hastily into the regions of Antioch. There he captured Gabelus [Jabala, 16 July] Laodicia [al-Lādhiqiyah, 23 July] and some other fortresses of the province by storm rather than by siege. The city of Antioch was struck with no small terror. But by common counsel the patriarch [Aimery de Limoges] and the prince [Bohemond III] promised the tyrant that they would surrender if the help they hoped for had not come within a given time.[52]

An inconsolable grief would have shaken all Christendom if such a renowned city, the city where the name 'Christian' had first been invented [Acts ch. 11 v. 26], had submitted again to the impure Gentiles. Our victors had expelled the Gentiles long before in a long and horribly dangerous war. But where was new help to defend the city to come from, and when would it come, and how could it come? There was no way in by land, and the sea route was blockaded by the enemy. The Christian ships stopped coming, because they feared that they would be ambushed by the Gentiles' galleys.

Chapter 14: King William of Sicily sends Margarit with fifty galleys and 500 knights to assist the Holy Land.

But those whom the Lord chooses to save can in no way perish. Behold, the longed-for ones come; those who were awaited arrive! The distinguished King William of Sicily sent the first relief force to the land, two counts, 500 knights and fifty galleys. Who can doubt that this was a miracle? With the help of the king's forces Antioch was held, Tripoli defended, Tyre saved, and the inhabitants of these cities kept secure from famine and the sword.

---

51. For Saladin's northern campaigns see Bahā' al-Dīn, pp. 125–38; 'Imād al-Dīn, pp. 125–48. On 3 July Saladin attacked Tortosa; the city fell but the Templars' tower held out, under the command of Master Gerard de Ridefort. Saladin continued north, capturing many towns and the Templar fortresses of Baghrās and Darbsāk.

52. Eight months (October 1188–May 1189): 'Imād al-Dīn, p. 144. After making this truce, Saladin went to Damascus ('Imād al-Dīn, pp. 145–8) and then went south to capture those Christian fortresses that were still holding out.

Margarit was in command of the royal fleet: a great man of action. Hastening ahead with his galleys, he boldly crushed pirates; then having proved that the route was safe, he encouraged others to follow. Forcing his rule on far-off islands, skilled by fortunate fate in all the dangers of the sea, he had won through his many victories the title of 'king of the sea'. Some also called him 'Neptune'.

Now the seafarers catch sight of Tripoli. The citizens notice their sails from a distance. But as the messengers of salvation approach: 'Fear, the worst augur in doubt', [Statius, *Thebaid*, Bk. 3 v. 6] fills them with foreboding. Without delay, they crown the walls, they climb the ramparts, still uncertain as to whether they should offer surrender or resistance. But when the ships come closer and they catch sight of the banners of the Cross and other insignia of the Christian religion standing high up in the poops, they raise an enormous shout, and the seas resound with mutual cries of greeting. The shore is filled with a crowd of people running to meet the fleet, and everyone burns with unutterable joy.

Among the rest, but before them in renown, was Henry de Danzy,[53] who lent timely assistance to the land.

So in a brief time a numerous and strong force assembled which preserved our coastal regions unharmed.[54]

53. Stubbs (1864), p. 28, note 5 and Mayer (1962), p. 272 identify this as Hervy III, lord of Donzy, Dépt. Nièvre, France.

54. 'Imād al-Dīn calls Margarit 'a bandit...one of the most ignoble rebels and the most deadly demons,' (p. 125) and says that he achieved nothing for the Christians (p. 126) yet complains about the help which the king of Sicily's fleet gave the Christians (p. 125). Roger of Howden, *Gesta*, 2 p. 54 states that Margarit controlled the coast so that the Saracens could not go up and down it.

Chapter 15: Crach Castle and Montréal are captured, after being besieged for two years by Saladin.[55] They are surrendered in exchange for the liberation of Reinfrid [Humfrey] and Gerard de Ridefort, master of the Temple.[56]

There is a castle which they call Crach [Kerak], where there was once a city called Petra of the Desert. It is now the seat of a metropolitan, but the prelate of the place retains the old name and is called the archbishop of Petra.[57] The castle stands in the inner heart of the kingdom. It was held under siege by the sultan's emirs for a long time; for if it were not for the fact that starvation overcomes even the safest places, that castle would have been secure from all attack.

There is also a castle which is called Montreal [Crac de Montréal, or Shaubak], which is twenty leagues from the city already mentioned, further towards Egypt. The tyrant had also sent his emirs here at the beginning of the war. Although the fortification of the place rendered it impregnable by storm, he intended to overcome its defenders by starvation through a lengthy siege. They did not erect siege machines nor attempt an assault. It would be ridiculous to try to pull stars from the sky or to have any confidence in storming the city when there was no approach open to attack.

When the siege had dragged out for almost two years, our people began to run out of supplies. But adversity cannot break the victorious spirit, and 'the more danger, the more honour'. In their perseverance our people endure the same harsh and difficult things that the Spanish bore

55. In autumn 1188 the Templars' castle of Ṣafad, the Hospitallers' castle of Kaukab (Beauvoir), and the castles of Kerak and Crac de Montréal (Shaubak) were still holding out. The last two belonged to Stephanie, Lady of Transjordan, and her son Humfrey IV of Toron, who was held prisoner by Saladin. Kerak fell first in November 1188, then Ṣafad on 6 December 1188, Kaukab on 5 January 1189, and Crac de Montréal last, in May 1189. IP1 ignores the Military Orders' castles and concentrates on those in Transjordan.

56. Incorrect. Gerard de Ridefort was released in May 1188; Humfrey of Toron in May 1189. 'Imād al-Dīn, pp. 104–7, is emphatic that Humfrey was not released until Shaubak had surrendered, in May 1189. Gerard de Ridefort was active against Saladin by July 1188, when he held the Templars' tower at Tortosa against Saladin: ibid., pp. 124–5.

57. The writer is confused by the fact that the two castles had similar names: the site of the ancient city of Petra lies near Crac de Montréal, not Kerak. MSS G, B and C call Kerak 'Erathum'.

at Saguntum, or the Romans at Perusium, as ancient witness narrates.[58] In their extreme need, they do not abhor what nature and custom condemn. Family feeling abandons its affection, love gives up its pleasures, for a father condemns his little child, a son his decrepit parents, a husband his bride. The noncombatants are ejected with tears and exposed to the mercy of the enemy, so that the warriors may fight for longer on the remaining food.

At last, wasted and half dead from hunger, they still earn a treaty of honourable surrender [May 1189]. They win for themselves the right to depart in freedom and the liberation of their lord Reinfrid [Humfrey IV] of Turon who was being held captive.[59] Similarly [May 1188] the master of the Knights of the Temple, Gerard de Ridefort, was freed on the surrender of certain fortresses. The marquis' father also went away free in exchange for certain Gentile captives.

Chapter 16: How a certain fool replied to Saladin when he was boasting about his victories.

By now [May 1189] Saladin was master of almost the entire kingdom. Everything proceeded at his nod. He luxuriated in arrogant elation. Boastfully extolling the law of Muḥammad, he claimed that recent events proved it to be greater than the Christian religion. While the victor was insolently bragging about his glorious successes in the presence of some Christians, a certain fool, known to the sultan for his biting wit, was inspired by God to mock him with this reply:

'God the Father of the faithful judged that the delinquent Christians should be rebuked and corrected and took you, O prince, to serve his purpose - just as a worldly father sometimes when he is enraged grabs a

58. Saguntum was captured by Hannibal in 219 BC after an eight-month siege. Octavian, later Caesar Augustus, starved out Mark Antony's supporters at Perugia in 41-40 BC.

59. Humfrey was lord of Kerak and Montréal through his mother Stephanie, lady of Transjordan. By 1188 she had been widowed three times: her husbands were Humfrey III of Toron, then Miles de Plancy and finally Reynald de Châtillon, executed after the battle of Hattin. 'Imād al-Dīn, pp. 105-7, gives a touching account of how Lady Stephanie, a 'virtuous and intelligent' woman, and her daughter-in-law, the lovely Isabel of Jerusalem, came to plead with Saladin for Humfrey's release in exchange for the surrender of the castles. The name 'Reinfrid' appears here in MSS B and C and seems to have been taken from Ambroise. G has 'Enfrid', while A has 'Gaufrid' (Geoffrey).

filthy stick from the mud with which to beat his erring sons, and then throws it back into the dungpit from which he took it.'

Chapter 17: The archbishop of Tyre announces the destruction of the Holy Land to the whole globe.[60]

While such things were going on in Palestine, the archbishop of Tyre [Joscius] had embarked on a ship and carried the news of this great disaster to the whole of Christendom. So the wound of this small country brought pain to all lands. Rumours flew to the ears of princes and declared to all the faithful that the inheritance of Christ had been occupied by the Gentiles; stirring some to tears and inflaming others to revenge.

Richard, count of Poitou, is the first to receive the cross. Richard, the great-hearted count of Poitou, was the first to receive the sign of the cross to avenge the Cross's injury. He preceeded everyone in this action, inviting them to follow his example. His father Henry, the king of the English, was already approaching old age. However, he disregarded his father's white hairs, and the kingdom - which was due to come to him by right - and the difficulties of so great a journey, and used no pretext to avoid the undertaking. The Lord, judging this man's constancy as worthy of reward, chose him first to incite all the others. And when all the other princes had either died or retreated, He retained him as executor of His affairs.

Although the count took the cross, he embarked on the pilgrim journey only after he was made king on his father's death.[61]

The king of France and the king of England take the cross.[62] A little later, King Philip of France and King Henry of England took the cross at Gisors. Princes of both kingdoms and an innumerable number of men from the ecclesiastical and secular militias [i.e. monks and knights] followed them in vow and act. But we shall speak below at greater

60. For what follows, see also William of Newburgh, pp. 271-5; Ralph of Diceto, pp. 29-30; Roger of Howden, *Gesta,* 2 pp. 29-30, *Chronica,* 2 pp. 325, 335; Gerald of Wales, *Liber de principis instructione,* pp. 239-40, *Expugnatio Hibernica,* pp. 365-6.
61. This sentence only appears in MSS B and C, and belongs to IP2. It links this chapter to the events described in Book 2.
62. Our writer uses a special verb, *crucizari,* literally 'to be crossed'.

length and more fully about these three princes and about the pilgrimage of King Richard of England and King Philip of France.[63]

The enthusiasm for the new pilgrimage was such that already it was not a question of who had received the cross but of who had not yet done so. A great many men sent each other wool and distaff, hinting that if anyone failed to join this military undertaking they were only fit for women's work.[64] Brides urged their husbands and mothers incited their sons to go, their only sorrow being that they were not able to set out with them because of the weakness of their sex.[65]

Men of the cloister take the cross with the rest. The attraction of this expedition spread everywhere. A great number went from cloister to camp, threw off their cowls, donned mailshirts, and became knights of Christ in a new sense, replacing alms with arms.[66] The prelates of the Church preached that soberness was the mother of virtue, exhorting everyone to give up fine food and clothing and reduce their usual luxury. It was laid down by the common agreement of the princes and bishops that all who stayed behind should pay a tenth on all their goods, to support the poor pilgrims. But with malicious greed many used this as an excuse to exact heavy and undue exactions from their subjects.

At this time King William of the Sicilians yielded to fate. His death was a regrettable loss to all the faithful, for he was close to the Holy Land and wished to assist it.

---

63. This sentence only appears in MSS B and C and acts as a link to Book 2.
64. There is an obvious British parallel to this in the white feather sent to young men who failed to enlist in the armed forces at the beginning of the First World War.
65. While the pope was anxious to prevent the presence of noncombatants on crusades, as the crusade was also a pilgrimage it was difficult to prevent anyone from joining the expedition. It is obvious from our writer's account of the siege of Acre (chs. 34, 50, below) that women were present in the crusaders' army. The contemporary Muslim accounts by Bahā' al-Dīn and 'Imād al-Dīn state that Christian women fought among the crusader infantry. But obviously many male crusaders would prefer to leave their wives behind to run the family estates or business. Riley-Smith, J. (1991), 'Family Tradition and Participation in the Second Crusade', indicates that noblewomen played an important role in spreading the crusading ethos. Our writer gives women a very positive role in encouraging men to take part in the crusade. See also Nicholson, H. (forthcoming), 'Women on the Third Crusade'.
66. Our writer approves, but in fact a monk's vows bound him to remain in one house and not to go wandering about. Again, the clergy were forbidden to shed blood. Hence monks were in theory barred from crusades. See Brundage, J. (1971), 'A Transformed Angel: The Problem of the Crusading Monk'.

Chapter 18: Frederick, the emperor of Germany, receives the cross, and issues a formal defiance to Saladin.

As time ran on, the emperor Frederick of the Romans took up the symbols of the holy pilgrimage. In both appearance and heart he declared himself the true pilgrim. His kingdom stretched from the Mediterranean to the North Sea, his glory continually increasing with his repeated victories, his reputation immune to insult; yet this great man gave up all the allurements of the world and humbly equipped himself to fight for Christ. His energy, especially in his declining years, was as astounding as it was praiseworthy. He was getting old, and had sons who seemed more fitted in age and strength for military undertakings than he. Yet, as if he thought they were not up to the task, he himself undertook the management of Christendom's affairs. As his sons insisted that they should either fulfil his undertaking with him or for him, he left the elder [Henry] to rule and took with him the other [Frederick], whom he had made duke of Swabia.[67]

The imperial majesty attacks no one without formal defiance. He always declares war on his enemies before attacking them. So the emperor sent a messenger with his sealed letter to Saladin, commanding him to give full satisfaction for his injuries to the whole of Christendom. Failing that, he was defied and should prepare for war.[68] The emperor's letter went as follows.

Frederick's letter to Saladin.

> Frederick, by the Grace of God, emperor of the Romans and forever Augustus, and magnificent conqueror of the enemies of the empire, to Saladin, president of the Saracens, who will flee from Jerusalem as the illustrious Pharaoh once did.[69]

67. From this point to 'the enemy's frequent attacks' in ch. 24, Gerald of Wales' *Liber de principis instructione* follows our writer word for word except for a few omissions. Mayer (1962), p. 182 argued that Gerald was using our writer's German source, and not IP1. *LFWT*, pp. 94–107, follows IP1.

68. The letter does not appear in MSS G or B. It does appear in Diceto, 2 pp. 56–7; Roger of Howden, *Gesta*, 2 pp. 62–3, *Chronica*, 2 pp. 356–7; *Libellus*, pp. 257–8; Roger of Wendover, 1 pp. 145–6, *LFWT*, pp. 94–6. Both this letter and the one which follows it are probably spurious.

69. Obscure, unless this is a reference to the defeat inflicted by King Nebuchadnezzar of Babylon on Pharoah Necho after Necho had established control over Jerusalem. Nebuchadnezzar went on to capture Jerusalem (2 Kings ch. 23 vv. 29, 33–5; ch. 24 vv. 7, 10–12).

Some time ago we received, as befits the magnificence of Our Majesty, your Devotion's letter which was sent to us on weighty matters and which - provided your words could be relied on - would have brought you advantage. We judged it fitting to communicate with your Magnitude by addressing you in a letter.

Now however, because you have profaned the Holy Land, which we govern by the command of the Eternal King as protector of Judaea, Samaria and Palestine, concern for our imperial office urges us to give due attention to the outrage of such presumptuous and culpable audacity. For this reason, unless you restore the land and everything you have seized and pay satisfaction assessed in proportion to your wicked excesses and in accordance with holy ordinances, we are fixing a date a year from 1 November[70] - so that we should not seem to be waging illegal war - when we shall test the fortune of battle on the Campus Taneos [the Field of Zoan, in Egypt - see Psalm 78 v. 13] in the strength of the Lifegiving Cross and in the name of the true Joseph [Christ].[71]

For we can hardly believe that you are unaware that these events of our time echo the writings of the ancients and the old histories. Surely you are not unaware of our predecessors' campaigns in both Ethiopias, Mauritania, Persia, Syria, Parthia - where our dictator Crassus met his premature fate at the hands of the Parthians - Judaea, Samaria, Maritima, Arabia, Chaldaea, and also Egypt, where, alas! the Roman citizen Antony, a remarkable man, who was endowed with all virtues except the splendour of self-control, served Cleopatra with immoderate passion, unfittingly for a knight sent on such important business. Surely you are not unaware that Armenia and innumerable other countries are subject to our authority? This is well known to the kings on whose blood Roman swords are repeatedly intoxicated, and you also will discover from your own experience what our victorious eagles may do with God's help; what the cohorts of various nations may do, the Teutonic fury, seizing arms even in

70. It is not clear which year is meant. Frederick did not set out until May 1189 and did not reach Cilician Armenia until June 1190. Perhaps the set date is 1 November 1190.

71. In contrast to the false Joseph, Saladin (Yūsuf).

peace, the indomitable people from the source of the Rhine,[72] the young Istrian who has never known flight, the lofty Bavarian, the cunning Swabian, the cautious Franconian, the Saxon, sporting with a sword, the Thuringian, the Westphalian, the agile Brabantine, the Lotharinian who does not know what peace is, the restless Burgundian, the lecherous[73] Alpine, the Frisian flying madly[74] ahead; the Bohemian, rejoicing beyond death; the Bolognese, fiercer than their wild beasts, the Austrian, the Bugresian, Illyrican, Lombard, Tuscan, those from the March of Ancona; the Venetian ship's mate, the nautical Pisan! In short, on that prearranged day, that day full of joy and delight and reverence for Christ, our right hand which you have accused of being weakened by old age will teach you that it has learnt to brandish swords.

We think that the sultan's reply to the emperor's letter also ought to be inserted into our little book, because it clearly shows the proud and confident state of mind in which the tyrant set out to resist. We propose to reproduce the simple language in which it was composed, changing absolutely nothing.[75]

To the sincere, friendly, great, lofty king Frederick of Germany; in the name of God the Merciful, through the Grace of God the One, the Powerful, the All-surpassing, the Victor, the Eternal, whose kingdom has no end. We give eternal thanks to Him, whose grace is over the whole world; we beseech Him to pour out His utterance over His prophets; and especially over our instructor His messenger Muḥammad, whom He sent to amend right law; which He will make to appear over all laws.

Now we give notice to the king, the sincere, powerful, friendly, great, amicable, king of Germany, that a certain man named Henry [count of Dietz] came to us, saying that he was your messenger. He brought us a certain document, which he said was from you. We have had the document read, and we

72. *Caput indomitum Rheni.* MS C has *caput indomitum Regni*, 'the indomitable people from the capital of the Empire'.

73. *Salaces.* MS C has *acies*, which probably means 'army' in this context.

74. Reading *in amente* for *in amento.* The *Libellus* has *in armento* which would mean 'under arms', or 'fully armed'.

75. This letter appears in all MSS of IP1 and also in *Libellus,* p. 259; Gerald of Wales, *Liber de Principis Instructione*, pp. 269–72; Roger of Wendover, 1 pp. 147–9; *LFWT*, pp. 96–8.

heard what your messenger had to tell us, and we are replying to those words.

So this is our reply to the document. What if you reckon up those who have agreed to come with you against us, and you name them and you say: 'the king of such and such a land, and the king of another land; and such and such a count, and such and such an archbishop, and marquises and knights'. If we wished to declare those who are in our service and who are intent on our command and ready at our utterance and who fight personally in our forces, it would not be possible to reduce them all to writing. And if you compute the names of the Christian races, there are more Saracen races, and they are larger than the Christian ones. And if there is a sea between you and the Christians whom you name, there is no sea between us and the Saracens, whose numbers cannot be estimated, and there is no impediment to their coming to us.

There are Bedouins with us, who would be force enough for us if we were to set them against our enemies. There are Turkemanns, who would destroy our enemies if we were to pour them out over them. There are our peasants who would fight strenuously if we ordered them to do so against peoples who were about to invade our country, and would be enriched by them and exterminate them.

How? We have warlike sultans with us, through whom we are able to hold our land without defences, and through whom we have acquired lands and conquered our enemies. All these most Pagan[76] kings will not delay when we summon them. And when you have assembled your army, as your document says, and when you lead an infinite multitude as your messenger described, we will come to meet you in the power of God.

Nor is this coastal land enough for us; but by God's Will we will cross the sea and obtain all your lands, by God's Strength. For if you come, you will come with all your forces, and you will be here with all your people, and we know that no one will be left in your land who would be able to defend it or to guard the land. And when God, by His Strength, has given us the victory over you, there will be nothing more for us to do except

76. Obviously this should be 'Muslim'. It was normal western European Christian practice at this time to use 'Pagan' to mean 'Muslim'.

to capture your lands easily by His Strength and Will.

For the united forces of Christianity have come twice against us in Babylon [Egypt], one time at Damietta, and the other time at Alexandria.[77] That was when the coast of the land of Jerusalem was in Christian hands, and both in the land of Damascus and in the land of the Saracens in individual castles each individual lord was acting independently. You know how the Christians retreated both times and the result of their campaigns. And now our people have been restored to their own regions, and God has added to us more affluent areas and gathered lands from far and wide into our dominion: the land of Babylon [Egypt] with its dependancies, and the land of Damascus, and the coastland of Jerusalem, and the land of Gesira and its castles, and the land of Roasia with its dependancies, and the region of India, with its dependancies, and through the Grace of God all this is in our hands; and the rest of the kingdom of the Saracens obeys our command. For if we command the most excellent kings of the Saracens, they will not hold themselves back from us. If we instruct the caliph of Baghdad, God save him! to come to us, he will rise up out of the high throne of his empire, and he will come to aid our excellence.

We have obtained through the virtue and power of God both Jerusalem and its lands. There remains in Christian hands the three cities of Tyre, Tripoli and Antioch, and these we will soon seize. But if you wish for war, and if God wills, so that it may be that we acquire the whole Christian land by His Will, we will come in the virtue of God to meet you as is written in your letter. On the other hand if you should seek peace with us, we will send to the commanders of the three places I have mentioned and order them to consign them to us without argument, and we will return the holy cross to you and free all the Christian captives who are in our whole land and we will have peace with you. We will permit you to have one priest at the sepulchre, and we will restore the abbeys which used to exist at the time of Paganism, and we will be good to them; and we will permit pilgrims to come, as long as we shall live, and we will have peace with you.

If the document which came to us by the hand of the said

77. During King Amalric's campaigns of the 1160s.

Henry was the king's document, we have written this document in reply, and may God elevate us to His Counsel by His Will! This document was written in the 584th year after the coming of our prophet Muḥammad, thanks be to God the Only One. And may God save our prophet Muḥammad and his offspring; and may He preserve the safety of the Lord Saviour, the victorious High King, unifier of the True Word, adorner of the Banner of Truth, reformer of the globe and law, the sultan of the Saracens and Pagans, the servant of the two sacred houses, and the sacred house of Jerusalem, the father of victors, Joseph son of Job, arouser of the offspring of Murmuraenus.[78]

Chapter 19:[79] The armed multitude the emperor assembled at Metz. He crosses through Hungary.[80]

The magnificent emperor regarded with contempt all the nonsense in this letter from the proud and faithless tyrant. He was filled with the anger worthy of a prince, and all his passions burned for war. The magnates of the whole empire followed him. By imperial edict all assembled together at Metz [27 March 1188][81] and unanimously proclaimed their vow to make this distinguished pilgrimage: '"This is the Lord's doing" [Psalm 118 v. 23] "which blows where it wills" [John's Gospel ch. 3 v. 8] and inclines human hearts where it wishes.'

Great princes armed themselves for war, yet they were not drawn by appetite for vainglory, not led on by money, not stirred by entreaty, but only by a desire for eternal reward through God and for God's sake. The Heavenly Wisdom on High had arranged for them to be freely called and to give their service freely to God, so that the imperial mag-

78. *Al-muḥyī dawlat amīr al-mu'minīn,* 'arouser of the kingdom of the rulers of the believers': see Mayer (1962), p. 250 note 1.

79. Stubbs (1864), p. 42 note 1, notes that from this point the chapter numbering in MS A, the only manuscript to number the chapters, becomes unreliable. His edition of the text followed the numbering of Gale's edition of 1687.

80. The best account of the Emperor Frederick Barbarossa's crusade is in *Historia de Expeditione Friderici*, the so-called 'Ansbert'. See also *Historia Peregrinorum*; *Epistola de Morte Friderici Imperatoris* (*EMFI*); William of Newburgh, pp. 326–30. The accounts in Roger of Howden's works, Ralph of Diceto and Ralph of Coggeshall are extremely brief. Gerald of Wales' account is almost identical to our writer, as is *LFWT*.

81. See 'Ansbert', p. 14.

nificence should have worthy companions. By the instigation of the Holy Spirit, they flocked together from everywhere.

Anyone who saw so many peoples and so many princes under one general would have believed that the ancient glory of the Roman empire had never passed away. There were bishops, dukes, counts, marquises, and as many other princes as could be in this army of Christ, but if we were to record their names and where each one came from it would be both troublesome for the writer and tedious for the reader and make our account too long.

By wise advice it was decreed that no one should set out on this journey who did not have sufficient means for a year of travel. A great many wagons were constructed for sick travellers so that the infirm should not delay the healthy and the crowd of sick and destitute should not perish on the way.

They discussed whether this great mass of warriors should travel by sea or by land. However it seemed that even an enormous fleet of ships would not be enough to transport so many thousands across the sea. The emperor was anxious to press on with his proposed undertaking, so he set out through Hungary.[82] So the king who had been the last to make his vow of pilgrimage hurried to be the first to discharge it.[83]

Chapter 20: The emperor is received by the king of the Hungarians, and the people follow his example and take the cross.

The king of the Hungarians, whose name was Béla [III, 1173–96], came joyfully to meet Caesar. He was a man with many natural gifts: a tall stature and a notable face; and if the rest were not enough, he would be thought worthy of a kingdom for the masterful grace of his face alone. This king hastened joyfully to meet the army of Christ. He received it hospitably, accompanied it on its route in friendship and by practical actions gave testimony of the fervour of his devotion.

82. The problem with the land route was that an enormous army would have to pass through the Christian Byzantine empire and the Muslim lands of the sultan of Iconium. In December 1188 the Emperor Isaac Angelus and the sultan of Iconium sent ambassadors to Emperor Frederick's court, concerned that the emperor was not really coming on pilgrimage but was intending to invade them ('Ansbert', pp. 15–16). Frederick sent the bishop of Münster and a number of noble counts to Constantinople to negotiate peace: see ch. 21, below.

83. He set out from Ratisbon (Regensburg) 11 May 1189: 'Ansbert', p. 17.

A great many of the local inhabitants were inflamed by his excellent example. They saw the holy army and were eager to join it. They looked forward to the rewards for those who strove and they did not fear the labour. At once they wished, they vowed, they followed. So it was clearly shown that the grace of the Holy Spirit allowed them no delay in their undertakings.[84]

Chapter 21: Having crossed the Danube, the emperor has to contend with the Huns, Alans, Bulgarians, Patzinaks, Macedonians, and the emperor of Constantinople.

Having crossed the Danube,[85] the emperor arrived at the farther mountain passes of Bulgaria. Huns and Alans, Bulgarians and Patzinaks rushed suddenly out from ambushes on to the Lord's people. These people have become confident bandits because of the inaccessibility and difficult terrain of their regions.

The emperor left Bulgaria and entered Macedonia. The land is fortified on all sides with high crags, obstructed with thorn bushes, entangled in narrow winding paths, and in addition the natural fortifications have been improved by man-made constructions. The aforementioned peoples had seized these narrow passes. The villainous emperor Isaac [Angelus] of Constantinople had sent them in advance to do this, so that they could either crush or impede the advancing army. However, our knights successfully overcame both the problem of the enemy and of the road.

So having crossed the Macedonian plains, they reached Philippopolis [Plovdiv: 24–6 August 1189].[86] This city used to be called Pulpudeba. It took its present name from the Roman emperor Philip, who was the first of all the emperors to become a Christian. He adorned the imperial glory with the title of the Christian profession.[87] When they heard that

---

84. See 'Ansbert', pp. 24–5 for the problems which the emperor encountered in Hungary.
85. The author's geography is inaccurate. 'Ansbert' states that Frederick had followed the Danube from Ratisbon to Vienna and then continued into Hungary travelling on the south bank of this river. So he had no further need to cross it. Leaving Hungary he crossed the River Drava and then the Sava where it meets the Danube, proceeding through Belgrade into Bulgaria.
86. They spent 11 weeks at Philippopolis: 'Ansbert', pp. 37, 52.
87. A short-lived emperor of the third century AD; it is unclear whether he actually became a Christian. In fact this city was named after Philip II of Macedon, the father of Alexander the Great.

the Latins were coming, the Greeks deserted the city, 'in great fear where no fear was due' [Psalm 53 v. 5].

The Greeks only had one reason for fear: they feared them because they did not love them. The Latins had not come to plunder other people's property, for they had enough of their own. They had not taken up arms against the Faithful, for they were persecuting the errors of the unbelieving Gentiles. This was that ancient and inexorable hatred which the Greeks conceived long ago against the Latins and which had now with the relentless passing of time descended into their posterity. Do you wish to know what sparked off this hatred? 'It is no crime, if it has good reason.'[88]

We can confidently put this forward as the cause: whereas the Latins are equally proficient in knowledge and arms, the Greeks know that they themselves are completely ignorant and unwarlike. This sparked off their hatred, and they are wasting away with jealousy of the good they see in others. Perfidious people, wicked and altogether degenerate generation! Their decline is the more extraordinary because they used to be so illustrious. It is as if gold were transformed into slag, grain into chaff, purity into dung or glory into confusion.

The Ancient Greeks undertook many military enterprises, and pursued many studies, but all that burning virtue has gone cold in their descendants and moved over into the Latin world. Those who used to be fountains are now trickles, or rather dry and exhausted hollows. There is no modern successor for the virtues of the Ancient Greeks, instead all are successors of their crimes, the deceits of Sinon and the tricks of Ulysses; and they continue the atrocities of Atreus.[89] As for their military skills, they fight with artifice, not arms. As for their good faith, they do you more damage as friend than as enemy.[90]

Although those people could not prevent our army's passing in the

88. This seems to be a proverb. It is repeated in MS C's additions to Bk. 6 ch. 37, p. 385 below.

89. For Sinon, see Vergil's *Aeneid*, Book 2. In the legend of the Trojan war, Sinon was the Greek who tricked the Trojans into taking the wooden horse into Troy. The horse turned out to be full of Greek warriors. Ulysses, or Odysseus, was one of the Greek leaders in the Trojan war; the wooden horse was his idea. Atreus, according to Greek legend, was King of Mycenae. His wife Aerope was seduced by his brother Thyestes. In revenge, Atreus served up their children for Thyestes to eat.

90. *Historia Peregrinorum*, p. 132 and *EMFI*, p. 173 also criticise the Greeks; 'Ansbert' includes a letter from Frederick to his son Henry in Germany complaining about the untrustworthiness of the Greeks, pp. 40–3.

abovementioned places, they did what they could. All the local inhabitants went up into the mountains, taking away all the comforts which can be bought. Those approaching found empty houses with everything removed.

The emperor had already sent the bishop of Münster on ahead with other princes to Constantinople to negotiate peace. That most villainous and cruel tyrant threw them into prison. He did not shrink from violating the immunity of ambassadors, which is sanctified by antiquity even among Barbarians, and approved by custom and commended by honour. However, he later released the interned envoys. This release was motivated more by fear than regard for the law, for he was afraid that the royal city would be destroyed if he did not quickly appease our people for the insult he had offered them.

It would have been fitting for that city to have been razed to the ground. If rumour is to be believed, it had recently been polluted by the construction of mosques, which the perfidious emperor had allowed to be built. He was obliged to do this by the terms of a treaty he had made with the Turks.[91]

By now the summer was passing and autumn was coming. Day and night were of equal length as if the sign of Libra held them in balance.

Chapter 22: The emperor Frederick winters in Greece; his peace with the emperor Isaac; the crafty words of the sultan of Iconium; he crosses the Straits of St George.

The magnificent emperor of the Romans marched towards Adrianople, to winter there. When he entered it [22 November 1189][92] he found it empty and deserted by its inhabitants. He set up his quarters there and waited for better weather before moving on.

The duke of Swabia, the emperor's son, feared that his idleness would appear to be self indulgence, and self indulgence would appear to be cowardice. He decided that the army needed exercise during its winter inactivity, and hastened to attack a certain castle which was not far from the city. Greeks had assembled there so that they could use it as a base for launching ambushes on the Latins. They trusted in its fortifications, but they were put to shame, for they were swiftly tamed, conquered,

91. See 'Ansbert', p. 39; Bahā' al-Dīn, pp. 198–201.
92. See 'Ansbert', p. 53.

bound and carried away as prisoners.[93]

When he heard this, the Byzantine prince feared the worst. Afraid that the whole empire would be destroyed, he hastily sent messengers to the emperor, promising to give hostages as security for peace, access to markets where they could buy food, and ships to carry them across the straits.[94]

Although many of his people considered it undesirable to make any peace with the tyrant, the emperor preferred to accept the terms as offered rather than delay his journey. Just before Easter [23–8 March 1190][95] he crossed that narrow strait which is known in popular parlance as 'St George's arm'. Although this strait is very narrow it is glorious because it flows past the great city of Constantinople and it divides the globe in two, bathing both Asia and Europe.

The sultan of Iconium was a crafty man and thirsty for Christian blood. Hiding his malignant intentions, he faked friendship towards our people on a fraudulent pretext so that he could catch them unawares and destroy them. He sent messengers to Caesar more than once while he was still in Greece, trying to persuade him to come and accusing the Greeks and the Greek prince of deceit. He promised that he would be a devoted and faithful friend of the Christians, would put his goods and his people at their disposal, and would give everyone access to markets and an unhindered passage through his lands.[96]

Now Caesar was too credulous, for he thought that other people were as highly principled as he. He commanded everyone with threats that when they entered Turkish territory no one was to plunder anything, but were studiously to observe the peace which had been agreed with the sultan. So it was that our people passed by an enormous quantity of booty which the sultan had deliberately sent to the entrance of the kingdom, and left it completely untouched. Alas for the mistaken judgement of men ignorant of what was to come! If only they had had prior knowledge of the future famine, their difficult journey and the ambushes set by the tyrant, they would have known that chance had offered them the

93. See 'Ansbert', pp. 53–4, and 58–9, 62 for other cities captured; also *Historia Peregrinorum*, pp. 146–8; *EMFI*, p. 173.

94. Peace was made 14 February 1190: 'Ansbert', p. 64.

95. For the dates see 'Ansbert', pp. 70–1 and *Historia Peregrinorum* p. 152, which record that Frederick and the army passed through Gallipoli and then crossed the Hellespont.

96. Bahā' al-Dīn, p. 183 states the opposite: the sultan of Iconium pretended to be the emperor's enemy but was really on good terms with him. 'Ansbert', pp. 67, 76 agrees with our author.

opportunity to provide for themselves in the face of great and imminent danger. Yet our people did not have so much confidence in the words of the faithless prince that they were off their guard. They kept ranks and marched fully armed.

The Emperor Frederick's army: number, ranks and organisation. And so all took up arms to advance into Parthia. There were around 3000 knights, and around 80,000 of the rest. There were seven bishops, one archbishop, two dukes, nineteen counts and three marquises. This remarkable army 'seemed not to have its like before nor yet its sequel after.'[97]

To prevent disagreements causing disorder in such a great confused mass the whole army was divided into three parts. The first part was assigned to the duke of Swabia, the last to the emperor, and the middle part was to guard the pack animals and the baggage. The army was a pleasure to behold as it proceeded.

It was wisely arranged. They did not all march together, nor spread out, but in troops; and although there were many commanding the parts, one governed the whole. This is the best arrangement in camp, and excellent in war. Just as the army perishes without a leader, so it is generally inefficient where there are many in charge contending on equal terms.

Fortunate empire! fortunate bosom of Germany! it has produced such great children, so many fruitful people, so many energetic warriors of Christ, for its own glory and the ruin of its enemies!

Chapter 23: The Christian army suffers ambushes and attacks through the treachery of the sultan of Iconium. It later wins a victory through which it overcomes the sultan, his son and the Turks and captures Iconium.

When our people had crossed into Turkish territory [27 April 1190],[98] they experienced no hostility for some days. This was the sultan's intention, as he wished them to pass unhindered into the heart of his kingdom, so that as they began to run short of food and the roads deteriorated they would be more vulnerable to attack.

97. Stubbs and Mayer identify these phrases as poetry. Mayer believes that they were in the German source used by the author of IP1. However, it is interesting that the compiler of IP2 also included the occasional lines of verse.
98. See 'Ansbert', p. 76.

That wicked traitor had seized the mountain precipices, the woodland thickets and the impassable rivers. He did not keep to the terms which he had so earnestly agreed upon, opposing them with arrows and rocks as they passed through. This was his market, his peaceful passage through his lands![99] This is how much trust can be placed in Gentiles! They always measure out virtue and fraud equally against their enemies.[100]

Furthermore, they are very anxious to avoid pitched battles or hand-to-hand conflict; they hurl missiles from a distance. For them it is no less honourable to flee than to put their enemy to flight. They attacked both ends of the army, now the rearguard, now the vanguard. If by some chance the army became divided in the narrow passes they would launch an attack on one part or the other.

Our people also passed sleepless and troubled nights, for the enemy made a terrific clamour around their camp. A rain of missiles pierced the tents. Several people were killed while they were asleep. The enemy threatened them continually, so that for six weeks they ate under arms and they slept under arms, never removing their mailshirts. What was more, they grew very short of food and water. When horses were killed in battle they drew relief and great pleasure from eating the horses' flesh and drinking the blood. So with the ingenuity which comes from necessity they found a new use for their mounts.

At one point [3 May][101] the going became particularly difficult, with steep cliffs and rough ascents up narrow paths. The first part of the army, led by the emperor's son, was passing through this when the Turks suddenly rushed out of ambush and fell on the rearguard from all sides. Confident of victory, they engaged them at close quarters with lances and swords. The dreadful news reached the duke's ears. Without delay he returned headlong the way he had come, unhesitatingly retracing the difficulties he had just rejoiced to have overcome, his anger indifferent to danger. Their horses were forced to gallop where they could hardly even walk. While he was rushing about hither and thither anxiously and off his guard, seeking his father, calling his father, a rock struck his helmet and knocked out his teeth; but still he remained unmoved and was not thrown from his horse. That fortunate child! In order to rescue his father he did not spare himself, but threw himself into danger. But in compensation for the wound he received he keeps an eternal mark of honour; for

99. This refers to the promises made by the sultan: see ch. 22, above.
100. For this, see 'Ansbert', pp. 76–81.
101. 'Ansbert', pp. 77–8.

whenever he parts his lips his empty mouth bears witness to the glory of his victory.[102]

At last after many heavy assaults they reached Iconium, where that wicked traitor had shut himself up within the fortifications of the city. Our people pitched their tents not far away, with no idea of what danger might threaten them the next day. By this time the solemn festival of Pentecost was almost over, and that night there was a terrible downpour, so heavy that it was felt as much inside the camp as outside.[103]

How Melchin, son of the sultan of Iconium, came against the emperor Frederick with an enormous army. When morning came [18 May][104] the clouds had gone and the sky was clear. Look! Suddenly with trumpets and drums and a horrible noise the Turkish army was bearing down on them spread out on every side. So great an army had never before been seen, nor could it be believed possible. You might read somewhere that there were 300,000 or more, but that would be a guess, for they could not be counted.

The sultan's son, named Melkin [Quṭb al-Dīn Malik-Shāh], had summoned all this multitude to arms, wishing to forestall his father-in-law Saladin by carrying off the victor's palm. He was confident of victory, trusting in the number and strength of his forces. Meanwhile the sultan ascended his highest tower and sat down to watch. From there he had a view of the adjacent farmland where the armies were about to fight. He hoped that what his boastful mind had foretold was about to be fulfilled.

The city of Iconium is captured and the army of the sultan's son Melkin is routed. Seeing that most of his army was terrified by the unheard-of size of the enemy force, the emperor displayed the confidence befitting a great-spirited prince. Raising his hands towards Heaven, in the sight of

---

102. As this sentence is written in the present tense the original source for this section was probably written before Frederick of Swabia's death in January 1191. Onlookers were apparently much impressed by this incident, as all the detailed accounts of the emperor's crusade record it. 'Ansbert' states: 'the duke of Alamannia happened to be wounded by a blow from a stone.' *Historia Peregrinorum*, pp. 158–9, has a similar account to our author, stating that the enemy broke one of the duke's teeth. *EMFI*, p. 175, states that the duke lost a top tooth and half a bottom one.

103. 'Ansbert' also records a heavy storm, on 17 May; but the army had encamped on 15 May (pp. 82–4).

104. 'Ansbert', p. 84; for this battle see also *Historia Peregrinorum*, pp. 168–70; *EMFI*, p. 176.

all he gave thanks to the Lord because now the inevitable battle was upon them, which had been put off until now because the enemy kept running away. All were inspired with immense enthusiasm at the sound of his voice. As they gazed on Caesar's joyful face, all received from this one man the incentive to be courageous. Although he was old he inspired youths, and although he was weak he inspired the strong.

'What god is as great as our God?' [Psalm 77 v. 13]. All that multitude was so certain of victory that they brought chains with them rather than swords, but they were overcome in a moment. At once the city was captured, and the enemy outside it was thrown down. On both sides there was massacre, carnage everywhere, on all sides heaps of the slain. The enemy were so densely packed that they could not flee; so the great numbers which had been their boast became their downfall. 'Now they press close, in hand-to-hand combat,' bows are broken, arrows do not fly, 'there is scarce room for swords; all is confusion.'

The battle with which the enemy had planned to destroy our people instead brings them glory. Hitherto the enemy had confined themselves to a fleeting war among thorn bushes and rocky chasms, but now battle was joined in open country. The Christians satisfied their anger, which had burned so many times in vain. The Turks discovered, whether they liked it or not, what those whom they had provoked at a distance could do hand-to-hand.

Divine Virtue supplied this notable victory. His faithful people were not undeserving of it, for there was chastity in the camp, and discipline under arms, in all and before all fear of the Lord, among all love for their neighbour, all of one mind in fraternal affection just as they were all partners in danger.

The emperor Frederick takes hostages from the sultan of Iconium and confirms the treaty with him.[105] When the city was captured and the sultan realised that the only fortification which he had left was the tower where he was, he sent at once to Caesar pouring all the blame on his son. He claimed that he was completely innocent, promised Caesar as much gold as he wanted, and promised that he would give him as many and whichever hostages he might order, to guarantee their treaty. Caesar, alas, was too easy-going! He accepted the offer and he conceded what the sultan begged for. It was hardly praiseworthy to free 'a violent and deceitful' man [Psalm 5 v. 6] when he had virtually captured him; it

105. 'Ansbert', pp. 86–7; *Historia Peregrinorum*, p. 170.

would have been more honourable to have killed him than to have preserved this great enemy of the Christian name unharmed.

The hostages were handed over and the peace treaty was confirmed, but the godlessness of that malignant traitor was not yet done. When the Christians were travelling far away from Iconium he attacked them, now with ambushes, now in open battle. The hostages were interrogated about these attacks and they concocted a lie which suited them: they claimed that these were wild Turks who were subject to no government, wandering with no fixed abode. Having nothing of their own, they were always after other people's property, either seizing it or stealing it.[106]

However, the Turks attacked the army less heavily, remembering that they had lost many of their own people. According to a conservative estimate, in the above battles 22,000 Turks had been consumed by the sword.

Chapter 24: The emperor Frederick comes to Cilician Armenia, where he drowns in the river Selef. His son the duke of Swabia is put in charge of the army.

Now the victorious army crossed the frontier into Armenia.[107] Everyone was delighted because they had left an enemy kingdom and arrived in a Christian country. But alas! They came into a calamitous land, which extinguished the joy and light of all.

Ascend to a high place and search out, if you may, the counsels of the Lord, Whose many judgements are 'like the great deep' [Psalm 36 v. 6]. Sometimes you will be amazed at what happens and sometimes you will be disturbed, so that you will learn to praise the Author of All in all things!

There is a place in the heart of Armenia closed in on one side by steep mountains and on the other by the course of the river Selef [Göksu]. While the pack animals and the baggage were crossing this river the victorious emperor waited. That renowned man was slightly above average height, with gold-red hair and red beard both mingled with grey-white; prominent eyebrows, burning eyes, cheeks short but wide; his chest and shoulders were broad; the rest of his appearance was also

106. 'Ansbert', p. 88: Frederick threatened to kill the hostages if the attacks continued; the attacks then stopped.

107. See 'Ansbert', pp. 88-9.

manly. He had a notable and amazing characteristic which is also recorded of Socrates: his expression reflected his steadfast mind, constant and unchanging, never clouded with sorrow, nor tense with anger, nor relaxed with joy. He held such respect for his native German language that although he was not ignorant of other languages he never spoke to ambassadors from other nations except through an interpreter.

For a long time the great man waited while the pack animals were going on in front. At last bored by the delay and wishing to get on with the journey he decided to cross the river at the nearest point, so that he could overtake the pack animals and return to the freedom of the road. O sea! O earth! O Heaven! That governor of the Roman Empire, forever Augustus, through whom the glory of Ancient Rome flourished again, its honour lived again, its power sprang up again: alas! he was carried away in the water and perished. Although his companions hurried from all sides to help him, the spark of his aged life was quickly extinguished [10 June 1190].

Many claim that his death came about because he decided to go swimming, but the gravity of his character makes this unlikely. It is unbelievable that he, a weak swimmer, should choose to risk himself, on whom so much depended, in treacherous waters. Conscience be witness, it is his death itself which is painful to us rather than the cause of his death. But what we read in scripture consoles us: 'But the good man, even if he dies an untimely death, will be at rest' [Wisdom ch. 4 v. 7].[108]

---

108. It is unclear how the emperor died. 'Ansbert', pp. 91-2 states that he was trying to cross the river. *Historia Peregrinorum* says he was trying to swim across to cool off and wash, and the current overpowered him (p. 172). *EMFI*, pp. 177-8, says that he had crossed the river and had lunch, decided to go swimming to cool off and drowned. Bahā' al-Dīn initially states, p. 184, that he died trying to swim across, but then quotes a letter from the *Catholicos*, head of the Armenian Church, stating that the emperor had gone for a cooling swim and been carried away by the current (p. 187). Both state that the emperor was pulled out alive but died a few days later. Ralph of Diceto, p. 84, states that he was crossing the river on his horse and fell in and drowned. Roger of Howden, *Gesta*, 2 p. 89 states that he was swimming alone in the river, but in his later *Chronica*, 2 p. 359, he gives the same account as Diceto. Ralph of Coggeshall's account is similar to Diceto and the *Chronica* (p. 24). Ibn al-Athīr says that the emperor went into the river to wash, but drowned (2 p. 24). 'Imād al-Dīn states that he was told by a Christian that the king of the Germans (*sic*) wanted to cross the river at a narrow ford and was carried away by the current and thrown against a tree. His men pulled him out, but he died. There was then a dispute over who should replace him as leader of the army, because his elder son was in Germany. Eventually his younger son took over command (p. 229).

If the mountains of Gilboa deserved to be deprived of dew and rain when the strong men of Israel were slaughtered [2 Samuel ch. 1 v.21], what fitting punishment shall we call down on this deadly river, which overturned the chief support of the whole of Christendom? There are those who say that that place had been fatally damned from ancient times, and the nearest rock preserved these letters which had been inscribed on it long ago:

'HERE THE GREATEST OF MEN SHALL PERISH.'

The emperor Frederick's body is divided in two so that it may be buried in two places. An explosion of grief brought the news to the ears of the army. Everyone was dismayed. Their sorrow was unparalleled in the annals of antiquity, the traditions of history or the fictions of fairytale. Even the laments of mothers bereaved of their children, the tears of brides bereaved of their husbands, or any other grief could not equal it. 'Lacking a model and unknown in any age,' [Lucan, *The Civil War (Pharsalia)*, Bk. 9 v. 169], it surpassed all tears and laments.

Many of the emperor's servants were present, his relatives and also his son; but they could not be told apart in the crowds of mourners where each and everyone bewailed the loss of their lord and father. Yet they were all relieved and all thanked divine providence that he had not departed this life while they were in infidel territory.

When the funeral rites were complete, they left that fatal place as quickly as possible. They adorned Caesar's body with regal magnificence to carry it to Antioch. At Antioch they boiled the body for a long time to separate the flesh from the bones.[109] The flesh was laid to rest in the church of the apostolic see of Antioch.[110] The bones were carried by sea to Tyre to be transported to Jerusalem.[111] It was indeed fitting and wonderfully ordained by the Lord that he who had contended so honourably for Christ should reside in the two preeminent churches of the Christian faith. He was a knight of both and he was divided between them: one was preeminent as the site of the Lord's Sepulchre and the other was distinguished as the see of the prince of the apostles [St Peter].

---

109. 'Imād al-Dīn, p. 228, corroborates this.
110. 'Ansbert', p. 92, agrees.
111. They never reached Jerusalem, however: William of Newburgh, p. 330, states that they were buried at Tyre.

The misfortunes endured by the German pilgrims in the land of Antioch after the death of Emperor Frederick. When the Christians arrived at Antioch [21 June 1190] after many long food shortages, they greedily overindulged and were choked by the sudden repletion. They had overcome enemies and famine only to be destroyed by peace and wiped out by too much food. When the greater part of the army had died by this shameful fate, many of the rest went home. A small number who were ashamed to go back fought under the command of the emperor's son [Duke Frederick of Swabia].[112]

The prince of Antioch [Bohemond III] handed the whole city and all its defences over to the duke. He decided of his own accord that the city should be entrusted to the duke for its better protection. This man of action would be able to protect its territories against the enemy's frequent attacks.[113]

The news that Emperor Frederick has drowned reaches Acre. The besieged Turks rejoice and the besieging Christians are depressed. Meanwhile the knights of Christ who had travelled by sea to assist the Holy Land were besieging Acre.[114] Confident in their own numbers and the strength of the city's fortifications, the besieged Turks held out obstinately against them, manning the city ramparts and struggling to return blow for blow on their attackers. Then, listen! an enormous shout goes up, and there is a clamour of exulting voices in the city! Climbing up the towers, Turks yelled insults at the besieging Christians outside.

'What are you doing, wretches? What more are you hoping for? You were expecting the imminent arrival of your emperor, but he's drowned! Your hope has disappeared and you can do no more to resist, as you see!'

Shouting these insults, they led a dance around the city, blowing trumpets, cawing as is their custom, with drums crashing and declaring the joy of their hearts in as many ways as they could. So they mocked and derided the Christians and aroused confidence and rash joy in their own side.

---

112. See 'Ansbert', p. 92; 'Imād al-Dīn, pp. 232–3; Bahā' al-Dīn, pp. 191–2, p. 198.

113. Bahā' al-Dīn claims, p. 270, that the duke forced Prince Bohemond to hand Antioch over to him. The duke of Swabia then went on to Tripoli and finally arrived at Acre in October 1190. See Bk. 1 chs. 44–5 and ch. 61, below.

114. 'Confident...western parts of the globe' is not in the G and A groups of manuscripts (IP1), but has been inserted by the compiler of IP2.

The Christians were shattered by this news. They were afflicted with incredible grief, almost desperate, mortally wounded by this bitter disaster, because it was true that they had expected to achieve their end with the emperor's help. So they could hardly believe what the Turks had said; but the latter claimed that it was true and that Saladin had told them.[115] For there were not enough Christians to control the entrances to the city or to prevent Turks from going in and out secretly.

Invoking God to help them, the Christians patiently awaited the arrival of the others whom they hoped were coming from the western parts of the globe. But to give a fuller account of the siege we shall have to backtrack.

Chapter 25: King Guy of Jerusalem is freed from imprisonment at Damascus and goes to Tripoli. Here he collects an army and hurries to Acre to engage the enemy.

After Guy, king of Jerusalem, had been held in chains at Damascus for almost a year, Saladin released him on the strict condition that he give up the kingdom and go overseas into exile as soon as possible, as we said above [ch. 10: May 1188]. The clergy of the kingdom judged that this oath should not be binding both because oaths entered into under duress are void and because the armies of the Faithful who were on their way would need him as chief and leader.

One piece of cunning deserves another! The faithless tyrant was cheated by his own bad example, for the man who slips lightly out of his promises invites others to treat their promises in the same way. That faithless man had broken the terms and good faith of the earlier treaty in which he had first promised to release the king [ch. 8, above]. Now he had forced the captive king to swear on oath that he would go into exile as soon as he was returned to freedom. Cruel liberty, which brings exile! Harsh liberation, which renounces a kingdom! But the Lord ordained that Belial's scheme would be destroyed. The tyrant lost his hopes of keeping the kingdom, and the clergy's judicial decision released the king from his excessive promise.

Distinguished warriors had come to avenge the injuries inflicted on the Cross. Summoned by their devoted fervour, from everywhere famous

115. Saladin heard the news of the emperor's death between mid-June and mid-July 1190 ('Imād al-Dīn, p. 231).

champions had come for your consolation, Jerusalem! Look! Already the whole globe fights for you, to fulfil what was said through Isaiah the prophet: 'I shall bring your descendants from the east and gather you from the west. To the north I shall say, "Give them up"; and to the south, "Do not obstruct them",' [Isaiah ch. 43 vv. 5–6].

The king had gone to Tripoli, as we said above [ch. 11], and many flocked to join him there. All glowed with a martial spirit, eager not only to protect the territories which they still held but to recover those they had lost. Their days were not idle while they were waiting at Tripoli. They launched frequent raids against the enemy nearby, striking down now 300, now more, with their victorious force.

The king's brother, Geoffrey de Lusignan, was especially conspicuous for his valour and shone out among the rest. He seemed to be inflamed against the enemy, as if he were fired more deeply than the others by personal grief. For although a single sorrow drove the rest to battle, this man was moved equally by the common cause of Christendom and by a personal desire to avenge his brother's injuries.

Chapter 26: The Christians besiege Acre on all sides. First the king comes to Tyre from Antioch, but the marquis does not let him into the city. Passing over this insult, he goes with the Pisans and no small army to Acre, which the Christians besiege by land and sea.

Not long after this, the king assembled his army and proceeded to Tyre. However, when he wished to enter the city the marquis would not admit him, although the city had been entrusted to the marquis on condition that it should be returned to the heirs of the king and the kingdom. Not content with this insult, the marquis heaped insult on injury. Everyone who tried to enter the city, whether they were the king's messengers or pilgrims, were harshly treated and 'are to him as heathen and publicans' [Matthew's Gospel ch. 18 v. 17].[116]

The marquis attacks the rebel Pisans. The Pisans possessed no small part of the city. They refused to be made partners in perfidy and

116. According to 'Imād al-Dīn, p. 163, and Bahā' al-Dīn, p. 144, the marquis said that he was acting on behalf of the kings of Europe and was awaiting their decisions and orders.

launched a commendable revolt in support of the king's rights. The marquis attacked them with many insults and civil war. The Pisans wisely decided to give way to him for the time being and retreated from the city to the army. Many others went with them.[117]

So the army camped outside on the plain. But no one was allowed to enter the city, not even to buy food. They all discovered that he whom they had hoped would help them was their enemy.

The marquis falls ill and kills his own doctors. Meanwhile the marquis was struck down by a familiar and recurring illness; but because this time it happened to be worse than usual he supposed that he had drunk a deadly potion. So a harsh edict went out against the doctors who make potions. Because of an unjust suspicion the innocent were destroyed, although their profession does not bring death but health to the sick.

Although many urged the king to attack the city he wisely overlooked the insult and hurried to besiege Acre with the best and largest army he could muster. There were 700 knights and many more of other ranks, gathered from every Christian nation. If we should care to estimate the size of the whole army together, its strength in numbers amounted to not quite 9000.

At length, after four months, King Guy led what army he had through a very dangerous place called Candelion [al-Iskanderūna]. Saladin was nearby at the time but did not know that he was passing.[118] At the end of August, that is on St Augustine's day [28 August 1189], that long and grievous siege of Acre began. At its courageous beginning it was two years since the Turks had captured the city, and the siege was to drag out for another two years.

When the Turks on the ramparts saw them coming from a distance, they were uncertain as to who was coming and why. But when they realised the situation they did not fear their arrival and they jeered at their intentions. The Pisans, seeing the journey by sea as easier because it was shorter, sailed to Acre in due order, and boldly seized the beach. They settled immovably on the sea shore and set up a steady and vigorous siege by sea. The king, on the other hand, with the rest of the army, decided to pitch his tents on the nearest mountain, which is popularly

---

117. Ambroise, lines 2737–42, agrees: the Germans and the Tiberias brothers were among those who went out to join the king.
118. 'At length...was passing' is not in IP1: cf. Ambroise, lines 2767–75.

called Mount Turon [Tell el-Mosallīyin, or Tell al-Maṣlaba].[119] Due to its good position one may observe from here all approaches to the city by land and sea. That mountain rises loftily on the eastern side of the city, and from it a clear view spreads out all around before the roving eye, far and wide across the plains.

Chapter 27: The Christians make an attack on the city, but Saladin comes up and they are attacked on both sides. They are cheered up by the arrival of a fleet of around 12,000 northerners.

On the third day after their arrival,[120] the Christians stormed the city, for it was going to be a long wait before they had stonethrowers[121] ready to hurl missiles, or other siege equipment. So, content with shields as protection, they put up ladders and climbed up. That day would have seen a quick and easy end to so many days of trouble and effort if the hatred of the ancient Enemy and a lying messenger had not obstructed them when success was within reach. The news came that Saladin was coming! Our people returned as quickly as possible to the camp, only to see that it was just a few advance guards. They were then more indignant than bitter at the victory that they had lost! Only a few had come, but terror had declared that they were innumerable. It is not unusual for fear to make things seem worse than they are.

At that time the sultan was laying siege to a castle called Beaufort

---

119. Bahā' al-Dīn, p. 156; 'Imād al-Dīn, p. 170; later Tell al-Fukhkhār. Ambroise, lines 2783-6, and Roger of Howden, *Gesta,* 2 p. 95, agree that the Christians camped here.

120. Most of the details in chapters 27 and 28 are similar to Ambroise's account, but arranged differently; e.g. in Ambroise, Saladin actually does arrive three days after the Christians' arrival (lines 2815-34), and James of Avesnes was commander of the Danish fleet (lines 2845-70). A letter from Theobald the Prefect and Peter son of Leo to the pope agrees with Ambroise that Saladin actually arrived on the third day (see Ralph of Diceto, pp. 70-1, trans. in *Conquest of Jerusalem*, p. 170). On the other hand the *Itinerarium*'s account of the fleet is endorsed by Roger of Howden and Diceto. It is not impossible that IP1 and Ambroise were drawing on the same material but interpreting it differently. The account in ch. 28 of the battle on Friday, however, is not in IP1. It only appears in MSS B and C and may have been taken from Ambroise - but the two accounts are not identical.

121. Latin: *Petraria*, French: *perrière*. Literally, a 'stoner'. The modern technical term is *petrarie*. Basically this was a large, vertically mounted slingshot.

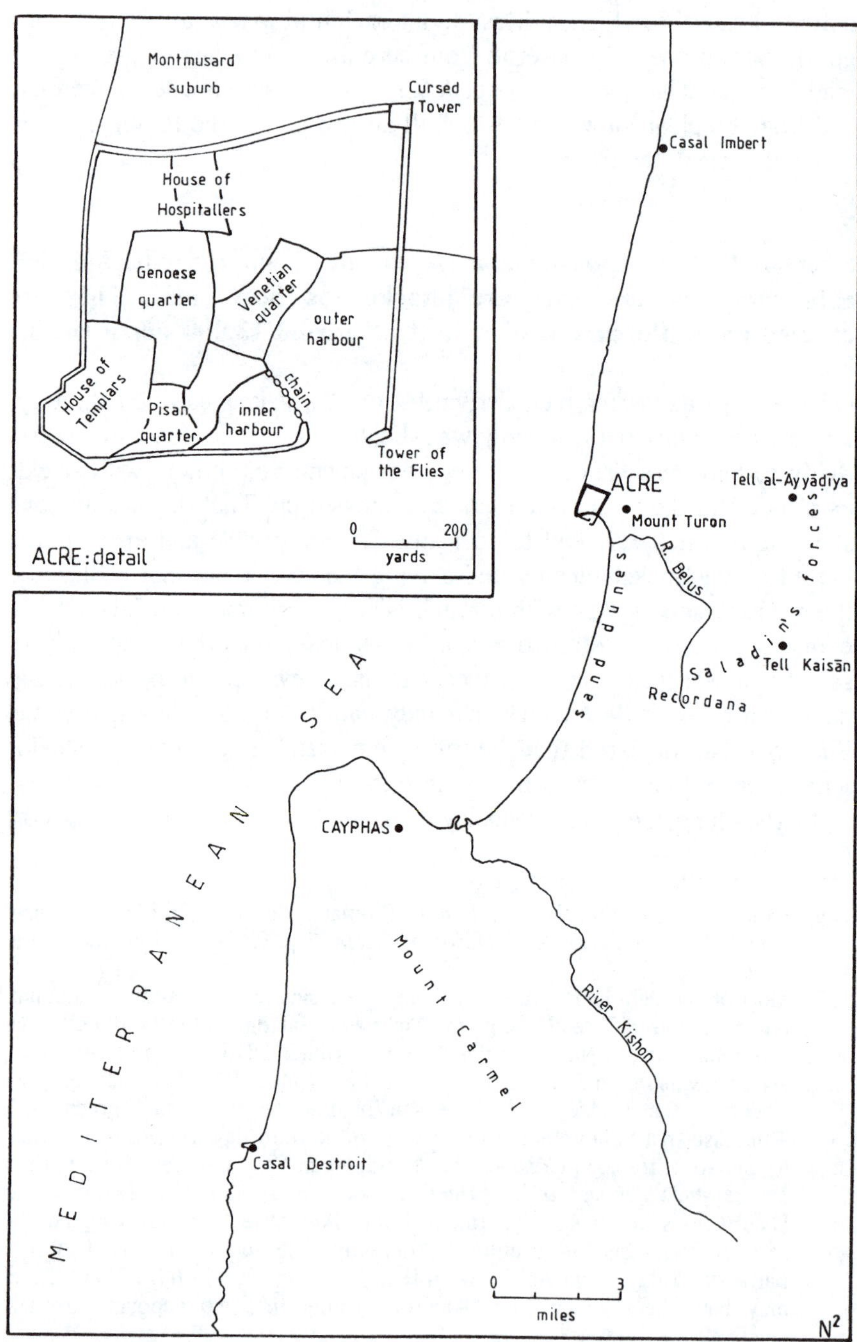

Map 2. The city of Acre and its environs.

[Shaqīf Arnūn].[122] Hearing what was happening, he hurried to Acre with a very large army. Those who were in Acre had informed him that a small number of Christians had disembarked, and that he could come and crush them in a moment, wiping memory of them from the face of the earth.[123]

As our people were outnumbered they were shut up between the enemy lines, threatened on all sides by the Turks. The Turks waged war on them in daylight and in the silent night. They also launched frequent raids against the mountain. Those who had come to besiege were themselves besieged.

While they were in these straits, 'the Dayspring from on high visited them' [Luke's Gospel ch. 1 v. 78]. Fifty ships of a type popularly called 'cogs' came with 12,000 armed warriors![124] They were so much the more welcome because they brought our people help when they were in such great straits. What comes through prayer is gratefully received; what is offered unexpectedly is more gratefully received; but we are most grateful for what comes to our aid in our direst need. However, we very often cease to believe that our greatest longings can possibly be granted, and we cannot credit something which we have longed for very much! Our people were in a tight spot, now under attack from the city side, now attacked from the outer side by Saladin's army. Surrounded and attacked alternately from this side and that, or from both sides at once, they were so perplexed that they did not dare lay down their arms nor was it even safe for them to eat.[125] When our people on the mountain summit saw the approaching fleet they did not dare to hope for such joy; and also those who were coming regarded the camp with suspicion when they saw it. But when they came closer and they caught sight of the symbols of the Christian faith, a shout went up from both sides, their

122. The castle of Beaufort or Belfort was held by Reynald of Sidon. Through trickery he had enabled his castle to hold out against Saladin, although he was taken prisoner and sent to Damascus: Bahā' al-Dīn, pp. 150–5. On 22 April 1190 Beaufort surrendered in return for Reynald's release. He then went to Tyre. He appears in ch. 63, below, supporting the Marquis Conrad's marriage to the Lady Isabel, and in Bk. 5 ch. 24, negotiating with Saladin on behalf of the marquis.

123. This sentence is in MSS B and C only and seems to be based on Ambroise.

124. For an account of the voyage of this fleet see *Narratio Itineris Navalis ad Terram Sanctam*, in Chroust, A. (1928). Ralph of Diceto, pp. 65–6, and Roger of Howden, *Gesta*, 2 p. 90, and *Chronica*, 3, p. 18, also describe the voyage.

125. 'Our people...them to eat', is only in MSS B and C; again it seems to be based on Ambroise, lines 2832–4.

emotions overflowed in joyful tears, they ran together from all sides and leapt into the waves to meet them.

That fortunate fleet travelled from the Northern Ocean, undertaking an untried journey, passing through many seas, around many lands, overcoming many dangers on the way. Crossing from Europe through African waters it came to help labouring Asia. The fleet was directed by Danes and Frisians. Coming from the harsh North they are naturally hardy and have three qualities useful in war: slender limbs, indomitable mind, and a devout fervent faith. A favourable wind accompanied them as they set out from their home port on to the deep, and to the delight of the seafarers both wind and seas were favourable. So the merciful Lord brought His champions unharmed and unhindered through so many dangers.

When the inhabitants of the lands which they sailed past saw the fleet, many were roused to action. English and Flemish alike at once embarked on ships and followed the fleet. Nor should I pass over in silence what a remarkable feat they achieved in passing: for they boldly stormed a certain city on the coast of Spain called Silves, swiftly captured it, slaughtered the Gentile inhabitants and gave the city to the Christians. After ordaining a bishop for the city, they went on their way as victors.

So, coming to Acre, they set up a camp in a place between the city and the Turks and turned their indomitable strength to destroying the enemy, not with frequent battles but with one continual conflict! Their extravagant courage and contempt for life threw them into so many attacks and dangers so often that not long after the city was captured there were hardly 100 men left alive out of the 12,000.

Chapter 28: James of Avesnes' arrival. The organisation of the siege. The attacks and dangers made on both sides by day and night.

The night after the Frisians and Danes came to land, James of Avesnes reached the longed-for shore. He was a man endowed with triple perfection: a Nestor in counsel,[126] an Achilles in arms,[127] better than Attilius

126. i.e. very wise. In Homer's *Iliad* Nestor was the king of Phlos in the western Peloponnese, a veteran warleader, and gave good advice at the siege of Troy. Our author draws a parallel between the sieges of Troy and of Acre in the Prologue and in ch. 32, below.

127. One of the Greek heroes of the siege of Troy.

Regulus at keeping his word.[128] He pitched his tents opposite the so-called 'Cursed' tower [see ch. 32, below]. The Templars pitched theirs a little further on.

As the greater part of the city was not yet under siege the enemy was able to come and go freely. Our people were anxious as to what they should do. They resented the enemy's freedom of movement, but the perimeter of the walls was too long and the army too thinly spread for a complete blockade. So they assembled their forces in troops and took it in turn to keep an armed watch on the entrances to the city, and for some days obstructed the usual communication routes. Then the Turks came out of the city and the camp, assembled forces from both sides, attacked our people and overcame them. They were easily able to break through our broken lines and a divided force quickly gives way. The Hospitallers were on guard duty that day. The Knights Templar came to their relief as they were falling back. The enemy pressed them hard but the Templars prevented them from breaking into the camp.

Meanwhile, one Friday [14 September 1189][129] the enemy made a very severe incursion at dawn, catching the Christians totally unawares. Coming out of the city in troops, a great many launched a most persistent attack, throwing the king's camp into confusion. The Turks assailed our people while they struggled to resist, with no small carnage on both sides. The Turks had the advantage principally because their attack was unexpected. While our people were hard-pressed and resisting manfully the Turks admitted into the city some camels which had been sent to them loaded with food and had just then happened to enter the camp. They also led one of Saladin's sons out of the city and brought him to his father, as our people were unable to prevent them.

For the Turks were able to keep going in and out because they were greater in military strength. They were truly the most preeminent men, chosen from all Paganism to hold Acre against the Christians, fit and ready for anything; certainly not inferior to our people. Virtue is praise-

---

128. A Roman consul and general in the third century BC. Captured by the Carthaginians in 255 BC during the First Punic War. According to tradition the Carthaginians sent him to Rome to treat for peace on condition that he return to prison if peace were not made. He advised the Senate not to accept the peace terms and returned to prison.
Our author gives James of Avesnes prominence because on his arrival he took over the leadership of the Christian army from King Guy: see ch. 43, below.

129. See Bahā' al-Dīn, p. 157; 'Imād al-Dīn, pp. 172-3. Ambroise, lines 2901-12, has an account of this battle, but not identical to this.

worthy even in an enemy.

Yet each day the army of the faithful grew and the multitude of ships flocking together struck the Gentiles with no little terror. But Saladin invented a story to reduce their fear. He claimed that the Christians took their ships away by night and when it was light the same ships returned again as if they had just arrived, to make it appear that they had more men than they had. He however was aware of the truth and was bitterly grieved that our people's strength was increasing daily. Yet, he concealed the cloud which was over his thoughts under an expression of lofty pride, making a pretence of being fearless and serene.

Chapter 29: The arrival of some French and English, Flemings and Germans and Marquis Conrad the guardian of Tyre.

By now very many people had come from the kingdom of the French:[130] among others the bishop of Beauvais [Philip of Dreux], a man more devoted to battles than books, who revelled in knightly pursuits. He would have been the equal of Turpin if he could have found a Charlemagne.[131] Count Robert,[132] brother of the aforesaid bishop, also arrived and the counts of Brienne [Erard III][133] and Bar and a great many Flemings.

There is a certain part of France which is called Champagne. Although the study of arms flourishes throughout the whole country, Champagne is uniquely privileged in knightly pursuits, excelling and surpassing everywhere else.[134] Martial youths from this area rode out powerfully and boldly deployed against the enemy the skills which they had practised in tournaments. They put off their imaginary practice-battles

---

130. Roger of Howden states that they arrived with James of Avesnes: *Gesta*, 2 p. 94; *Chronica*, 3 p. 20.

131. In the epic accounts of Charlemagne's campaigns such as the *Chanson de Roland* ('Song of Roland'), Archbishop Turpin of Reims was both the emperor's religious adviser and one of his leading warriors.

132. Count of Dreux. This sentence is only in MSS B and C and seems to come from Ambroise.

133. Mayer (1962), p. 314. His brother Andrew was killed on 4 October 1189: see ch. 30, below. Erard died later: Roger of Howden, *Gesta*, 2 p. 148.

134. This description of Champagne is particularly interesting as the Countess Marie of Champagne (1164-81) was a patroness of the famous poet Chrétien de Troyes, whose Arthurian romances form the basis of our knowledge of the knightly code of conduct, chivalry, at this period. Her son Count Henry arrived at the siege of Acre in August 1190: ch. 42 below.

and turned their pugnacious minds to real war. Again, the great warmth of their devotion led some English and French to give up waiting for their kings and to hurry on ahead so that they could serve the King of kings.

Another illustrious and powerful man came from Germany. They call him *landgraf* in the Teutonic language.[135] As the word itself indicates, this means 'count of land'; the title reflecting his office, as it were. He persuaded the marquis to come to Acre [24 September 1189], although the latter was opposed to King Guy. The marquis had refused to come before because of the disagreement between himself and the king.

We know that the rules of History demand that from time to time the names of individual princes who had a role in the management of affairs should be recorded in writing. They themselves sometimes aim for this, having a sort of itch for glory. On the other hand, always dragging material out in this way tends to become wearing to the ears, and the discerning audience finds it tedious. So we will keep our list of the princes short, but when the course of events offers the opportunity we will say which individual performed what memorable feat. As we prefer to be brief rather than wordy at this point, we decline to record all the names of the many arrivals.[136]

How King Guy with the Templars and Hospitallers and with other pilgrims who were there stormed the Gentiles' camp, but they were attacked by the townspeople and many fell on both sides. Among others fell Gerard de Ridefort, master of the Temple, with many others: i.e. 1500 of our people [4 October 1189].[137] So as the number of the faithful had increased to the point where the army was large enough to undertake difficult military operations, it was unanimously decided that they should set out to attack the neighbouring Gentile camp, which had so often attacked them.

The enemy had pitched their pavilions on a certain mound [Tell

135. Ludwig III, landgrave of Thuringia, one of the leading magnates of Germany. He joined James of Avesnes in commanding the Christian army: see ch. 43, below.
136. Only MSS B and C have this final sentence.
137. For this battle see Roger of Howden, *Gesta*, 2 p. 94; *Chronica*, 3 p. 21; Ralph of Diceto, p. 70; the letter of Theobald and Peter son of Leo, *Conquest of Jerusalem*, p. 170; *Conquest of Jerusalem*, pp. 82–3; Bahā' al-Dīn, pp. 162–9; 'Imād al-Dīn, p. 178; Ibn al-Athīr, 2 pp. 10–14; Ambroise, lines 2957–3095.

al-'Ayyāḍīya][138] standing opposite Mount Turon, which we described above. A vast plain lay between the two camps, the wide area providing a suitable battlefield. The Christian army descended from the camp into the plain, where it was arranged in ranks which were then divided up into troops. Those more lightly armed with bows and crossbows went first. The main strength of the army followed, a brilliant sight with their horses and arms and their various insignia. Their faces and bearing declared the passion of their minds. They were the hope of the faithful and the terror of the enemy.

When the ranks of the army had been put in marching order, King Guy, the Templars, the Hospitallers, the count of Brienne and the landgrave proceeded in order, each with their unit.[139] One person, carried away with pleasure at the sight of the army, dared to say: 'What power can overcome it, what great number can resist it? God can do nothing for us nor our adversaries! Our own valour will win us the victory.' This was certainly a most evil and damnable remark which made human rather than Divine power responsible for the outcome of the battle, since without God we can do nothing [John's Gospel ch. 15 v. 5]. Sad experience and the outcome of events proved this.

The Turks stood as if in one mind to defend their camp. As our people came nearer, the unit of infantry which marched in front divided into two, allowing the cavalry to charge boldly between them into the enemy. The Gentiles turned in flight, deserting their camp. The Christians stopped pursuing them, and greedily plundered the booty. Pavilion ropes were cut, and the courageous count of Bar seized the tent of the sultan himself.

Meanwhile, a vast body of the enemy sallied out from part of the city which was not under siege and marched to the mountain by indirect routes. In fact they deliberately advanced with twists and turns so that our people would be uncertain as to whether they were going to attack the army or the camp. They could then suddenly attack the army and cut it off from behind.

The knights of the Temple, who are second to none in renown and devoted to slaughter, had already charged through all the enemy lines. If the rest of the Christians had pressed on after them and pursued the enemy with equal enthusiasm, that day they would have won a happy

---

138. Bahā' al-Dīn, p. 160.

139. This sentence is only in MSS B and C. It is similar to Ambroise, lines 2967–8.

victory over the city and the war. But the Templars went on too far in their pursuit of fortune and their own inclinations. The townspeople suddenly rushed down on them. Yet although they were innumerable numbers crushing just a few, they only triumphed after much slaughter of their own forces.

There the master of the Temple, Gerard de Ridefort, whom we mentioned above, fell slain. Happy man! The Lord conferred such great glory on him, giving him the laurel wreath which he had earned in so many battles and making him a fellow of the college of martyrs. When he saw his troops being slaughtered on all sides, and was urged by his companions to flee so that he would not perish, he replied: 'Never! It would be shame and scandal for the Templars. I would be said to have saved my life by running away and leaving my fellow-knights to be slaughtered.' He could indeed have escaped had he wished, but he fell slain with the slain.[140]

Our people's misfortune: they are slaughtered because one German's horse ran away. Elsewhere, while the Germans were greedily pillaging the enemy's camp, look! that ancient Deceiver pointed out to them that a horse which belonged to one of the Germans was running away.[141] He and his companions ran after it. Seeing them eagerly chasing it, some people thought that they were fleeing. This tiny but fatal cause threw the whole army into confusion, and everyone's thoughts turned to flight. They were also attacked by a rumour which redoubled their fear: the shout went up that the townspeople had gone to plunder their baggage. At that their ordered battalions were thrown into disorder, their units dispersed, no one paid attention to their standards. The leaders themselves rushed headlong into flight and scarcely anyone had the courage to remain.

---

140. 'When he saw...slain' is only in MS C, and is identical to Ambroise, lines 3021-34. Ambroise never hints that the Templars went on too far. Another account of the master's death is in a contemporary poem about the siege of Acre, published by Prutz, H. (1881), 'Ein zeitgenössisches Gedicht', 478-9. This was apparently written in the Christian camp before June/July 1190 and again it praises the Templars highly and gives no hint that they were rash. The fact that IP1 does imply that the Templars were partly to blame for their own deaths by charging too far is persuasive evidence against its author being a Templar. Ibn al-Athīr states that Gerard de Ridefort was captured and Saladin had him executed (2 p. 12).

141. Only MS C states that the horse's owner was a German. A and G omit the horse as a cause for the retreat.

Chapter 30.

The Turks were amazed when they saw the Christians thrown into confusion, but did not know why this had happened. Realising that they had unexpectedly won a victory, they recovered their confidence and turned their horses around. Their knightly practice, as against their religious practice, is to give way when they are being attacked and to attack those who are giving way. For if you pursue, they flee, but if you flee, they pursue.

In this sad and unfortunate confusion, Andrew de Brienne was killed by the Turkish onrush while he was courageously calling out to the others not to run away. His valour had raised him so far above all the French that he was regarded as first among knights, while all the rest contended for second place. His brother, the count of Brienne, knew that he had fallen and passed by him, but although his brother called to him for help he was afraid to stop. So cowardice declined the glory which chance had offered.

In contrast, when another knight who was fleeing saw that James of Avesnes had been thrown off his horse, he immediately gave him the horse on which he was sitting. So by his own death that laudable man ransomed his lord from death.

Also King Guy went to help the marquis when he was being crushed by the enemy. Despite previous injuries and the rivalry between them, he showed humanity to that undeserving man and rescued him when he was about to perish. The king's brother, Geoffrey de Lusignan, had taken on responsibility for defending the camp. When he saw that the army was thrown into confusion and that everyone was struggling to get away he hastily left his post and, anxious for his brother's safety, ran forward to stem the rout.

O! wretched reversal of fortune! The Christians went out in confidence, and returned in confusion; they went out in ranks and returned in a rout; conquerors, they put the enemy to flight, and were then conquered and fled back themselves. So may human presumption realise what humanity and what human strength may do without the power of the Lord's right hand! May He powerfully work victory in His own, who shows constancy to those who fight for Him and bestows a crown on those who overcome! They had presumed that they would conquer in their own strength, thinking it impossible to find an enemy they would fear. Yet soon afterwards they found that enemy was much too close, and lost 1500 of their own people.

There was a certain knight named Ferrand who hid himself amongst the dying and was stripped and left for dead. When night came he returned to the camp but he was so disfigured by his wounds that his people could not recognise him and he was barely able to persuade them to let him in.

Poetic licence or a long treatise would go on to describe various incidents of the battle and the different ways people died. We are constrained by the need to be brief, and may say not 'how' but only 'what' happened. Saladin ordered the Christian corpses to be collected together and thrown into a nearby river. His intention was that they would be carried downstream by the current, striking fear into those who saw them, and as they rotted they would pollute the water.[142]

Chapter 31: Our people's numbers increase daily. They concentrate on making trenches round their camp on the landward side, while being seriously troubled by the Saracens.

Considering it best to refrain from open battle for a while, our princes pressed on with laying out the boundaries and fortifications of the camp. They heaped up a turf rampart and dug deep trenches from sea to sea to defend the tents. The marquis and the Hospitallers boldly laid siege to those stretches of the city wall which were still free from siege. Now at last the whole city was blockaded by land and sea.[143]

The Turks were a constant threat. While our people sweated away digging trenches, the Turks harassed them in relays incessantly from dawn 'till dusk. So while half of them were working the rest had to defend them against the Turkish assault. What sort of people were these who bore the unceasing attack, while the air was black with a pouring rain of darts and arrows beyond number or estimate?

Our forces laboured on with every effort. The Turks grieved at their progress. In repeated engagements you would have seen first one side and then the other thrown down and trampled underfoot; such is the fortune of war. So our people struggled on for quite some time like this; but the Lord grieved over them, and did not altogether abandon those who

142. For this detail see also Bahā' al-Dīn, p. 168; 'Imād al-Dīn, p. 186; Ambroise, lines 3087–98.

143. From this point to the end of the chapter is not in MS G, and so was not in IP1.

had placed their hope in Him. Each day He increased and strengthened the number of the Faithful. Princes, dukes, counts and great numbers of lesser degree streamed together from various parts of the globe. These are their names:

The earl of Ferrers [William de Ferrers I, earl of Derby];[144] Nargevot de Toci [Narjot de Toucy];[145] Ancelin [Ansier/Anselm] de Montréal;[146] Geoffrey de Gienville [Joinville]; Otto de la Fosse; William Goeth; the viscount of Châtellerault;[147] the viscount of Turenne [Raymond II];[148] the castellan of Bruges [Jean de Neele];[149] the archbishop of Pisa [Ubaldo Lanfranchi].[150] Also Count Bertulf;[151] Count Nicholas of Hungary; Count Bernard; Count Jocelin;[152] Count Richard of Apulia; Count Alebrand; Ingelram de Fiennes;[153] Hervey de Gien;[154] Theobald of Bar[-le-duc];[155] Count John of Loegria; another Count John, of Seis. Also some Danish magnates and 400 Danes came with the nephew of the king [Knut VI] of Denmark. Then there was Guy de Dampierre[156] and the

---

144. Died at the siege in autumn 1191: see the letter of the archbishop of Canterbury's chaplain in *Conquest of Jerusalem*, p. 171; Roger of Howden, *Gesta*, 2 p. 148.
145. Mayer (1962), p. 374.
146. Later died at the siege: Roger of Howden, *Gesta*, 2 p. 149. Ralph of Diceto alleges (pp. 82–3) that at his death he confessed that he, the bishop of Beauvais, Count Robert of Dreux, Guy de Dampierre, the landgrave and the count of Gadres had been in treasonable negotiation with Saladin. In return for generous gifts they prevented the princes from launching an attack on the Muslims and allowed the Christians' siege castles to be burnt.
147. Died during the siege: Roger of Howden, *Gesta*, 2 p. 149.
148. Died in 1190, during the siege: Roger of Howden, *Gesta*, 2 p. 148.
149. Mayer (1962), p. 364.
150. Mayer (1962), p. 375.
151. Possibly one of the two Count Bertolds listed by Roger of Howden, *Gesta*, 2 p. 148 note 10; if so, he died during the siege.
152. A Count Jocelin of Apulia died at the siege: Roger of Howden, *Chronica*, 3 p. 88. Alternatively, this could be Jocelin III de Courtenay, titular count of Edessa, uncle of Queen Sybil.
153. Engeram de Fiennes in *HGM*, line 4559. Died at the siege: Roger of Howden, *Chronica*, 3 p. 88.
154. Stubbs (1864), p. 28 note 5, believed that this was the Hervy III of Donzy who appeared in ch. 14, above. Mayer (1962), pp. 317 and 370, stated that this was Hervy IV, lord of Donzy and Gien and count of Nevers, Dépt. Nièvre; presumably the son of Hervy III.
155. Count Theobald I of Bar-le-duc: Mayer (1962), p. 379.
156. Diceto accuses him of negotiating with Saladin: pp. 82–3. In 1213 he was one of those who gave evidence to the papal legate about the divorce of the Lady Isabel from Humfrey IV of Toron and her marriage to the marquis: see *Conquest of Jerusalem*, p. 172.

bishop of Verona [Adelard][157] and some Roman citizens.

All these and many other future martyrs and confessors of the Faith came to shore and were joined to the number of the Faithful. They really were martyrs: no small number of them died soon afterwards from the foul air, polluted with the stink of corpses, worn out by anxious nights spent on guard, and shattered by other hardships and needs. There was no rest, not even time to breathe. Our workers in the trench were pressed ceaselessly by the Turks, who kept rushing down on them in unexpected assaults. The Turks reduced them to exasperation before the trench was eventually finished. Then they organised the siege and tried to bring pressure to bear on the city.

Chapter 32: A description of the city of Acre and its neighbourhood.

The subject demands that we should give a brief geographical description at an appropriate point in the narrative. We believe that such a description would not be out of place, for our work may supply clearer knowledge about this great city which is already famous for its grandeur and the various events of the war. For if the ten-year war made Troy famous, and the Christian triumph made Antioch more illustrious [during the First Crusade] then Acre will certainly win eternal fame, for the whole globe assembled to fight for her.

The city is triangular in shape: narrower on the west, more extended on the east. More than a third of its perimeter, on the south and west, is enclosed by the flowing waves. Its harbour is not as good as it should be. It often fails to protect vessels wintering there so that they are smashed to pieces, because the outcrop of rock which runs along parallel to the shore is too low to break the force of waves in a storm. Since that rock seemed suitable for washing out the entrails of animals, in ancient times sacrifices used to be celebrated there; and because the sacrificial flesh attracted flies, the lone tower which stands on it is called the Tower of Flies.[158]

There is also a tower called the Cursed Tower, which is situated on the wall which surrounds the city. If common report can be believed, it got its name like this: it is said that this is where the silver was made in

157. Mayer (1962), p. 381.
158. See also ch. 58, below.

exchange for which Judas the Traitor sold the Lord.

A city called Ptolemais was formerly situated on top of Mount Turon, which lies in the vicinity of the city. For this reason some people make the historical error of calling Acre 'Ptolemaida'. The hill they call 'the Mosque' rises close to Mount Turon. Ancient witness states that the tomb of Memnon is in this hill, but as for how he was brought here, we have neither read nor heard.[159]

The river which flows to the city is called the Belus [Nahr Na'mān]. It has a narrow bed and is not deep, but Solinus claims no little glory for it, including it among the wonders of the world and stating that it has sands like glass.[160] For there was a sandy ditch whose sands provided material for the manufacture of glass. To outward appearance the sand was completely useless; but if it was melted in a furnace, through the secret virtue of that place it soon took on the appearance of glass.

Not far from the river they point out a low rock near to the city, where they say the three parts of the world, Asia, Europe and Africa, all meet. Although between them they contain all the other districts of the world, that place alone belongs to none of them and remains distinct and independent.

Mount Carmel rises loftily on the south side of the city. We know that Elijah the Tishbite had his modest dwelling here, and his cave can still be seen.[161]

Although a description provides a pleasant diversion, we will omit the delights of the surrounding areas for the present, so that our martial pen may return to its original path and hurry on to other things.

---

159. Memnon: King of Ethiopia, son of Tithonus and Aurora. A legend later than Homer states that he was killed at Troy by Achilles. Another legend states that he survived the Trojan war and ruled for five generations in Ethiopia. A statue was identified with him, which was said to sing at dawn. It stopped singing after the Roman emperor Septimius Severus attempted to repair it in the late second century AD.

160. Gaius Julius Solinus wrote the *Collectanea Rerum Memorabilium*, probably soon after AD 200. This was a geographical summary of parts of the known world. Almost all the material was taken from Pliny's *Natural History* and Mela's *De Chorographia*. Stubbs (1864), p. 76 note 8 remarks that the surviving remains of Solinus' work say nothing about this river, but Tacitus' *Histories* 5, 7 state that at the mouth of the River Belus are sands which are fused with natron to make glass.

161. This Elijah is the famous Old Testament prophet. In the early thirteenth century there were many hermits living on Mount Carmel. Their loose association eventually developed into the order of Carmelite friars.

Chapter 33: The townspeople suffer such a shortage of food that they offer to surrender the city. Saladin assists them by sending fifty galleys which drive away our galleys.[162]

Since our people had blockaded Acre on all sides, the townspeople began to suffer from a grave food shortage once they had eaten all their provisions. Their situation was so serious that they offered to give up the city if they were allowed to depart freely with life and limb. The princes regarded these conditions as totally unsatisfactory. They had decided either to wait until utter necessity left the enemy at their mercy or preferably to press on with all their energies to win glory by taking the city by storm.

While the negotiations about the surrender of the city dragged on, the sultan equipped fifty galleys with adequate supplies of men, food and weapons, and sent them to maintain his forces in Acre. So on the eve of All Saints [31 October 1189][163] all the ships approached together. They were spotted from a distance. In their uncertainty the people were divided, making various predictions: some declared that the enemy was at hand, some were confident that aid was coming for the Christians. While they were still unsure as to who was coming, the ships suddenly rushed headlong into the city. They also forcibly took into the city with them one ship of ours, laden with food, which they encountered on their way into the harbour.

Now that they had enough food to continue fighting for longer, they pursued our people with taunts more bitterly than usual. Not content with pillaging our supply vessel, they mercilessly killed the sailors and everyone they found in that ship, hanging their bodies round the walls of

---

162. What follows has been altered by the compiler of the base manuscript for MSS A, B and C (IP2). MS G, following IP1, describes the arrival of fifty supply vessels which led to a naval battle, on 26 December 1189. This date is endorsed by 'Imād al-Dīn, pp. 198–200, who depicts the battle as a great Muslim naval victory. Ambroise, lines 3143–96, describes the arrival of fifty supply vessels on 31 October 1189, which led to a skirmish in which a Christian ship was captured. He then says that both sides spent the winter manufacturing siege machines, and the Germans made a great windmill, which the Muslims thought was another siege machine (lines 3225–32). IP2 has split IP1's description of a naval battle in half, making one skirmish around supply vessels on 31 October 1189, and one naval battle on 26 December.

163. This date is not in MS G, which treats this skirmish and the battle which follows as a single engagement on 26 December.

the city on All Saints' Day. What is more, the aforesaid enemy galleys kept watch over the entrance and exit to the city harbour, so that no one would dare to come to our people's assistance for fear of falling into their hands.

Ships come from Babylonia [Egypt] to the city of Acre. But on the day after the Lord's birthday [26 December 1189] one of our galleys incautiously went to investigate a fleet coming from Babylonia, thinking that they were Christians coming to help us. With it went a little lightweight skiff of the type popularly called a 'galliot'.[164] Expecting to find friends, it rather rashly hurried on ahead into the midst of its enemies. The sailors called out in greeting, but no answering voices broke the peace; there was only a suspicious silence. When the wretched sailors noticed this they immediately leapt into the sea and swam away, escaping death as best as they could.

So, that part of the sea fell under the enemy's control. Our galleys, which were far fewer in number, fled secretly to Tyre, leaving the enemy free entry and exit by sea to the besieged city.

At that time the Germans had put a great deal of work into constructing a milling machine for grinding grain. Horses walked in a circle, driving the creaking millstones round. The Turks watched in fascination as the mill operated, thinking that it was some instrument to destroy them or for use in storming the city. For they had never before seen an ass-driven mill of this sort in that country.[165]

Chapter 34: The battle between the enemy fleet and the fleet of our people and the marquis. Our people's victory.

It was nearly Easter [25 March 1190], and the weather had improved. The marquis, who had fallen back on Tyre in order to repair his fleet, now returned at our people's request with an enormous quantity of equipment and plenty of warriors, weapons and food. Our people again won

164. A small galley: the Latin is *galio*.
165. The description of the mill is not in MS G (following IP1), and seems to have been inserted by the compiler of IP2 from Ambroise's work, but differently. Ambroise, lines 3225–32 says that it was a windmill, but Mayer (1962), p. 321, states that there were two windmills at Tyre in 1187 – so windmills were not new to the country. However, horse-drawn mills must also have been familiar to the Muslims.

control of the sea and cleared the way for ships to approach more safely. For, thanks to the princes' mediation, the king and the marquis had been reconciled on the basis that the marquis would hold Tyre, Beirut and Sidon, and as the king's faithful man, he would concentrate all his power on promoting the interests of the king and the kingdom. But headlong ambition always leads a greedy and wicked heart astray: burning with the desire to gain the kingdom, he broke his sworn word. He pretended outwardly to be a friend while concealing his enmity within.

The townspeople resented losing the freedom of the seas, and resolved to see what they could achieve by naval battle. So they brought out their galleys two by two and, keeping good order as they advanced, they rowed into deep water to meet the ships coming to attack them.[166]

Meanwhile our people went on board their warships. Taking a leftwards course they withdrew to a distance, giving the enemy a clear road. The enemy ships approached. Our people prepared to engage them. Clearly there was nowhere to hide, so they determined to meet the enemy onrush head on.

Since we have mentioned naval matters, we think it appropriate to describe the battle fleet briefly and explain what kind of ships are used nowadays and what sort the ancients constructed.

Among the ancients, several banks of oars were required in ships of this kind, one above the other in steps. When they were worked, some oars had to be very long to reach the waves, and some were shorter. They often had three or four banks of oars, and sometimes five; but we read that some of the ships at the battle of Actium [31 BC] when Mark Antony fought Augustus, had six. Battleships were called 'liburnas'. Liburnia is a part of Dalmatia where the fleet at the battle of Actium was mostly constructed. For this reason it became the custom among the ancients to call warships liburnas.[167]

---

166. Ambroise also describes a sea battle at this point, but his account is different from the *Itinerarium.* He states that the marquis returned from Tyre after Easter (line 3269) and immediately engaged in a naval battle, which was followed by an attack on the besiegers' camp from the land side. The Muslim sources do not mention this sea battle, and neither do the other European sources. The compiler of IP2 seems to have tried to reconcile the accounts in IP1 and Ambroise by adding some of Ambroise's details to IP1.

167. The liburna was the standard warship of the Roman fleet in the first and second centuries AD. It was a small galley, usually with two banks of oars but sometimes with only one. It was effective in battle but relatively slow and unmanœuvrable in a chase: Haywood, J. (1991), *Dark Age Naval Power*, pp. 48–9, p. 142 note 5.

Yet all that ancient magnificence has faded away and vanished: for a battlefleet, which once charged the enemy with six banks of oars, now rarely exceeds two. What the ancients used to call a liburna now has a longer waist and modern people call it a galley. Long, slender and low, it has a piece of wood fixed to the prow, commonly known as a 'spur', which rams and holes the enemy's ships.

Galliots have only one bank of oars, are short and manœuvrable, more easily steered, run about more nimbly, and are more suited for hurling Greek fire.

As they advanced from both sides into battle our people arranged their ships not into straight lines but curved, so that if the enemy tried to break through they could be surrounded and crushed. They formed crescents like the moon, with the stronger ships at the front, which could inflict a more violent attack while repelling the enemy's assault. Shields were placed closely together all around the upper decks. The rowers sat in the lowest deck, to leave those on the upper deck with more space for fighting.

The sea was completely calm and quiet. It seemed to have quietened itself in preparation for the battle, so that no rolling wave would cause a shot or an oarstroke to miss. As they met, trumpets sounded from both sides, mingling terrible blasts. They opened hostilities by hurling missiles. Our people called on divine aid, worked the oars with all their strength, and drove their prows into the enemy ships. Soon battle was joined: their oars entangled and they fought hand-to-hand. They bound their vessels to each other with grappling irons, and set fire to the decks with the incendiary oil which is popularly called 'Greek fire'.

Greek fire: and how it can be put out. Greek fire has a noxious stench and bluish-grey flames, which can burn up flint and iron. It cannot be extinguished with water; but it can be put out by shaking sand over it. Pouring vinegar over it brings it under control.[168] What could be more dangerous in a conflict at sea? What could be more savage? Such various fates await the combatants! - either they are burned to death, or drown in the waves, or die from their wounds.

Our people steered one galley carelessly, exposing its nearside to the enemy. Greek fire was thrown on to it, set it alight, and Turks jumped on

168. 'This medieval forerunner of napalm' as Aubrey Galyon calls it (1978), p. 337, was made with pitch, sulphur, oil, resin and naphtha and could burn on water.

board from all sides. The terrified rowers immediately vanished into the sea, but a few knights who were impeded by their heavy armour and who did not know how to swim, put their trust in fighting through sheer desperation. It was an unequal fight, but in the Lord's strength a few overcame many. They slew the enemy and triumphantly brought back the half-burnt vessel.

The enemy had invaded another ship, driven out the warriors and captured the upper deck. Yet those who were assigned to the lower deck struggled to escape with the help of their oars. A marvellous and miserable struggle ensued, with the oars pulling in different directions and the galley driven now this way by our people's efforts and now that way by the Turks. However, our people won. The Christians attacked the Turks who were rowing on the upper deck, dislodged and defeated them.

The other side lost a galley in this naval engagement, and a galliot with its crew. Our people returned safe and sound, bearing a solemn triumph.[169] The victors dragged the enemy galley back with them up on to dry land and left it on the shore to be plundered by our people of both sexes who came running to meet them. Our women pulled the Turks along by the hair, treated them dishonourably, humiliatingly cutting their throats; and finally beheaded them. The women's physical weakness prolonged the pain of death, because they cut their heads off with knives instead of swords.

No naval battle like that was ever seen before. It was so destructive, completed with such danger and won at such cost.

Chapter 35: Meanwhile the Turks on the outer side try to fill in our trenches with earth, making fierce attacks on our people positioned within them.[170]

Deeply grieved at our people's victory, the army of Turks on the outer side of the camp relentlessly rushed in a mass against our people who were in the now-completed trench. Their intention was either to fill up the trench by throwing earth back into it, or to destroy the defenders. Our people met their attack with difficulty, struggling with enormous

169. From here to the end of the chapter is not in MS G (following IP1), and seems to be based on Ambroise, lines 3309–14, 3323–6.

170. This chapter and the first sentence of chapter 36 are not in MS G. The compiler of IP2 seems to have taken them from Ambroise, lines 3331–76.

effort, seemingly unequal to such an innumerable multitude. The number of attackers seemed to increase constantly and they had to keep a guard on the city side as well in case the townspeople broke out and charged down on them.

Among their opponents was a fiendish race, forceful and relentless, deformed by nature and unlike other living beings, black in colour, of enormous stature and inhuman savageness. Instead of helmets they wore red coverings on their heads, brandishing in their hands clubs bristling with iron teeth, whose shattering blows neither helmets nor mailshirts could resist. As a standard they carried a carved effigy of Muḥammad. There was such an enormous crowd of this violent race as they rushed on the trench that no sooner had some been knocked to the ground than others followed.

The enemy's unceasing assaults had our people so bewildered that they did not know where the next attack was coming from. Nowhere was safe; they had no rest; they were hard pressed on all sides. Now they were on watch against attacks from those besieged in the city; now they were under constant threat from those on the outer side; and now even from the seaward side, where the enemy's galleys waited in ambush to admit approaching Turks into the city and prevent Christians from coming to our assistance.

Chapter 36: Our people storm the city with three wooden towers. The townspeople offer to surrender. While the Christians are harassed by the enemy on the ground, their siege machines are burnt.[171]

At length, through Divine Providence their adversaries were thrown back and repulsed. Our princes then pooled their efforts to build siege machines to storm the city. They constructed three mobile towers out of seasoned wood. The landgrave was responsible for the first, the Genoese the second and the rest of the army the third. They vied with each other in the construction of these massive structures, building them tall with wooden beams and boards. They were mounted on rollers, which with the aid of some mechanical ingenuity enables them to be easily moved.

171. For what follows see Bahā' al-Dīn, pp. 178–80; 'Imād al-Dīn, pp. 214–9; Ralph of Diceto, p. 84. Ambroise's account is similar but not identical (lines 3395–432).

To prevent the machines catching fire, the builders covered them all round with cloths and rawhides. To prevent shots from stonethrowers damaging the vulnerable construction they stretched rope netting out in front. The tops of the towers were above the battlements and ramparts of the city, and were full of crossbowmen and archers. People who fought with staffs and pikes occupied the middle levels. Each camp also had its stonethrowers which stood to one side to defend the siege towers as they were led out and to break down the enemy's walls. The towns-people were already in utter despair and offered to surrender the city if they were allowed the freedom to depart and to take their possessions with them.[172] Our people refused. They pressed on with every effort to bring the completed siege machines up to the walls, while the towns-people resisted manfully, giving their opponents as good as they got and retaliating in kind.

On the Sunday after Ascension Day [5 May 1190] the siege machines were moved next to the walls and they attacked the city from dawn to dusk. Then the outer Turkish army rushed on them in troops with great force and poured into the trench! By attacking the rear of those assailing the city they hoped to draw off the assault and scatter their forces completely. So our people were hemmed in on both sides and divided between the two. They went different ways, some to defend the army from those charging down on them from the rear, while others concentrated on storming the city, and so their military strength was reduced. In the meantime, the enemy set our siege machines on fire. No effort could extinguish them; they were burnt up by Greek fire and left useless.

And so by an unlucky accident they lost the triumph they had hoped for. Its loss was the sadder because previously it had seemed so certain.

Chapter 37: Famine among the townspeople; succour from three ships.[173]

By this time the besieged were suffering from such a serious lack of food that they ate their horses and did not spare other types of beasts. Starvation incited them to forbidden foods, and they forgot the law of Muḥam-

172. From here to 'left useless' is not in MS G. The compiler of IP2 may have taken it from Ambroise's account, but the two accounts are not identical; for instance, Ambroise says that the attack took place on a Thursday.

173. This chapter is not in MS G. The compiler of IP2 seems to have taken it from Ambroise, lines 3433-56.

mad if only they could satisfy their ravening hunger. Meanwhile they hurled the older Christian captives lifeless outside the walls, because they reckoned that old age made them useless for work. They kept the younger captives alive because they could be used as labourers.

While the Turks were in these straits three supply vessels arrived. The sailors, fearing an attack by our people, suddenly rushed headlong into the city and some of them were drowned, but the ships and their cargoes of food were saved. Then the besieged dissolved into unrestrained joy as if their every wish had been granted. With cymbals and flutes and high-pitched wailing voices they declared that all was well. This celebration was made as a gesture so that no one would think they had suffered any loss.

Chapter 38: Saladin assembles the armies of all his kingdom and attacks our army. Our people manfully resist him; his son is killed and he retreats in confusion.[174]

Saladin meanwhile had drawn together forces from the whole of Asia, from India to the Tigris, from the Tigris to the Euphrates, from there to the waves of the Mediterranean, and led them all together into battle. Innumerable races streamed from Africa, the Nadabares, the Gaetuli, and Numidians.[175] There were also peoples deformed through adapting to the southern sun: they are called Mauros or Mauritanians from the Greek word *Mauron*, which means black. Thus two parts of the world attacked the third. Europe, which alone – and not entirely – acknowledged the name of Christ, struggled against the other two.

Furthermore, Saladin enlisted many as mercenaries. The great expense was met by money which had been collected over a long period, for the

174. The only other source which includes this battle is *LFWT*, pp. 124–5, which seems to have copied it from IP1. 'Imād al-Dīn does state at this stage of the siege that new armies were arriving to join Saladin: he had summoned them to help him face the Emperor Frederick's army (pp. 221–3). They included the atabek of Sinjār, the lord of Jazīra, the son of the lord of Mosul and the lord of Irbil, but there is no mention of African forces or anything on the scale the *Itinerarium* describes.

175. Our author uses classical names for modern races. Nadabares could be the Nobades of southern Egypt/Libya, or the Nabataens of Arabia Petraea; Gaetuli (Virgil, *Aeneid* Bk. 4 vv. 40–1) were a tribe of what is now central Algeria; Numidae are listed with the Gaetuli by Virgil as a tribe of what is now north-east Algeria.

Gentiles had laid down by common agreement that the dying should bestow a third of their possessions on those who defended their law. Besides this, some came without pay on a sort of pilgrimage and proceeded to fight against Christians in defence of the ceremonies of their law.

The tyrant poured out this multitude gathered from all over the place in a bold attack on our people, elated and confident that he would either take them all captive or exterminate them with the edge of the sword. Now, we read that the army of King Darius of the Persians was 700,000 strong: this helps us to estimate the size of this multitude, because his army could be numbered but there was no certain number to this.[176] That immense plain which stretched from sea to sea and spread far and wide was not large enough for so many thousands; and although the fields were broad and spacious still the densely-packed ranks complained that the place was cramped.

The Christians, threatened on one side by the townspeople and on the other by the enemy army, strenuously bore both attacks. Stationing guards in the trenches, they drove back first one side and then the other from breaking into the camp. The assault began on the Saturday before Pentecost [19 May 1190] and lasted for eight days, with great slaughter on both sides as evidence of the heat of the battle. Our people found the holy day no holiday. Yet the Spirit of Virtue gave them strength against the enemy: He who once taught the apostles to preach now inflamed His knights to fight. By public edict, everyone was forbidden to go outside the camp; there was no need to go looking for a fight when they could find a challenge nearby. Such a great number of attackers rushed on them that arrows fired at random found a target, and no one bothered to aim a blow when the dense crowd provided so many potential targets.

On the eighth day one of Saladin's sons was killed by a shot from a crossbow. His death brought the attack to a halt and struck terror into the enemy army. Many returned to their homelands. After seeing the Christians contend so vigorously against such an enormous horde, they shuddered at the thought of ever engaging them in battle again.

---

176. Herodotus (Bk. 4 ch. 87) states that Darius I, King of the Persians, invaded Scythia with 700,000 men.

Chapter 39: Again, the townspeople are hungry and relieved by galleys.[177]

Meanwhile famine attacked the townspeople. The sultan sent them corn vessels from Egypt, sailing with the south wind. There were twenty-five of them, of which three were larger than the rest. While they were attempting to run between the Tower of Flies and the nearby reef two were smashed on the rocks but the third reached the harbour safely. Our people's galleys had deflected them from their course as they were approaching. However, one of them pursued the fleeing vessels too rashly, struck the rocks and was wrecked.[178]

Chapter 40: The misfortune which befell our people in a battle on St James' day, [25 July 1190] undertaken without the princes' consent.[179]

Time passed, and the army grew listless from long inaction. The common people, greedy for excitement, began to accuse the princes of being cowards and started agitating for a fight. All were equally enthusiastic. They resented the Gentile camp being so close: the greedy were aroused by hope of plunder, while those of martial mind yearned for the glory of victory. In the heat of the moment they hatched a hasty plot, and all prepared themselves for battle, without seeking their princes' agreement.

The princes tried to restrain the rash daring of the common crowd as far as they could. Even the patriarch forbad them on pain of excommunication to challenge the enemy or engage in the dangers of battle without consulting the princes. However, nothing had any effect; neither the princes' dissuasion nor the patriarch's threat. Madness overcame good

---

177. This may be the naval battle of 12 or 13 June mentioned by Bahā' al-Dīn, pp. 181-2, and 'Imād al-Dīn, p. 224. Bahā' al-Dīn depicts it as a Muslim victory while his colleague sees it as indecisive.

178. The text now picks up the narrative from the point where our author broke off at the end of ch. 24, after the death of the Emperor Frederick I.

179. This was a significant battle, and despite what the *Itinerarium* says other writers imply that the whole Christian army was involved. See Roger of Howden, *Gesta*, 2 p. 142 - dating it after the divorce of the lady Isabel; Ralph of Diceto, p. 84; 'Imād al-Dīn, p. 237; Bahā' al-Dīn, p. 193; the archbishop of Canterbury's chaplain, translated in *Conquest of Jerusalem*, p. 171; Ambroise, lines 3457-94 - which differs from the *Itinerarium*.

advice, impulse overcame reason, and the multitude took command. Whenever an impulse seizes the common people, they think that rashness is a virtue, judge that what they want is best, do not stop to think about the outcome, flee correction and despise direction.

On St James' day, that mournful and inimical day, the ill-fated troop of common knights sallied forth from the camp. Although they advanced under arms, they had not taken full account of the dangers ahead. A remarkable band of young warriors indeed, youths of action, ready to yield to none! If only they had had a chief; if only they took advice before setting out to daring deeds; if only they thought as much about battles as they did about booty! But the host had no commander; it was each knight for himself, each their own leader. They hardly recognised their own standards, let alone followed them; a great many ran on ahead, their minds on plunder rather than the battle in which they were about to die.

The Gentiles saw these troops advancing on them. They deliberately withdrew a little, wavering and fearful, and leaving their tents filled with all sorts of valuable things as they did not stop to take their baggage with them. They halted at the bottom of the nearest mountain to gather their lost strength and sent spies to find out what our people wanted and what they had come for.

At that time the sultan's nephew Takieddin [al-Malik al-Muẓaffar Taqī al-Dīn 'Umar ibn Shāhanshāh, lord of Hamah][180] had his tents pitched towards Castle Imbert [al-Zīb].[181] He was a man of action and resolve, of inhuman wickedness and implacable cruelty, and he had a deadly hatred of the Christian name. The aforementioned crowd hurried towards his camp, all inflamed by their lust for plunder. Hardly pausing to look around for any ambushes thereabouts, in a moment they were fighting over the spoils. Most gorged themselves on the quantities of food they found, laying down their arms and lying about as relaxed as if they had

180. Michael the Syrian, Jacobite patriarch of Antioch 1166–99, describes him in his chronicle as 'a violent, malicious man and enemy of the Christians.' He died 10 October 1191 after a campaign in Cilician Armenia. Michael states that he was struck down by the Lord for his cruelty to Christians: Bk. 21 ch. 7: 3 p. 403. His father was Saladin's elder brother.

181. IP2 calls it 'Casal Imbert' – see Bk. 3 ch. 1, Bk. 5 chs. 8 and 11, below. A casal was a village.

been invited to a banquet.[182]

When they realised what was going on the Turks rushed on them from all sides with terrible yells, as is their wont, and won an easy triumph over the scattered and stupified mob. None of them thought of battle; everyone fled. But they were on foot, weighed down with armour and exhausted by thirst and the heat, and so were unable to escape an enemy pursuing them swiftly on horseback. They were put to flight and dispersed in all directions. No one was spared, no prisoners were taken. The Turks' rage could not be satisfied, and even when they were sick of killing their anger drove them on. Wherever their fear drove them, the Christians met with death; no one could escape the disaster. Everywhere the enemy, everywhere slaughter! The wounded were beyond number; the dead were reckoned at 5500.

Our princes heard the roar and saw the carnage, but pretended not to notice. Hard, inhuman and pitiless! – they saw their brothers being cut to pieces in front of them yet made no attempt to rescue them from death, although their only crime was that they had left the camp after they had been forbidden to do so. Some held back out of cowardice rather than because of their offence. Yet the archdeacon of Colchester, Ralph d' Hautrey,[183] assisted the afflicted and helped the stumbling. He was a man of remarkable height and appearance, graced by a double laurel wreath, outstanding in both the ecclesiastical and secular militias, for he was renowned both for his learning and his feats of arms. Later on, after he had performed a great many remarkable feats in this same siege, he departed this life with a happy and praiseworthy death.

Seeing their people's success, the townspeople made a ferocious sortie and attacked the pavilions, shooting fire from close range.

---

182. Ambroise mentions the attack on the tents, but does not say whose tents. 'Imād al-Dīn states that the tents of Saladin's brother al-'Ādil ('Saphadin') were attacked (p. 238). Taqī al-Dīn had left the camp a week before: Lyons and Jackson (1982), p. 314.

183. Or Hauterive. He is named in MS C, and *LFWT*, p.126. These writers could have found the name in Roger of Howden, *Gesta*, 2 p. 142, or Ralph of Diceto, p. 84.

Chapter 41: Ships of pilgrims come to assist our people.

After this pitiful slaughter our people's strength was much reduced. Then fortune smiled on them more sweetly and Favonius [the west wind] began to blow, bringing vessels loaded with troops. Meanwhile, the Gentiles' ships proceeded stealthily. Equipped with Christian symbols and imitating the Christians' speech, they mingled with our ships; then suddenly and unexpectedly slipped into the city.[184]

Chapter 42: The men who came to assist our people, and their ranks: laity and clergy, of the upper and lower class.[185]

Then the Lord, who does not abandon those who hope in Him, regarded our people and saw that they had been made perfect by purification in the fire of long tribulation and severe trials which had pierced them to their very souls. Grieving over them, He brought them strong helpers from the farthest ends of the earth, renowned men, powerful in battle. The hordes of new arrivals not only restored the army to its previous strength, but actually increased it.

The first to land was the count of Troyes, Henry of Champagne, with a strong force of knights.[186] Subsequently a great many others followed.

---

184. Bahā' al-Dīn, pp. 204–5, states that the Muslim sailors dressed like Christians, shaved off their beards, set up crosses in conspicuous places on the ships and even put pigs on the decks in order to pass as Christians (August–early September 1190). Ibn al-Athīr, 2 p. 29, agrees but omits the pigs.
185. This chapter is not in MS G. Ambroise, lines 3499–520 has the same material down to the count of Chalons. He then goes on to cover the material in chs. 47–59 of the *Itinerarium*, returning at line 3897 to discuss the material in chs. 44–6. The compiler of IP2 obviously had other sources of information on those who arrived at the siege at this point.
186. The nephew of King Richard of England and King Philip II of France. Henry's mother Mary was daughter of Duchess Eleanor of Aquitaine by her first marriage to King Louis VII of France. That marriage was later annulled and both Louis and Eleanor married again. Eleanor married Henry of Anjou, later king of England: Richard was her third son. Philip's mother was Louis' third wife. Because both these kings were his uncles, Henry came to be the 'compromise candidate' in the struggle for control of the kingdom of Jerusalem. He gained the kingship after his marriage to the heiress Isabel of Jerusalem in 1192, although Isabel and he were never crowned. Bahā' al-Dīn, (p. 197) gives 'Count Herri' the credit for restoring the strength of the Christian army after the defeat of 25 July.

These are their names, in the order of arrival: Count Theobald of Blois; but death carried him off within three months.[187] Other arrivals were Count Stephen [of Sancerre],[188] and the count of Clermont [Ralph],[189] the count of Chalons[-sur-Saône],[190] Manassier de Garlande, Bernard de St Valéry[-sur-Somme],[191] Count John of Pontigny,[192] Erard de Châtinay, Robert de Boves,[193] Alan des Fontaines, Louis d'Assela [Arceles],[194] Walter d'Arzillières, Guy de Châtillon[-sur-Marne][195] with his brother Lovell, Guy de Maciers [Mezières?], John de Montmirail,[196] John des Arches [d'Arcis-sur-Aube].[197] The lord of Camte in Burgundy also came, and Gaubert d'Aspremont, Clarembald de Noyers and the bishop of Blois, the bishop of Toulon [Desiderius],[198] the bishop of Ostia [Octavian],[199] the bishop of Thérouanne, the bishop of Brescia, the bishop of Asti [William].[200]

There was also the patriarch of Jerusalem [Heraclius], the archbishop of Caesarea [Monachus], the bishop of Nazareth [Lethard II].[201] The bishop-elect of Acre was also present,[202] the archbishop of Besançon [Thierry de Montfaucon],[203] Archbishop Baldwin of Canterbury,[204] and Bishop Hubert of Salisbury.[205] In addition there was the archdeacon of

---

187. Seneschal of France. He had been count of Blois and Chartres since 1152. Mentioned again in ch. 61, below. Roger of Howden, *Gesta*, 2 p. 148, notes his death.
188. His death is mentioned in the letter from the archbishop of Canterbury's chaplain: see *Conquest of Jerusalem*, p. 171.
189. Hereditary Constable (chief military commander) of France: Mayer (1962), p. 365; see *HGM*, lines 2913, 3056–9, 3696: 'One of the best knights of the world,' line 7511. See ch. 78, below.
190. William II: Mayer (1962), p. 378.
191. Mayer (1962), p. 364. *HGM*, line 836. Roger of Howden, *Gesta*, 2 p. 149 mentions his death at the siege.
192. Or Ponthieu? Mayer (1962), p. 371.
193. Died at the siege: Roger of Howden, *Gesta*, 2 p. 149.
194. Died at the siege: Roger of Howden, *Gesta*, 2 p. 147.
195. Mayer (1962), p. 369.
196. Mayer (1962), p. 371: viscount of Meaux and castellan of Cambrai.
197. Mayer (1962), p. 371.
198. Mayer (1962), p. 380.
199. Mayer (1962), p. 374.
200. Mayer (1962), p. 363.
201. Hamilton (1980), p. 405.
202. Died at the siege: Roger of Howden, *Gesta*, 2 p. 147.
203. Mayer (1962), p. 364.
204. Arrived at Acre around 29 September 1190: see his chaplain's letter in *Conquest of Jerusalem*, p. 171.
205. Arrived with the archbishop of Canterbury: Ralph of Diceto, p. 84. They set

Colchester, Ralph d'Hautrey, of whom we have spoken before. The abbot of Chalons also came and the abbot of Esterp [St Pierre de Lesterps].[206] There was also a certain priest who harassed the enemy constantly and tirelessly with shots from his crossbow.[207]

A great number of Normans also came: Walkelin de Ferrers, Robert Trussebot, Richard de Vernon and his son, Gilbert de Tillières[-sur-Avre][208] with a strong force of warriors. Ivo de Vipont also came,[209] in addition to Ranulf de Glanville former justiciar of England,[210] Gilbert Malmain and Hugh de Gournay.[211]

A great many others came besides these from the farthest frontiers of the world. The sum of them is beyond numbering; and even if we knew it, it would be tedious for the audience if we were to name them all.

Chapter 43: Count Henry of Champagne is put in command of our army.

As we have already said, Count Henry of Champagne had landed first. He was at once entrusted with the command of the army. James of Avenses and the landgrave had held it hitherto, sometimes jointly and sometimes in turn; but the landgrave had become unwell and deserted the camp to return to his own country. Although he had performed many illustrious feats and won much honour, his shameful departure tarnished the brilliance of his glorious deeds.[212]

---

out with King Richard of England but sailed straight to Tyre from France, not stopping at Sicily as the kings of France and England did.

206. Mayer (1962), p. 367.

207. It would be tempting to think that this is the author of IP1 – but this chapter is not part of IP1.

208. Mayer (1962), p. 368. Died at the siege: Roger of Howden, *Gesta*, 2 p. 148.

209. A tale of his courage is told in ch. 53, below.

210. Chief justiciar of Henry II of England: on Richard's accession in 1189 he resigned and took the cross. He arrived with Archbishop Baldwin of Canterbury and Bishop Hubert Walter, but died before 21 October 1190: see the letter of the archbishop's chaplain, *Conquest of Jerusalem*, p. 171.

211. After the fall of Acre, King Richard put him in charge of his share of the hostages: Roger of Howden, *Gesta*, 2 p. 180. See *HGM*, lines 10935–9, 10945–52, 10953–6: a wise and bold knight.

212. He died on his journey home: Roger of Howden, *Gesta*, 2 p. 148. Our author's remarks and the fact that Ralph of Diceto accuses him of treasonable correspondence with Saladin (pp. 82–3) indicates the depths of the divisions and mutual distrust in the Christian army.

Chapter 44: The duke of Swabia, son of the Emperor Frederick of Germany, comes to Acre at the instigation of the marquis and stirs up trouble.

At that time the emperor's son, [Frederick] the duke of Swabia, was staying at Antioch. His father had died a short while before, as we recounted above (ch. 24). The princes commanded him to remain there and attack the neighbouring Gentile territory. This was sound and useful advice, for if the enemy were under attack on several fronts they would be generally less effective because their efforts would be dispersed. The marquis took this message to the duke. He was a disloyal ambassador, interpreting the message maliciously to sway the duke into believing that the princes were procuring his absence because they were jealous of him and wanted to keep the glory of capturing the city for themselves. In fact someone claimed that the marquis had received 60,000 bezants from the sultan in return for persuading the duke to leave the Antioch area.[213]

So the duke came to Acre, where he stirred up trouble.[214] For there is an ancient and ongoing dispute between the French and the Germans, with the French kingdom and the German empire struggling for supremacy.

---

213. According to Bahā' al-Dīn, p. 207, and 'Imād al-Dīn, pp. 250–1, the duke left Antioch in late August with his troops; the marquis met him at Tripoli in early September 1190 and escorted him back to Acre by sea. Bahā' al-Dīn regarded the duke as a powerful individual and a great danger to Islam, but was aware that the princes of Acre feared that the duke would deprive them of their authority (pp. 212–3). 'Imād al-Dīn dismisses the duke and his forces as so depleted that they were no longer a danger to Islam (p. 233).

214. Bahā' al-Dīn: Duke Frederick arrived at Acre 7 October (p. 213). The Christians' morale rose enormously at his arrival. He at once began attacks on the city, making a raid on the Muslims and building siege machines, although these were burnt.
The *Itinerarium* mentions him only once more, ch. 61 below. The duke died of the plague 20 January 1191 (William of Newburgh, p.330; *Conquest of Jerusalem*, pp. 89–90).

Chapter 45: How the marquis aspired to be king, with the duke of Swabia's aid.

In eagerly seeking the presence of the duke, to whom he was related,[215] the marquis was secretly advancing his own cause. He hoped that through the duke's influence he would be able to gain the throne of the kingdom. Chance smiled on him and allowed him greater hope of achieving his desire: for untimely death carried off the queen and her children by King Guy.[216] In order to elucidate this point, we will briefly describe the royal dynasty from its origins.

Chapter 46: The genealogy of the kings of Jerusalem. The failure of the royal line was the cause of the marquis' ambitions on the kingdom.

Fulk, father of Geoffrey count of Anjou, was elected as king of Jerusalem on account of his unique virtues and married Melisende, the daughter of his predecessor King Baldwin [II].[217] They had two sons, Baldwin (named after his grandfather) and Amalric.

When the elder of the two[218] had acquired the royal sceptre he married the niece of Manuel [Comnenus], prince of Byzantium, whose name was Theodora. He captured Ascalon most victoriously [1153], but passed away without children.

His brother was successor both to his virtue and his kingdom.[219] He

---

215. The Marquis Conrad's mother was the sister of King Conrad III of Germany and of Frederick of Hohenstaufen, the father of Frederick Barbarossa, the duke's father. The marquis was therefore the duke's first cousin once removed.

216. Queen Sybil of Jerusalem and her daughters Alice and Maria died before 21 October, 1191. See the letter of archbishop of Canterbury's chaplain, *Conquest of Jerusalem,* p. 171. The children are named in the Lyon *Eracles*: *Conquest of Jerusalem*, p. 95. As Sybil and Guy had married at Easter 1180 (see *Conquest*, pp. 149–50) the eldest child could have been ten by the time she died.

217. Fulk (1131–43): Count Geoffrey of Anjou was father of Henry II of England. Queen Melisende acted as regent for her son Baldwin III until 1152. She died in 1161. She was widely admired for her political skills: see Mayer, H. (1972), 'Studies in the History of Queen Melisende of Jerusalem'.

218. Baldwin III, 1143–63.

219. Amalric: reigned 1163–74. He invaded Egypt four times in the 1160s.

compelled Babylonia [Egypt] to pay tribute. He married twice, and raised various progeny of both sexes. His first wife was named Beatrix [Agnes de Courtenay], daughter of the count of Edessa [Jocelin II]. He married her before he succeeded to the throne. The marriage was condemned by the clergy because they were related by blood, and so they were divorced. However, he had two children by her, a daughter named Sybil, and a son called Baldwin.

After his father died Baldwin was crowned, although he was underage and suffered from leprosy.[220] With a small force he miraculously defeated Saladin and 60,000 Turks [Battle of Montgisard, 1177].

He was swiftly released from human affairs. He appointed as his successor in the kingdom Baldwin, the son of his sister, who had married William, the marquis' brother. Baldwin was crowned. But he was very young and died soon afterwards, in his seventh year.[221]

The boy's father had died long before. Guy de Lusignan, who was a native of Poitou, had come to visit the Holy Sepulchre, and married the boy's mother, Sybil. Afterwards when she claimed her father's throne he too received the symbol of royal power. He was the father of her four daughters. However, death unexpectedly carried them and their mother off in a short stretch of time, causing accusations against Guy and prompting the marquis' ambitions of becoming king.

After King Amalric had put away his first wife he married a second, named Maria, who was related to the emperor Manuel. They had two daughters. One of them departed this life at a tender age, but the other, called Elizabeth [Isabel] was married to Enfrid of Turon [Humfrey IV of Toron] before she had attained marriageable age.[222] By the law of succession the inheritance of the kingdom now devolved upon her. So the marquis plotted to take both: to snatch his wife from Enfrid, and the royal sceptre from Guy.[223]

* * *

220. Baldwin IV, 'the leper king', 1174-85.
221. Baldwin V, 1185-86.
222. According to William of Tyre, Isabel was betrothed in 1180 when she was eight, which was below the canonical age for marriage: see *Conquest of Jerusalem*, p. 96 and note 165.
223. The account of the siege continues at chapter 58.

Chapter 47: A collection of the miracles which took place during the siege.[224]

It is said that the fortunes of war favour first one side and then the other, turn and turn about. Meanwhile many incidents occurred which were no less miraculous than amazing and which are not unworthy to be brought to the attention of posterity.

Chapter 47a: One of the townspeoples' stonethrowers crushed all our siege machines by its force, but one of our men who was struck was not injured.[225]

There were plenty of stonethrowers in the city, but one of them was unequalled for its massive construction and its effectiveness and efficiency in hurling enormous stones. Nothing could stand against the power of this machine. It hurled really incredible lumps of rock: 'violent action, far-hurled stones; the blow smashed everything, whatever it struck.' If the stones met no obstruction when they fell, they sank a foot deep into the ground. This machine struck some of our stonethrowers and smashed them to pieces or at least rendered them unusable. Its shots also destroyed many other siege machines, or broke off what it hit. It fired with such force, and its blows were so effective, that no material or substance could withstand the unbearable impact without damage, no matter how solid or well-built it was.

This machine hit one of our men on the back with a stone of immense size. He was standing with his back to it, suspecting nothing, not thinking that a stone could reach so far. But that stone did not injure the man in the least. He did not even move. The stone rebounded off his back as if he was a mountain of iron, and fell harmlessly near by. When the man saw it he had more horror on his face than he had had pain from the blow.[226]

---

224. The miracles which follow are not in MS G, and so were not in IP1. For a discussion, see the Introduction, pp. 12–14.
225. Ambroise, lines 3529–60, but not identical to this.
226. Instead of refering to an iron mountain, Ambroise says that if the man were a tree or a block of marble he would have been broken in two, but the stone rebounded from him. He says nothing about the expression on the man's face.

I ask you, wouldn't you attribute his escape to divine compassion? Wouldn't you see in this the great works of the Lord, whose clemency always waits upon those who are fighting for Him? I shall set out His works so that His magnificence may be honoured everywhere!

Chapter 48: A bolt fired from within the city at one of our people went through all of his armour but was unable to pierce a piece of parchment with God's name written on it which was hung on his chest.[227]

One of our men-at-arms was in the ditch outside the city walls. He wandered back and forth, searching for the weak spots in the walls, and firing the crossbow which he was carrying in his hand at the enemy. At last he halted. His armour was quite adequate for an infantryman: his head was protected by an iron covering; he also had a mailshirt and a tunic made of quilted linen, popularly called a 'doublet'. Its skilful cross-seaming makes it difficult for a weapon to pierce it.

While he was standing, looking up, suddenly a Turk fired a crossbow bolt at him with great force from the top of the wall and struck him in the chest, piercing all the armour, i.e. the iron headpiece, and the mail shirt and doublet. Yet it stopped when it hit a certain amulet which he wore hung from his neck across his chest, and it bounced back bent and blunted, as if it had hit an iron plate.

Wasn't this obviously God's work? This bolt which went through so many layers of iron bounced back blunted by a scrap of parchment! It is said that that man carried God's Holy Name written on that piece of parchment hung round his neck, and iron cannot pierce it. God is indeed an impregnable wall to those who trust in Him.

227. Ambroise, lines 3561–81. He dates this to April–May 1190, but our author, normally so keen on dates, does not date it. Ambroise does not describe the man's wanderings in the ditch.

Chapter 49: An unarmed knight in the middle of answering a call of nature is attacked by a Turk armed with a lance, and knocks him down with a stone.[228]

A mounted Turk came unexpectedly charging down on one of our knights who, as was the custom, had gone out of the camp to answer a call of nature and was squatting down at the edge of the trench around the camp. The knight had scarcely finished his business when he noticed the Turk coming down on him from the flank. He got up quickly to dodge his attacker or, if God allowed, to meet his attack as effectively as he possibly could, although he was completely unarmed. When the Turk reached out to impale him on his lancehead, he bent down a little and through God's protection the blow missed. 'The horse gallops by, the blow flies into thin air.'

Annoyed that his attempt had failed, the Turk again charged down on the knight, brandishing his spear. What could that knight do, unarmed, on foot, alone and exposed like booty to the enemy? Calling on the help of God, who is always present with His people through grace, he waited until his attacker was almost on top of him and then seizing a stone which he had happened to find 'he threw it at his enemy, at the bare face below the helmet.' It hit the Turk on the temple, and he fell stunned from his horse, broke his neck and died.

The knight caught hold of his horse, quickly mounted and returned to his people. Someone who had seen this incident told another, and so it became notorious in the camp.

228. Ambroise, lines 3583-624. Ambroise's version is different: the knight was alerted to his danger by shouts from the Christian army; picked up two stones; and the Turk was killed when the stone hit him on the forehead, not by the fall from his horse. Neither version seems superior to the other.

Chapter 50: While the faithful are filling in the city ditch with earth, a woman who dies in the ditch instructs that her body should remain there instead of earth.[229]

Among those carrying earth to fill the ditch around the city so that it could be captured more easily was a certain woman. With great care and persistence she laboured on to get the job done. She worked without stopping, untiringly coming and going, encouraging the others as she went. Yet her zeal brought about the end of both her life and her labour.

That crowd of all ages and sexes was continually going back and forth together again and again to complete the job as quickly as they could. While this woman was busy depositing the load of earth she had brought, a Turkish sniper shot her with a dart, and she fell writhing to the ground. As she lay groaning with the violence of her pain, her husband and many others came running to her side, and in a weak voice she tearfully begged her husband for a favour.

'Dearest lord, by the sacrament of marriage, by our long-ago marital vows, I entreat and implore you, my darling, not to let my corpse be removed from here when I am dead. No, because I may no longer live to labour towards the completion of this work, let my body have a place in the work so that I can feel I have achieved something. Let my corpse lie in the ditch instead of earth; in a little while it will become earth.'

She implored the whole crowd standing around her to do this, and not long after she gave up her spirit. O admirable faith of the weaker sex! O zeal of woman worthy of imitation! Even after death she did not cease to work with the workers, for even when dying she wished to continue in the work.

---

229. This is our author's only favourable anecdote about a woman. Note his anxiety to assure us that she was a woman of good repute, respectably married and respectful of her husband. He is anxious to distance her from the women of ill repute described by 'Imād al-Dīn as coming to assist the crusaders with their services: pp. 202–3. Ambroise tells the story at lines 3625–60, stating that even the barons helped carry stones on their warhorses and packhorses. He is less anxious to underline the heroine's married state. On the besiegers' eagerness to fill in the ditch, see Bahā'al-Dīn, p. 247.

Chapter 51: A Turk's horse caught in a net.

One of our common people was unrolling his net and stretching it out outside the camp, to keep the Turks out or trap them if they made an assault. Suddenly a Turkish horseman came charging swiftly down on him. When the commoner saw him rushing towards him he turned and fled, even though he had not completely finished his task. The Turk found that he could not catch up with him as he had already got into the camp. Giving up the pursuit in disgust, he went back and began to pull up the net.

He tore up some of the pegs to which the net was attached and then began to roll it up; but in his careless haste he caught it round the head of the horse he was sitting on, covering it. The horse, which was a rather fine animal, did not deign to be caught in a net. It reared up and began to spin round in a circle to free itself, but only became more and more entangled.

Some of our people saw this and went rushing out. The Turk realised that his horse was tied up, swiftly jumped off and fled on foot. He outran his pursuers despite having lost his horse, for 'fear gave wings to his feet' [Virgil, *Aeneid*, Bk. 8 v. 224].

With great care and effort his beautiful horse was eventually disentangled from the net, which it had torn to shreds. All those who had come rushing out decided by common judgement that the commoner from whose net it had been extricated should have it in compensation for his torn net.

Chapter 52: Ditto, a Turk's horse caught in a trap.

In response to the frequent unexpected Turkish assaults our princes decided to make secret traps and hide them in the ground so that they could not be seen. So one day while some of our young warriors were having a practice-session on the plain outside the camp, shooting arrows at a target, some Turks came charging down on them on horseback. Because our people were unarmed and fewer in number they turned and retreated into the camp. One of the pursuers overtook the others, as if he was showing off his horse's speed. Then suddenly the horse was caught in mid-gallop in a trap! – and neither its rider's desires nor efforts could free it.

The Turk, preferring to lose his horse rather than his head, jumped down and fled unharmed on foot back to his people. It was decided that his horse should be given to the owner of the trap in which it was caught, i.e. Count Robert of Dreux.

Chapter 53: Ivo de Vipont[230] with a small force killed eighty pirates.

Three sailors were taking one of our knights, Ivo de Vipont, to Tyre in a small ship. He was accompanied by ten companions. Some Turkish pirates spotted them when they had already sailed far from port. They rowed out in their galley from a place near the land where the sea whirls and surges, and bore down on their ship. There were around eighty of them.

When the sailors saw them approaching swiftly they were petrified with fear. 'Lord God, alas for us!' they said to each other, 'we're caught! We'll be cut to pieces.'

'What, O ye of little faith,' said Ivo de Vipont to them, 'are you afraid, when in a moment you will see them dead?'

When the galley, driven by the force of the oars, seemed about to ram the ship with its prow, Ivo leapt into the galley and instantly began to behead Turks with the axe he was carrying in his hand. When his companions saw that his work prospered they were encouraged and jumped into the galley to join him, mercilessly beheading all the enemies they found or taking them captive.

Thus those who placed their hope in God were given a triumph, for He did not allow them to be conquered. It was their unfeigned faith which gave them strength, rather than a large number of fighters; because it is of no consequence to God whether there are few or many. He gives strength for the battle and total victory.

230. Ambroise did not include Ivo de Vipont in the list of new arrivals after the battle of 25 July 1190, and does not include this story. Perhaps the compiler of IP2 had information about Ivo de Vipont not available to Ambroise.

Chapter 54: How an emir's genitals were burnt up by Greek fire with which he had planned to burn our siege machines.[231]

The townspeople happened to discover that a great crowd of our people had gone out of the camp, as they were in the habit of doing to look for essential fodder for their animals. Led by their emir, a famous and powerful man named Bellegemin [Ḥusām al-Dīn 'Abū'l-Haijā' al-Samīn], they made a sudden sortie from the city and rushed on our people, catching them off their guard. After some had been killed on both sides, our people repulsed their attack and drove them back into the city. Only the emir, who was more spirited than the others, remained behind for longer. He had earlier boasted that he would destroy our siege machines which were ready to be moved up to the city walls, either by smashing them with iron or burning them up with Greek fire. Now he struggled zealously to achieve this.

The others had already fled, leaving him alone; but he pressed on, hoping to achieve his aim. Then one of our knights charged against him and threw him from his horse. The flask in which he was carrying the Greek fire was broken by the fall, and the inextinguishable liquid set alight the Turk's genitals, and the other, respectable, parts of his body. And so his plan to harm us led to his own destruction.

Chapter 55: A Turk bringing Greek fire to the city by swimming is caught in a net by our fishermen.[232]

Not far from land, some of our fishermen let out their nets to catch fish. Through the pursuit of this occupation they met their own needs and also supplied great comfort to the hungry by selling them fish. So it happened one day as the sun was setting and their nets were out that one of our people sitting some way away on the shore saw far out to sea the

231. Ambroise has a similar account, lines 3661-700.

232. Ambroise's history does not include this story. Bahā' al-Dīn tells the career of the swimmer 'Aisa (or 'Īsā), who used to carry letters and gold into the city of Acre by swimming, and died in late August/early September 1190. But 'Aisa was drowned, not captured (pp. 205-6). 'Imād al-Dīn places this incident after 16 September 1190 (p. 250). He mentions several instances of messengers swimming back and forth, e.g. pp. 215-6, 244; but the principal method of communication between the Muslim forces was by carrier pigeon: e.g. pp. 211, 244.

head of a man swimming; the rest of his body was covered by water. The man who had seen him pointed him out to the fishermen, who determinedly rowed their boat in pursuit of the swimmer to find out what this strange creature was. When the rowers got nearer to him they observed that he was a Turk. Terrified by their shouts, he retreated, but they rowed quickly after him and caught him in their own nets.

He was a very skilled swimmer who had earlier passed through their nets carrying something hung round his neck. He was actually carrying Greek fire in an otterskin bag to those besieged in the city. The Turks used to send this fire to the besieged in this way, using swimmers, because they reckoned that this was the most convenient and secret method of doing it.

The fishermen returned to land with their captive and explained the matter to everyone in order. They led him in chains through the army with the bag in which he had carried the fire, harshly beating him and jeering at him, severely mangled and at last beheaded him; so he was dismissed to rest in peace.

So it is proven that God has care for His own, for He 'frustrates the purposes of the nations; He foils the plans of the peoples' [Psalm 33 v. 10], and He reduces to nothing the hostility of the malevolent enemy.

Chapter 56: A Turk who arranged to urinate on the Lord's cross is pierced in the groin by a bolt and killed.[233]

We judge that this should not be kept silent, although it is onerous to relate 'and horrific to hear.' In order to offend the Crucified One and bring disgrace on our faith, the Turks used to stand on the city walls in full view of the Christians and beat with rods icons and pictures which they had found in the city, representing the mysteries of the Christian religion. They would flog as if they were alive, and spit on them, and treat them ignominiously in many other ways, as they pleased. One day one of our people saw a Turk acting like this, waving a cross with the image of Our Saviour on it about with obscene movements, with filthy and sinful miming actions and blasphemously shouting impious words against our religion. At last he pulled out his genitals, contemptuously intending to water that illustrious object with drops of urine. Spurred by

233. Ambroise, lines 3701–30, has a similar account.

zeal, the Christian fired a crossbow bolt at the blasphemer, and 'with lethal wound transfixed the Turk in the groin.'

And thus as he died he perceived the futility of attempting anything against God.

Chapter 57: A Parthian archer who did not keep to an agreement is killed with an arrow by a Welsh archer.[234]

One day the slingers and archers of both armies, and all those skilled in hurling missiles, were challenging each other and firing shots from a distance at each other in turn, for amusement and practice. Eventually the rest went their separate ways, but a certain Parthian went on firing missiles at a Welshman on the opposite front line, trying hard to hit him. The Welshman, who was no beginner with the bow, fired back at him, returning shot for shot.

Then the Parthian called a truce, approached until he was within earshot and began to negotiate with him. 'Which country are you from?' he asked. 'What name do you call yourself? It would give me great pleasure to know, for I have certainly found you to be a doughty archer. So that you will more willingly reveal what I ask, let me tell you that I am a Parthian, trained in the art of archery since boyhood. I am called Grammahyr.[235] My reputation is great among our people, for I am famous for my remarkable deeds and distinguished for my victories.'

The Welshman told him his homeland and his name.[236] 'Let us prove,' said the Parthian, 'which of us has greater skill in this art. We will each draw our bow and fire a single arrow at the other in turn. You will stand still first and I will fire the first arrow at you, and then I will be the target and you will fire at me in the same way.' The Welshman agreed. Then the Parthian fitted an arrow to his bow. He placed his feet apart as that art requires, stretched his hands wide apart, his eyes on the target, and bent his bow: but 'the arrow flies into the void, piercing nothing.'

The Welshman, unscathed, demanded his part of the agreement. 'I

234. Also in Ambroise, lines 3731–70, but with some differences. This anecdote can be regarded as a 'Welsh joke' of the type mentioned by J. S. Brewer (1861) in his introduction to Gerald of Wales' *Opera*, 1 p. lxii note 1.

235. Ambroise calls him 'Grair', (line 3741).

236. But our author does not tell us his name. Ambroise (line 3739) calls him Marcaduc.

won't,' the Turk replied. 'No, you can face another arrow, and then I will get two fired by you.'

'You are not standing by the agreement,' the Welshman replied. 'You are not observing the terms you laid down. If you do not face your turn, however unwillingly, I shall be forced to postpone the punishment God may demand for your tricks, until such time as He wills.'[237]

The words were scarcely out of his mouth when in the twinkling of an eye he shot that Turk in the chest, even as the Turk was searching in his quiver for a bolt suitable for firing at his adversary. As no bone barred its course, that arrow 'went through the Turk's body and came out his back.'

Then the Welshman said: 'You don't stand by the agreement, so I don't stand by my word.'[238]

The Christians were exhilarated by these and similar successes. They resolved to bear their adversities with eager faith and fervent hope, saving themselves for the prosperity to come.

* * *

237. The Latin here is unclear; apparently our Welshman is speaking Latin with a Welsh accent. Ambroise's Welshman simply says 'That's fine by me.'

238. The joke is that the Welshman, after his long and involved speech declaring that he will postpone the Parthian's punishment, promptly shoots him, thereby 'welshing' on his promise.

Chapter 58: A naval battle between the Turks and our people. Our people strive to seize the Tower of Flies with towers and siege machines fixed in their galleys, but our siege machines are destroyed by fire [25 September 1190].[239]

The blockade of the city from the seaward side had been delegated to the Pisans and others who were skilled in handling ships. They had erected in their galleys a siege machine, constructed with much care. It was like a castle with battlements, built higher than the city walls, providing an easy means of firing missiles at the city. They also built two siege ladders with many rungs so that they could capture the city ramparts. They covered all these things and the galleys with hides to prevent their being damaged by iron or shots.

When everything was ready they approached the Tower of Flies and laid siege to it with violent shots from crossbows and missiles. Those inside it put up a stiff resistance. The two sides were evenly matched and the honours were even: whenever our people killed one of theirs they immediately returned the compliment. Then, even worse, 2000 Turks came out of the city in galleys to relieve those under siege in the tower. They attacked the Pisans from the rear, hoping to crush them or drive them away.

Our glorious and elite warriors moved the siege machines as close as they could to the said tower, and immediately attempted to throw enormous anchors into the tower. They also threw whatever suitable missiles lay to hand, boulders or darts. Other warriors had been assigned to naval warfare. They struggled energetically to repel those attacking from the seaward side. The anchors were fixed into the tower, and the shields, bucklers and targes which were attached to it fell off or were

239. This chapter and the two following are not in MS G, so were not in IP1. They seem to have been taken almost entirely from Ambroise's history, lines 3771–822. Bahā' al-Dīn gives the date for this attack and describes the Tower of Flies: 'the Fly-Tower, which is built on a rock at the entrance to the harbour, and is surrounded on all sides by the sea. It protects the harbour, and every vessel [coming in] that gets past the tower is safe from attack by the enemy. The besiegers were anxious to get possession of it in order to make themselves masters of the port, when they could effectively close it against vessels and prevent provisions entering the city' (pp. 210–2). See also 'Imād al-Dīn, pp. 253–5. This attack took place before the arrival of the duke of Swabia at Acre.

crushed.[240] The tower was attacked for a long time with amazing, unbearable force. Invincible was their valour, as fresh fighters continually replaced those who were exhausted. Clouds of darts mingled with the horrible crash of missiles; larger projectiles flew whistling through the air.

At last, unable to sustain the weight of battle, the Turks fell back. Our people brought up scaling ladders and prepared to storm the walls! Realising that final disaster was imminent, the Turks resolved to resist with all their valour. They dropped huge lumps of rock at our people as they climbed up the ladders, crushing them and throwing them off. Then they also hurled Greek fire at the tall castle, which eventually caught fire. When those inside saw what had happened they were forced to descend and retreat in frustration.

Meanwhile on the seaward side our people slew an incalculable number of their Turkish assailants. So although on the tower side our people were bewailing their lack of success, those assigned to the seaward side took a heavy toll of the enemy.

At last the siege machines were destroyed by the devouring flames, as were the castle and the galleys in which they were fixed and the scaling ladders. Then the Turks dissolved into excessive joy. Wailing with high-pitched voices, they mocked our people over their misfortune, 'wagging their heads' [Matthew's Gospel ch. 27 v. 39].

The Christians were devastated by this. They were no less distressed by the insults heaped on them than by their losses. However, they were cheered by the fact that pilgrims were arriving with increasing frequency. As their numbers grew their force grew stronger.

---

240. Various sorts of shields were attached to the tower for decoration and protection.

Chapter 59: The townspeople, with some loss to themselves, burn up the archbishop of Besançon's battering ram with Greek fire.[241]

Meanwhile the archbishop of Besançon [Thierry de Montfauçon] had a siege machine built with great care and expense. They call it a 'ram' because it is pushed backwards and forwards with repeated and frequent blows like a ram, and demolishes walls, no matter how solidly built. The ram was strongly covered all round with iron plates, and when it was finished the archbishop intended to use it to destroy the wall.

Count Henry had had another ram built. It was fortified and strengthened with every possible effort, so that one would have thought that nothing could damage it. The rest of the magnates and nobles of the army also had various types of siege machines constructed, each according to their means or at shared expense. Some made 'sows' with spikes,[242] some pikes, others stakes, or whatever they had either seen before or devised for themselves.

A day was set when they would all attack the wall with the devices they had made. The archbishop moved his ram forward to shatter the wall. It was roofed over like a house. Inside it had a long ship's mast, with an ironcovered head. Many hands drove it against the wall, drew it back and aimed it again with even greater force. So with repeated blows they tried to undermine the face of the wall and break it down. As they shook the wall with repeated blows, the roof of the ram kept its operators safe from all danger of attack from above.

The Turks on the walls defended themselves manfully. They collected a huge heap of old dry wood on top of the machine, which of course they could easily set on fire. At the same time their stonethrowers were continually hurling enormous boulders at it. At last they dropped Greek fire on top. As it ignited the wood those inside the machine found the

241. This attack took place early October 1190 (Bahā' al-Dīn, p. 214). According to Bahā' al-Dīn, the duke of Swabia was the commander, and was responsible for constructing the siege machines. Our author's account is very similar to Ambroise, lines 3823–96, but Ambroise only mentions the ram, not the other siege machines; Bahā' al-Dīn supports our author's evidence of other machines being used as well (p. 214). Roger of Howden, *Gesta*, 2 p. 144 and *Chronica*, 3 p. 73 mentions a battle on 1 October when four siege machines were burnt by the Saracens with Greek fire.

242. *Sues rostratas*. Stubbs (1864), p. 456: the *sus* was a shed of wood used to protect sappers and miners while they dug under the wall. The spike or beak dug into the base of the wall and broke up the stone, just as a sow's snout digs up the earth.

growing heat of the fire unbearable. Realising that the whole machine was going to be destroyed, they left it and pressed on with the attack using what other devices they could. The Turks kept on tirelessly hurling missiles at the ram, hoping either to crush it with enormous lumps of rock or to burn it with their incendiary oil.

Great was the strife and contention between the Christians and the Turks. One side pressed on with all their might to extricate the ram while the other courageously resisted them and defended it. Once the ram was set on fire the Turks kept feeding the flames. The fire burnt the whole machine to ashes, sparing nothing.[243]

The Christians had already retreated, grieved at the failure of their efforts. On the other side the Turks were dancing and shouting loudly, jeering that our hopes were in vain and that the Christians' valour was nothing compared to their own people. Yet they did not insult our misfortune with impunity. Their own forces had suffered the loss of eighty Turks, one of those who died being a prominent emir who had commanded this operation. Yet they deliberately concealed all these losses in order to hide their setback from our people.

Our princes realised that their hard work and expenses did not seem to be having the success that they desired. Shattered by so many severe setbacks, they decided to slacken their efforts and refrain from assaults on the city for a while.[244]

---

243. Bahā' al-Dīn, p. 214, describes the ram and states that it was captured by the Muslims. He also describes another siege machine called a 'cat' which clung on to the wall, and which was burnt.

244. At this point Ambroise inserts information regarding the death of Queen Sybil and the problem of the succession to the kingdom of Jerusalem: lines 3897–909. Ambroise has muddled the order of events: he says that the queen died 'after August', but the attack on the Fly Tower took place late September and the attack with the ram in early October. The Lyon *Eracles* dates the queen's death to late July 1190: *Conquest of Jerusalem*, p. 95. The compiler of IP2 has put events into the correct order.

Chapter 60: A fleet of fifteen ships is sent from Alexandria to the townspeople, but many perish.[245]

Meanwhile, not much after Michaelmas [29 September 1190] a fleet of fifteen ships came from Alexandria to relieve the besieged. The ships sailed in extraordinary pomp and splendour, each at a short distance from each other. They arrived as the sun was setting, but because the wind was quite strong they were not able to adjust their course. Seeing our army, they were very much afraid that our people would come out to meet them, since they would not be able to escape. But the Christians did not dare to do this because the night was coming on and the wind was strong.

So the fleet advanced in close formation and charged towards the Chain.[246] Behind followed three of the larger ships, known as 'dromonds', while in front sailed the galleys, which are lighter and more manœuvrable in an attack. As they charged in confused order into the harbour they ran into great difficulties with ships running into each other, while two ships ran on to the rocks and smashed, and almost all those in them drowned. The Christians mocked and derided them in their peril, and beheaded those who were carried into their harbour by the force of the waves. The violence of the wind drove the largest galley into their harbour. It was well loaded with food. They seized it, killed the crew and kept the rest for themselves.

The rest of the ships were carried into their intended harbour beyond the Chain. The townspeople were overjoyed at their most welcome arrival. Carrying innumerable illuminated lanterns they went out to meet the new arrivals and hastily admitted them into the city with much honour. These reinforcements increased their numbers so much that they expelled from the city those less able to fight. They feared that otherwise they would impede their defence and be more of a hindrance than a help to them by consuming their food supplies.

And so the days passed.

---

245. Ambroise, lines 3909–60, is similar but not identical. Bahā'al-Dīn does not describe this specific incident. He mentions the loss of a ship between 12 and 22 October 1190 (p. 217) and the arrival of three ships in mid September (pp. 209–10: also 'Imād al-Dīn, p. 248, on 16 September). He also mentions two Christian ships which ran aground in a storm between 12 and 22 October and were captured by the Muslims (p. 217).

246. The Chain was a chain hung across the harbour entrance as a security measure. It was raised at night to prevent ships going in or out. For a description of the Chain at Tyre, see *Conquest of Jerusalem*, p. 69.

Chapter 61: With Archbishop Baldwin in command of the army, our people are drawn up in battle array to attack Saladin. Saladin flees with his people to the mountains.[247]

Meanwhile the common people began to murmur about the lack of activity by the princes. They were tired of the siege and began to complain about the cost of the idle blockade. The magnates had discussed for quite some time what would be the best course of action. At last they all came to a decision to challenge the enemy on the outer side to a general engagement, for if the enemy army were defeated they would be able to attack and capture the city more easily.

On the day after St Martin's day [12 November 1190] as Phoebus' rays [the sun] grew cooler with the approach of winter, our princes led our battalions out of the camp into the plain and marshalled them in accordance with military practice. We watched them advance with their various standards, here the knighthood of the Temple, here the Hospitallers, here various nations brandishing their banners. It was a delightful and stimulating sight. Their great number was astonishing, their valour aroused our confidence in a victory, and their diversity was a pleasure to see.

The clergy claimed no small share of military glory. Fighting faithfully for the Faith, abbots and bishops led out their cohorts and joyfully contended for God's Law. Baldwin, venerable archbishop of Canterbury fought among the rest; but he outstripped them all. He was old and infirm, so that military action was difficult for him, yet his perfect virtue enabled him to transcend his natural weakness. He had a banner carried high in front of his troops on which was depicted the glorious martyr Thomas.[248] He had procured for the martyr a seemly and worthy following: 200 knights and 300 men-at-arms followed his banner and fought in that holy man's pay. He took charge of the camp in conjunction with the duke of Swabia [Frederick] and Count Theobald of Blois. He also discharged the duties of the patriarch [Heraclius], who was then ill in bed, by absolving and blessing the whole army as it set out.

---

247. With this chapter we return to the original text of IP1. The abortive battle of 12 November is also described by Ambroise, lines 3861–4002; Roger of Howden, *Gesta*, 2 p. 144 and *Chronica*, 3 p. 73; 'Imād al-Dīn, pp. 263–4; and Bahā' al-Dīn, pp. 223–4. The Muslim sources and Ambroise state that when Saladin withdrew the Christians continued to advance, leading to the battle at the Bridge of Da'ūq, ch. 62, below.

248. Thomas Becket, archbishop of Canterbury: see note on ch. 12, above.

The heroic bishop of Salisbury [Hubert Walter] could not bear to be absent from the expedition. He played an honourable role in the war: his virtues made him a knight in battle, a leader in the camp, and a pastor in ecclesiastical matters.

The sun was setting as the army, having come a short way, halted and pitched its tents. The townspeople made a sortie into the empty camp to plunder the baggage. Our people met them with all their strength, preserved their own unharmed and put the attacking Turks to flight.

That night Saladin ordered his pavilions and other equipment to be carried into the mountains, and he burned everything which they could not carry off at that moment. This was clearly the action of a beaten and despairing mind: he destroyed his own possessions, abandoned his position, and retreated into the mountains, avoiding a battle in level country.[249] When he found a defensible position he made a stand and placed numerous infantry and archers in the way of the approaching army; so that at least they could inflict injury from a distance, although they were afraid to engage them at closer quarters. So our people, cheated of the opportunity of a battle in level country and not able to pursue the enemy through the steep mountains, turned back without loss or glory.

Chapter 62: Some of our people go to Cayphas for food and return. The Turks fight them but are defeated [13 November 1190].[250]

After this they heard that food was to be had at Cayphas [Haifa]. As they were very much in need of this, they turned in that direction. When our people had come *en route* to a place known as Recordana [Tell al-Kurdāni, 13 November], the Turks rushed out and attacked them, thinking that they were fugitives from the camp! Some threw darts, some

249. Bahā' al-Dīn, pp. 223–4: Saladin's advance guard left al-'Ayyāḍīya and went to Tell Kaisān. The baggage went to Nazareth and Qaimūn. The sultan, however, remained at al-'Ayyāḍīya. Bahā' al-Dīn states that the advance guard retreated to draw the Christians on as they marched to Haifa (see following chapter).

250. This chapter is not in MS G, and so was not in IP1; it was added by the compiler of IP2. It is similar but not identical to Ambroise, lines 4003–90. For these events see Bahā' al-Dīn, pp. 226–8; 'Imād al-Dīn, pp. 265–6. In adding this account, the compiler of IP2 improved the historicity of the *Itinerarium*.

leapt on them with lances; some with dreadful shouts, some blowing trumpets like hunting horns.

That night our people pitched their tents on the plain and lay quietly until morning. When morning came, an enormous number of Turks appeared, surrounding our army on all sides! Our people were absolutely terrified at the sight of such a great horde, but they took up their arms, drew up ranks to repel assault, and went out in due order to meet them. However, the Turks did not dare to attack their battle formation. As our people advanced they slowly fell back, although the size of their army was beyond reckoning.

Hearing that, contrary to what they had thought, there was no food to be had at Cayphas because the Turks had carried it away, our people prepared to travel back to Acre. They suffered no little trouble and danger on the journey, for the Turks harassed them continually, making frequent assaults on them. At the spring or source of a certain river which flows from there towards Acre [Ra's al-'Ain], the two armies clashed and there was a great slaughter of fine horses before the armies parted.

Our army proceeded on one bank of the river, while the enemy host was on the other bank, harassing and threatening our people without pause and firing missiles at them from a distance. Some pursued our people from behind, tormenting them so much that our infantry, men-at-arms and archers who made up the rearguard,[251] had to march looking backwards, firing arrows constantly at their pursuers.

The following night they pitched their pavilions not far from the river. They had little rest but a lot of worry, because they had to repulse open assaults and beware of hidden ambushes. The opposition never ceased their constant, continual taunts and provocation.

There is a bridge over which they had to cross the river [Bridge of Da'ūq: 15 November 1190]. The Turks had already seized it. Because they had not had the time to destroy the bridge before our people arrived, as they had intended,[252] they massed their forces, made a stand in the middle of the bridge and tried to prevent a crossing. Our people realised that only force would make them give way. Then Geoffrey de Lusignan, the king's brother, with five other elite knights, charged powerfully into them and scattered them in an instant. Thirty of them were thrown into the water, never to emerge again because they drowned. So

251. Ambroise says: 'The king of England's men and the Templars formed the rearguard,' lines 4044–5.

252. 'Imād al-Dīn states that the Christians were destroying the bridge: p. 266.

they conceded the road, albeit unwillingly. Everyone crossed freely and returned to the siege of Acre.[253]

Chapter 63: The wiles employed by the marquis to marry the heir to the kingdom, i.e. Reinfrid's wife [Isabel], in order to acquire the kingdom; although Reinfrid was still alive.[254]

For a long time the marquis had entertained hopes of becoming king, but he now saw a means of obtaining his desire open to him. He promised himself confidently that he could get the kingdom if he could take the wife of Reinfrid [Humfrey IV of Toron] from him and marry her himself. He yearned for this with all his heart and applied all his skills to obtaining it. Adopting an indirect approach to start with, he complained about the state of the government, claiming that the king was not up to managing affairs of state, and now that his wife had been taken from him he had no right to rule, since another daughter of King Amalric was still alive.

First he laid these arguments before the people, but he was also careful to canvass the princes' support, winning some over with gifts and getting others to join him because they were related to him. He lured some by flattery, put some under obligation to him by favours, and drew in some by promises. He was such an industrious man and had so many clever arguments at his fingertips that he easily obtained everything he

253. Our author does not return to the military events of the siege until 8 June 1191, in Bk. 3 ch. 1. Bahā' al-Dīn informs us (pp. 229-31) that on 23 November the Christians were defeated in an ambush and several were captured. Saladin then sent his troops away for the winter, relieved the city garrison (pp. 232-5) and rebuilt the city wall. On 31 December 1190 seven grain ships coming to the city were lost in a storm (p. 234); Bahā' al-Dīn regards this as the first warning that the city would fall. The second sign was the collapse of a large part of the city wall on 5 January 1191 (p. 234). In ch. 93 (p. 236) he mentions the death of Duke Frederick of Swabia on 20 January 1191 from fever and the Christians' grief at his death. Our author omits this. Roger of Howden, *Gesta*, 2 p. 144 and *Chronica*, 3 p. 73 mentions an attempt by the besiegers to scale the walls of Acre in December 1190. The Germans lost their ladder, but the English kept theirs. This is probably the attack of 31 December 1190 mentioned by 'Imād al-Dīn, p. 277.

254. For this see also Ambroise, lines 4112-65; 'Imād al-Dīn, p. 304; Ralph of Diceto, p. 84; E-B, pp. 267-8; *Conquest of Jerusalem*, pp. 95-6, and 172-4. MS G of the *Itinerarium* names Isabel's husband more correctly, as 'Enfrid'. Apparently the compiler of IP2 changed the name to Reinfrid, probably because Ambroise calls him Reinfrid.

desired. He surpassed the deceits of Sinon, the eloquence of Ulysses and the forked tongue of Mithridates.[255]

But because ecclesiastical sanction prevents the marital bond from being indiscriminately put asunder, that cunning man composed a new accusation through which he might steal Reinfrid's wife. He persuaded the princes that she could be separated from her husband without breaking the law, because she had been married while she was underage and without her own consent.[256]

Reinfrid himself had conceived the hope of winning the kingdom through his wife. He was more like a woman than a man: he had a gentle manner and a stammer.[257] This poetical quotation describes him:

> As nature doubts whether to make a man or girl,
> You are born, O lovely, a boy who's almost a girl.[258]

He intended to inherit the kingdom himself, basing his claim on the right of his wife. But his claim was unwise. The princes ordered him to produce his wife on a certain day; then he lost both his bride and the

---

255. On Sinon and Ulysses see p. 57 above, and note 89. Mithridates is Mithridates VI, Eupator Dionysius (The Great), who ruled 120–63 BC. He was king of Pontus in northern Asia Minor, and fought a series of wars against the expanding power of Rome. He was famed for his cunning, courage and organising ability.
256. Isabel was betrothed to Humfrey in 1180, when she was eight, and married him in 1183, when she would have been eleven or twelve: see *Conquest of Jerusalem*, p. 44 note 27, p. 96 note 165. Twelve was the normal age for heiresses to marry in the kingdom of Jerusalem.
257. Bahā' al-Dīn states that Humfrey was a man of high rank in the kingdom of Jerusalem, and acted as an interpreter between the sultan and the Christians (p. 288). The French continuations of the work of William of Tyre, which seem to preserve the opinion of a part of the Palestinian Frankish nobility, have a very low opinion of Humfrey, regarding him as a coward because he had submitted to Queen Sybil in 1185 rather than supporting the Ibelins, who wanted to make him king (*Conquest of Jerusalem*, p. 27). In the context of the divorce, Humfrey is accused of having a cowardly heart and being trained like a woman (ibid., p. 96). The marquis' supporters persuaded him to give his wife up by telling him that he could not govern the kingdom, as it would be too much trouble and hard work for him. In fact, when a papal legate made enquiries in 1213, witnesses of the divorce gave evidence to show that Humfrey loved his wife and had had no intention of giving her up: ibid., pp. 172–4.
258. MSS A, B and G state that the quotation is from Virgil; Stubbs (1864), p. 120, and Mayer (1962), p. 352 state that it appears in Virgil's *Catalecta* (1617), ed. Scaliger, Leyden, p. 177. MS C omits the reference to Virgil, and in fact this quotation is not now thought to derive from Virgil.

kingdom through the marquis' machinations. What a crime, a worthy subject for satirical attack and tragic declamation! It was more disgraceful and a greater injury than the rape of Helen, which is generally condemned.[259] For Helen was stolen secretly, when her husband was away, but this wife was violently abducted in her husband's presence.

To preserve appearances, the girl was put into the hand of sequestrators while a clerical court debated the case for a divorce. So the marquis approached the clergy with gifts and guiles. He sounded out all whom he believed supported him; he poured out enormous generosity to corrupt judicial integrity with the enchantment of gold.

Word of this dreadful crime came to the ears of the most holy metropolitan of Canterbury. His pure heart was shocked; as protector of the law, he was furious. The patriarch, as we have said, was ill and had entrusted his duties to the archbishop.

While he discharged them with due vigour, the marquis' accomplices threatened to appeal against the sentence pending in the divorce case. He had three leading accomplices, Reginald lord of Sidon, Pagan of Cayphas Castle [Haifa], and Balisan [Balian II of Ibelin]. The deceased count of Tripoli would have been a fitting fourth member in this council of consummate iniquity.[260] For a swarm of crimes had streamed eagerly together into them, as if into their rightful home: the treachery of Judas, the cruelty of Nero, the wickedness of Herod, and everything the present age abhors and ancient times condemned.[261] What is more, Balisan had married King Amalric's widow, who was the girl's mother [Maria Comnena]. Steeped in Greek filth from the cradle, she had a husband whose morals matched her own: he was cruel, she was godless; he was fickle, she was pliable; he was faithless, she was fraudulent. The marquis had cajoled them with gifts and promises into instructing the girl

---

259. In classical myth Helen was abducted by Paris, sparking off the Trojan war.
260. Pagan or Pain of Haifa is mentioned again as an opponent of King Richard (and therefore of King Guy) in Bk. 2 ch. 38. Reynald of Sidon and Balian of Ibelin appear again in Bk. 5 ch. 24 negotiating with Saladin on behalf of the marquis. Balian's brother, Baldwin of Ramla, was one of the leading opponents of the coronation of Guy in 1186, calling the king '*fol et musart*' – a blithering idiot: see E-B, pp. 135–6, and *Conquest of Jerusalem*, pp. 26–7. When Guy was crowned, Baldwin left the kingdom in disgust, and Raymond III of Tripoli became recognised as the leader of the nobles opposed to Guy: E-B, pp. 138–9; *Conquest*, pp. 28–9.
261. These examples are drawn from a combination of history and Christian legend. Judas betrayed Christ; Nero murdered his wife and stepson and persecuted the early Christians; Herod had all the infants of Bethlehem murdered.

to bring an action against Reinfrid. She should claim that she had married him against her will, that she had always protested against it, and the marriage should not be valid since she had never given her consent to it.

She was easily persuaded to do this, for a woman's opinion changes very easily. 'For fickle and ever changeable is a woman' [Virgil, *Aeneid*, Bk. 4 vv. 569–70]. The female sex is weak, her mind is changeable, and she rejoices at each new embrace, lightly spitting out those she knows and swiftly consigning them to oblivion. The girl is easily taught to do what is morally wrong, willingly accepted her advisers' shameful instructions, and soon she is not ashamed to say that she was not carried off but went with the marquis of her own accord.[262]

Spurning the law, the princes were rather inclined to give the marquis both the kingdom and the girl. The most holy archbishop of Canterbury[263] saw that justice and equity had been confounded and turned upside down and ecclesiastical sanction obliterated. He also perceived that the clergy and some of the bishops, i.e. those of sounder mind and more fervent zeal, were murmuring against this iniquitous marriage, as far as they dared. Then he pronounced the sentence of excommunication against those contracting and consenting to it.

Nor was this without good reason, for he carried her off and slept with her while her husband was still alive; he took her into his house and married her – with the bishop of Beauvais presiding over the marriage; and he had a wife who was still alive in his own country, and another in

---

262. The Lyon *Eracles* states that Isabel was in love with Henfrid and was only persuaded to leave him after much bullying by her ambitious mother (*Conquest of Jerusalem*, pp. 95–6). When the case was investigated by the papal legate it was stated that Isabel was bullied by the marquis' allies into leaving her beloved husband and that she only gave way because she thought she had no choice: *Conquest of Jerusalem*, pp. 172–4. She was only eighteen. 'Imād al-Dīn describes her as a beautiful young woman, with face white as the morning and hair black as night, faithful and devoted to her husband Humfrey (pp. 105–6) – the only Christian woman he describes in such detail. He disgustedly notes that she was pregnant by Humfrey when she was forced to marry the marquis (p. 304) – but this is unlikely, as no birth was later recorded. In the *Itinerarium*'s version of events our writer appears to be blaming the woman for events beyond her control.

263. From this point MSS A, B, and C leave MS G. IP1 went on to describe the death of the archbishop, as below, ch. 65, and then ended. A, B, and C's account of the divorce from here to 'what the Holy Church judged wrong', approximates to Ambroise, lines 4125–44, but in a different order, and also approximates to Ralph of Diceto, p. 86. From 'On the same day', the account seems to be following Ambroise, lines 4145–65.

the city of Constantinople,[264] both noble, young and lovely, and quite suited to his requirements. Thus, they alleged, he had committed triple adultery.

The clergy spoke out as best they could against doing what the Holy Church judged wrong. However, the marquis' accomplices strove to excuse him. They claimed that as a condition of contracting the marriage the marquis had pledged that he would send supplies of food from Tyre to the army, which was very much in need of them.[265] But he scorned his oath, and irreverently transgressed his pledge of good faith. He who is unfaithful in little things is not afraid to commit greater crimes.

On the same day that the long desired nuptials were celebrated, some of our people who had been at the marital drinking-session were returning in twos and threes after dawn when they were attacked by Turks who rushed down on them out of an ambush, and some of them were killed. This was the beginning of many disasters. The butler of Senlis was captured there [Guy III of Senlis]; it was never known afterwards whether the Turks kept him prisoner or killed him. Twenty were captured or killed.[266]

Chapter 64: The marquis returns to Tyre and fails to keep his oath to send famine relief to our people.[267]

The marquis, his wishes fulfilled, at once returned swiftly to Tyre with his spouse and his people. Everyone hoped that he would gladden their hearts by supplying them with food, as agreed. But they hoped in vain. He did not send so much as an egg to the famine-striken army. Either he forgot his earlier agreement, or he was ungrateful for what they had

---

264. Theodora Angela, sister of the emperor Isaac Angelus. Conrad had married her in the spring of 1187 and abandoned her in July 1187. She was still alive in 1195–98 when she converted the monastery of Dalmatios into a convent, presumably for her retirement: Brand (1968), pp. 80, 84, 119.
265. This reasoning was repeated to the papal legate in 1213: *Conquest of Jerusalem*, p. 173.
266. Ambroise adds: 'In this way the marriage was paid for' (line 4165). Roger of Howden, *Gesta*, 2 p. 150, also mentions the butler's capture. Apparently the butler of Senlis had challenged Humfrey in the divorce court, claiming that the lady Isabel had never agreed to the marriage and offering to prove it by battle. Humfrey refused to fight: see *Conquest of Jerusalem*, p. 96. The title 'butler' was given because the lords of Senlis were hereditary cupbearers to the king of France.
267. Ambroise, lines 4166–78.

done for him! No, that lying perjurer did not even give permission for those who wished to sail to the army with essential foodstuffs! Therefore a great famine developed in the army, little or nothing could be found to eat, and nothing was brought by ship.

Chapter 65: Baldwin, archbishop of Canterbury, dies.[268]

The archbishop of Canterbury had heard that the army had lost all discipline, concentrating on taverns, prostitutes and games of dice. Seeing now that this was true, he could not bear such lack of self-restraint, and was so discouraged in spirit that he wearied of life.

One day he was receiving even more frequent reports of this sort of behaviour, the worst he had heard yet. General ills are difficult to remedy, but he knew that while humanity has the care, God has the cure. He sighed deeply. 'Lord God,' he exclaimed, 'now Holy Grace must rebuke and correct them. Let it be well-pleasing to your Mercy to carry me away and allow me to quit the whirlwind of this present life. I have been in this army for long enough.'

As if the Lord had heard his request, not a fortnight after making this speech he began to feel a little stiff, and then became weak and feverish. Within a few days he fell happily asleep in the Lord.[269]

Chapter 66: The harsh famine and the enormous price of goods, for which they cursed the marquis.

Meanwhile famine raged, torturing the middle classes as well as the common people with continual distress. The onset of famine was the more severe because of the marquis' desperate prevarications, although he had secretly sent grain to those whom he had enlisted as his accomplices and supporters in his illicit and abominable business.

Already even the leaders of the army could scarcely obtain the little

268. This account is not in Ambroise. Ralph of Diceto notes the archbishop's death, p. 88.

269. MSS C and G add: 'We say confidently that he sleeps in the Lord, for he led a laudable life which knew no blemish and his death was no less miraculous than mournful for the whole of our army.' G continues: 'It is permissible to digress a short distance to relate evidence briefly and succinctly in order to include testimony to virtue, provided the intended brevity is not upset by lengthy treatment of the subject.' IP1 ended here.

nourishment needed to sustain life.[270] Winter was coming on, which used to be a time of plenty and prodigal luxury, flowing with all sorts of good things to eat. But now times had changed to shortage and austerity, and the belches of their greedy gullet were not caused by overeating as they used to be but by their empty stomachs. The voracious table had already consumed all their sustenance, but the fervent hunger of youth was unsatisfied. They ran out of even basic essentials, they wasted away with hunger. The more they lacked plentiful supplies, the worse their burning torment became. The threat of unsettled weather approaching also increased the severity of the famine somewhat.[271]

Certainly, poverty is usually more unpleasant for those brought up in splendid affluence.

What more can I say? A measure of wheat, a small measure which one could easily carry under the arm, was sold for 100 gold coins. A hen was sold for twelve shillings and an egg for six pence. The prices of other essential foodstuffs can be calculated from these.

Then they curse and damn the marquis
Who stole their consolation;
He cheated of their food those
In danger of starvation.[272]

Chapter 67: Perishing with hunger, our people devour the corpses of their horses, including the offal.[273]

It is said that need drives folk to crime, and intercedes for mercy for them; and God created all things for humanity, and gave them into our hands so that they might be a help for us.

So, rather than let humans die while beasts of burden were spared, they slew their precious warhorses and consumed the horseflesh with pleasure, sometimes without having even skinned the animals first. A horse's offal was sold for ten shillings. They flocked together eagerly

---

270. From this point, IP2 and Ambroise virtually break into song. See the Introduction, pp. 12, 14.
271. Bahā' al-Dīn, p. 236, also describes famine and plague in the Christian camp.
272. Ambroise's refrain is shorter and always the same: *Lors malsdisent li marquis/par qui il erent si aquis,* – 'then they cursed the marquis, who got them into this mess'.
273. Ambroise, lines 4229–42.

anywhere a horse was known to have been killed, either to buy or to steal. Starving people rushed in crowds to the corpses of dead animals like vultures to a corpse. So they devoured the bodies of their mounts. Those who used to carry them, vice versa, they now carried in their stomachs. A horse was worth more dead than alive. This part of the Gospel seems not inappropriate for them: 'Wherever the carcass is, there will the vultures gather.' [Matthew's Gospel ch. 24 v. 28] – the mystic interpretation aside; we are not intending to detract from its dignity!

Such was the pressure of famine that when they had slaughtered a horse none of the offal was regarded as waste; every part, no matter how vile, was greatly valued. They wolfed down the offal and head, and when they had avidly consumed – no, devoured – everything, the wise ones licked their fingers, so that anything left there was taken by the tongue rather than wiped away with a napkin.

Then they curse and damn the marquis,
Who stole their consolation
He cheated of their food those
In danger of starvation.

Chapter 68: Anyone who had any food ate it in secret.[274]

As time passed the terrible famine grew very serious from the shortage of foodstuffs. If anyone had anything edible they hid it away under lock and key for their own use so that it would not be violently taken from them, because there was not enough to satisfy the need of more. So it came about that little was put out for sale, and those who had anything did not distribute it for others to share. Everywhere the poor went without.

Then they curse and damn the marquis,
Who stole their consolation,
He cheated of their food those
In danger of starvation.

---

274. Ambroise, lines 4243–52.

Chapter 69: Those who used to live in luxury ate grass.[275]

Wherever they happened to see grass growing, noblemen and potentates' sons, those who were once delicately nourished, devoured it. They resorted to dire fodder to quench their violent hunger, eating grass like beasts! Necessity led many people to plant herbs which were suitable for food and effectively dispelled their hunger pangs. So the immensity of the famine transformed herbs which they would once not even have looked at or considered suitable for human use into the sweetest food for the famished.

Then hear the voice of the people wailing,
Cursing the marquis' perfidy,
For he's indifferent to their suffering
And all their misery.

Chapter 70: The people perish from the rains and hunger.[276]

Besides, the excessive rain caused people to contract a dangerous sickness. That unheard-of downpour – constant, continuous – inflicted such great injury on the army that in their terrible distress their limbs swelled up and their whole body was swollen with liquid as if they had dropsy. The violence of the disease was such that some people's teeth fell out, torn away completely at the roots.

O the laments of each of them, O the grief of all! Even those who were unharmed grieved over the miseries of the others. Each day saw the funerals of their comrades; every single day they performed the funeral rites of 1000 dead.[277] Some, although only a few, recovered from the illness. As their appetites were increased after their sickness, they suffered excessive misery in the famine.

Then hear the voice of the people cursing
The marquis' perfidy,
For he's indifferent to their suffering
And all their misery.

275. Ambroise, lines 4253–64, but in a different order.
276. Ambroise, lines 4265–73, but in a different order.
277. Among those who died was Duke Frederick of Swabia; Count Henry of Champagne also fell sick. 'Imād al-Dīn adds that Count Theobald died (p. 278).

Chapter 71: The starving fight at the bakehouse.[278]

Whenever it became known that bread was baking in an oven, a crowd formed of people shouting out: 'Here's money, have whatever price you want for your bread, if only you'll give me plenty.' Each person begged to be served first, bidding for the bread, bread which they did not yet have and perhaps would never get, as each violently carried it off for themselves. Sometimes it happened that someone wealthy bought a large part of the bread. Then there was grief and lamentation and shouting from the poor, wailing as if in one voice when they saw the rich carry away that little bit of bread which could have profited the poor in some way if it had been divided up and distributed among them. They eagerly offered for the bread whatever price the seller asked. Because there was too little to meet the demand of such a great crowd, tempers were frequently lost around bread ovens, and there were disputes, quarrels, resentment, and some fights as they vied bitterly in uncertainty as to who would get what they all wanted.

> Then hear the voice of the people cursing
> The marquis' perfidy,
> For he's indifferent to their suffering
> And all their misery.

Chapter 72: The starving nibble bones gnawed by dogs and consume filth.[279]

But who can write or describe such great misery, such great common suffering? Some were driven mad by starvation and seen rushing around like rabid dogs and seizing on bones found by chance, which had been thrown to the dogs and gnawed for three days. Although there was nothing left to gnaw they nibbled, sucked and licked them, not doing themselves any good but having some sort of pleasure as if they were nibbling the memory of where meat had once been.

What should we add to this? The enemy harassed them with constant attacks from both sides. But when they killed them in sudden attacks they were reckoned to be gentler than the terrible famine, because their

---

278. Not in Ambroise, nor in MS C.
279. Not in Ambroise.

swords brought an instant end to life and misery, whereas starvation killed slowly, with long torture. Indeed, often those who had lost their sense of shame through their hunger, for sorrow! fed in sight of everyone on abominable food which they happened to find, no matter how filthy, things which should not be spoken of. Their dire mouths devoured what humans are not permitted to eat as if it were delicious.[280]

Then hear the voice of the people cursing
The marquis' perfidy,
For he's indifferent to their suffering
And all their misery.

Chapter 73: Even noblemen steal when they cannot afford to buy bread.[281]

On the basis of the evidence worthy of being recounted it is possible to judge the great extent of the famine, and see that for those who sustained it patiently in the flesh it could be reckoned as a form of martyrdom. But perhaps a murmur of doubt stands in the way of their receiving the grace of merits; for many unworthy deeds were committed under the pressure of necessity.

There were some who were ashamed to beg in public because they came from noble stock. But as they were less afraid to sin in secret than to seek sustenance by begging in public, they used to steal bread. So it happened that someone was caught in this sort of robbery, and tied up very tightly with a strap. The bound man was put under guard in the house of his captor, who was a baker. And while the members of the household pressed on busily with their many tasks, the captive's hands came untied through his wriggling or somehow. As it happened, he was seated next to a pile of fresh bread; he ate some secretly, without anyone noticing or realising what he was doing. When he had eaten enough, he took up one loaf of bread in his hand, and sprang out free. Returning safely to his comrades, he told them the whole story and distributed the sole loaf which he had carried off for them to share among them. But what was that among so many? The morsel irritated the throat and excited hunger rather than calming it.

280. This could mean dead dogs or rats; or even human corpses.
281. The first paragraph is not in Ambroise; for the rest, see lines 4279-314.

Then hear the voice of the people cursing
The marquis' perfidy,
For he's indifferent to their suffering
And all their misery.

Chapter 74: Many people apostatize because of the severity of the famine.[282]

This cannot be related or heard without deep sorrow. Some of our people broke down in the face of the excessive severity of the famine, winning salvation for their bodies, but incurring damnation for their souls. After the greatest tribulation had been partly overcome, they fell away and fled to the Turks. Not hesitating to apostatize from their faith, to prolong their temporal life a little they won perpetual death with wicked blasphemies. O calamitous exchange! O shameful crime, worthy of what punishment? O foolish ones, 'short-lived like oxen' [Psalms 49 v. 12] fleeing death which will inevitably come soon, but not escaping an endless death! If the just live by faith, [Romans ch. 1 v. 17], treachery must be death. But, at length, those who happened to recover their senses purged their consciences.[283]

Then they curse and damn the marquis,
Transgressor of his word,
And call evil down upon him,
And deadly woe.

Chapter 75: Two companions buy thirteen beans for a penny.[284]

There were two companions, comrades in calamity and misery, who were in such need and sore straits that they had only one coin between the two of them, one commonly called a penny Angevin. With that one coin they hoped to get themselves something to eat. But what should they do? The little that they had would be reckoned as slender substance even if there had been plenty of good things for sale. They had nothing

282. Ambroise, lines 4315–32.
283. Reading *resipuerant* from MS A, rather than *respuerunt*, in B and C.
284. Ambroise, lines 4333–60.

more except their armour and clothes.

They discussed in detail for a long time what they would buy with that sole coin, and how to avert the pressing evil of that day. At last they reached a decision: they would buy some beans, since they were the cheapest thing on sale. And so with much persuasion they finally succeeded in buying thirteen beans for the penny. After they got home they found that one had a maggot hole in it, and was not fit to eat. By mutual decision, they made a long journey and after lengthy enquiries finally found the vendor. After much supplication he eventually deigned to exchange the faulty bean for an undamaged one.

O what a great exchange, won through humble begging after seeking far and wide! We can guess how much satisfaction they had from those beans, which they consumed in a moment! We reckon that it should be weighed by the reader's judgement rather than describing it with the pen.

> Then they abhor the marquis,
> Transgressor of his word,
> And call evil down upon him,
> And deadly woes.

Chapter 76: The starving consume carobs, and die from drinking wine.[285]

A sort of fruit which was growing on the trees was put on sale, seeds enclosed in a pod like peas, known commonly as a 'carob', sweet-tasting and delectable to eat. The needy filled themselves with them, because there was a larger supply of these than of other things. So there was a well-trodden path to the place selling them, because although they were not thought to be worth much they were something.

Because those who were ill ate little, either because they had nothing to eat or because they could not eat, the wine they drank made them overheat and very many of them choked. This was either due to the strength of the wine, because it was not moderated with food, or due to their illness which had made them too weak to bear strong wine.

In fact there was a reasonable enough amount of wine for sale, but much wine and little food is not good for the human body. It is best to

---

285. Ambroise, lines 4361-80.

take both in equal moderation. But the curses on the marquis did not rest, as he was the cause of the great shortage.

They always abhor him,
Transgressor of his word,
And call down evil on him,
And deadly woes.

Chapter 77: Those who are starving consume meat in Lent.[286]

Even at the beginning of that Lent, which is called 'the Start of the Fast' [Ash Wednesday] their pressing hunger compelled some of them to eat meat; not because there was a plentiful supply but because it was the easiest food to get hold of.[287] However, afterwards, when things grew easier, they repented and did suitable penance.

Over and above all these things, all that winter love between everyone grew so cold from fear of shortage that a friend would not even share with a friend in necessity. 'O ye of little faith!' [Matthew's Gospel, ch. 8 v. 26], doubting that 'God is love' [1 John ch. 4 v. 16] and thinking that if they gave what they had to others they would go short of necessities themselves. The vice of parsimony grew so strong, with everyone holding on to what they had, that they hid anything they had, so that those who had something were thought to have nothing.

So what do they wish for the marquis,
All these complaining voices?
Certainly all would pronounce him guilty
Of causing so many dangers!

286. The first sentence is a rough equivalent to Ambroise, lines 4381–96. The second paragraph is like Ambroise, lines 4397–412.

287. During the period before Easter, the forty days of Lent and Holy Week, Christians traditionally have not eaten meat or eggs, as an outward sign of repentance.

Chapter 78: With the encouragement of the bishop of Salisbury and some others, the wealthy make a collection to feed the poor.[288]

The communion of the faithful had been damaged beyond measure. No one cared about the poor and needy. This shameful lack of faith was spread among all. The bishop of Salisbury [Hubert Walter] strove to correct this situation, teaching that nothing is greater than charity, nothing more welcome to God, nothing more fruitful than giving. By this effective persuasion he induced everyone to open their hands to share with their neighbour, to give to the needy, to sustain those who were perishing, because otherwise by neglecting another's necessity they might fail to obtain their own. As it is said: 'Anyone who is able to save the feeble from death and fails to do so actually brings about their death' [Gratian, *Decretals*, pt. 1 dist. 83 pt. 1]. He showed them that a person who avoids helping another when the opportunity is offered is guilty of causing their death, as we are commanded to give something to drink to a thirsty enemy and something to eat to a hungry one [Romans, ch. 12 v. 20]. Moreover, the bishop of Verona was stirred into giving similar exhortations, as was the bishop of Fano in Italy.

So at their necessary encouragement and insistence a collection was made for distribution to the poor. Those whose hearts God had touched gave so many and such great things as gifts to the needy that the starving were most amply filled. At the same time through the cooperation of God's grace the distributions did not reduce the means of those who gave. Then a new joy appeared, then the lips of many blessed their benefactors, then welcome mercy flowed down upon them, when the powerful poured out compassion on the afflicted. That notable man Walkelin de Ferrers and Robert Trussebot were foremost in carrying out these matters. No less enthusiastic were Count Henry of Champagne, Jocelin de Montoire, and also the count of Clermont and the leader of the action, the bishop of Salisbury.

Through the care and effort of these people and others, everyone con-

288. Ambroise, lines 4413-62. From here the compiler of IP2 follows Ambroise, until the end of Book 1. For the role of Hubert Walter, bishop of Salisbury, see also Roger of Howden, *Gesta*, 2 p. 145, *Chronica,* 3 pp. 69-70. Ralph of Diceto, p. 88, states that Bishop Hubert acted as executor of Archbishop Baldwin and took care of the poor. He includes a copy of a letter written by Bishop Hubert to Richard fitz Nigel, bishop of London, describing the situation in the besiegers' camp in early 1191: translated in *Conquest of Jerusalem*, pp. 171-2. In 1193 Bishop Hubert was made archbishop of Canterbury.

tributed according to their means towards a distribution 'to all according to their need' [Acts ch. 2 v. 45]. Their hearts had been frozen under the dead ashes of avarice, but when the divine grace blew upon them, they blazed up in charity. Because they were converted like this and became merciful, the Lord regarded them and magnified His mercy in them, as it is said, 'Return to me, and I will turn back to you, says the Lord,' [Malachi ch. 3 v. 7].

Chapter 79: After the arrival of a ship known commonly as a Dromond with a cargo of grain, what was sold yesterday for 100 gold coins is today bought for four gold coins.[289]

While everyone was pressing on with pious works, God led a ship to them! It was loaded with grain, and its arrival very much alleviated the previous food shortage. For the great dearth of bread was not caused by a lack of wheat but by vendors demanding an inflated price from the buyers, so that with their oppressive business methods they could make a lot of money. Greed will stoop to anything!

That ship, which was rather small, arrived on a Saturday, I think. And on the Sunday following, through the dispensation of God the giver of all good things, a measure of grain which was previously sold for 100 gold coins was reduced by the arrival of one little ship to four gold coins. Meanwhile a new delight arose in the people, and the only ones who were sad and resentful were the greedy merchants, because the profits that they had been making would be reduced. But so what? There is no counsel against God, because He does all things, 'whatever He wills' [Psalm 115 v. 3].

Chapter 80: A fire burnt down the house and grain of a Pisan who wished to store grain for the future.[290]

A certain Pisan who sold grain had kept wheat untouched for a whole year, until such future time as he could sell it at what price he wished. For he had hoped that the famine would be worse, and if he ever sold any, he sold it at his own price and on his own terms to those who could

289. Ambroise, lines 4463–97; see also Roger of Howden, *Gesta*, 2 p. 145.
290. Ambroise, lines 4498–512.

not do without it.

God showed by a clear sign that this was wicked. It happened that the Pisan's house, which was full of wheat, was suddenly set violently on fire. Although very many came running to put the fire out, all their efforts were futile, and everything was immediately burnt up.

Chapter 81: Everyone eagerly bestows food on the poor, and those who ate forbidden food are given penance to perform.[291]

Therefore everyone pressed on eagerly with works of piety, contending with all their strength to distribute alms. Each was driven by zeal to surpass their neighbours in generosity, thinking that the more lavish they were in providing necessities to the needy, the more welcome their service would be to God. Also, those who had eaten meat in Lent out of necessity - as was said above - repented of their crime. They each received correction from the aforesaid venerable bishop of Salisbury and undertook with devotion to carry out the appropriate penances he laid on them.

The end of the first book; the beginning of the second.

291. Ambroise, lines 4513-26.

Here begins Book 2

Chapter 1: The kings of England and France.

After Easter King Philip of France arrived [20 April 1191], and Richard, king of the English, not much later [8 June 1191]. To give you fuller information about the course of their journey, it seems best to go back and begin the narrative with their departure from their countries, following the order of events until we arrive at the abovesaid siege of Acre.

Chapter 2: Both the French and English eagerly take the cross.

Reports of events such as those I have been describing spread throughout the world. Everywhere people heard that the cities of the Holy Land had been captured by the infidel, holy things given over to abuse and to be trampled underfoot, and Christians pillaged and taken away as captives. Then kingdoms were shaken and empires moved by the exhortations of Pope Gregory VIII, who was very much the man of action. An enormous number of people of various nationalities, especially French and English, were roused into putting their devotion into practice, taking the sign of the Holy Cross and hastening to help the Holy Land with all their strength. Like David, they burned to punish the Philistines who taunted the labouring hosts of the God of Israel with their Goliath [1 Samuel ch. 17].

The supreme Pontiff diligently urged them to do this to obtain mercy for all their sins. By the authority with which he was endowed he absolved anyone who immediately undertook this pious and necessary work from their guilt for past sins they had committed, maintaining that those whose more fervent zeal drove them to undertake the journey without delay would merit more blessing.

This journey was the more commendable because its cause was so just. This service was many times more excellent because the divine mystic Promise has many times increased the holiness of that forsaken place. It is dedicated by God's birth in humanity, His dwelling and His suffering, and set apart from all other regions by divine election. It seems

Map 3. The route taken by the German crusaders and King Richard's crusaders to the Holy Land.

KEY
Route of German Crusade
Route taken by Crusaders of Richard I, as described in Book 2
Budapest
UNGARY
Sava
Belgrade
Morava
Danube
BULGARIA
Maritsa
Philippopolis
BLACK SEA
CONSTANTINOPLE
ASIA MINOR
ICONIUM
Selef
ANTIOCH
Margat
Tortosa
Famagusta
Tripoli
Rhodes
CYPRUS
Limassol
Beirut
Crete
ACRE
NEAN
SEA
JERUSALEM
Alexandria
Cairo
EGYPT
N2

imperative that it be rescued from the heathen who seized it, because God commanded that they should not enter His Church [Psalms 95 v. 11, Hebrews ch. 4 v. 3].

Hence people eagerly ran to receive the cross from bishops, with lively zeal and pious competition. Already it was not a question of who was wearing the cross, but rather who was not yet girded with such a pious burden! Henceforth songs were silent, dainty dishes and luxurious clothes given up; disputes laid to rest; a new peace formed between old enemies; legal actions terminated in settlements; and whatever the case, even those divided by inveterate hatred were recalled into new goodwill because of this recent development. What more can I say? By the inspiration of God all were of one mind. A single cause called all to the pious labours of pilgrimage.[1]

Chapter 3: King Henry of England and King Philip of France and an immense number of people take the cross between Gisors and Trie.

Meantime Richard, then count of Poitou, was the first to be marked with the cross.[2] An immense number of people took the cross with him. However, they did not set out on the journey at that point, because their departure was delayed by a dispute between two kings: viz. King Philip of France and King Henry of England, Count Richard's father. A long-standing feud, arising from relentless and almost constant rivalry, had driven these two kings into mutual attacks on each other as it had their ancestors, the French and Normans.[3]

At last, after great efforts by an archbishop [Joscius] from the land of Jerusalem – Tyre, in fact – a day was fixed for a meeting between Gisors and Trie[-Châteaux] to negotiate a peace settlement between the two kings. The said archbishop had come as a messenger to rouse some of

1. See Bk. 1 ch. 17, above.
2. *Cruce insignitur.*
3. This sentence is similar to Ambroise, lines 87–90. Henry II was duke of Normandy as well as king of England and count of Anjou. He was descended from William the Conqueror, duke of Normandy and king of England, through his mother Matilda the Empress. Ever since Normandy became virtually independent of the king of France in the early 10th century, the kings of France had regarded the rulers of Normandy as a threat to their security, while the rulers of Normandy resented the king's claim to exercise authority over them.

the Faithful and recruit them as helpers to recover the land of Jerusalem. He had been especially sent to the king of England because his virtues were famous far and wide, surpassing those of all the kings of the entire earth – his wisdom, and glory, and wealth, and power.[4] On the day of that assembly [21 January 1188],[5] after different opinions had been voiced and various speeches made, both kings came to the decision that they would both receive the cross and both leave their land. Both seemed to be taking a wise precaution here, because if one of them happened to stay behind, he would invade the country of the one who was on pilgrimage. So neither of them dared to go without the other.

At last after great difficulty their joint decision was ratified, with the blessing of the aforesaid archbishop and the kiss of peace. Each of them took the cross.[6] An immense number of people of both sides also took it, partly from love of God and for the remission of their sins, and partly out of respect for the kings. There was such an enormous rush that day of people receiving the cross that people almost fainted in the crush from the unbearable heat: things certainly became very heated.

But their delay in actually setting out on the journey should be absolutely condemned. This was the work of the Enemy of the human race, who is always stirring up relentless hatred and fostering perpetual discord.[7] At his instigation the dispute between the aforesaid kings revived, and the slightest cause hatched a brood of quarrels. Because of their diabolical principles, each was ashamed to allow himself to be brought low without retaliating, for fear of damaging his honour and reputation. As if people would think that he was cowardly and powerless because he was subject and obedient to justice!

---

4. See Mayer, H. (1982), 'Henry II of England and the Holy Land'.
5. Roger of Howden, *Chronica*, 2 p.335.
6. *Crucizatur* – lit.: 'is crossed'. 'An immense number...no obligation to vow', (ch. 4) is like Ambroise, lines 144-74. Ambroise states that he was present at this assembly. Presumably our author was not, as he does not repeat the claim.
7. *Historia Peregrinorum*, pp. 128-9, also blames the work of the devil for the breakdown of relations between Henry and Philip and the consequent postponement of their crusade.

Chapter 4: King Henry of England dies.

The end of King Henry's life brought an end to this dispute. So death at last prevented him from carrying out the vow of pilgrimage which he had earlier put off fulfilling when he was in good health. As a vow to do something ought to be completely voluntary, when it has been made it definitely ought to be kept. A person who is bound by a voluntary vow should be absolutely condemned if it remains unfulfilled through negligence, because there was no obligation to vow.[8]

So King Henry died in Normandy,[9] on the eighth day after the feast of the Holy Apostles Peter and Paul [6 July], in the year of Our Lord 1189, and he was buried at Fontevrault.

Chapter 5: Count Richard of Poitou is crowned king of England.

In the same year, after his father's death, Count Richard of Poitou spent about two months setting affairs in Normandy in order and then crossed the sea to England.[10] On St Giles' day [1 September] he was received with a solemn procession at Westminster; and on the third day after, i.e. the ordination day of St Gregory the pope [3 September] - which was a Sunday - he was solemnly anointed king. By virtue of his office Archbishop Baldwin laid hands on him, and performed the service, assisted by a large number of his suffragans. He was crowned in the presence of his brother Count John [of Mortain] and his mother Eleanor [duchess of Aquitaine] - who following the death of King Henry and on the command of her son Richard, the prospective king, had been released from the custody in which she had been held for around ten years. Also present were earls, barons and knights and an infinite crowd of humanity. King Richard was confirmed in his possession of the kingdom.

King Richard was anointed as king in the year of Our Lord 1189, on the 3rd September, on Sunday, when the Sunday letter was A, in the

---

8. Yet Henry claimed to be making plans to set out on crusade: Ralph of Diceto, pp. 51-4, includes copies of letter from him to Frederick I, Isaac Angelus and Béla of Hungary telling them that he is going on crusade and asking for safe passage through their lands; see also Roger of Howden, *Gesta*, 2 p. 38-9 and *Chronica*, 2 pp. 342-3.
9. King Henry died at his castle of Chinon, in Anjou.
10. Roger of Howden, *Chronica*, 3 p. 8, states that even before Richard was crowned he started to collect a fleet for his crusade.

year after the leap year.[11] Many people were forecasting many things then, because 'unlucky day' was written over that day in the Calendar; and it certainly was an unlucky and bitter day for the Jews of London, because they were destroyed that day.[12] In the same way, that year the Jews who had settled in various places throughout England suffered much evil.[13]

After three days of feasting worthy of a king in the royal palace at Westminster, King Richard with fitting munificence distributed gifts beyond number or price to each of his guests in proportion to their rank.[14] He delighted all his subjects with his actions and his incomparable superiority. The Governor of the Ages had conferred on him a generous character and endowed him with virtues which seemed rather to belong to an earlier age. In this present age, when the world is growing old, these virtues hardly appear in anyone as if everyone were like empty husks; and so they are wonderful and memorable in the few people where they do appear. King Richard had the valour of Hector, the heroism of Achilles; he was not inferior to Alexander, nor less valiant than Roland.[15] No, he easily surpassed in many respects the most praiseworthy figures of our times. Like another Titus,[16] 'his right hand scat-

---

11. In the ecclesiastical calendar the seven letters A to G are allotted to the days of the year in rotation, so that 1 January = A, 2 January = B, and so on. The Sunday or Dominical letter is the letter which falls on the Sunday that year. Once the Sunday letter for a year is known, one may calculate on which day of the week any date in that year will fall. A leap year has two Sunday letters. In the Book of Common Prayer the change falls on 29 February, but in our author's calendar it fell on the 25 February.
12. William of Newburgh calls it an 'Egyptian' day, as if it were a presage of the Jews' death, he says (p. 294).
13. The Jews were massacred at King's Lynn (January 1190) Norwich (February 1190) Stamford in Lincolnshire, York and Bury St. Edmunds (March 1190).
14. This sentence is from Ambroise, lines 105–7.
15. Hector: in the legend of the Trojan War, he was the elder brother of the Paris who stole Helen, and leader of the Trojan defence. He was killed by Achilles. Renowned for his courage and sense of honour, he was regarded as one of the 'Nine Worthies' in the Middle Ages. Achilles: the leading Greek hero in the same war. Alexander: Alexander the Great. Roland: hero of the popular epic poem *La Chanson de Roland*, where he is killed fighting a desperate rearguard action against the Muslims, and so an obvious comparison for the crusading King Richard. In legend he was the nephew of the emperor Charlemagne and his most outstanding warrior.
16. The Roman emperor Titus Flavius Sabinus Vespasianus, son and successor of the emperor Vespasian, and famed for his humanity. He was said to have regarded a day as wasted if he had not given anyone help that day.

tered help.' Also, which is very unusual for one so renowned as a knight, Nestor's tongue and Ulysses' wisdom[17] enabled him to excel others in every undertaking, both in speaking and acting. His skill and experience in action equalled his desire for it; his desire did not betray a lack of skill or experience.

If anyone perhaps may think that he could be accused of rash actions, you should know that he had an unconquerable spirit, could not bear insult or injury, and his innate noble spirit compelled him to seek his due rights. So he may not unreasonably be excused. Success had made him better able to do everything, since 'Fortune favours the brave,' [Virgil, *Aeneid*, Bk. 10 v. 284]. So, although Fortune works her will as she pleases, King Richard 'could not be overwhelmed by the hostile waves of life,' [Horace, *Epistolae,* Bk. 1 no. 2 v. 22].

He was tall, of elegant build; the colour of his hair was between red and gold; his limbs were supple and straight. He had quite long arms, which were particularly convenient for drawing a sword and wielding it most effectively. His long legs[18] matched the arrangement of his whole body. With the not insignificant addition of his suitable character and habits, his was a figure worthy to govern.

He gained the greatest praise not so much for his noble birth as for the virtues which adorned him. But why should I labour to extol such a great man with immense praises? 'He does not need another to commend him, although he has deserved it fully; fame accompanies the deed.' He far excelled others both in his good character and in physical strength. He was memorable for his military power; his magnificent deeds overshadowed all others, no matter how glorious. He would have been thought really fortunate - speaking in human terms - if he had not had rivals who were jealous of his glorious deeds. The sole reason for their hatred was his greatness; because you will never torture the envious more than by serving virtue.

17. Another reference to Greek heroes of the Trojan War. Nestor was the venerable and wise old king; Ulysses the clever one.
18. Lat: *tibiarum longa divisio*, lit.: 'a long division of the legs', which gave him a good seat on a horse.

Chapter 6: King Richard settles the affairs of his kingdom and celebrates Christmas in Normandy at Lyons. Following the agreement between him and the king of France, he goes to meet him at Vézelay at the feast of St John the Baptist [24 June].

So when the coronation festivities were over, as was said above, King Richard stood in his father's place and received securities of their loyalty[19] from the magnates of the country, as is the custom, in token of their subjection to him. Then leaving London he toured the country, and afterwards he made a pilgrimage to Bury St Edmunds, as St Edmund's feast day [20 November] was then approaching. From there he went to Canterbury.

Some of the bishoprics had earlier fallen vacant and had been held in his father's hand.[20] At King Richard's command, bishops were elected and then enthroned with the king's consent. Richard [fitz Neal] the treasurer was elected to be bishop of London, Godfrey de Luci to Winchester, Hubert Walter to Salisbury, and William Longchamp to Ely. The king also made the last his chancellor and justiciar of the whole of England.[21] In a similar way the same king had bishops ordained to the vacant bishoprics in his other lands.[22]

Having prepared what was necessary for his journey, and put the kingdom of England in order as far as the short time allowed, he returned to Normandy without delay [11 December 1189],[23] and kept the festival of Christmas at Lyons[-la-Forêt]. For his intention to set out on his pilgrimage and discharge his vow troubled him constantly. He judged that a delay would be dangerous while the debt was still outstanding. So he wrote to the king of France that he himself had got everything ready for the journey, and that he should also set out hastily, arguing from his father's example that 'delay is always dangerous to those who are prepared.' [Lucan, *The Civil War*, Bk. 1 v. 281].

---

19. *Fidelitatis securitate*. Note the use of 'security' rather than the more familiar '*iuramentum*' for 'oath'. There is no mention of homage, although presumably that was included. I have translated '*fidelitatis*' as 'loyalty' in preference to the archaic 'fealty' or the rather clumsy 'fidelity'.
20. For this paragraph, see Ambroise, lines 229-32; William of Newburgh, p. 300; Ralph of Coggeshall, pp. 28-9.
21. See Appleby, J. (1965), *England Without Richard*, p. 35.
22. Normandy, Anjou, Aquitaine. Ireland was ruled by Count John, Richard's younger brother. From this point the account begins to follow Ambroise more closely (from line 234).
23. Roger of Howden, *Chronica*, 3 pp. 28, 30.

So in the year of Our Lord 1190, when the Sunday letter was G, the kings met at Dreux to discuss the arrangements for their journey. Many people contributed their opinions, and while they were talking a messenger suddenly came to report that the queen of France [Isabel] had died.[24] This bitter news was a terrible blow to the king of France. He was so completely devastated that he was on the verge of deciding to abandon his plans for the pilgrimage. And, listen: more devastating news came – King William of Apulia had also passed away! A great many people were shattered by all these adversities coming against them. As if they were held back by a superstitious fear of bad omens, they shrank from continuing with the undertaking, and their burning zeal went completely cold.

The pious undertaking which had seen so much planning and such solemn arrangements might have been finished, and what had been arranged to win merit might have turned into damnation and disgrace. Yet by the inspiration of God, who guides our steps [Proverbs ch. 16 v. 9], in whose hands are the hearts of kings [Proverbs ch. 21 v. 1], they resumed their strength, and were stimulated to go on and set out on their journey so that they would not be accused of being idle cowards. They arranged to set out on the Nativity of St John the Baptist [24 June], so that the two kings and their entourages would meet together at Vézelay[25] on the eighth day after that date.

So, not long after this, King Philip of France left the city of Paris, which is the capital of the kingdom of France, with much necessary equipment. He went to the shrine of St Denis where he entrusted himself to the saint's prayers and merits. In this way he began his pilgrimage, accompanied by an enormous multitude. The duke of Burgundy [Hugh III] and the count of Flanders [Philip d'Alsace] set out with him on his pilgrimage.

It would be impossible to describe the progress of each of them with their respective forces. On all sides you would see people flocking together from everywhere and assembling, forming one army from many. Those who were going mingled tears with their dear ones, relatives or friends, who watched them lovingly as they set off. As friends departed, they were unable to restrain themselves from bursting into tears of affection or grief.

24. Isabel de Vermandois died on 15 March 1190: Rigord, p. 97. He calls her Elizabeth.

25. Vézelay: in the département of Yonne, about 40 km SSE of Auxerre and 14 km WSW of Avallon.

Chapter 7: At Tours, King Richard orders his fleet to go on ahead, sailing round Spain through the straits, and wait for him at Messina.[26]

King Richard was at Tours with an elite force of knights. The city and its suburbs were crammed with such an enormous number of people that the crowds were colliding with each other because the roads and streets were too narrow for so many thousands.

So by urgent royal command the royal fleet was assembled and ordered to proceed in due order.[27] It numbered 108 ships, not including other ships which were to follow soon. The fleet set out at the king's request. With prosperous course and in close formation the seafarers avoided unharmed the dreadful sandbanks, the terrible dangers from rocks and the stormy straits of Africa [Gibraltar] and all the other dangers of the sea. As if the winds had plotted together to serve them, they came to port at their chosen destination, Messina.[28] As he had commanded, they waited here for the arrival of the king, who was coming with his forces by the land route.

When the king set out from Tours with his comrades the roar of the great multitude made the local people tremble. Who could describe the size of his company, the different varieties of weapons, the nobles' retinues and the forces of elite warriors? – or the troops of infantry, the masses of crossbowmen? Those who watched them as they set out in due order felt such deep emotion that they were moved to tears. They both mourned and cheered their new lord the king. They mourned him because although he had only just begun his reign he had not yet tasted the sweetness of rest; he had completely and immediately deserted everything. They cheered him because he was a man of great prowess who had taken up this difficult and necessary undertaking, this commendable journey, as if he had been chosen by God.

---

26. The first two paragraphs are from Ambroise, lines 303–22. The third paragraph starts like Ambroise, lines 323–39, but is longer. The final paragraph is not in Ambroise.
27. Roger of Howden, *Gesta,* 2 pp. 110–1 and *Chronica*, 3 p. 36 sets out Richard's arrangements for his fleet and the names of the commanders. Ambroise appears to have sailed with the fleet, because he has no details of the precise route followed by the pilgrims, and he refers to those with the fleet as 'us', (lines 553–5). Richard received the staff and scrip of a pilgrim at Tours: Roger of Howden, *Chronica*, 3 pp. 36–7.
28. 14 September 1190: Roger of Howden, *Chronica*, 3 p. 54. *Gesta*, 2 pp. 115–24 and *Chronica*, 3 pp. 42–54 give a detailed description of the voyage to Sicily.

O what pitiable sighs there are at the departure! O how they groan as they embrace and say their farewells to those going away! O eyes heavy with tears! As dear ones talk together they interrupt themselves with sobs and kisses; friends can hardly bear to part and can never finish talking. Those who are setting out put on solemn expressions, pretending that their minds are strong although their heart grieves. They make a long drawn-out speech as they leave, as if they are hanging on to say more. Often having said farewell they stand talking for longer, and as if to put off the moment of departure they repeat themselves, so that they always seem to have more to say. But at last they drag themselves away from their wellwishers, leap from the hands which clutch them and are whisked away.[29]

Chapter 8: In accordance with their agreement the two kings meet at Vézelay.[30]

So in the first year after his coronation, King Richard of England set out on pilgrimage from Tours. From Tours he went to Azay [le Rideau], thence to Montrichard, then on to Selles [sur Cher], and from there to Chapelle d'Angillon. From there he went to Donzy and then to Vézelay, where the two kings had arranged to assemble their forces.

The endless throng seemed beyond numbering. The mountains and valleys were filled with pitched pavilions, and all around far and wide the face of the earth was covered with tents. The camp covered the cultivated fields of the plain so that from a distance it looked like a new city, with the most impressive variety of pavilions of different styles and shape, divided into different colours.

There you would have seen a martial band of youth: assembled from various regions, fit and ready for war. It seemed that they would easily master the whole breadth of the globe, overcome the countries of every nation, penetrate the retreats of sundry peoples. You would have reckoned that no rough terrain, no fierce enemy could defeat them, and that

29. The inclusion of a second farewell scene is puzzling. It is not in Ambroise, who has already described goodbyes (the end of our ch. 6). It may be no more than a literary *topos*, included for effect, or it may represent what the compiler of IP2 himself saw.

30. Ambroise omits the details of Richard's route; for the rest of the chapter, see lines 340–56.

they would never give way before any injury – as long as they supported each other in one mind with united strength and mutual assistance. For although an army may glory in its great numbers, be protected by its weapons and burning with passion, if disputes arise within it or friends fall out it is routed and destroyed. Military discipline and common purpose hold the army together so that its external enemies cannot defeat it, but when the common bond is broken it is completely overwhelmed, torn to pieces by its own members. For 'every kingdom divided against itself is laid waste' [Luke's Gospel ch. 11 v. 17].

Chapter 9: At Vézelay the kings make a treaty and promise to wait for each other at Messina. Thus they both reach Lyon-sur-Rhône at the same time.

There the two kings concluded a treaty of mutual security: that each would keep faith with the other, and that they would share equally everything they acquired by right of war. Moreover, whoever arrived first at the city of Messina, the capital of Apulia, would wait there patiently for the other to follow.[31]

After this, those who had come to see off members of their family and friends who were going on the pilgrimage set off homewards.[32] The kings started out ahead with their companies, and made the arrangements for their journey. They frequently paid their respects to each other with great munificence, showing each other mutual honour and esteem. The whole army was of one mind on the march. They completed their daily stages with eagerness and joy, without any complaint or dispute.

As they passed through cities and towns the locals were very impressed at the sight of the great crowd with so much equipment and such a clatter of arms, and the sections of people from many different regions and how they marched with such discipline. 'Wow!' they said, 'What's all this about – this great crowd of people, this powerful army? Who could stand against their force? What a beautiful company, what handsome youths! O happy parents, who have such fine children! They must be grieved to see you go. Which countries produced such good-looking youths? Where were such pleasing young soldiers conceived? Who do you think could be in command of such a great crowd? What authority

31. For this paragraph see Ambroise, lines 365–75.
32. This sentence is not in Ambroise.

could control legions of such valour?'

They said this and things like this, and escorted them with good wishes as they passed by. They also declared their devotion by giving whatever assistance they could, offering them water in containers of various sorts – a very welcome service to those tired by the journey.[33]

So the troops advanced in order in distinct daily stages.[34] They went briskly from Vézelay to St Leonard's at Corbigny, from there to Moulins-Engilbert, and then on to Mont Escot. From there they went to Toulon [sur Arroux], to le Bois Ste. Marie, thence to Bélleville, then on to Villefranche [sur Saône], and from there to Lyon-sur-Rhône.

As the speed and uncertain depth of the river made the crossing difficult, they halted there for some days to enable the army which had already arrived to cross, and to wait for those who were following on to catch up. At last when the river was crossed, the kings had their pavilions set up on the other side of the river and resided in the open air. Part of the army was lodged in the town, as many as it would hold, part in the suburbs, and in the open country. There you would see countless people hailing from various regions, set apart by the positions of their tents and their different sorts of weapons. It was thought that they numbered over a 100,000, and still they kept pouring in.

When the king of France and his company set off for Genoa the king of England accompanied him for a short distance, to show him friendship and honour.[35] The king of France had long before engaged the Genoese to transport him over the sea, because they are very experienced mariners. The kings had decided, as was said before, that whoever arrived first at the Sicilian city of Messina should wait for the arrival of the other.

---

33. For 'The kings started out ahead...tired by the journey', see Ambroise, lines 376–406.
34. 'So the troops...Lyon-sur-Rhône' is not in Ambroise. The rest of the chapter corresponds to Ambroise, lines 415-44.
35. Ambroise states that the two kings set out together and travelled together until their roads parted: lines 437–8. But Ambroise does not appear to have been with the army at this point, as he gives no details of the route the pilgrims took.

Chapter 10: After the departure of the king of France for Genoa, the bridge over the Rhône collapsed under the weight of people on it. King Richard embarked at Marseille and arrived at Messina.

A great crowd of pilgrims was still flocking in from everywhere. In their haste, they poured across the bridge over the Rhône, which is rather narrow. This was unwise, because part of the bridge collapsed under their weight, together with those who were on it. The bridge was extremely high, and more than 100 people fell from it into the water. The current is so strong and rapid that anyone who fell from such a great height would be unlikely to escape alive. But those who had fallen in shouted loudly and begged for help and, astonishingly, they were pulled unhurt if exhausted from the water. Only two were drowned. Their bodies were destroyed, but their spirits live in Christ, in whose service they were taken.

Those who had been behind them were at a complete loss. Each asked worriedly where or how they were going to cross the Rhône because it was impossible to cross the broken bridge. They were absolutely at their wits' end. King Richard, whose capacity for firm action was never shaken, was sorry for those who needed to cross the river. When he found out about this accident he swiftly had a bridge constructed out of little boats fastened firmly together, the best possible in such pressing circumstances. They were able to make some sort of crossing over these boats, although slowly and with difficulty. The king and the army were delayed for three days because of this incident.[36]

Some of them went to the nearest port, Marseille; some went to

---

36. Ambroise (lines 449-500) gives a slightly different account of this incident: when the army knew that the kings had gone, they got up early to cross the Rhône. Those who went across first crossed safely but when a great crowd followed them a span of the bridge collapsed. He says nothing about Richard building a bridge of boats, but says that they crossed as best they could in little boats, and it took three days to cross. Gaston Paris attributed this difference to bad translation by the author of the *Itinerarium* from Ambroise's French. Certainly there are places where our author seems to have translated carelessly, but this need not be one of them. Roger of Howden, who also went on the crusade but was with the fleet (as Ambroise may have been) says that the bridge collapsed as the two kings and their entourages were crossing it (*Gesta*, 1 p. 112). So we have three accounts of the same incident. Our author is the only one who gives a precise route for the crusaders, which suggests either that he was on crusade himself or he had information from someone who was - see Introduction, p. 13. I am therefore inclined to prefer his version of this incident.

Venice and some to Genoa, or to Barletta or Brindisi. A great many set out for the port of Messina, the destination of the two kings.

Three days later, the king left Lyon, and the same day the bridge was dismantled. From Lyon we[37] crossed through Viaria by Hauterives, from there to La Motte de Galaure, then on to St Bernard's at Romans, from there to Valence, after that to Loriol, after that to Paleys, from here to S. Paul de Provence [Trois-Châteaux]. After that we crossed through Mondragon and from there to Orange. After that, crossing through Sorgues, we rested at Bonpas near Avignon. After that we went to Sénas and from there to Salon [de-P.], after that to Martigues on the sea. From Martigues to Marseille, where we stayed for three weeks. Then we embarked on the sea on the day after the Assumption of the Blessed Virgin Mary in the first year after King Richard's coronation [16 August 1190].

We crossed between two islands, of which one, Sardinia, was on the right while Corsica was on the left. There is a very narrow strait between them. From there we sailed between two mountains which are always burning, one of which is called Vulcano and the other Strombeli.[38] Then we sailed through the Faro [Straits of Messina], which is very dangerous. After that we reached the city of Messina. King Richard's fleet was there; as we said before, he had sent it on ahead of him.

Chapter 11: The city of Messina; King Richard's sister the Queen of Sicily, and her dowry; and Tancred.[39]

You should be informed that the city of Messina is full of copious quantities of good things. It has a pleasant and very convenient location, within Sicily close to Reggio, which it is said was once conferred on the famous Agoland for his service.[40] The city of Messina stands at the entrance to Sicily. It abounds in every good and essential thing, but its people are

37. From here to the end of the chapter is not in Ambroise. Now the compiler of IP2 seems to be recounting personal experience. See the Introduction, p. 13.
38. These are two of the Lípari islands, which lie north of Sicily.
39. Ambroise, lines 511–34.
40. In the epic poem *La Chanson d'Aspremont*, Agoland is king of Africa and invades Calabria (lines 315, 319). Ambroise says simply: 'Risa, which Agoland took by his enterprise', (lines 515–6). Gaston Paris believed that the author of the *Itinerarium* had mistranslated Ambroise's French. In Bk. 5 ch. 21, below, he translated the same incident correctly. Yet it is odd that an educated clerk did not know this story about Charlemagne.

cruel and the very worst sort. Their king, Tancred, was very richly endowed with different sorts of wealth, amassed by his ancestors who had ruled in Sicily from the time of Robert Guiscard.[41]

At this time the queen of Apulia [Joanna] was staying at Palermo. She had recently been widowed of her husband King William. As King William had died without an heir his widowed queen and the dowry assigned to her were being held in wardship by the aforesaid King Tancred, who had succeeded King William in the kingdom.[42] This widowed queen was the sister of King Richard. As he was concerned about her, he compelled King Tancred to give the queen full satisfaction for the dowry due to her.

Chapter 12: The injuries which the Griffons at Messina inflicted on our people before the king's arrival.[43]

As was said above, that frequently mentioned fleet of the king's was waiting at Messina for the king to arrive. The fleet had an astonishing number of ships,[44] and was fully equipped. It was said that nothing like it had ever been seen there: it was so large, and so much work had gone into fitting it out. Moreover, many sorts of people had been assigned to look after the fleet. They were camped on the seashore in pavilions and tents of various types. Before the king's arrival they avoided staying in the city because of the insolence of the godless citizens.

The citizens were a wicked bunch, commonly known as Griffons.[45] Many of them were the offspring of Saracen fathers, and they were

41. A Norman adventurer invested in 1059 by the Pope as duke of Apulia, Calabria and Sicily, on condition he conquer them. This was done by Robert and his brother Roger. Robert died in 1085.
42. Tancred was the illegitimate son of William's brother. The other claimant to the kingdom of Sicily was Emperor Frederick I's eldest son Henry, who had married William's aunt Constance.
43. Ambroise, lines 539–58.
44. Ambroise calls them 'eneckes', or sneckas, a word derived from snekkar, a long and narrow Scandinavian ship with twenty rowers. The snecka was used as a transport vessel in the North Sea. In the *OED*, 'snack' is the preferred form of the name.
45. Griffon: a derogatory term, which could be used to designate Muslims, e.g. *Le Charroi de Nimes* (1931), line 976. Our author uses it to mean persons of Greek origin; Sicily had been part of the Byzantine empire until the late eleventh century.

absolutely opposed and hostile towards our people.[46] They inflicted daily insults on them, poking their fingers in their eyes, calling them 'stinking dogs', and mocking them in many other ways. What is more, they secretly killed many of our people and threw their bodies into the sewers – a crime for which some of them were later convicted.[47]

In these ways and a great many others they taunted our people and showed their great hatred for them, exercising their wickedness as far as they dared. Our people were driven to fury, but if they had tried to fight back and retaliate in kind they would have been completely wiped out of the city, because they were outnumbered, and pilgrims,[48] and inferior in strength. But the enemy acted without foresight, because they forgot that their kings would soon arrive.

Chapter 13: The splendour of first the king of France's arrival at Messina and then the king of England's.[49]

It is a recognised custom that when a king in particular or the prince of some country is on the march, his progress should be as distinguished and grand and project as much authority as the power which he actually holds. He should not appear less than he is; no, his appearance should match his actual power. The king's splendour should reflect his royal office; his exterior appearance should declare his inner virtue. As it is commonly said: 'The man that I see, I expect you to be.'[50] What is more, appearance is governed by character. Whatever sort of character the ruler has, it is naturally reflected in outer appearance.

The king of France is a man of such great name, whose edict is obeyed by so many princes and so many nations,[51] that when it was announced in the city of Messina that he was approaching the port local people of every age, every sex, and whatever condition leapt up to see such a renowned king. But he was content with only one ship; and as if

46. Ambroise says 'us', implying that he arrived at Messina with Richard's fleet (lines 553–5).
47. The next paragraph is not in Ambroise.
48. And so unarmed – at least in theory.
49. See, for Philip's arrival, Ambroise, lines 559–600; but Ambroise is longer.
50. Old French proverb: *'Tel te voi, tel t'espoir'*. See Morawski, J. (ed.) (1925), *Proverbes*, no. 2324; Ambroise, line 570.
51. Rather an exaggeration for 1190, although truer by 1220 when this work was probably written in its present form.

he was avoiding human gaze, he took himself secretly into the city's castle harbour. Those waiting on the shore for his arrival accused him of being timid and jeered him, saying that this king could not easily accomplish great deeds of valour since he was so wary of human gaze. So, disappointed in their hope of seeing him, they returned indignantly to their homes.[52]

Then, when rumours spread that the nobleminded king of England was approaching,[53] the people rushed out in crowds, wanting to see him. Pouring on to the shore they struggled to stand where they could see him coming in. Look! Far away they saw the sea covered with innumerable galleys, and from afar the sound of war-trumpets echoed in their ears, with clarions resounding clear and shrill. As the fleet came nearer, they saw galleys rowing in good order, adorned and laden throughout with various sorts of weapons, with countless standards and pennants on the tips of spearshafts fluttering in the air in beautiful array. The prows of the galleys were each painted differently, with shields glittering in the sun hung on each bow. You would have seen the sea boil as the great number of rowing oars approached. The ears of the onlookers rang with the thundering of war-trumpets - known as *trompes* - and they were thrilled with delight at the approach of this diverse uproar.

Then, behold the glorious king! - with the troops of sailing galleys like an accompanying escort, he stood out on a prow which was higher and more ornate than the rest, as if to see things unknown or to be seen by the unknown. Willingly putting himself on show for all to see, he was carried towards the densely packed shore.

Elegantly dressed, he came ashore, where he found the sailors whom he had sent on ahead waiting for him with others in his service. They received him joyfully and brought forward the warhorses and his noble horses which he had entrusted to them for transportation. The locals flocked in from all sides to join his own people in escorting him to his lodging. The common folk talked among themselves about his great magnificence, which had left them stunned. 'This man is certainly worthy of authority! He deserves to be set over peoples and kingdoms. We had heard of his great reputation, but the reality that we see is far greater.'

---

52. 'Those waiting...to their homes' is not in Ambroise.

53. 23 September 1190 (Ralph of Diceto, 2 p. 84; Roger of Howden, *Gesta*, 2 p. 125; *Chronica*, 3 p. 55). The *Gesta* agrees that Richard's arrival was impressive. Ambroise, lines 593-600, is much shorter and lacks the vivid description.

Meanwhile trumpets resounded together, harmoniously blending alternate notes, so that they made a sort of jarring harmony of tones [Lucan, *The Civil War*, Bk. 1 v. 98]. They produced a prolonged tuneful even sound in which each somehow cancelled out the others' variations, thus creating a constant tone.

Chapter 14: The injuries our pilgrims suffered at Messina from the Lombards.[54]

When the Griffons saw the kings' impressive landings their arrogance was somewhat checked. They realised that the kings were stronger and more glorious than they. But the Lombards murmured insolently, and did not cease in their struggle to provoke our people with taunts and insults. They threatened to invade our camp, kill our people and carry off their possessions. They were led on by jealousy, because some of the pilgrims had been chatting to their wives – but they did this more to annoy their husbands than with adultery in mind.

So on this pretext and aroused by malice, the Lombards and the common people of the city[55] were always harassing our people as much as they could. They especially hated them because they had discovered from their ancestors that they had once been subjugated by our people.[56] So they created whatever difficulties they could for our people, and they increased the height of the fortifications of the towers around the city and dug deeper ditches around. Then to arouse them to fury still more they provoked and shamed them with repeated insults and affronts.

---

54. Our author uses 'Lombard' to denote Italians in general. For what follows, see Ambroise, lines 605–26. The Sicilians' hostility to the crusaders is understandable, as the crusaders must have constituted a serious drain on the local economy as well as a threat to law and order.
55. *Communa civitatis*. This could mean the common people, or the government of the city; but the former seems more likely in the context.
56. This must refer to the conquest of Sicily by the Norman adventurer Robert Guiscard and his brother Roger and their descendants in the eleventh and early twelfth centuries. But they hardly stood for the whole Anglo-Norman race, as the writer implies.

Chapter 15: There is a fight between us and the Lombards over one loaf of bread which a women was selling.[57]

One day it happened [3 October 1190][58] that one of our men was bargaining with a certain woman over a fresh loaf of bread which she had put out for sale.[59] As they negotiated he suggested fixing a certain price. Then the woman suddenly flew into a great temper because he had offered less for the loaf than she wanted, and attacked the man with a stream of abuse, barely restraining herself from hitting him with her fist or pulling out his hair. Then, at the sound of the woman's commotion a crowd of the citizens suddenly gathered, who violently seized that pilgrim, beat him mercilessly, tore out his hair, and after maltreating him in many other ways left him virtually trampled to death!

There was an outcry, but King Richard tried to restore peace and goodwill. He issued an assurance that he had come in peace, and simply with the intention of performing his pilgrimage. Nor did he cease pleading for peace until each side had promised to keep the peace and returned peacefully to their homes.

Chapter 16: The Lombards attack King Richard's men. Then the king besieges, storms and captures the city, and places his standards on the city towers. The king of France is jealous, and gives assistance to the Lombards.[60]

But it is always the intention of the ancient enemy of the human race to disturb the peace and arouse unrest. Through his instigation the struggle between citizens and pilgrims broke out again the following day [4 October],[61] and the renewed dispute was even more dangerous.

The two kings were negotiating with the justiciars of Sicily and the leading citizens of the city over a treaty to ensure mutual peace and security. Then a cry went up that the locals were killing the king of England's men! The king shrugged this off, mainly because the Lom-

---

57. Ambroise, lines 627–44.
58. Roger of Howden, *Chronica*, 3 p. 56; *Gesta*, 2 p. 127. He says that there was a disturbance, but does not mention the bread.
59. Ambroise (line 628) calls her Ame – to rhyme with *femme* – but this may be simply for the rhyme.
60. Ambroise, lines 645–830.
61. Roger of Howden, *Gesta*, 2 p. 128; *Chronica*, 3 p. 56.

bards assured him that it was not true. Then a second messenger came, crying that the locals had attacked the pilgrims. The Lombards had themselves just come from the conflict, but they intended to get round the king with lies. So they were persuading him that it was not so when a third messenger appeared, running in at breakneck speed, and shouted loudly that this was an evil sort of peace when swords were already hanging over their necks. Then without delay the king hurried out of the conference and set off on horseback with the intention of breaking up the quarrel and pacifying those involved.

There were two very crafty and deceitful Lombards who had instigated the city mob's attack on the pilgrims. Cloaking their guile with lies, they assured the king that they had just come from there, and no evil had been done. These were their names: Jordan del Pin and Margarit.[62]

When King Richard arrived at the place he found that people from both sides had congregated and were already groaning over their mutual blows. They were now not only wrangling with words but also with fists and staves. When the king tried to break up the fighting, the incensed and defiant Lombards hurled a stream of abuse at him. Refusing to put up with their ridicule, he at once put on his armour, took up his weapons, shut them up inside their city and laid siege to it, taking them by surprise.[63]

Meanwhile, the French, unsure of what their lord the king would do, were running about looking for him, when he hurriedly left the conference place and took refuge in the palace where he was lodged!

The whole city was in confusion. Each person snatched up whatever weapon happened to come to hand and boasted to each other that come what may they would put up a defence. The Lombards went to the king of France, begging and imploring him to aid and defend them. They and theirs would submit to his authority and will; they would even surrender the city to him, if only he would counter the king of England's relentless attack on the city. At once the king of France took up his arms. According to what someone who knew the truth told us, he was more ready to assist the Lombards than the forces of the king of England, although he

62. Margarit is the famous admiral of Bk. 1 ch. 14. Ralph of Diceto, p. 86, states that Jordan del Pin and Margarit were commanders of Messina, and they fled in secret, taking their families with them. Roger of Howden, *Gesta*, 2 p. 128, states that Margarit was one of those negotiating with the two kings; in *Chronica*, 3 p. 57 he added Jordan del Pin.

63. *Obsidione subita*: sudden or unexpected siege.

had previously bound himself to him by oath and given his word that he would give him aid and keep good faith with him everywhere.[64]

The city gates had been barred, and guards placed on the ramparts of the city walls. Then there was a loud shouting, and noise and confusion on this side from the attackers and on the other side from those driving them back. There was a general rush to arms. Each armed themselves, snatching up such weapons as madness [Virgil, *Aeneid*, Bk. 1 v. 150] and hasty impulse supplied. The French united with the Lombards: they acted by common counsel and assembled together as if they were one people. Those outside did not know that their allies had become their adversaries.

At the beginning before the city gates were closed some Lombards went out to attack Hugh le Brun's[65] lodging. They were pressing on relentlessly with the attack, when King Richard discovered what was going on and swiftly turned that way! When they saw him coming they all immediately turned and fled, scattering in a moment like sheep fleeing wolves. So they ceased their threatening words and assaults! The king pursued them as they fled. They headed for a postern gate in the city wall, not even daring to look back at him, let alone fight - although the king did not even have twenty of his men with him when he first charged on them, or so it is said. As they entered the postern gate he unhorsed some of them and killed them. That was the last time *they* would ever attack the pilgrims!

Realising that this was getting serious and the attack was in earnest, the Lombards resisted with all their might. They filled the ramparts of the city walls, throwing rocks, firing arrows and a rain of crossbow bolts, and attacking their besiegers in any way that they could, to make them cease their assaults or at least reduce their strength. In the heat of their initial defence they inflicted many injuries on some of our people. Some were mortally injured, others were bruised, and some suffered fractured limbs. Amidst the dense clouds of flying bolts and arrows and stones and rocks being thrown down, we lost among others three knights: Peter Tirepreie, Matthew de Sauley, and Ralph de Roverei.

Had the Lombards had Christ's true faith and respect for justice, they would have been able to inflict enormous slaughter on our people, and

---

64. *Gesta*, 2 p. 129, agrees: King Philip did nothing to help King Richard and harmed him as much as he could.

65. Count of La Marche, part of King Richard's possessions as count of Poitou. He was a brother of Guy and Geoffrey de Lusignan. Roger of Howden also mentions this attack: *Gesta*, 2 p. 128 and *Chronica*, 3 p. 57.

defeat us by weight of numbers. Instead they fully deserved to suffer through their own arrogance and impiety, which had led them to inflict such undue injury and damage on our innocent people.

It was reckoned that the crowd of citizens and others defending the city was more than 50,000 strong. You would have seen men making the fiercest assaults as they tried many ways of breaking into the city: some boldly shooting bolts, others cutting down gates; first this side falling back, now that side. Our galleys tried to seize the harbour opposite the palace and besiege the city from the seaward side; but the king of France prevented them, and some of those who had entered and refused to fall back happened to be killed by arrows. On the landward side the attack was pressed most fiercely where the king of England was. He was uniquely skilled in warfare. Part of his army attempted to cut the hinges of the gates, but when they were not successful they climbed a high hill next to the city and went to a postern gate which the king of England thought that the citizens had overlooked. He had noticed it on the second day after his arrival when he and two companions were going round the city spying out the land as a precaution against future need.[66] They boldly made a great charge through this gate and entered the city, broke down the city gates and let the rest of the army enter. They either captured or killed any citizen who stood in their way or resisted them, and invaded the city in a body. Many of the Lombards and our people fell in that conflict.

The citizens did not dare to fight face-to-face with those who were entering the city on all sides and had already all but seized it. So they fired missiles at them with all their might from the tops of houses, tower ramparts and upper rooms, struggling to hold back the attackers by whatever means they could. Nevertheless, the city was already captured.

The victors swept through it led by the king, who was the first in every attack. He was the first to enter the city; he was always at their head, giving his troops an example of courage and striking fear into the enemy. Around 10,000 men followed him through the city, looting everything in it. You would have heard horrible cries and a confusion of voices, here from our people urging each other on in pursuit, there from Lombards fleeing, screaming with fear. Our people redoubled their blows and put anyone they found to the sword, like crops to the scythe. When our people seized houses, the Lombards leapt off the roofs and from the upper floors. They were more afraid of falling into their ene-

66. This detail about how Richard found the postern gate is not in Ambroise.

mies' hands than of having an unlucky fall, because they were aware of how cruel they had been and despaired of gaining mercy because they knew they did not deserve it. The city was quickly and manfully subdued, with no sign of anyone who might dare to raise even a murmur of resistance.

What more can I say? King Richard had captured Messina by right of battle at the first assault more swiftly than any priest could sing Matins.[67]

Many more of the citizens would have died, but the king, moved by mercy, ordered that they be spared. Who can estimate how much money the citizens lost? All the gold and silver and other precious things which were found became the property of the occupying army. What is more, their galleys were set on fire and burned to ashes, to prevent them from fleeing and recovering their strength to resist. The victors also carried off the noblest women for themselves. When the great undertaking was complete, the French suddenly saw King Richard's standards and banners on the walls and towers of the city! The king of France was so violently shaken by this that he conceived a lifelong hatred for the king of England. 'He conceived mischief' [Psalm 7 v. 14] for an opportune time, which he later revealed when he struck at Normandy.[68]

Chapter 17: The king of France is jealous because only the king of England has his banners on the towers. So the king of England humbles himself and concedes that the banners of both be placed there together.[69]

The king of France was jealous of the king of England's success. He found his noble character unbearable, and regretted having had no part in the glory which the other had won through his own sweat and superior qualities. Despite the agreement between them, he had not offered the king of England a helping hand against the relentless enemy - as he was bound to do by the terms of their treaty - even when his people were in very great danger and great slaughter was going on before his

67. The first service of the day, sung before dawn.
68. Philip invaded Normandy in 1194. William of Newburgh, p. 325, agrees that Philip turned against Richard when he saw Richard's banners on the walls of Messina.
69. 'The king of France...had their lodging', is not in Ambroise. For the rest, see lines 831-63.

very eyes. Instead he had resisted him with all his strength. In brazen violation of his oath, he had hindered him for a long time by whatever means he could from seizing the entrance to the city, which was where he and his people had their lodging. After the city had been captured and the king of England's banners had been placed on the walls, as was described above, the king of France with the support of his counsellors sent instructions to King Richard to have his standards taken down from the tops of the walls and his own erected, as a sign of respect for his superior rank.

Indignant at this command, King Richard remembered recent events, weighed up the rights of partners in a partnership and did not even bother to reply. He did not wish to give up what he had won or hand over his victory to a man who was not just idle but had also broken his oath and acted in opposition to him.

Mediators interceded between them, and at last King Richard's indignation cooled, and the abusive words ceased. He put up little resistance to the coaxings of his companions, although he had appeared invincible in the face of his enemies' attacks. He accepted the king of France's request that he should hand over the towers he had captured to joint custodians until they could obtain King Tancred's decision on the matter. So he who remained strong and unbending in the face of threats and bragging words bent before flattery and entreaties! The standards of them both were erected on the walls for the time being, while he tested the king of France's reliability and friendship.

Chapter 18: Messengers are sent to Tancred, instructing him to give compensation for his offences and restore the queen's dowry. The king of France secretly sends instructions to the opposite effect.[70]

So it was decreed by common counsel that they should send messengers to King Tancred of Sicily to gain compensation for the outrages his people had committed and to discover what in his opinion should be done about recent events. In addition, King Richard instructed King Tancred to provide his sister, the queen of Sicily, with an adequate dowry and her share of her husband the king's treasury, which belonged to her by

70. 'So it was decreed...names have been forgotten', see Ambroise, lines 863–86. The rest is not in Ambroise.

right.[71] There was also the matter of a gold table to be equally divided with the wife of its late owner. The messengers on this occasion were [Hugh] the duke of Burgundy and Robert de Sabloel,[72] and some others whose names have been forgotten.

Meanwhile, the king of France was still seething and eaten up with envy over King Richard's noble character and success. He began to raise objections over the booty which had been taken when the city was captured, demanding his share under the agreement they had made. When King Richard was unwilling to agree to his demand he threatened him with big words and hurled abuse at him. He kept on trying to infuriate him with sly insinuations and boastful taunts, attempting to make out that King Richard had violated their agreement and friendship.

More indignant than crushed, King Richard decided not to keep company with this deceitful man any longer, and arranged for his ships to be summoned and his baggage loaded on to them, ready for his departure. He preferred to proceed alone with only his own forces to complete his pilgrimage with God as his leader and guide, rather than to associate with a jealous man; as the common proverb says, 'Better to be alone than in bad company.'

When the king of France was informed of this, he managed to repair the damage through mediators. Once again they were allied in a fixed bond of friendship, retaining the equal division of all future acquisitions [8 October 1190].[73]

---

71. For the history of this dowry, see Bk. 2 ch. 11 above, and note 42.
72. The future master of the Temple, from 1191 to 28 September 1193; see Demurger, A. (1993), *Vie et Mort*, p. 395. He was previously one of the commanders of Richard's fleet and one of the treasurers of the crusade: Roger of Howden, *Chronica*, 3 pp. 36, 42, 45, 53, 58–9, 62. It is not known when he joined the order of the Temple; he was not a Templar in October 1190.
73. Roger of Howden, *Gesta*, 2 p. 129 and *Chronica*, 3 pp. 58–60 gives the text of the treaty, which deals with (a) the property of pilgrims who die on the pilgrimage; (b) gambling: only knights and clerks may gamble, and may lose up to twenty shillings in twenty-four hours; servants and men-at-arms within the kings' lodgings may also gamble; (c) loans taken during and before the pilgrimage; (d) those who abandon their lord's employment during the pilgrimage; (e) trade within the camp; (f) royal coin; (g) sale of meat (which must be fresh); (h) sale of wine; (i) the price of bread, fixed at a penny a loaf; the rate of exchange is one English penny to four Angevin pence. A committee was set up to administer this treaty.

Chapter 19: King Tancred gives an ambiguous response, at which the king of England is incensed. The Lombards refuse to supply his people with food.[74]

Meantime the messengers were discharging their mission according to their instructions, and examining King Tancred's response to the orders they had brought. But the king spoke ambiguously, assuring them that the kings would receive compensation over all the matters which had been communicated to him at a council of the magnates of his country properly convened in respect to time and location and procedure. It is said that the king of France had sent a letter to King Tancred instructing him not to give way to the king of England's demands, but to stand firm and protect his rights in everything. He could be absolutely certain that he would be faithful to him and would never fail him for King Richard's sake. There is one persuasive piece of evidence in favour of the truth of this story: King Tancred loaded the king of France's messengers with valuable gifts, but he did not even give an egg to those of the king of England.

When the messengers returned and made their report to the kings, King Richard said: 'There is no need for a long discussion and lengthy speeches. As King Tancred will not give compensation of his own accord, I must expend my own efforts to correct the error of his ways as far as I can.'

So everything[75] was in confusion. The king of France's support made the locals bolder and they oppressed King Richard and his people as much as they could contrive. They prevented them from buying the food that such a large army needs, and decreed that nothing could be put out for sale, so that they would be forced to submit to the local authorities.

---

74. See Ambroise, lines 886–950, but not all in the same order.
75. MS C says 'the kings were in confusion'; A and B say 'things were in confusion.'

Chapter 20: The construction of Mategriffun, and the two kings' disagreement.[76]

King Richard put a great deal of work and care into constructing a castle, which he called 'Mategriffun' [Griffon-killer].[77] The Griffons were absolutely infuriated because he intended to use this building to destroy them. The completed construction was placed on a suitable hill next to the city. As the Griffons had forbidden, as far as they could, any sort of food from being put out for sale, the army would have been in difficulty if it had not been able to rely on the things which the fleet had brought. They employed all their enmity against the army, trying to harm it as much as they could. Guards watched over the city by night, while on the other side the pilgrims set watches, taking precautions against their attacks.

Meanwhile the kings were divided by disagreement, and the king of France was showing open support for King Richard's opponents. A large section of the nobles worked hard to restore peace between them, going back and forth between the palace and Mategriffun, trying to soften the anger of the two kings. But they worked in vain. Each blamed the other and claimed that he had received a great many grounds for offence. Both of them refused to give way to the other: the king of France felt he would demean himself if he committed himself to the judgement of an inferior, while King Richard thought he would be dishonoured if he submitted to a man whose feats were less impressive than his own.

---

76. See Ambroise, lines 937-40, 957-75. See also Roger of Howden, *Gesta*, 2 p. 138; *Chronica*, 3 p. 67; Ralph of Diceto, p. 86.
77. This was a 'prefab' wooden castle which could be slotted together and erected, then taken down and transported elsewhere. King Richard's other siege machines were similarly constructed: see Bk. 5 ch. 39, p. 316 below.

Chapter 21: Tancred makes peace with King Richard. He gives him 40,000 ounces of gold[78] for the queen's dowry and the marriage of Arthur.[79] The two kings and the citizens also make peace.

Everything was fluctuating in uncertainty,[80] and King Tancred realised that danger could arise if disagreement continued, as he had learnt that King Richard would not give up his efforts once he had begun until he had got what he wanted. So he sent noble messengers[81] to offer peace and seek friendship. He assured him in an appropriately convincing manner that insofar as it lay with him he did not wish to continue angering such a great man, as this endangered his own people. Instead he was prepared to offer him money to make a treaty of friendship, if he so wished. He would give 20,000 ounces of gold for the dowry of the queen of Sicily, King Richard's sister, and in addition he would give another 20,000 as the dowry of a daughter of his, a talented and attractive girl, if King Richard wished her to marry his nephew Arthur of Brittany.

King Richard gave his assent to these terms, and the matter was concluded after much work by messengers from both sides. A sum of money was received, i.e. 40,000 ounces of gold; and the queen was handed over unconditionally to her brother King Richard. A firm peace was agreed and confirmed in writing, and everyone's disagreements were completely laid to rest [11 November 1190].[82]

When King Richard saw that he had received the compensation he had wanted, he decided of his own accord that the sum of money which he had received from King Tancred should be shared equally between himself and the king of France. Although he was not bound by the terms of the alliance to divide the money received for his sister's dowry he wished to do so out of pure liberality. This brought him glory and approval and wiped out his enemies' envy to some degree.

On the advice[83] of the venerable Walter, archbishop of Rouen, it was

---

78. See Spufford, P. (1986), p. 59. The gold *uncia* was the standard unit of currency in Sicily: it was divided into thirty *tari* or *tareni*, each of which was divided into twenty *grani* or grains.
79. King Richard's nephew, son of Richard's younger brother Geoffrey and Constance, heiress to the county of Brittany. Geoffrey had died in 1186. Arthur was now aged about three.
80. 'Everything was fluctuating...laid to rest', is in Ambroise, lines 977-1028.
81. Ambroise says that he sent a son of a chancellor and a knight, his constable (a high-ranking military commander): lines 979-80.
82. Roger of Howden, *Gesta*, 2 pp. 136-8; *Chronica*, 3 pp. 65-6.
83. 'On the advice...goodwill was restored' is in Ambroise, lines 1029-47.

proclaimed that all the gold and silver and any sort of money which the victorious force had looted from the citizens should be completely restored to them, on pain of the Church's curse. So everything was restored and peace was made, at least to outward appearance. The citizens rejoiced in security, the pilgrims rejoiced in peace and tranquillity. The city was guaranteed against harm, and legislation was passed against disturbers of the peace. The citizens and pilgrims went in and out without offence or disagreement. Everything was restored to pleasant harmony. One and all rejoiced. Now necessary foodstuffs for humans and horses were laid out for sale at a reasonable price. The kings' friendship blossomed again, and through the mediation of justice universal goodwill was restored. But although the king of France was outwardly cloaked with an appearance of affection, the undying rivalry conceived in his heart remained within. Jealous of King Richard's brilliant deeds, 'he concealed a crafty fox within his smooth breast' [Persius, *Satires*, no. 5 v. 117].[84]

Chapter 22: King Tancred and King Richard meet each other at the city of Catania [1 March 1191].[85]

Staying at Palermo, King Tancred was greatly amazed at what he heard about King Richard's magnificence and his glorious deeds. So he sent very noble messengers to ask him to meet him in person at Catania, saying that he was very anxious to see him face to face because in the past he had been greatly impressed by reports he had heard of his fine character and exceptional valour. The city of Catania is situated midway between Messina and Palermo.

King Richard assented, and set out to meet him at the place they had decided, accompanied by a glorious company of his most noble princes. When they met, as they had agreed, each of them was delighted by the other's arrival, and was at pains to show every regard to the other. They made a solemn treaty of mutual affection, an alliance which confirmed in perpetuity and in every respect the peace that had been made

84. Roger of Howden, *Gesta*, 2 p. 161, describes a peace made between Richard and Philip in March 1190, after the meeting between Richard and Tancred in chapter 22.

85. Roger of Howden, *Gesta*, 2 pp. 158–9; *Chronica*, 3 p. 97. This episode is not in Ambroise.

between them. Then the kings each gave and received gifts with regal munificence. When all this had been done with due solemnity the parting was brisk. King Tancred went back to Palermo, and King Richard to Messina.

Chapter 23: King Richard gives generous gifts to knights and others who were short of money because of the delay at Messina [February 1191].[86]

All that summer the knights had incurred heavy expenses in the aforesaid unrest and disturbances, and were resentful at the long, idle delay there. They objected that their brothers in Christ were constantly struggling in the siege of Acre while they idled their time away in Messina. They had already used up most of what they had to no advantage, since they had been forced to give back what they had acquired by right of war when they looted the captured city.

Moved by these widespread complaints, King Richard surpassed all hopes with his regal openhandedness. He gave so many gifts to all those in need according to their rank that each had more than enough. The knights were greatly consoled by this generous distribution of gifts of gold, silver and other things. Noble Palestinian women, widows and virgins who had been deprived of their inheritances and exiled from their homeland, also received copious wealth. Because of this action King Richard received everyone's gratitude and favour. Yes, he even bestowed at least 100 shillings on the infantry and lesser men-at-arms! His example also prompted the king of France to give many gifts to his people. So joy blossomed again in the people, and those who had been shattered by sorrow were raised up by welcome largess.

---

86. Roger of Howden, *Gesta*, 2 p. 157; *Chronica*, 3 p. 95; Ambroise, lines 1053–79. Richard delayed at Messina partly because the army arrived so late in the year that the weather was too unsettled for a safe sea crossing: see ch. 26, below. He also wanted to obtain his sister Joanna's dowry, to help finance his crusade. In addition, as we have seen in ch. 22, he wanted to establish good relations with the king of Sicily, as Sicily was an essential supply base for the crusader states in the Holy Land and much of the traffic to and from the Holy Land went through Sicily.

Chapter 24: King Richard keeps Christmas with great festivity. He invites the king of France and all the people to a feast at Mategriffun, and gives very generous gifts.[87]

The noble festival of Christmas was at hand, which should be celebrated with such distinguished solemnity because it played such a necessary part in the redemption of the human race. In honour of this festival, King Richard respectfully invited the king of France to dinner. Through a public crier he also called every soul to spend the great day with him in joy and gladness.

The king of France came at his request with a huge company of magnates. A numerous crowd also came. What more should I say? It is not difficult to force the willing! Would anyone have deliberately been absent from King Richard's feast? They were honourably received in Mategriffun, the castle which he had built against the locals' opposition, and seated at table according to their rank. Who could list the varieties of dishes, or the types of drinks, or the finely dressed crowds of servants? If you want to know, make a mental estimate of King Richard's noble character and deduce from this how fine that feast was. You would have seen nothing unbecoming or out of place; everything was costly and admirable. The cups and dishes on which food and drink were brought in had been manufactured only from gold or silver; all the vessels were golden or silver, with wonderfully intricate embossing or subtly engraved and chiselled with the shapes of humans or beasts and set with precious stones. In addition, 'above all, the approach of happy faces,' ensured the universal pleasure of the guests.

What more is there to say, except that everyone enjoyed themselves very much, with plenty of choice food and drink and the servants' cheerful wit?

When the great feast of celebration was over, King Richard had various exceptional and valuable treasures laid out. In honour to the king of France, he compelled him – in a friendly way – to choose the best of them for himself. No less, to round off the festival perfectly King Richard gave each person gifts of incalculable value in accordance with their

---

87. Ambroise, lines 1080–108; he claims to have been present at the Christmas meal (line 1091). In the final paragraph, 'No less, to round off...scattered help' is not in Ambroise. See also Roger of Howden, *Gesta*, 2 p. 150; *Chronica*, 3 pp. 92–3.

rank. He used to regret that he had wasted a day when he had not given anything away. His generosity could only be compared to that of the emperor Titus, whose 'right hand scattered help.'[88]

Chapter 25: The Pisans and Genoese attack the guards on King Richard's fleet.[89]

That same day the Pisans and Geneose got drunk on neat wine and attacked the guards on King Richard's fleet; it is not known on what provocation. They launched a strong assault, and in their violent charge a heavy toll was inflicted on both sides. On the following day they recalled the previous days' slaughter, and as if they regretted not having finished off the job, they launched a new premeditated attack. As they cruelly slaughtered each other King Richard rushed up. He succeeded with difficulty in restraining their relentless rage and forced them to separate.

Chapter 26: The arrival of Queen Eleanor and Berengaria, King Richard's wife-to-be. First the king of France and then the king of England depart for the Holy Land.

Therefore in the year of Our Lord 1191, when the Sunday letter was F, the people rejoiced as the days grew longer after the snowy and idle winter months. They were tired of the lack of action caused by their long stay in Messina, but now more suitable weather for sailing was coming.[90] For the kings stayed in the city of Messina with the whole army from Michaelmas, as was said above, until after the end of Lent.

So they discussed the crossing, claiming that a further delay would be inconvenient for various reasons. Calmer weather was coming; their supplies would run out if they remained here; they were inactive and not achieving anything; they sympathised with those who were toiling in the siege, and regretted that their assistance had been delayed so much.

While they were each making arrangements to begin the journey,

---

88. See pp. 145–6 above, and note 16.
89. Not in Ambroise. See Roger of Howden, *Gesta*, 2 pp. 150–1; *Chronica*, 3 p. 93; he states that King Philip also helped King Richard to separate those who were fighting.
90. 'For the kings...delayed so much' is like Ambroise, lines 1109–20.

messengers came running to inform King Richard that his mother Queen Eleanor was hurrying after him. She had travelled a great distance, but was now very close, and had brought with her a noble young woman,[91] daughter of the king of Navarre. Her name was Berengaria and she was the king's intended wife. Attracted by her graceful manner and high birth,[92] he had desired her very much for a long time - since he was first count of Poitou. So her father the king of Navarre had entrusted her to King Richard's mother so that she could take her to King Richard and he could take her as his wife before he set off on his planned journey across the sea. Everyone was delighted at their arrival.

Meanwhile[93] the king of France had made arrangements for his journey and the transportation of all his equipment. He set out with his whole fleet in a favourable wind on the Saturday after the Annunciation of the Blessed Mary [30 March 1191]. King Richard and his more prominent nobles accompanied him for some distance in his galleys as he set out. But King Richard himself was not yet ready for the crossing. He had not yet gathered all his ships together for loading his horses and baggage; he did not yet have all the supplies that he thought necessary; and, as was said, he had received the news that his mother was coming to him with the aforementioned young woman. So after he had let the king of France depart in peace on his voyage, he crossed the Faro to the city of Reggio, as he had learnt that his mother the queen was there with Berengaria. He welcomed them with great joy and brought them back with him to Messina.[94]

After a short stop, he gave his mother the queen leave to go and asked her to take over the guardianship of his kingdom jointly with the aforementioned Archbishop Walter of Rouen, a man of great virtues. Gilbert de Gascuil also went back with them. It was through Gilbert's treachery that the king of France later won the famous castle of Gisors which has a very strong site on the frontier between France and Normandy and had been entrusted to his safekeeping. But King Richard kept the aforenamed young woman with him, as he was going to take her as his wife. Queen

91. *Puella*, which also means 'girl', and 'virgin'.
92. William of Newburgh calls her: 'a virgin of famous beauty and prudence,' (p. 346); Ambroise says she was: 'A wise girl, a noblewoman, good and beautiful,' (lines 1141-3) and calls her King Richard's 'dru', i.e. his love; Richard of Devizes ungraciously describes her as 'more prudent than pretty,' (p. 26).
93. 'Meanwhile...a straight route in front of them', is like Ambroise, lines 1124-201. Philip sailed straight to Acre, arriving on 20 April.
94. See also Roger of Howden, *Gesta*, 2 p. 161; *Chronica*, 3 pp. 95-6.

Eleanor departed by barge for Salerno and from there went on to Normandy.[95]

Having prepared everything necessary for his journey, the king hurried to follow the king of France as quickly as he could, as they had arranged. He appointed Robert de Thornham to direct and watch over the fleet.[96] Then he sent his aforesaid fiancée and his widowed sister, dowager queen of Sicily, on ahead in the first line in the ships which they commonly call 'dromonds'. They sailed directly towards the east. He had also assigned some knights and a numerous crowd of servants to comfort and guard the women. Ships of this type are slower than others because of their weight, but stronger in construction.

The great mass of galleys[97] did not move until the king had dined, as a precaution against any problems. Then bidding farewell to the locals he and the whole army went on board, ready to set out. When that great throng of ships was ready to move off, the rowers plied their oars and it moved out into the ocean, committing itself to the favourable winds and the waves. The city of Messina may justly and uniquely boast that never in times past had such a great fleet left its shores, and neither perhaps would its like ever be seen again.

On the seventeenth day after the king of France's departure, i.e. the Wednesday after Palm Sunday,[98] King Richard followed with a numerous fleet of ships. As breezes blew, sailing and rowing by turns they passed through the middle of the Faro and proceeded into the open sea, struggling to catch sight of the dromonds which were on a straight route in front of them.[99] The king had laid down that as far as possible the ships should never be separated, unless they were scattered in a storm. So the galleys deliberately reduced their speed in an attempt to stay with the flotilla of slower transport vessels, to protect the many and comfort the weaker.

95. This last sentence is not in Ambroise. Roger of Howden, *Chronica*, 3 p. 100 says that Queen Eleanor went via Rome.
96. This detail is not in Ambroise.
97. Ambroise calls them *eneckes*, i.e. sneckas.
98. 10 April 1191. But Roger of Howden, *Gesta*, 2 p.162 and *Chronica*, 3 p.105 says 'four days before Maundy Thursday,' presumably meaning Monday 8 April. Perhaps Roger of Howden's ship had set out before our author and Ambroise did. There is also an error here: seventeen days after Philip's departure was 16 April, which was after Easter (14 April) - Richard set out before Easter. The Wednesday after Palm Sunday was eleven days after Philip's departure. Ambroise simply says that Richard set out in the Wednesday of Holy Week.
99. From here to the end of the chapter is not in Ambroise.

Chapter 27: The winds are still at first and then stir up the sea. The dangers which King Richard's fleet endured as far as Crete and from Crete to Rhodes.[100]

Then we suddenly felt the wind drop, so that we had to drop anchor and remain stationary between Calabria and Mont Gibel [Monti Iblei?]. The following day, Maundy Thursday [11 April 1191] He who 'brings the wind out of His storehouses' [Jeremiah ch. 10 v. 13] sent us a wind which kept up all day, but it was so weak that the fleet moved quite slowly. Then the following night it was completely still. On Good Friday [12 April] a violent contrary wind struck from the left, 'with which the turbulent sea seethed from the depths,' with great rollers and rising gales. Everyone was terrorstruck at the crash of waves colliding and the creaking of the ships in the violent winds. The sailors completely abandoned their efforts under the winds' assault, for the helm could not control the ships when they were being tossed about like this. The line of ships was broken up as they went in different directions and they were carried they knew not where. Then they entrusted their steering to God alone, for they believed that they were beyond human aid. For the sake of our Saviour who freely deigned to bear undeserved suffering for us on that day, we resolved to bear everything patiently, as far as human weakness may.

As the widely scattered ships drifted separately, people began to feel sick as their stomachs revolted against so much tossing. The seasickness greatly reduced their awareness of the danger! As evening came the strength of the wind and the angry sea gradually quietened. The wind which remained was quite favourable, so the sailors recovered their strength and confidence and tried to proceed on a straight course.

In all that great confusion the king remained unshaken. He never gave up encouraging the others and urging them to be confident and hope for an improvement in conditions. It used to be his custom to have in his ship an enormous lighted candle in a lantern, which was placed aloft to give light to all around and show the sailors the way. He also had extremely experienced sailors who had withstood the winds' violence as far as

100. Ambroise, lines 1204-312, except for details of Mount Camel. Roger of Howden, *Gesta*, 2 pp. 162-3 gives a shorter account of Richard's voyage to Cyprus. Ambroise and IP2 use the first person plural for this voyage; as IP2 seldom uses the first person and does not always use it when Ambroise does, this suggests that the compiler of IP2 was also travelling with the fleet.

human skill could. So they all struggled as best as they could to follow the royal ship, guided by the king's burning light.

The king also remained stationary for some time waiting until the fleet which had been scattered in the storm saw the light and gathered around him. The king looked after the fleet like a hen caring for her chicks!

The following night we sailed with a favourable wind without running into obstacles or danger. It was the same on Easter Saturday [13 April] and on the great festival day of Easter and from then until Wednesday [17 April]. That day we saw the island of Crete. The king headed for it, to rest and to assemble the fleet. All the ships came except for twenty-five which the king was very upset about.[101] Among the steep mountains of the island of Crete is one peak higher than the rest, like the apex of the mountains, which is called Camel [Iráklion]. Sailors who know these seas say that this point on the island represents the midpoint between Messina in Sicily and the city of Acre in Palestine.

On the following day, Thursday [18 April], the king and all the multitude returned to the ships. They set sail and pressed on their way. But then, as the evening drew on, the wind became stronger! Although it was not excessive, it drove the fleet powerfully forward with no little force, with swelling sails and masts a little bent so that it looked like a flock of birds in flight. This wind kept up all that night, and at dawn it carried the whole fleet violently with sails lowered to the island called Rhodes.

There was no port for us to steer into; it was deep water right up to the land. However we had a refreshing rest there, the sweeter because it was so much needed. We rested until the following Monday [22 April] when we landed on the island of Rhodes.[102]

The city of Rhodes used to be enormous, not much unlike Rome. It is almost impossible to guess what it was like, because there are so many ruined houses and ruined towers with only part still standing and remains of walls and buildings of remarkable and wonderful workmanship. Some

101. 'Among the steep...to the ships' is not in Ambroise. The writer of IP1 and the compiler of IP2 made a point of inserting interesting geographical details into their work. This was a tradition in historical writing and lent their work authenticity.

102. Ambroise says that they arrived one evening in a narrow inlet and disembarked the following day. Ralph of Diceto, p.91, says that they reached Rhodes around 20 April. The different dates may reflect the fact that the fleet was split up by the winds and arrived at Rhodes over a period of a few days.

monasteries still remain, but they are largely deserted although many lived there in ancient times. Although the city is now destroyed by age, its great site testifies to the fact that it once had a very large population. Some inhabitants are to be found there - very few, though - who sold us essential foodstuffs.

As the king was ill we stayed there for some days. The king was waiting for the arrival of the stray ships we had lost and his galleys which always accompanied him. He also made inquiries about that savage tyrant the emperor of Cyprus, who used to detain pilgrims who landed on his island.

Chapter 28: King Richard leaves Rhodes through the Gulf. The queens' arrival at Cyprus.[103]

Rhodes is a rich and fertile island. After spending ten days there, we returned to the fleet and set out on our journey again, on the first day of May. With sails set we were carried into the most dangerous place in the whole sea, called the Gulf of Satalea [Antalya].[104] Four seas meet there in continual conflict, forcing each other back as they collide. We were about to enter the Gulf when a contrary wind rushed on us, forcing us to draw back as far as our starting point! That wind kept changing its direction; without delay it then bore down on us from behind, even stronger and more terrifying than before, and drove us with a great blow into the Gulf. Frightened of its strength, we worked as best as we could to get quickly through that dangerous place and its raging waves. The royal ship was always first, keeping a constant course.

When the weather had calmed, the king raised his eyes and saw far away across the restless expanse of the sea an enormous ship coming towards him. It was the sort they call a 'buss',[105] returning from the land of Jerusalem. Eager for news, he quickly sent messengers to ask the people in the ship for information on the siege of Acre. When asked, they replied that the king of France had already arrived safely at the siege, and was busily engaged in constructing siege machines, while he waited

103. Ambroise, 1313-54, but see note below.
104. On this gulf see also Roger of Howden, *Chronica*, 3 pp. 158-9.
105. A transport vessel.

for the king of England to arrive.[106] The king of France had landed at the port of Acre on the Saturday after Easter [20 April] and with great determination was applying care and effort to the capture of the city. He had stonethrowers erected facing the Cursed Tower – the king of France was lodged beside that tower – and other siege machines constructed for smashing the walls. The ditches around the city had been filled with earth and siege machines brought up to the walls, and the stonethrowers kept hurling, and the wall had been partly demolished. But the Turks had fought back and not much later they succeeded in burning up the siege machines.

When he had learnt all this from the said sailors in the passing buss King Richard was in the best of heart. Then he turned his attention to other pressing matters. He was struggling to make the best of an unfavourable wind which was blowing only in occasional gusts. Yet after toiling for some time his fleet was unable to make headway against the adverse winds and repeated swelling waves. Tossed by the billows, it was forced back into deep water.[107] However, the buss from Lyon, in which the queens were [Joanna and Berengaria], had already been driven to port at the city of Limassol on the island of Cyprus. Yet they did not go ashore but dropped anchor and remained stationary far out at sea.

Chapter 29: The many misfortunes which befell the Holy Land. The emperor of Cyprus caused it particular injury.[108]

Was the land of Jerusalem guilty of some sin, so that she deserved to be punished and so heavily scourged? Was it because she was guilty of some crime that so many obstacles hindered her assistance, and aid was put off by so many delays? No, it is more credible that the wickedness of her defenders caused the long delay and led to her redemption being long suspended. There is much clear evidence that divine help was held

106. 'The king of France...burning up the siege machines' is not in Ambroise. Roger of Howden, *Gesta*, 2 p. 169, agrees on the date of King Philip's arrival and what he had been doing.

107. 'He was struggling...into deep water' is not in Ambroise.

108. Ambroise, lines 1355–400. For Richard's capture of Cyprus see also Roger of Howden, *Gesta*, 2 pp.163–8; *Chronica,* 3 pp. 105–11; the Lyon *Eracles* in *Conquest of Jerusalem*, pp. 100–4; the Colbert-Fontainebleu *Eracles* in ibid., pp. 176–9; Neophytus, 'De Calamitatibus Cypri', trans. Stubbs, W. (1864), *Chronicles and Memorials*, 1, pp. clxxxiii–ix; Ralph of Coggeshall, pp. 30–1; William of Newburgh, pp. 350–1; Ralph of Diceto, p. 92.

back from that land 'because the people that live there are so wicked' [Psalm 107 v. 34]. As a result, the distinguished men who were expected to bring strong support were carried off unexpectedly. What should we make of the death of the illustrious emperor of Germany, whose glorious beginnings were disgraced by his unfitting end? Or who can describe the sorrow at the death of the late glorious and very wealthy King Henry of England? With his money the city of Tyre was preserved undamaged; it had also been hoped that the Holy Land would be recovered through his wisdom and prudence. What should be said about the death of William, the great king of Sicily? After he had made all the necessary preparations for his pilgrimage, and had sent the oft-desired help so many times, he was taken by unexpected death. All these things and many others increased the difficulty of recovering the Holy Land. Each of them alone would have been bad enough.

One thing surpassed all these. I mean the island of Cyprus, from which the land of Jerusalem used to receive no little benefit each year. But now because of the tyrant who had usurped the imperial power in the island, it had thrown off the yoke of obedience and refused to give anything. This man was named Cursac [Kur Isaac, i.e. Lord Isaac: his name was Isaac Ducas Comnenus], and was the most wicked of all bad men. He surpassed Judas in faithlessness and Ganelon in treachery.[109] He pursued all who professed the Christian religion with shameless determination. He was said to be friendly with Saladin, and that they had drunk each others' blood as a sign and witness that they were allies, as if by external mingling of their blood they really became related by blood. Later on there were clear indications that they had in fact done this. The tyrant's confidence was increased by this alliance and he cast off all the obedience he owed, falsely usurping the title of emperor. He used to capture all the pilgrims who came to the island, either of their own accord or blown by violent winds, and extort ransoms from the wealthy and enslave the poor ones.

Therefore, when he was informed that an unknown fleet had arrived in those parts, he resolved to seize and hold captive all those who were on board and plunder their money, as was his custom.

---

109. Judas Iscariot betrayed Christ; Ganelon betrayed Roland, Oliver and the rest of Charlemagne's rearguard to the Muslims in the epic poem *La Chanson de Roland*.

Chapter 30: The shipwreck and adversities suffered by some of our people. They are captured, imprisoned, break out and win a victory over the Cypriot islanders.[110]

On the Eve of St Mark the Evangelist [24 April 1191] a little before sunset, a dark bank of cloud covered the sky. Suddenly stormy gusts of wind blew up, rushing against the sailing ships and throwing up great waves. Some of King Richard's ships which had been scattered by the gusting winds before he could arrive were endeavouring to land on Cyprus, but the stormy waves opposed them, the wind threw them back and they were carried on to the rocks. Although the sailors tried with all their strength to withstand the raging wind, three of the king's ships were smashed to pieces by the rushing waves not far from land, and some of those in them were drowned. Some, however, happened to grab hold of pieces of the ships' equipment. They were carried by the waves or rather tossed by the storm to land, arriving battered, exhausted, naked and penniless.

Among others who drowned was Roger, surnamed Malchiel,[111] the keeper of the king's seal, and the seal was lost. Later, however, the seething waves threw Roger's body on to land, and some common person found the seal and brought it to the army to sell. So the seal was bought back and returned to the king.

The locals joyfully allowed those who escaped from the shipwreck to land, pretending that their intentions were peaceful. As if they sympathised with their misfortune, they took them to a certain neighbouring castle to recover. As for those who came to shore safe and sound, they took their weapons from them and similarly put them in custody. They claimed that they did this for their own sakes, because if they came in armed they would look like spies or invaders. The Griffons[112] assured them that they did not dare do anything else until they had consulted the emperor.

Our nobles were sorry for the our shipwrecked people who were being held in custody and sent them clothing and other necessities. Stephen de Turnham [or Thornham], the king's marshal and treasurer, also sent them plenty of necessities, but when this reached the entrance to the castle where they were, everything which had been sent to the detainees was

110. Some of the material in this chapter is in Ambroise, lines 1401–25; most of it is not.

111. For his death see also Roger of Howden, *Chronica*, 3 p. 105.

112. As above, a perjorative term for those of Greek extraction.

plundered by the Griffons and the city guards. As yet the Griffons had not shown their enmity openly. They deceived them with flattery and deceitful words, saying that they would not be allowed to leave until they had informed the emperor of what had happened, and deceitfully promising to provide them with all their necessities in the meantime. The magnates of the province were called together and decided that they would take as many of the pilgrims captive as they could by trickery and kill them.

When our people were informed of this they shut themselves up in the castle of their own accord with the intention of defending themselves manfully. The locals killed some of them and laid siege to the castle. The pilgrims, weighing up the danger which threatened them, consulted together and chose to undertake the risks of battle rather than to prolong the danger of famine and falling into the hands of the infidel persecutors of Christians. So they made a sortie from the castle into the field in troops. They were unarmed; the locals surrounded them and began to kill them. Then the Christians conceived boldness from despair and strove to resist as best as they could. They inflicted no little slaughter on their attackers with only three bows, which they had kept with them unknown to the locals.

One of those there was Roger de Harcourt,[113] a knight of great prowess. He mounted a mare[114] which he happened to find and instantly knocked down and dispersed the crowd of Griffons. Also the Norman William du Bois, who was a very skilled archer, untiringly fired arrows and darts this way and that, routing them.

When our knights who were still in the ships realised what was going on, they armed and advanced quickly to help them. The Griffons opposed their landing as best as they could, firing bows and crossbows. Nevertheless, with God's protection, they sallied out of the ships and reached the port without loss. At last the Griffons scattered and yielded the road. Then our pilgrims came out of the aforesaid castle. Defending themselves continually, they reached the port where they found our people who had sallied out of the ships and the Griffons resisting them, fighting with all their strength. Our two forces combined their strength, routed the locals and captured the port.

113. MSS A and B and Ambroise call him Roger de Hardecourt. A Roger de Hardeincourt appears in *HGM*, line 4599. The Harcourts were a noble Norman family with extensive holdings in England.

114. Knights did not generally ride mares; it was regarded as shameful for a knight to do so. See Chrétien de Troyes, *Le Conte du Graal*, lines 6908–11.

The queens' buss was standing there. As was said above, the buss had arrived safely at the port of Limassol before the king's arrival, but those on board had not dared to go on shore because they did not know the state of the country and they were afraid of the cruelty and treachery of the emperor.

Chapter 31: King Richard's arrival on Cyprus.[115]

As evening approached on that same day when the pilgrims escaped from the aforesaid castle as was described above – a Thursday – the emperor of Cyprus arrived, having been informed of the pilgrims' arrival [2 May 1191]. When the pilgrims complained to him about the injuries done to their people and the money which had been taken the emperor promised them full redress and that the money belonging to those who were shipwrecked would be restored to them. He also gave them four hostages as a guarantee that he would keep his word. Under these conditions the pilgrims gained free entry and exit to and from the town of Limassol. Meanwhile the emperor summoned together the warriors of his whole empire and assembled an army of great strength.

On the day after his arrival the emperor sent a message to the queens couched in amicable but fraudulent words. He informed them that they could come ashore safely, and by his unconditional decision they could be assured of suffering no trouble or difficulty from any of his people. They refused. The next day the emperor sent many presents to the queens, on the pretext of honouring them: bread and ramsmeat and excellent wine from Cyprus grapes, which is said to be the best in the world.

On the third day, a Sunday, he again tried to get round the queens and seduce them with flattery and deceit. The queens were in a tight spot. They began to waver, anxious that if they submitted to the emperor's persuasions they would be taken captive. On the other hand, they were afraid that he would attack them if they persisted in their refusals – they had not yet been informed of the king's arrival and the success of the royal fleet. In order to hold the emperor off for a while they gave a noncommittal reply, assuring him that they would disembark on the following day and entrust themselves to the emperor's judgement. On the basis of this promise the emperor held back.

115. This chapter is not in Ambroise.

While the queens were burning with gnawing anxiety, God sent them prompt help. On that same Sunday, while they were gloomily discussing and bewailing their situation to each other and gazing out across the sea, two ships appeared in the distance among the foaming peaks of the rolling waves, sailing rapidly towards them, tossing about like little crows. The queens and those with them were still doubtful as to what this was, when they caught sight of some other ships following them. An enormous number of ships followed immediately behind, heading directly towards the port at great speed. Guessing that this was the royal fleet, they were overjoyed, the more so because help is the most welcome to those who have despaired of it.

So! After many unpleasant exertions, King Richard was brought to the island of Cyprus by the guidance of God! On the feast of St John at the Latin Gate [Monday 6 May] King Richard arrived with his whole company at the port of Limassol. However, he remained on board his ship.

Chapter 32: King Richard and his forces rout the emperor and his forces, first in a naval engagement and then in a land battle.[116]

When he was informed about the danger those who were shipwrecked had been in, and about the other things which had happened in the meantime, he was deeply grieved. On the following day, i.e. the Monday, he sent two knights as envoys to the emperor. He requested him amicably to compensate him and his people for the wrongs they had suffered and for the belongings of those shipwrecked to be restored in full to the king's satisfaction. The emperor, however, was extremely indignant at this command. As if the greatest injury had been inflicted on him, he burst out into abusive words. 'Phooey, my lord,' he said derisively to the king's messengers, the king of England was nothing to him! He prided himself greatly on the imperial rank which he had usurped; exuberant at having remained unpunished for so long, he now thought he could do whatever he liked.

The envoys reported his reply to the king. Furious at the emperor's arrogance, the abusive reply, and the losses of his own people, he shouted out an order to all his forces: 'To arms!' They immediately obeyed.

When he was armed he and all his people rode forward in small boats

116. Ambroise, lines 1449-64.

called 'snekas'[117] to seize the port. The emperor resisted them with a large army as they came to shore. He had obstructed those entering the port in whatever way he could, with every sort of obstacle and barrier placed all round the port entrance. There were house doors and torn-out windows, barrels and stakes, benches and planks from steps and long pieces of wood laid crosswise. There were different sorts of shields and old galleys and other ships, abandoned long ago and rotting at their mooring and all kinds of utensils. In short, the Griffons had assembled on shore as an obstruction every portable object of wood or stone which could be found in the city of Limassol.

In addition, the emperor, in full armour, marched up and down the shore with his forces. How becomingly the emperor's people were equipped! – with their armour of fine workmanship and most costly multicoloured clothes, riding on warlike horses foaming and champing on the bit, and beautiful mules. Ready for battle, they paraded up and down with countless pennants and most costly banners fluttering in the air. The intention of this display was either to prevent our people from advancing further, or to engage them in battle more effectively. As our people prepared to make a landing, they tried to distract them with horrible shouts like growling dogs, heaping abuse on us as if we were dogs, and taunting us that we were trying to do the impossible.

They had some crossbowmen and archers, and five well-armed galleys on the shore, full of young warriors skilled in naval warfare. Our people seemed to be no match for them, rowing in to seize a blocked harbour, exposed in tiny fragile skiffs; they were at a huge disadvantage because they were tired after their long and constant tossing at sea, and because they were on foot and overburdened with their weapons. On the other hand, the locals were fighting on their own soil and organised everything as they wished.

So as our people approached in order in their skiffs they decided to attack those nearest first, i.e. the crossbowmen and archers who were firing on them from the galleys. Our crossbowmen turned their aim on them and after a lengthy struggle firing arrows at each other and killing a great many Griffons the rest fell back because they could not sustain the weight of the fighting. Under the thick cloud of flying arrows three or four gave up and leapt into the sea. To escape the arrows they immersed themselves to die in the waves, striking into each other while they struggled to flee to safety.

117. See note 44 on Bk. 2 ch. 12 above.

Our people captured their galleys and our people's ships reached the land. Then our crossbowmen and archers, emboldened by their first success, fired a rain of bolts on those who were guarding the landing place. The Griffons could not withstand our people's attack, and immediately fell back and took themselves on to firmer ground. Their crossbowmen and ours kept firing arrows and bolts relentlessly without a break, so densely that the sky seemed to grow dark with them and the rain of bolts turned the bright day into night. The whole city seethed with people and the whole area was taken over by crowds of crossbowmen relentlessly firing their weapons. Victory was in doubt, still unsure of which side she favoured. Our people struggled with all their strength to return blow for blow, but they were getting nowhere.

Then the king, realising that our people were not bold enough to get out of the skiffs and advance on to the shore, took the lead himself in jumping out of his barge into the sea, and boldly attacked the Griffons. The rest of our people imitated his resolve, accompanied the king on both sides and strove to put the Griffon resistance to flight. As our people rushed on them their army fled, cut to pieces.

There you would have seen a rain of flying bolts and Greeks thrown down and running away; you would have heard the roar of the combatants, the groans of the fallen, the howls of the fleeing. Our people drove the routed Greeks back, continually killing as they went, first into the city and then from the city into the adjacent plain.

As the king pursued the fleeing emperor, he acquired a nag or packhorse with a bag behind its saddle. He quickly mounted from the ground into the saddle, which had cords instead of stirrups. Then he hurried to attack the emperor, shouting: 'Lord emperor, I challenge you to single combat,' – but the other paid him no attention and fled.

So the king captured the city of Limassol. He had the queens escorted out of the buss and lodged in the town, where after all the hardships and unpleasantness of the sea they relaxed in peace and security.[118]

118. The final paragraph is not in Ambroise.

Chapter 33: Ditto, a fight between the king and emperor; the king's victory; the emperor's flight to Nicosia.[119]

That night the king stayed in his pavilions. He had his horses led out of the sneckas. However the emperor was not afraid of him, thinking that he did not have any horses. He approached within two leagues of the king and spent that night in a tent.

The following day around the ninth hour [3 pm on 7 May] the king set out on horseback and found some Greeks not far away, standing with their splendid banners in an olive grove by the road. They fled at once, and the king pursued them. But since our horses had not yet recovered from continually standing for a whole month and being shaken about at sea, they pursued at a gentle pace to spare them. Eventually in the distance they noticed the emperor's army, which had spent the night in the next valley. When they saw them, our people stopped the pursuit and made a stand, but the Greeks set up a horrible racket, shouting and hurling abuse at our people.

Roused from his sleep by the noise, the emperor mounted his horse and he and his whole army slowly advanced towards our people. He came as far as a nearby hill where he would be able to see what happened in the engagement. The Greeks kept firing bows and crossbows and shouting at our people, who remained unmoved. A certain armed clerk came to the king, named Hugh de la Mare.

'My lord king,' he said, 'it would seem well-advised to avoid engaging such a great and powerful crowd of opponents at this moment.'

'Lord clerk,' the king replied, 'it is best for your profession to stick to your scriptures, leave the fighting to us, and concentrate on keeping yourself out of the thick of it.'

However, some others also advised the king against engaging such a large army, as he then only had around fifty knights with him. Yet their trepidation only made him more courageous. Putting spur to horse, he charged into the enemy, broke through and scattered their battleline, destroying them on this side and that. In a moment he routed the lot of them.

Since his opponents realised that his army was growing larger as his forces assembled, their courage melted away and they began to flee. Those who had swift surefooted horses escaped, but all the common in-

---

119. Ambroise, lines 1565–700; see also Roger of Howden, *Gesta*, 2 p. 164, *Chronica*, 3 p. 107–8. Roger supplies the date.

fantry who could not flee so easily fled no further when the king arrived: they were slaughtered *en masse* and fell everywhere. While the emperor was urging and encouraging his people to fight the king came up behind him, put spur to horse and threw him off his horse with his lance. He was at once given another horse and escaped into the crowd in flight, but he lost some of his companions there.

How many noble horses you would have seen slain there, how many mailshirts and helmets lying on the ground with swords and lances, pennants and many sorts of standard thrown down, and the countless bodies of the dead rolled in blood, or still breathing their last.

The emperor realised how bold our people were and saw that his own were routed. Seeing that he was the only survivor, he did not forget the spur but fled at great speed into the mountains. The king transfixed the emperor's banner bearer with his lance, and gave orders for that noble and remarkable banner to be kept for himself.[120] Our cavalry pursued the fleeing Greeks as closely as they could for two miles. Then they turned back and returned peacefully at a gentle pace. The people turned to plunder, and carried off much booty: arms, costly silken clothes. They also took the emperor's tent and everything that was found in it: gold and silver plate, the emperor's own bed with great finery, and all its bedding; mailshirts, helmets and choice swords, horses, mules; and an enormous quantity of booty in the form of flocks and herds, that is cows and oxen, sheep and goats, mares and fine foals, pigs, hens and poultry. They also found choice wines and a great deal of food. They took an army of prisoners, a huge crowd of people – in fact they became bored with plundering, because there was so much of it. In brief, everybody was stuffed with so much booty, everyone was so fully laden that they would not even bother to look at anything offered to them, no matter how valuable it was.

When this was over the king put out an edict by public crier. All the locals who wanted peace could freely come and go, unhindered by his people, and enjoy guaranteed liberty. If any regarded the king as an enemy, let them beware that they did not fall into his hands; for he declared that he would be an enemy to any who regarded him as one. They would be to him what he was to them.

The emperor engaged the king and his army in battle many times

120. He sent it to the abbey of St. Edmund the Martyr at Bury St Edmunds, Suffolk (Roger of Howden, *Gesta*, 2 p. 164; *Chronica*, 3 p. 108; and see Bk. 6 ch. 37, p. 386 below).

after that, and on each occasion he suffered great losses.[121] At last he took refuge in a very strong castle called Nicosia, sad and bewildered that he could not make progress as he wished.

Chapter 34: King Guy's arrival in Cyprus.[122]

On the following Saturday [11 May], three galleys appeared far out to sea. Everyone wondered what they wanted and where they were coming from. The king, who was always ready for anything, not to say reckless, went out to meet the arrivals in a small rowing boat, inquiring who they were and where they came from.

When they replied that this was Guy de Lusignan, king of Jerusalem, the king immediately returned at speed and ordered that dinner should be prepared without delay for his approaching guests. So when King Guy landed he received him with the greatest reverence and made him very welcome.[123]

This same Guy had come to King Richard to seek his counsel and aid because the king of France had decided that the marquis, who was mentioned earlier, should be made king of Jerusalem and King Guy deposed. King Richard received him cordially, and honoured him with gifts, as he was poor and destitute. He gave him 2000 silver marks,[124] and twenty cups worth 105 marks, two of which were of purest gold.

---

121. This sentence is not in Ambroise. Roger of Howden states that the Cypriot nobles came and submitted to King Richard on 8 May (*Gesta*, 2 p. 164).

122. Ambroise has the first sentence and the third paragraph of this chapter: lines 1701-34. See also Roger of Howden, *Gesta*, 2 p. 165; *Chronica*, 3 p. 108.

123. Roger of Howden, *Gesta*, 2 p. 165, states that the arrivals were King Guy, Geoffrey de Lusignan, Humfrey IV of Toron, Raymond prince of Antioch (presumably Raymond, eldest son of Prince Bohemond III of Antioch), Bohemond son of Raymond of Tripoli (presumably Bohemond count of Tripoli, younger son of Prince Bohemond III, who had succeeded Raymond III of Tripoli) and Leo, brother of Rupin, prince of Armenia. For obvious reasons, Humfrey of Toron was supporting King Guy against the marquis.

124. A mark was two thirds of a pound.

Chapter 35: The wedding of King Richard and Berengaria.[125]

On the following day, a Sunday, on the feast of St Pancras [12 May 1191] King Richard and Berengaria, daughter of the king of Navarre, were married at Limassol. The young woman was very wise and of good character. She was there crowned queen. The archbishop of Bordeaux was present at the ceremony, as was [John] the bishop of Evreux, and the bishop of Bayonne, and many other magnates and nobles. The king was merry and full of delight, pleasant and agreeable to everyone.

The king's galleys arrive.[126] After the wedding had been solemnly celebrated in royal style, one day all his galleys came into port! He had been waiting for them anxiously. They were handsomely equipped and defended with weapons so that no one ever saw better or more secure ships. He added the five abovementioned galleys which he had captured from the emperor. So the king had forty armed galleys, which were better than sixty of anyone else's.

Chapter 36: The conference between the king and the emperor and how peace was made.[127]

The king was encouraged because everything was proceeding well, believing that fortune was smiling on him. He urged and ordered his army to be prepared and ready for anything. So that the emperor should not catch them unawares with an attack he had watches set at night and organised sentries to guard the camp. The king intended to pursue the emperor with his army everywhere he went until he captured him or forced him to surrender. However, following mediation and great efforts by the master of the Hospital of Jerusalem [Garnier de Nablus], a conference was fixed between the king and emperor.[128] The emperor was extremely distressed by the loss of his people and because he had been shamefully driven to Nicosia, where he had fled from the king. His fear

---

125. Ambroise, lines 1735-44. Roger of Howden, *Chronica*, 3 p. 110: the king's chaplain Nicholas performed the ceremony, and John, bishop of Evreux, crowned Berengaria queen.
126. Ambroise, lines 1745-54.
127. Ambroise, lines 1759-832, but without the description of Richard and some details.
128. 'However, following...king and emperor' is not in Ambroise.

of the king's pursuit was increased by the fact that he could not rely on receiving assistance from the locals, because they hated him.[129]

Before the king's arrival [11 May][130] an enormous number of people from both sides assembled on a very wide plain between the sea and the royal highway, next to the city of Limassol. The king appeared later, regally dressed. The Spanish horse on which he had seated himself was 'by nature of firey heart.' It was elegantly formed, very large with flicking ears. It was high-shouldered, with a long neck, a broad chest, sound legs, broad hooves, and so handsome in all its lines that no painter could reproduce them perfectly, even with a great deal of work. Restless as if it were preparing to gallop, it disdained 'to be held dallying in a bridle' of gold, and with its feet in reverse order it leapt up on its fore feet, so that it seemed to be advancing backwards.

The king leapt on to this horse, and seated himself on a saddle sparkling with gold, glittering red and with many other colours gleaming between. On the rear of the saddle a pair of snarling little golden lions faced each other, each holding one forepaw stretched out towards the other as if to tear each other to pieces. The king also wore golden spurs on his feet. He wore a tunic of rose samite with a cloak over it; the cloak had the shapes of little half moons lined out on it, glowing white in solid silver, and shining orbs like suns scattered densely.

Thus adorned, the king advanced. He was girded with a doughty sword with a golden hilt, hanging from a silken crossbelt. The scabbard was of fine workmanship, its edges indented with silver. He wore a cap of 'scarlet'[131] on his head, embroidered by a skilful hand in gold thread with the shapes of various birds and beasts. He also carrying a baton in his hand, showing with his every gesture that he was an exceptional knight. The sight of him was a pleasure to the eyes.

After many proposals had been put forward on both sides between the king and emperor, the emperor offered to swear to be the king's faithful man in all things, and to bring fifty horsemen with him in God's service to the land of Jerusalem, to be at the king's disposal and wish. So that no doubt would remain in the king's mind over his trustworthiness, he offered to give security by handing over all his castles and fortifications to royal custodians. In addition, he would give 3500 marks in

129. 'Before the king's arrival...a pleasure to the eyes', is not in Ambroise.

130. This date is given by Roger of Howden, *Gesta*, 2 pp. 165–6; *Chronica*, 3 pp. 108–9. Apparently this conference took place on the same day that King Guy arrived on Cyprus.

131. A cloth from Stanfort in Flanders, red or brown.

compensation for the money which the king's people had lost, or which had been taken from them. At such time as the king should judge that the emperor had fought faithfully with his men in performance of the service due under the agreed terms, his land would be returned to him with the castles and fortifications just as before, except that there would be mutual friendship between them from henceforth.

The king laid the proposed peace terms before his people for them to judge whether the royal honour would be damaged in any way by such an agreement, and whether everyone found it acceptable. They replied that it was entirely compatible with the king's honour and that they were pleased with it in all respects. The king informed the emperor of their approval. The emperor then at once swore to the king that he would faithfully observe all the above terms, and the kiss of peace was given. So in this way they made an alliance.

When the council had broken up the king came back. As a pledge of peace and affection he at once sent back to the emperor his tent which he had captured in the aforesaid battle. In addition, he also sent him the plate which had been plundered from his tent. The emperor at once had the tent set up on the site of the said conference.

Chapter 38:[132] The emperor flees by night through Famagusta to Candaira. The capture of Nicosia by the king.[133]

The following night, the emperor fled swiftly away under the cover of darkness mounted on an excellent dun horse.[134] He went at the instigation of a lying knight of his named Pagan de Cayphas [lord of Haifa],[135] who had claimed that King Richard intended to seize the emperor that very night and put him in chains. The emperor, alarmed, left his tents, his excellent warhorses and all his household equipment and fled at nightfall to his city of Famagusta.

When the king heard this he began to follow him in his galleys, declaring that he had broken his oath and was in breach of faith. King

132. There is no Chapter 37 in Stubbs' edition of the text.

133. Ambroise, lines 1833–958; see also Roger of Howden, *Gesta*, 2 p. 166; *Chronica*, 3 p. 109.

134. Latin: *equo favello peroptimo.* Ambroise calls the horse *Fauvel*, a French name for a dun-coloured horse.

135. See Bk. 1 ch. 63, p. 123 above: one of the Christian nobility of Palestine, an ally of the Marquis Conrad.

Guy was entrusted with the responsibility of leading the army overland to the aforesaid fortification of Famagusta. On the third day he arrived there and found it deserted of people. The emperor had realised that he would not be able to withstand a siege there securely and would be shut up without a means of escape; so he hid in rough, forested terrain, intending to ambush our people as they passed through.

King Richard arrived at Famagusta in his galleys. He ordered that the port be strictly watched so that the emperor could be apprehended if he should try to escape. They stayed there three days. While they were there messengers came to King Richard from the king of France: the bishop of Beauvais and Drogo de Merlo, a noble and renowned man. They urged him to hurry and cross to the siege of Acre because, they claimed, the king of France would not attack the city until he arrived. Continuing in a similar vein, they added abusively that instead of coming speedily with his forces he had given up essential business and was concentrating his efforts on useless exercises; he was arrogantly persecuting innocent Christians when close by there were still so many thousands of Saracens whom he should be attacking; although he seemed so valiant, when it came to engaging the Saracens he turned out to be a coward. The king was incensed and replied in words unfit to be recorded. All their efforts to dissuade him from his undertaking were in vain, although they pressed him very hard. He was busy enough harassing the Greeks, and not without good reason: for it seemed very much in the general interest to subjugate the island of Cyprus because it is so indispensable for the land of Jerusalem.

So he ignored the messengers and moved his army to Nicosia. Each carried their own supplies because it was a deserted region. They advanced drawn up in order of battle because they had learnt that the emperor was lying in wait for them. The king proceeded in the rearguard, to repel any sudden chance attack. Suddenly the emperor and almost 700 Greeks leapt out of hiding! Their crossbowmen made great efforts firing darts at our vanguard, but our people kept themselves together in disciplined order and did not allow themselves to be dispersed. The emperor advanced gradually from the flank, as if to spy out our lines; then made a disordered charge, intending that our battle lines would scatter of their own accord at the sight of him or that he could find the king and shoot him. When he discovered the king in the last rank he fired two poisoned arrows at him. This roused the king to furious anger. Putting spur to horse, he charged the emperor, intending to run him through with his lance. However, the emperor evaded his attacker and fled at a very rapid gallop to his castle called Candaira [Kantara], extremely gloomy and bewildered that his plans had failed.

The king did not pursue the emperor far. He was sure that he would not catch him, for the emperor had a bay horse of such speed and stamina that no one ever saw another, no matter how nimble, which could be compared to it. So the king turned back towards Nicosia with his army and great booty of noblemen who had fallen in the battle. All the citizens of Nicosia came out to welcome the king and admitted him as their lord. The king received them in peace and had their beards shaved off as a symbol of their change of lordship.

When the emperor heard this he was beside himself with fury. He had as many of our people as he could seized and had one of their eyes put out, or their nose cut off, or an arm or foot mutilated, exacting whatever revenge he could to soothe his rancour. The king received homage from the most noble Greeks, who seemed to throw off the emperor's yoke of their own volition. The king felt a little unwell, and stayed at Nicosia to rest and recover.

Chapter 39: The capture of three castles, in one of which the emperor's daughter and his treasury were captured.[136]

King Guy meanwhile besieged three castles with the king's army, which the king had divided into three: Cherinas [Kyrenia], Didimus [Dieu d'Amour or St Hilarion], and Buffavento. The first two he captured quickly, commanding operations himself because he knew the level routes and rough terrain. The fortress of Cherinas was heavily besieged, with the army divided to attack from both land and sea. Those within, despairing of aid, surrendered the castle to King Guy. He found inside the emperor's daughter, who was living there. Her father loved her more than any other creature. The emperor's treasure was also kept there. When the emperor heard this, he was so overwhelmed with violent grief that he almost went out of his mind.

King Guy hung King Richard's banners from the battlements of the towers and arranged guards. Then he led the army to another castle, known as Didimus. It was very strong in situation and completely impregnable. Those within prepared to defend themselves and fired stones and

136. Ambroise, lines 1963–2013; see also Roger of Howden, *Gesta*, 2 p. 167; *Chronica*, 3 pp. 110–1.

darts at the besiegers for some days, until on the emperor's orders the castle was surrendered to King Guy. He placed the emperor's daughter in it to be guarded in case an attempt was made to carry her off. From there he returned with the army to Nicosia, where King Richard had been ill, as was said above. As soon as he recovered from his illness he besieged a castle called Buffevento, which was also thought to be impregnable.

Chapter 40: The emperor comes from Candaira to Nicosia, throws himself at the king's feet and surrenders Cyprus to him.[137]

Alas for that great imperial opulence! Alas for that land which was so fruitful with all good things! Alas for the fortresses surrendered, which were so strongly sited that they seemed impregnable to all siege machines, unless they were surprised by treachery or hunger!

The emperor realised that fate was against him: his only daughter, who was his whole life, had been captured; his fortresses had been captured or surrendered, and his subjects had long been alienated from him so that he was tolerated rather than loved. He saw that no hope of resistance remained. Unwillingly but out of necessity he decided to seek peace and mercy.

So he sent messengers to King Richard to plead his case and bend the king's heart to pity. Then he followed them down from the fortress of Candaira in mourning clothes and with face downcast. Coming to the king he humbled himself at his feet. Down on his knees, he declared that he submitted completely to the king's mercy: he would keep neither land nor castle but would have King Richard as his lord from henceforth, on condition only that he did not throw him into iron chains. Moved by pity, the king raised him up, made him sit at his side and brought his daughter out for him to see. When he saw her he was overjoyed: he hugged her affectionately and kissed her insatiably again and again, while his tears flowed copiously. This happened on the Wednesday next after the feast of St Augustine [31 May 1191] just before Pentecost. He did not throw the emperor into iron chains; he put him in silver ones.

---

137. Ambroise, lines 2014–59, except for the first paragraph. See also Roger of Howden, *Gesta*, 2 p. 167; *Chronica*, 3 p. 111. The *Gesta* dates the emperor's surrender to 1 June.

Chapter 41: Cyprus is subjugated and set in order by the king. The king prepares his journey and sends his army back to Limassol.[138]

So the king won the island of Cyprus in fifteen days and entrusted it to his people for them to inhabit. He found all the towers fortified and the castles stuffed with much treasure and various riches: gold cups and plate, and salvers and silver pots and cauldrons and great casks; and golden saddles, bridles and spurs, with precious stones of great virtue. What is more he found clothes of 'scarlet' and silken garments of wonderful design and very costly. In brief, whatever different sorts of wealth Croesus[139] is recorded as having possessed, King Richard found that the emperor had amassed it. He plundered everything necessary for his expedition as if it had been collected for him. For opportunity never abandons one who is great in soul, while abundance deserts the person of deceitful mind.

When he had done this, the king sent his army back to the city of Limassol, where the queens and their household were with the baggage. He ordered that no effort should be spared in repairing the ships in preparation for the sea crossing. The king entrusted the emperor to the custody of King Guy.[140] He gave his daughter, who was a little child, to his queen to be cared for and educated in their customs.

Chapter 42: As the king's fleet rows from Cyprus towards Acre it spots an enormous Saracen ship crammed full of every good thing. The king immediately captures it [7 June 1191].[141]

When he had done this, the king turned his attention to making a rapid sea crossing. Favourable winds were blowing; when they had arranged the baggage, the fleet cast off from the shore. The queens and their entourage advanced in busses on to the high seas. The king had left

---

138. Ambroise, lines 2060–92.
139. The last king of Lydia, late 6th century BC; famed for his wealth. Ambroise does not have this classical reference.
140. The emperor remained in prison until 1195, when he was released by Aimery de Lusignan. He died soon afterwards: Brand (1968), p. 124.
141. Ambroise, lines 2093–298; Roger of Howden, *Gesta*, 2 pp. 167–9; *Chronica*, 3 pp. 111–2; William of Newburgh, p. 352; Ralph of Coggeshall, p. 32; Ralph of Diceto, pp. 93–4.

industrious men as custodians and warriors in Cyprus,[142] with orders that they should send him essential foodstuffs later: wheat and barley, and meat of every kind of animal, of which there are plenty on Cyprus.

Then a rumour went about and more and more reports were received that Acre was about to be captured! When the king heard this, he gave a deep and heartfelt sigh. 'God forbid that Acre should be won in my absence,' he said, 'for it has been besieged for so long, and the triumph – God willing – will be so glorious.'

Then he made speedy preparations and went on board one of his better and larger galleys at Famagusta [5 June].[143] Impatient of delay as was his wont, he always advanced first in the front line with the rest of the galleys, suitably equipped, following on all sides. Anyone would have been justified in fearing a hostile encounter with them!

As they ploughed across the sea at the greatest speed, they caught their first sight of the holy land of Jerusalem. The first castle to meet the eye was called Margat [Marqab: a Hospitaller castle] then Tortosa, which is sited on the coast, and next Tripoli, Nephin, and Botron. Not much after the tall tower of Gibeleth [Jubail] appeared. After that a ship appeared in the distance this side of Sidon towards Beirut, full of Saracens [7 June].[144]

These Saracens were the elite of the whole of Paganism and had been sent by Saladin to aid the besieged in Acre. Since they realised that they would not have a clear entrance into Acre because the Christian army was on the watch for them, they had pulled back a little into the sea and 'looked for the time and the hour' when they could rush swiftly into the port unhindered. The king noticed the ship, and calling one of his sailors, Peter des Barres, he commanded him to row quickly and ask who was in charge of the ship. The reply came back that it belonged to the king of France. The king approached it in burning haste, but he found that there was no sign of the French language, nor any Christian symbol or flag to give him confidence in their reply.[145] Examining the ship from close

142. Roger of Howden names them as Richard de Camville and Robert de Thornham: *Gesta*, 2 p. 167; *Chronica*, 3 p. 111.

143. Roger of Howden, *Gesta*, 2 p. 168: he took with him King Guy, Count Bohemond of Tripoli and Raymond of Antioch and sent Ralph fitz Geoffrey to Tripoli with his prisoner the emperor of Cyprus.

144. Roger of Howden, *Gesta*, 2 p. 168; *Chronica*, 3 p. 112. Roger states that Richard tried to put into Tyre but was turned away. He then encountered the Great Ship.

145. This first investigation by Peter des Barres and the first reply is not in Ambroise; he simply has Richard coming up and looking at the ship. Roger

quarters, he was astonished at its enormous size; its solid bulk with the firmest jointing topped with three very tall masts. One side was covered with green tarpaulin[146] and the other with yellow. It was put together on all sides so neatly that nothing could be better, and it was crammed with plenty of all sorts of food.

Someone later said that they had been at Beirut when that ship was being loaded with heaps of stuff, 100 camel loads of every sort of weapon: great piles of crossbows, bows, bolts and arrows. There were seven Saracen emirs and 800 elite Turks on board, and overwhelming quantities of every kind of food, beyond calculation. They also had plenty of Greek fire in phials, and 200 very deadly snakes to destroy the Christians.

The king sent others to seek more definite information. They now altered their story and replied that they were Genoese, heading for Tyre.[147] While everyone was uncertain of what to make of this change, someone in our galleys firmly asserted that he was sure that it was a Saracen ship. The king asked him to explain himself. 'I will allow you to cut off my head,' he replied, 'or hang me on a gallows if I don't prove before your very eyes that this is a Saracen ship. They are already going away fast, so send another galley after them quickly whose rowers don't offer them a word of greeting. Then we shall see what their intention and faith really are.'

At the king's command a galley rowed very swiftly after the ship and rowed alongside without calling a greeting to its sailors. The people in the ship immediately fired bolts at them from bows and crossbows. Seeing this, the king instantly ordered an attack on the ship. Missiles flew this way and that like rain. Then the rowers on the ship slackened their pace and the ship moved more slowly, because there was not enough wind to drive it. So our sailors rowed many times quickly round the ship, but their scrutiny failed to reveal any point of attack. The ship seemed so big, solidly constructed in very strong material; and it was defended by a garrison of warriors who defended themselves strongly, shooting at them without a pause.

---

of Howden, *Gesta*, 2 p. 168 and *Chronica*, 3 p. 112, agrees that the sailors of the Great Ship claimed to be French, but he agrees with Ambroise that only one boat was sent to challenge the Great Ship. He says Richard did not believe the claim because the king of France had no ships like this one.

146. This seems to have been a waterproof cloth made of matted fibres.

147. According to Ambroise, the sailors claimed to be English (lines 2190–3); perhaps his version of the story reflects French antipathies towards the English.

Our people were unable to stand up under the shots fired from the great height of the ship. The defenders were assisted by natural motion, because it is easier for missiles to damage those below because they naturally fall point first. At a loss and despairing, our people quietly asked each other what King Richard the unconquered, the noble-spirited, thought about this situation. He shouted loudly at his forces: 'Surely you're not going to let this ship get away untouched? Shame on you! Are you turning into cowards, getting idle after so many triumphs? It is not yet time for rest, "while the foe remains freely offered to you by fate." The whole world knows that you all ought to be hanged on the cross or suffer the ultimate penalty if you let these people get away.'

So our sailors made a virtue of necessity, eagerly threw themselves into the sea, dived under the ship and tied up the rudder with ropes to turn the ship and impede its progress. Others crept up with great care and perseverance, grabbed hold of cables and jumped into the ship. The Turks met them with determination and cut them to pieces as they boarded, cutting off here an arm, there a hand, or heads, and throwing the bodies into the sea. When the rest saw this they seethed with anger and thirst for revenge. Gaining courage, they made a more bitter assault, climbed over the ship's bulwarks and fell on the Turks, slaughtering them as they bravely resisted. The Turks gained boldness from despair and tried with all their strength to resist the attacking sailors, cutting off here a foot, there a hand and even a great many heads. At last the sailors charged them with all their effort and drove the Turks back into the prow of the ship, but other Turks burst out of the ship's hold and resisted in a body, choosing either to die bravely or manfully to repel their enemy.

Certainly those were remarkable young Turks, ready for war and well armed. They fought for a long time, and many fell on both sides. The Turks persevered strongly and resisted with every effort and eventually their combined strength compelled our people to fall back and abandon ship.

Then the sailors returned to the galleys and circled the ship looking carefully for the best place to attack it. The king however realised that this would be dangerous for his people and that it would not be easy to capture the Turks with their arms and food and all the rest of the things which were in the ship, without destroying the ship. So he ordered each galley to ram the ship with its spur, i.e. the iron-covered beak on the prow. The galleys drew back; then with many strokes of the oars they slammed forward to hole the sides of the ship. The ship was stove in;

and as soon as a passage was given to the waves water flowed in and it began to sink. To escape death in the ship the Turks leapt out into the sea. They died there nonetheless because our people met them with weapons, killed some and drowned the rest. The king however kept thirty-five alive, i.e. emirs and those who were skilled at constructing siege machines. All the others perished, and their weapons were lost; the snakes were drowned and scattered by the waves of the sea.

If that ship had reached the siege of Acre safely, the city would never have been captured by the Christians. God brought this about to damage the infidels and help the Christians who hoped in Him through the service of King Richard. With the help of favourable fortune, the king always gained his object in the business of war.

Seeing what had happened from far off in the mountains, the Saracens were devastated. They informed Saladin [11 June].[148] On hearing the news he pulled out his hair and tore his beard in his furious rage. Afterwards he sighed, and burst into these words: '*O Alla kibir ychalla*!' which means, 'O God, the great and all-powerful,[149] now I have lost Acre, and my beloved elite troops in whom I had such faith. I am crushed by such a bitter fate.' According to those who saw this, there was weeping and wailing in the Saracen army. They carried on a terrible lamentation over this misfortune. In their grief they cut off locks of their hair and rent their clothes and cursed the hour and the constellations under which they had come into Syria. For in that ship all their outstanding young warriors had perished, in whom all their confidence had been placed.[150]

The end of the second book, the beginning of the third.

---

148. Bahā' al-Dīn, pp. 249–50.
149. "*O Alla*...all-powerful,' is not in MSS A and B, which have simply 'O God.'
150. For Bahā' al-Dīn this was the last of the signs that the city would fall. He and 'Imād al-Dīn, however, state that Richard had already arrived in Acre when the ship was attacked on 11 June; and they state that it was not sunk by the Christians: the Muslim captain scuttled it. The Muslims were overwhelmed by the catastrophe, but the sultan heard the news 'with perfect resignation to God's will,' (Bahā' al-Dīn, pp. 249–50). 'Imād al-Dīn reports that the Muslims had already captured five of the English ships and a fast galley, which were taken ashore at Beirut (p. 292).

Book 3

Chapter 1: King Richard's arrival at Acre.[1]

So when the ship had been destroyed and everything had been successful, King Richard and all his retinue hurried on joyfully and eagerly towards Acre, where his desire carried him. With a favourable wind behind them, the following night the fleet dropped anchor before Tyre. In the morning the fleet weighed anchor and hoisted sail, and after a short voyage Scandalion appeared, which has already been mentioned [al-Iskanderûna: Bk. 1 ch. 26]. Then, passing Casal Imbert [al-Zīb], in the distance the tall tower of the city of Acre came into view, and then little by little the rest of the city's fortifications.

Acre was surrounded by an enormous besieging force. There were people from every Christian 'nation under heaven' [Acts ch. 2 v. 5], the elite of the Christian people, well-fitted for war and unremiting labour. By that time they had been besieging Acre for a long time and had suffered many trials and tribulations, constant exertion, lack of food and many other hardships, some of which have been described already.

Beyond the Christian army, the Turkish army also came into view. It was a countless horde, covering the mountains and valleys, hills and plains, with its tents of various designs and iridescent colours pitched everywhere.

They also saw the pavilions of Saladin himself, and the tents of his brother Saphadin [al-Malik al-'Ādil Saif al-Dīn Abū Bakr Aḥmad ibn Ayyūb] and Takieddin [al-Malik al-Muẓaffar Taqī al-Dīn 'Umar ibn Shāhanshāh ibn Ayyūb, Saladin's nephew], agent of Paganism. He kept watch over the coast and the harbour and launched frequent assaults and very serious raids on the Christians. King Richard surveyed the whole of their army, appraising it.

When it was announced that he had arrived in the port, the king of France and the magnates, nobles and chiefs of the whole native army came in procession to meet him. Having longed so much for his arrival they received him with joy and exultation.

1. Ambroise, lines 2299-337.

Chapter 2: The joy, songs and processions which greeted King Richard's arrival.[2]

King Richard landed at Acre with his company on the Saturday before the feast of the Blessed Barnabas the apostle, in Pentecost week [8 June 1191], and the land shook with the Christians' rejoicing. The whole of the people were overjoyed and acclaimed their good fortune with sounding trumpets. They were led out in joy [Isaiah ch. 55 v. 12] and there was great rejoicing among the people because the 'treasure of all nations' had come [Haggai ch. 2 v. 7]. The besieged Turks, on the other hand, were terrified and devastated by his arrival, for they realised that because of the great number of the king's galleys they would no longer be able to go in and out.

The two kings accompanied each other joyfully from the port, showing each other every respect and deference. Then King Richard retired into the tent prepared for him and made plans for how the siege should be conducted. He considered with great care how the city could be seized in the shortest time: what means, what cunning, what siege machines must be used.

Tongue cannot tell, pen cannot do justice to the people's joy at his arrival. The night was calm and the air clearer than usual, as if it was smiling on him. Trumpets blew on this side, horns sounded on the other; here pipers played a shrill tune together, there drums crashed and *troinas*[3] buzzed in deep harmony; and the combination of various sounds formed a charming symphony.[4] It would have been difficult to find anybody who was not praising and rejoicing, each in their own way. Some testified to the joy of their hearts by singing popular songs, others recited 'epic tales of ancient heroes' deeds', as an incitement to modern people to imitate them. Some gave the singers wine in costly cups,[5] others passed the night in a great dance, the mean and the great mingled together regardless of rank.

Their joy was increased by the fact that King Richard had brought Cyprus under our authority, because the island is so profitable - even essential - and would be of such useful service to the army.

---

2. Ambroise, lines 2338-78; Roger of Howden, *Gesta*, 2 p. 169; *Chronica*, 3 p. 112. 'Imad al-Dīn, p. 297, and Bahā' al-Dīn, p. 249, agree the details of the last paragraph in this chapter.
3. A type of wind instrument.
4. Compare Bk. 2 ch. 13, p. 158.
5. Or 'toasted them with wine in costly cups': *Hi cantantibus vina propinant...*

In additional demonstration of the joy which filled their hearts wax lights and flaming torches shone everywhere to drive away the night shadows. With the profusion of lights bright day seemed to replace night, so that the Turks reckoned that the whole valley was on fire.

Chapter 3: The Pisans submit to King Richard. The Turks challenge our people to battle.[6]

The Pisans were astonished at the greatness and glory of King Richard. They came before him and offered him homage and loyalty, submitting themselves of their own accord to his authority and committing themselves to serve him.

Now, the crafty Turks resented the king's prestige. Perhaps they were cunningly pretending that his arrival had given them fresh boldness, or perhaps they wanted to provoke a speedy engagement. On Sunday morning [9 June] some Turks exposed themselves to attack by wandering about outside the city firing arrows aimlessly, as if for practice. From time to time they came closer and seemed to be on the point of crossing the deep ditch. They audaciously harassed and irritated our people with this perverse insolence.[7]

Chapter 4: The gifts both kings conferred on the needy knights. King Richard is sick.[8]

The great companies of both kings were combined, forming the whole Christian host into one army. The king of France had arrived on the eighth day after Easter. With him had come the count of Flanders [Philip d'Alsace], the count of St Pol [Hugh IV],[9] William de Garlande,[10] William des Barres,[11] Drogo d'Amiens, William de Merlo,[12] and the

---

6. The first paragraph is not in Ambroise. See Roger of Howden, *Gesta*, 2 p. 170; *Chronica*, 3 p. 113.
7. At this point, lines 2387-408, Ambroise breaks off his account and goes back to recount the events of 1187.
8. Ambroise, lines 4527-50, 4570-99.
9. Count 1174-1205. See *HGM*, line 5995.
10. See *HGM*, line 7476.
11. Mentioned several times in *HGM*, lines 2135, 2929, 4083-5, 12277; known simply as 'le Barrois', indicating his renown. See also Bk. 4 ch. 10, below.
12. *HGM*, line 11269; brother of Drogo de Merlo, or Merles.

count of Perche [Rotrou III].[13] Another man also returned there with them, who has already been mentioned: the marquis, who held Tyre and had aspired to the throne of Jerusalem. But why enumerate them one by one? There was not a man of great authority or renown in France who did not come, then or later, to capture Acre.

Then at the following Pentecost King Richard came, as was said, with an army and warlike valour. He later learnt that the king of France paid each knight three gold coins a month, and as a result had won the favour and gratitude of everyone. King Richard did not wish anyone to seem superior to him or even his equal in dealings of any kind. He ordered a proclamation to be made to the whole army that he would pay a fixed rate of four gold coins a month to each knight who wanted employment, regardless of country of origin.

So King Richard was universally extolled. It was declared that he surpassed everyone, not only in his merits and grace but also in the gifts he gave and his noble character.

'This is the man whose arrival we longed for so much,' they said. 'So when is the assault? The most outstanding king in the world, more skilled in warfare than any other Christian, has come. Let God's will be done!'

Everyone's hope hung on King Richard. However, when he had been there some days he contracted a very serious illness, commonly called 'Arnoldia'.[14] This was due to the unfamiliar climate of that region, which did not agree with his natural constitution. Nevertheless, he had his stonethrowers and mangonels and his castle erected in front of the city gate. Every care was applied to their construction and arrangement.

13. Died at the siege: Roger of Howden, *Gesta*, 2 p. 143.
14. Roger of Howden, *Gesta*, 2 p. 170, agrees. Ambroise calls it Leonardia (line 4603). It caused loss of hair and fingernails, affected the mouth and lips and could also cause blindness. 'Imad al-Dīn (p. 307), and Bahā' al-Dīn (p. 253), stress the severity of Richard's illness. Both these writers (pp. 309–10 and p. 252 respectively) state that Richard had already begun negotiations with Saladin.

Chapter 5: While King Richard was ill, the king of France manfully stormed the city. But Saladin attacked the outer ditches and the Turks in the city manfully opposed him and burnt the king's siege machines. As a result the king fell ill from grief.[15]

The king of France, disgusted at the great delay in launching an assault, sent word to King Richard that it was a suitable time to make an assault and that a proclamation should be made instructing the army to attack. King Richard replied to his messengers that he was still unable to act, both because his body was still wracked by pain and because some of his forces had not yet arrived due to adverse winds. However, he hoped that they and the fleet would very soon arrive, bringing materials for constructing siege machines.

The king of France did not think that he should give up his plans for this reason. He ordered that a proclamation be made to the army that an assault would be launched. So on the Monday after the feast of St John the Baptist [1 July][16] the king of France had his siege machines set up and ordered all his people to arm themselves. There you would have seen a countless horde of armed warriors suitably equipped with weapons, so many shining mailshirts, so many glittering helmets, so many noble whinnying horses, so many white coverings, so many elite knights, that it was reckoned so many had never been seen there before. There were so many men-at-arms of great prowess and boldness, so many pennants, so many banners of various workmanship!

They arranged for some to remain to defend the outer ditches against possible attack by Saladin and the threatening Turkish army. Then the armed troops approached the city wall and launched a very fierce assault on it, with crossbows and siege machines shooting bolts and stones without a pause. When the besieged Turks realised that they were coming they raised to heaven such an uproar and bellowing of war trumpets that the air seemed to resound with thunder and flashing lightning. Some of them were assigned to the sole task of banging on basins and tambourines, beating drums and making a racket in various other ways as well as raising smoke from a fire, as a prearranged signal to Saladin and the outer army to come to their assistance.

15. Ambroise, lines 4600–92.
16. Events appear to be out of order here: this date is rather late in relation to events preceding it, the events of chapters 6 and 7 seem to be recapping on events in June, while chapters 8 and 9 recount events of 2 and 3 July.

When the Turks on the outer side saw and heard this they charged forward together, bringing with them material of any sort to fill in the ditch so that they could cross more easily and attack our people. However, they were unable to carry this out. Geoffrey de Lusignan, a knight of extraordinary prowess, resisted them magnificently and drove them back from the barricade, which they had already seized from our people. He killed more than ten of them with the axe he was wielding; no one he struck got away alive. He also captured a great many alive. He bore himself with such confidence and agility that every mouth declared that never since the time of those renowned knights Roland and Oliver[17] had any knight been worthy of so much praise. He recovered the barricade, but only with the greatest effort and difficulty.

Hordes of Turks kept pouring relentlessly in and for a long time the outcome of the struggle was in the balance. It was such a serious battle and unbearable conflict, with such horrible blows and loud cries from the contenders that those who were attacking the city and intensely trying to fill in the ditches outside the city walls were forced to fall back and completely abandon the assault. For they lacked the forces to storm the city while at the same time defending themselves on the outer side from Turkish attack.

Many of the French were killed by bolts from crossbows, by stones, darts or Greek fire. Then there was a great weeping and wailing among the people.

'O why did we wait so long for the kings' arrival?' they lamented. 'What pointless hope! Now they have come, and we are no better off; in fact we are even worse off than we used to be. What we longed for is worth less than we hoped.'

While our French were laying down their arms, the Turks hurled disgraceful taunts and insults at them because they had been unable to complete what they had begun. They also threw Greek fire and gradually broke up the king of France's siege machines which he had built with such care, and other implements of war. It was said that the king of France was thrown into such furious rage that he fell sick from grief. He was so distraught that he would not mount his horse.[18]

17. Heroes of the epic poem *La Chanson de Roland*.
18. Bahā' al-Dīn says that Philip was suffering from a wound: p. 253.

Chapter 6: The army is devastated by the kings' sickness, but it is comforted by the arrival of many sneckas.[19]

The army was becoming increasingly demoralised. The troops were devastated and grief-stricken by the kings' ill-health, for there was no longer a prince or duke who fought 'the Lord's battles' [1 Samuel ch. 18 v. 17]. To heap sorrow on sorrow, the count of Flanders had already met a premature death [1 June].[20] The army was extremely distressed at this, and only the arrival of many sneckas brought them some comfort. Following a peaceful voyage, a very great number of bishops and magnates arrived to aid the Christians, each with their retinues.[21] These were their names:

The bishop of Evreux; Roger de Toony [Tosni],[22] and several of his brothers and relations with the surname de Corneby;[23] Robert de Newburgh; Jordan de Hommet;[24] the chamberlain of Tancarville;[25] Earl Robert of Leicester;[26] Gerard Talbot;[27] Ralph Taisson;[28] knights with the surname Torolens;[29] [Ralph][30] the viscount of Châteaudun; Bertram de Verdun;[31] Roger de Harcourt;[32] the knights of the des Préaux family;[33]

---

19. Ambroise, lines 4693–736, but with a shorter list of names. For sneckas, see note 44 on Bk. 2 ch. 12 above.
20. Roger of Howden, *Gesta*, 2 p. 168; *Chronica*, 3 p. 111.
21. These are the reinforcements Richard was expecting at the start of the previous chapter.
22. See Bk. 4 ch. 17, p. 247 and Bk. 6 ch. 4, p. 341, below.
23. Paris, G. (1897), p. 568 judged that this should be 'Tourneby.'
24. See Bk. 6 ch. 14, p. 353 below.
25. Paris, G. (1897), p. 567: William II of Tancarville, hereditary chamberlain of Normandy.
26. Robert de Breteuil: created earl in Sicily by Richard on the death of his father. After the crusade, while Richard was a prisoner in Germany, he held Rouen against King Philip of France, until being captured in 1194. A large ransom was paid for his release. He died young, in 1204, and the earldom was divided between his sisters.
27. Ambroise has Gilbert Talbot: line 4719.
28. See Bk. 6 ch. 33, below.
29. Ambroise, line 4725, has 'Tozeleis.'
30. Paris, G. (1897), p. 535.
31. In *HGM*, lines 8226–32, he is one of King Henry II's household knights. Roger of Howden, *Gesta*, records that on 21 August 1191, after the capture of Acre, he was given the task of guarding the Hospital of St John. He died at Jaffa a year later: 2 pp. 149–50.
32. See note 113 on Bk. 2 ch. 30, p. 181 above.
33. Named in *HGM* as five brothers, Peter, Roger, William, Engerran and John: 'Between Rouen and Le Mans there were not five better brothers, nor so

Warin fitz Gerald;[34] the de la Meres;[35] Henry fitz Nicholas; Ernald de Grandeville and the Stutevilles; William Marcel; William Malet; William Bloez;[36] Chotard de Loreora; Roger de Saty; Andrew de Chavigny;[37] Hugh le Brun [de Lusignan];[38] Geoffrey de Rancon; Ralph de Mauleon;[39] William des Roches;[40] Geoffrey de la Celle; Hugh de la Fierté – he had taken part in the capture of Cyprus and had come to Acre from there.

The two kings were still unwell, but the Lord kept them safe to aid the Christians and recover the city.

Chapter 7: The two kings' stonethrowers and the stonethrowers belonging to the army of the Faithful shatter and demolish the Cursed Tower and a long stretch of the wall.[41]

The king of France made a swift recovery from his illness and concentrated on constructing siege machines and placing stonethrowers in suitable places. He arranged for these to fire continually day and night. He had one excellent one which he called 'Bad Neighbour' [*Malvoisine*]. The Turks in the city had another which they called 'Bad Relation' [*Mal Cousine*] which often used to smash 'Bad Neighbour' with its violent

good in arms, even counts or viscounts', (see lines 4662–74). They were Normans by birth. John, Peter and William went on crusade: William later saved King Richard's life (Bk. 4 ch. 28 and Bk. 6 ch. 36).

34. See Bk. 4 ch. 33, p. 276 below.
35. Ambroise and *HGM* only mention one. *HGM* mentions Robert de la Mere, a Norman knight (line 4307). However, Paul Meyer notes that he had a brother named William (*HGM* 3 p. 61).
    The names after these are not included by Ambroise.
36. See *HGM*, lines 16914–5.
37. *HGM* describes him as 'a knight of the count of Poitiers' son, renowned for his noble prowess', (lines 633–5). In 1189 he fought for Richard while the latter was still count of Poitiers, against King Henry II (*HGM*, lines 8662–80). Richard rewarded him by marrying him to the heiress of Châteauroux (line 9392). After Richard's death in 1199 he appears as an ally of the Lusignans in Poitou against King John. His fame as a knight was such that in the fourteenth century he was one of the characters in a romance of the third crusade called *Saladin*, part of the second version of the epic Crusade cycle.
38. See Bk. 2 ch. 16, p. 161 above.
39. See Bk. 6 ch. 14, p. 353, and ch. 22, below. Paris, G. (1897), p. 559: he was the father of the famous knight and poet Savaric de Mauleon.
40. Fought for King Henry II in his last war against Count Richard and King Philip of France: *HGM*, line 8817. From 1199 he was seneschal of Anjou, Maine and Touraine. Later went on the Albigensian crusade.
41. Ambroise, lines 4741–808.

shots. The king kept rebuilding it until its continual bombardment partly destroyed the main city wall and shattered the Cursed Tower. On one side the duke of Burgundy's stonethrower had no little effect. On the other the Templars' stonethrower wreaked impressive devastation, while the Hospitallers' also never ceased hurling, to the terror of the Turks.

Besides these, there was a stonethrower which had been constructed at general expense, which they called 'God's Stonethrower'. A priest, a man of great probity, always stood next to it preaching and collecting money for its continual repair and for hiring people to gather the stones for its ammunition.[42] This machine at last demolished the wall next to the Cursed Tower for around two perches' length [11 yards or 10 metres].[43]

The count of Flanders had had a choice stonethrower, which King Richard had after his death, as well as another which was not so good. These two constantly bombarded the tower next to a gate which the Turks frequently used, until the tower was half-demolished. Besides these, King Richard had two new ones made with remarkable workmanship and material which would hit the intended target no matter how far off it was. He also built a very strongly constructed machine with steps for climbing up into it. Commonly called a 'belfrey', it was closely covered with a layer of hides, rope netting and very solid wooden boarding so that it could not be destroyed by a missile from a stonethrower nor by Greek fire nor be damaged by anything else.[44] He also had two mangonels prepared. One of these was so swift and violent that its shots reached the inner streets of the city meat-market.

King Richard's stonethrowers hurled constantly by day and night. It can be firmly stated that one of them killed twelve men with a single stone. That stone was sent for Saladin to see, with messengers who said that the diabolical king of England had brought from Messina, a city he had captured, sea flint and the smoothest stones to punish the Saracens. Nothing could withstand their blows; everything was crushed or reduced to dust.

Yet the king was confined to bed suffering from a severe fever, completely wretched because he saw the Turks insolently challenging and attacking our people with increasing frequency but he could not engage them in battle because he was ill. He suffered more torture from the insolent Turkish raids than from the burning fever.

---

42. Ambroise does not give this detail.
43. Roger of Howden, *Gesta*, 2 p. 173 states that this happened on 3 July, before the battle in ch. 9 below.
44. A belfrey was also described in Bk. 1 ch. 36.

Chapter 8: While the king of France is attacking the city, the Turks use Greek fire to burn up all the siege machines, the cat and the king of France's *cercleia*.[45]

The city of Acre has such a very strong position and it was defended so carefully by elite Turkish troops that it seemed very difficult to capture it by storm. The French had already expended a great deal of care on constructing siege machines and devices for demolishing the walls, but all in vain. Whatever the French manufactured at great expense the Turks demolished, either by pouring Greek fire over it unexpectedly or with other incendiary devices.

Among other siege machines and implements which the king of France had made to destroy the city wall, he constructed with great determination an implement which would climb up the wall. It was called a 'cat' because it clung like a cat to the wall as it crept up it to seize it. He also made another contraption, very firmly constructed from frames of stiff cane, which they called a *cercleia*. This framework was covered in rawhide. The king himself used to sit under it with crossbow at the ready, on the look-out for Turks appearing on the top of the wall. Then he would shoot them unexpectedly as they stood between the battlements.

Then one day while the French were busily trying to fix the cat on to the wall the Turks with violent determination threw a heap of dry wood down from the walls, piling it up on top of the cat! Then they immediately threw some Greek fire on top. They also threw some on the framework which the French had put so much work into constructing, and to cap it all they set up a stonethrower to fire at it. Suddenly everything was burned to ashes or destroyed by the shots of the stonethrower!

At this the king of France was thrown into a violent rage. He began to curse all those under his command, using terrible language, abusing them and telling them that they were dishonoured because they did not seek suitable revenge from the Saracens for inflicting such things on them. He was still raging with anger as day drew towards evening, and he had a public crier proclaim that an assault would be made on the following day.

45. Ambroise, lines 4809–40. The *cercleia* was a circular hut.

Chapter 9: The king of France's army undermines the walls. The Christians standing in the ditches manfully repel the Turks who make a very heavy attack on them from the outer side [3 July].[46]

So in the morning they all armed themselves. They placed preeminent and picked warriors of exceptional valour in the outer ditches as a precaution against any problems or unexpected Saracen attack. Saladin had boasted that he would cross the ditches in strength that day and would finally demonstrate his great valour by crushing the Christians. However, he did not keep his word: he did not come himself,[47] but his ferocious and unwavering army came with Takieddin[48] its manager. They poured into the ditch in a body and struggled violently to cross. The French were not slow to resist and tried to drive them back, with no little slaughter on both sides. The Turks left their horses so that they could fight less impeded on foot. It was a bitter battle: they fought hand-to-hand with drawn swords, and daggers and two-headed axes, and clubs bristling with sharp teeth. These struck, those fell; these shouted, those groaned; a great many perished *en masse*. The desperate Turks attacked, and the magnificent Christians threw them back; yet it took an enormous effort because such a great number of Turks was pressing in so relentlessly. They were inflamed with twofold heat, because it was summer.

The other part of the army had been sent to attack the city. They were either firing bolts or trying to undermine the walls or hit them with repeated shots from siege machines or creep up them. Fearing their great spirit the Turks in the city raised Saladin's ensign. This gave a signal to the Turks on the outer side to come hastily to their aid, or at least to attack the French so as to drive them away.

When they saw this, Takieddin and the Turks on the outer side attacked with greater determination, throwing themselves against our people with all their strength. They violently filled the ditch while our people fought back just as strongly, placing themselves with God's help like a wall against the invaders, and repulsed them.

Meanwhile the king of France's sappers were gradually advancing underground with their subterranean burrowing. They succeeded in

---

46. Ambroise, lines 4841–87: for date see Roger of Howden, *Gesta* 2 p. 173; *Chronica*, 3 p. 117.
47. Bahā' al-Dīn, pp. 258–61, states that Saladin did take part in this battle.
48. The text gives 'Kahedin' in this chapter, but for the sake of clarity I have altered the name to the form which is given elsewhere in the text.

destroying the foundations of the wall, filling the breach with wood. They then set fire to it. At once the fire burned up the wood which was supporting the wall and a great part of the wall subsided so that it leaned slightly but did not fall completely to the ground. A great number of Christians ran forward to enter, while Turks ran to drive them back. How many banners you would have seen there, how many ensigns of various shapes! The wicked Turks fired Greek fire at our people. As the wall had not collapsed completely the French brought up scaling ladders and struggled to climb it, while the Turks placed ladders on the other side so that they could defend the breach.[49]

Chapter 10: Aubrey Clements climbed the wall by a ladder but was killed by the Turks.[50]

A memorable deed occurred there which should not be passed over in silence. There was a man renowned for his valour and his great skills as a warrior, named Aubrey Clements. He observed that the French were sweating with toil yet making little progress. Aroused to passion, he moved into action. 'Either I shall die today,' he said, 'or God willing I shall enter Acre.'

So saying, he boldly scaled a ladder, and reached the top of the wall, where he killed many Turks who ran up from all sides to attack him. The French followed him up the ladder, but there were so many of them that the ladder could not bear their weight and they all fell to the ground. Some were crushed to death, while others were pulled out very seriously injured. The Turks shouted out at their disaster, their joy increased by the severity of the French misfortune.

Aubrey Clements was left alone on the top of the wall, where the Turks surrounded and crushed him, stabbing him to death with countless darts. So the truth of his statement was confirmed: as he had foretold, that day he died a martyr, for he could not enter Acre when all aid had deserted him. The whole army was devastated at his loss, and abandoned the assault to lament and bewail his death. He was certainly a man of very great authority and family and of exceptional valour.

---

49. For this, see Bahā' al-Dīn, p. 261.
50. Ambroise, lines 4888–908. See also Bahā' al-Dīn, p. 260. He calls Aubrey 'a Frank of enormous stature', who was eventually killed by being burnt by Greek fire. Aubrey Clements was lord of Mez in the Gatinais and marshal of France.

Chapter 11: While the French enter the Cursed Tower from the outside the Turks enter it from the inside, working against the sappers.[51]

Not much after, the French sappers' zealous mining excavated an underground passage under the Cursed Tower. They supported the roof on logs of wood. However the Turks were digging the other way under the ground and reached the same part of the foundations. There both parties made a peace agreement: the Turks would leave unharmed, and they agreed in exchange to set free some of the Christian captives whom they held in chains. When the Turks in the city discovered this they were very upset and they blocked the underground passages through which they had gone out.[52]

Chapter 12: Although King Richard is still unwell, when he attacks the city with his people he kills many with a crossbow held in his own hand. His sappers and stonethrowers throw down a tower [5 July].[53]

King Richard had not yet completely recovered from his sickness. However, he was eager for action because he was very anxious to capture the city. So he arranged for his forces to storm the city, hoping that perhaps by divine grace he might gain his wish. He had an interwoven framework called a *cercleia* built, constructed with great care. He decided that it should be brought out into the ditch outside the city wall. His most skilled crossbowmen stood underneath it. He had himself carried out to it on a silken bed, to discourage the Saracens with his presence and encourage his own people to fight. There he used his crossbow, with which he was skilled, and killed many by firing bolts and darts at them.

His sappers also dug a subterranean passage under the foundations of the tower at which his stonethrowers were firing. They thrust wooden material into the breach and set fire to it. With that and the repeated blows from the stonethrowers the tower suddenly fell to the ground with a crash.

51. Ambroise, lines 4909–26.
52. At this point negotiations for the surrender of the city began: see ch. 15 for events of 4 July.
53. Ambroise, lines 4927–46. For date see Roger of Howden, *Gesta*, 2 p. 174.

Chapter 13: King Richard's men manfully attack the city, while the Turks manfully repel them. King Richard's crossbow kills a man wearing Aubrey Clement's armour.[54]

The king considered the difficulties which they had encountered; how warlike their enemies were, and that courage is needed at critical junctures. He decided that the best way to arouse enthusiasm in the young was to offer a reward rather than to force them by commands, because everyone is attracted by the smell of money. So he resolved that a public crier should announce that everyone who took one stone from the wall next to the aforesaid tower would receive two gold coins from the king. Later he promised three gold coins, finally four: so that for each stone that anyone took from the wall they received four gold coins in payment. You would have seen youths leap forward, and men-at-arms of great valour rush to the wall and eagerly keep on pulling out stones, as greedy for glory as for gain. Even among the darts of their adversaries they boldly pressed on with the destruction of the wall. A great many of them were wounded and had to abandon the work; others gave up because they were afraid of the mortal danger. Some the Turks manfully drove back from the wall - their shields and armour were unable to protect them. The wall was extremely high, and not a little thick. However, men of valorous spirit overcame the danger and took a great many stones from the body of the wall.

The Turks rushed down on them in a body, struggling to throw them back from the wall. They were so anxious to repel their adversaries that they forgot their armour and unwisely exposed themselves almost unarmed to their enemies' fire. One of the Turks had donned the armour of the abovementioned Aubrey Clements and was evily flaunting himself in it, standing out boastfully on the highest part of the wall to arouse our people's anger. King Richard fired a lethal shot into the middle of his chest from his crossbow.

Grieved at his death, the rest of the Turks ran up recklessly to avenge him. (It was thought that their grief was lessened if they could do this.) They showed themselves to be extremely daring, as if they feared neither darts nor missiles. They struck, they pushed forward, they pressed on our people like wild things. There were never more outstanding warriors or better defenders than these, whatever their beliefs. The mind is astounded and recoils at the memory of their deeds. Not even the strong-

54. Ambroise, lines 4948-88.

est armour, double layered mailshirts or doublets could withstand the violent shots of crossbow bolts and darts in that critical engagement. At the same time the Turks were digging out from inside the city and our sappers were forced to retreat. Then the Turks began to shout loudly, as they had achieved their objective.

Chapter 14: Our squires and the Pisans manfully climb up the tower which had been shattered, in order to break into the city. The Turks repulse them courageously, using weapons and Greek fire [11 July].[55]

At last the aforesaid tower fell to the ground under the repeated shots from our stonethrowers and the removal of stones. King Richard's men had stopped sapping and the assault ended. Then our squires[56] took up their arms. They were greedy for glory and victory, and fit and ready for battle. The banner of the earl of Leicester was there, and the banner of Andrew de Chavigny and of Hugh le Brun. The bishop of Salisbury also came to the assault, very handsomely equipped, as well as a great many others.

At around the third hour [9 am] i.e. the hour for dinner, the men of valour and the outstanding squires set out to attack the aforesaid tower. They boldly climbed up it immediately. When the Turks saw them they began to shout, and the whole city was aroused! Snatching up their arms, the Turks came running up densely packed and fell on the squires who were nimbly coming up. The squires struggled to enter the city; the Turks struggled to repulse them. Both sides assembled in a body, they fought hand to hand, right hand grasped right hand, sword struck sword. Some caught hold of each other, some pushed, some struck, some fell. There were few squires, whereas the Turks' numbers were continually increasing. The Turks also threw Greek fire at them. As the squires could not stand up under its burning they were at last forced to retire.

They descended from the tower. Some of them had been killed by weapons and some burnt up by that pernicious fire. Then the Pisans, greedy for glory and revenge, climbed up up that tower in full force; but

55. Ambroise, lines 4989–5040. For date see Roger of Howden, *Gesta*, 2 p. 178; *Chronica*, 3 p. 120.

56. *Armigeri.* Usually means squire, i.e. 'armour-bearer', although it can mean a man-at-arms. At this period squires were not necessarily trainee knights but fighting men in the service of knights.

the Turks rushed down on them like wild things. They were in such a violent frenzy that although the Pisans bore themselves outstandingly they were unable to withstand them and had to retreat and leave the tower.

There was never a race as effective in war as those Turks. That day the city would have been captured and the business ended if the Christians had taken wise advice and the combined strength of the whole army had gone to fight. As most of the army was having dinner at that time, the operation was undertaken rashly, so that it could not succeed.

Chapter 15: Praise for the Turks in the town. Out of desperation they send Mestoc and Caracois to our kings to gain a delay until they could reach an agreement with Saladin. But they returned without success [4 July].[57]

What should be said about that unbelieving people who guarded the city? They certainly ought to be admired for their valour in war and their integrity. If only they had held the right faith, there would be none better - according to human reasoning, that is.[58] Yet they feared our people's resolute spirit, and not without good reason, for they had seen elite troops come from the whole breadth of Christendom to destroy them. What was more, the walls had been partly demolished or broken down, and a large part of their forces had been mutilated, killed or disabled by wounds.

Although there were still 6000 Turks within the city, as well as their leaders Mestoc [Saif al-Dīn 'Alī ibn Aḥmad al-Mashṭūb] and Caracois [Bahā' al-Dīn al-Asadī Qara-Qūsh], they had given up hope of aid. They realised that the Christian army was absolutely devastated by the death of Aubrey Clements and the death of their sons and relations who had fallen in battle and that the Christians were ready to die bravely or to

57. Ambroise, lines 5067-156. For date see 'Imād al-Dīn, pp. 312-3, and Roger of Howden, *Gesta*, 2 p. 174, and *Chronica*, 3 pp. 117-8. Note that the besieged tried to surrender the day after the battle when Aubrey Clements was killed, chs. 9-10 above, and before the events of chs. 11-14. The change in the order of events here is probably partly to build up the tension; but it also allows our writers to include more of the deeds of King Richard and imply that King Richard was responsible for the defenders' decision to surrender.

58. Cf. the description of the Muslim Baligant in *La Chanson de Roland*: 'God, what a knight, if only he were a Christian!' (line 3164).

conquer the Turks, but that they would consider nothing honourable besides these options.

By common counsel and assent the besieged sought a truce in which they could inform Saladin of the state they were in, as he had previously promised them on oath according to the rites of the Gentile superstition that he would either send them swift aid or enable them to leave the city honourably.[59] In order to obtain this petition the two most noble Saracens and most renowned of the whole of Paganism, Mestoc and Caracois, came to our kings with the promise that if Saladin did not send them help quickly they would surrender the city. The only condition was that all the Turks who were in the besieged city should be allowed to leave freely with their weapons and all that they had and go wherever they wished.

The king of France and almost all the French agreed to this condition, but King Richard absolutely refused to agree. He stated that it should not be conceded, because after such a long and laborious siege they would be entering a city stripped of everything valuable. When they realised King Richard's opinion, Caracois and Mestoc returned to the city, their mission a failure.

Meanwhile Saladin had heard the messengers sent by the besieged. He instructed them to endure with perseverance and manfully continue to defend the city as they had done so far, as they could be sure that very adequate aid would certainly come to them shortly. He claimed that messengers had informed him that a huge military force would certainly come soon from Babylonia [Egypt] in the ships and galleys which he had summoned earlier. He had instructed Muleina[60] that they were to reach them within eight days regardless of any excuse. If perhaps these forces did not come as arranged, he promised them on oath that he would get from the Christians the most favourable peace terms possible and unconditional permission to leave the city.

Having heard him out, the messengers returned to the city, where they repeated Saladin's promises and persuaded the besieged to continue the resistance. So the anxious Turks were kept in suspense, waiting for assistance to come.

---

59. 'In order to obtain...their mission a failure', is not in Ambroise.
60. This is the Molan, or caliph of Egypt, but our writers are mistaken: there was no longer a caliph in Egypt. See Bk. 1 ch. 4, above.

Chapter 16: While our people are manfully attacking the city many of the Turks flee from it out of desperation.[61]

Meantime the Christians' stonethrowers kept up a constant battering of the walls, day and night. The besieged were shaken, distressed and distraught at this; 'filled with alarm they panic' [Psalm 48 v. 5]. Giving way to their fears, some of them hurled themselves from the walls at night in their terror in an attempt to escape, not bothering to wait for the promised aid.

A great many of them begged to be given the sacrament of Christian baptism. There is justification for doubting the extent of their merits, since they asked for this more as a means of escape from the danger which threatened them than from the inspiration of divine grace; but there are many routes to salvation.

As messengers ran constantly back and forth it became clear to Saladin that it would be too dangerous for the Turks to hold on to the city any longer, as they could not defend it against the Christians.

Chapter 17: The peace terms the besieged made with the Christians, with Saladin's advice [12 July 1191].[62]

Realising that delay would be dangerous, Saladin at last decided to approve the petitions of the besieged. Those who were most influential in persuading him to do this were his emirs, satraps [provincial governors] and powerful friends who were parents, relations and friends of the besieged.[63] They claimed that as Saladin had given a promise on oath to the besieged in accordance with the rites of those who worship the Muḥammadan law he was obliged to procure honourable terms of freedom for them when they were in dire straits. Otherwise, under the rights of war [*jure belli*], they could be seized and put to a derisive and shame-

61. Ambroise, lines 5157–67; first and last paragraphs only.
62. Ambroise, lines 5167–224, but with substantial differences. See also Bahā'al-Dīn, p. 267; 'Imād al-Dīn, p. 318; Roger of Howden, *Gesta*, 2 p. 178; *Chronica*, 3 pp. 120–1.
63. 'They claimed...Christian hands.' is not in Ambroise. The following paragraph is included by Ambroise, lines 5120–36, under the negotiations of ch. 15. IP2's description of the negotiations is more detailed and shows a greater interest in legal rights than that of Ambroise. This may reflect developments in the theory of law in the thirteenth century, and the writer's greater education.

ful death, making the Muḥammadan law – which his ancestors had carefully observed as far as they could – appear worthless. His own dignity and reputation would be also greatly damaged if those who venerate Muḥammad fell into Christian hands.

They also asked Saladin to act on the matter because these crack Turkish troops had been obedient to his every request, and had been confined for so long in that siege, defending the city for him for such a great length of time. He should also remember the wives of the besieged and their pitiable families, whom they had not seen now for three years, since the start of the siege. They also said that it was better to surrender the city than to lose such doughty people.

With these and similar arguments Saladin's princes won him over. So that their plight should not be 'worse than before' [Matthew's Gospel ch. 12 v. 45] he agreed that they should make the best peace terms that they could. So they discussed and prepared the peace terms they thought would be most appropriate.

When the messengers brought back the decision of Saladin and the satraps, the besieged were overjoyed. Their leaders went out to our kings and offered through an interpreter to surrender Acre unconditionally and to give back the Holy Cross and 250 noble Christians whom they were holding captive![64] When they realised that our people did not find these terms satisfactory they offered 2000 noble Christians and 500 lesser captives; Saladin would have a search made throughout all his lands to find them. When they left the city the Turks would take only the shirts on their backs, leaving behind their weapons and everything else including foodstuffs. In addition, they would give the two kings 200,000 Saracen talents in exchange for their lives. As a guarantee that they would keep these terms, they would give the more noble and eminent Turks in the city as hostages.[65]

Our kings conferred together with their wiser men to decide whether they should concede these terms. At last all were agreed that they should accept what was offered and agree to the terms. When oaths to uphold the treaty had been given, the terms set down in writing and hostages given, they could withdraw empty-handed from the city.

---

64. Ambroise does not include this first offer.
65. For the full terms of the peace treaty see Lyons and Jackson (1982), p. 330.

Chapter 18: The Turks give hostages as security that they will hand over the Cross, money and captives within a month. They then leave the city and the Christians enter. The kings divide everything equally between them.[66]

On the Wednesday next after the Translation of the Blessed Benedict [12 July] hostages were given and received from among the more powerful and noble emirs. A time limit of one month[67] was fixed for the return of the Holy Cross and finding the captives. When the news of what had happened spread and everyone heard that the city had surrendered, the foolish common people were furious. However, the wiser were justifiably delighted that they had won the city quickly and without danger, as they had not been able to capture it earlier even after a long siege.

A public crier announced that no one should venture to do or say anything to insult or provoke any of the Turks. Nor should they fire any more missiles at the walls or at any Turks they might happen to see on the ramparts.

The Christians watched with very curious eyes as those Turkish people wandered around on the top of the walls that day on the point of leaving the city. They admired these outstanding and memorable warriors who were men of admirable prowess, exceptional valour, very energetic in the practice of war and renowned for their great deeds. No less, as they came out of the city almost empty-handed the Christians were stunned at their fine bearing and appearance, which remained unaltered by adversity. Even extreme necessity had hardly been able to reduce them to pleading for mercy. Even now as they came out defeated they were not gnawed by anxiety or depressed by the loss of their property. Their expressions remained resolute; in fact their fierce appearance made it seem that they had won the victory. However, their superstitious rite and the miserable error of idolatry perverted and corrupted these strengths.

At last when all the Turks had come out, the gates were opened and the Christians, commanded by the two kings, entered the city freely with dancing and joy and exulting at the top of their voices, glorifying the Lord and giving thanks because God had shown His people great mercy [Luke's Gospel ch. 1 v. 58] and He had visited and redeemed His

66. This chapter is not in Ambroise.
67. Roger of Howden says forty days: *Gesta*, 2 p. 179; Ibn al-Athīr says two months, 2 p. 46.

people [Luke's Gospel ch. 1 v. 68]. The kings' banners and multiform flags were raised high over the walls and towers.[68] The city was divided equally between the two kings; they also divided weapons and food-stuffs they found into equal shares. The sum total of the captives was also reckoned up and divided by lot. The nobleman Caracois fell into the king of France's part, and a great number of the rest. Mestoc was in King Richard's share, with all the remainder. In addition the king of France had the Templars' noble palace and all that went with it for his share, while King Richard had the royal palace in which he placed his queens with their girls and maids. So each peacefully received his share.[69]

The army was lodged throughout the breadth of the city. After such great protracted agonies in the long siege they were now free to enjoy themselves and be refreshed with much-desired rest. The night following our entrance into Acre, because he was afraid of our people, Saladin withdrew with his army from his position and occupied a mountain further away [Shafar'am].[70]

Chapter 19: The vile and shameful manner in which the Turks had treated our holy things while they held the city.[71]

When the city was surrendered four years had already elapsed since it was taken by the Saracens [9 July 1187–12 July 1191]. It was surrendered, as was said, on the day after the Translation of St Benedict. The state of the churches inside the city was horrible to behold, and even now it is distressing to remember the shocking things seen within them. For which of the faithful could gaze dry-eyed on the face of a venerable image of God's Son Himself crucified, or of some saint, which had been disfigured or dishonoured in some way? Who would not shudder at the

68. Richard of Devizes recounts (pp. 46–7) that one of the longstanding leaders of the siege, Duke Leopold V of Austria, also erected his banner on the walls of the city with the two kings'. Richard had it torn down, greatly offending Leopold. The sequel is told below, p. 383.
69. Roger of Howden, *Gesta*, 2 p. 186 and *Chronica*, 3 pp. 121–2, states that when the nobles who had been taking part in the siege for the last two years saw that the two kings had taken all the spoils, many went home because they had spent all their money and could not afford to stay.
70. Bahā' al-Dīn, p. 269.
71. Ambroise, lines 5225–44. 'Imād al-Dīn confirms, p. 33, that the Muslims had turned the Christian churches in Acre into mosques.

horrific description of how that impious Turkish people abusively destroyed altars, and threw holy crosses on the ground, and beat them in contempt? They set up their mosques in places of sanctity, and having removed all signs of human redemption and the Christian religion, put in all the filth of their Muslim superstition.

Chapter 20: The disagreement between the two kings over the marquis and King Guy, and how peace was made between them.[72]

As time passed, an enormous disagreement arose between the two kings over the aforementioned marquis. The king of France favoured him and had decided to give him all his share of everything gained in the Holy Land and his entitlement to future gains. Being sympathetic to the plight of King Guy, King Richard was unwilling to give his assent to this concession as it seemed more appropriate for King Guy. The kings were in disagreement over this point for quite some time.

Eventually through the mediation of the princes and leaders of the people they made peace on these terms: as the marquis was recognised to have married the heir to the kingdom, and also in compensation for the assistance he had shown the army during the siege, he would receive hereditary possession of the county of Tyre, i.e. Tyre, Sidon and Beirut. Geoffrey de Lusignan, King Guy's brother, would receive the county of Joppa [Jaffa, now part of Tel Aviv Yafo], i.e. Joppa and Ascalon,[73] in compensation for his toils and efforts. If King Guy should happen to die before the marquis, then the marquis would be crowned with the royal diadem and succeed King Guy on the throne because he had married the heir to the kingdom; although he had done so wickedly and forcibly in hope of becoming king, as was said above [Bk. 1 ch. 63]. However, if King Guy, the marquis and his wife should all be taken from human affairs together while King Richard was in that region, then it would be left to King Richard's judgement to dispose of the kingdom as he wished. The general strife was ended by these terms [27 July].

72. Ambroise, lines 5041–66: Ambroise places these events before the events of chapter 15. Roger of Howden, *Gesta*, 2 pp. 171, 183–4; and *Chronica*, 3 pp. 113–4, 124–5, shows that the dispute erupted before the city surrendered, but the final settlement was made after Acre was occupied by the Christians. See also William of Newburgh, pp. 353–4.

73. Roger of Howden, *Gesta*, 2 p. 184 and *Chronica*, 3 p. 125, has Caesarea [Qesari] instead of Ascalon.

Chapter 21: When the city had been surrendered, the king of France prepared to return home. Everyone was amazed, tried to dissuade him or cursed him.[74]

So this was how things stood: the city had been surrendered and the end of July was approaching, the month within which the Turks had promised to return the Holy Cross in exchange for the release of the hostages. Then the rumour spread through the army that the king of France, on whom the people had hung their hopes, wished to go home and was making great preparations for his journey [22 July]![75] How shameful, how outrageous, wanting to leave when there was still so much pressing business to be done! It was his duty to guide this great crowd of people, to encourage the Christian people in such pious and necessary work and to ensure the progress of such an arduous undertaking! What was the use of his eager intention to complete that long journey when he was going to return so quickly? What an extraordinary way of discharging a vow, when he had hardly entered the country and had such brief triumphs against the Turks!

What more can I say? The king of France claimed that he had decided to come on pilgrimage because of illness, and his vow was now discharged as far as it had been given. However, particularly because he appeared fit and well when he took the cross with King Henry between Trie and Gisors, there was no evidence to support his assertion.[76]

Yet the king of France's reputation should not be completely blackened. He had expended a great deal of effort and expense in that country, in storming the city. He had given aid and support to a great many people, while the very authority of his presence had brought about more quickly and easily the completion of that great undertaking. As the most

---

74. Ambroise, lines 5245–304, but shorter; William of Newburgh, p. 357.

75. Events are again out of order. The events in ch. 20 took place 27 July; the events in ch. 21 on 22 July: Roger of Howden, *Chronica*, 3 pp. 123, 124–5.

76. Ambroise states that the king of France said he was going home because he was ill, but illness is no excuse for the king who led all other kings (lines 5257–62). Another reason was that following the death of the count of Flanders (ch. 6 above) Philip wished to return to France to exert his rights as liege lord of Flanders (William of Newburgh, p. 357 and Roger of Howden, *Chronica*, 3 pp. 125–6). 'Ansbert', p. 100, says that the king of France could no longer bear the arrogance of the king of England. Rigord, pp. 116–7, states that Philip was ill and was suspicious of Richard's negotiations with Saladin.

powerful and most prestigious of Christian kings he certainly deserved to capture the city. Yet because he had greater strength and more outstanding prestige than others he was held to have a greater responsibility for the recovery of that desolate country, destitute of aid, which the Gentiles had entered to pollute. According to St Gregory: 'When more gifts are given, the reasons for giving the gifts also increase' [St Gregory the Great, *XL Homiliarum in Evangelica Liber*, Bk. 1, Homily 9, 1], and 'where some have been given much, much will be required of them' [Luke's Gospel ch. 12 v. 48].

When everyone was informed of the king of France's unyielding wish to return home, and that he would not give way to his people's groans or tearful entreaties, the French would have renounced their obedience to his authority and rejected his lordship over them, if it were possible. They called down on the would-be departer every adversity and misfortune which could fall on a mortal in this miserable life. Nevertheless the king made arrangements for his journey as quickly as he could, leaving [Hugh] the duke of Burgundy as his representative in that country and with him a vast number of people. He also sent a request to King Richard to lend him two of his galleys; King Richard willingly ordered two of the best to be given to him. But the king of France later showed how ungrateful he was for this favour.

Chapter 22: The king of France swore to King Richard that he would keep the peace towards his people and lands until King Richard returned home.[77]

King Richard was of the opinion that the king of France should make an agreement with him to preserve mutual good faith and security. For just like their fathers they revered each other with tender enmity cloaked in love, which it is believed will never cast out fear in their descendants [ironic misquotation of 1 John ch. 4 v. 18]. Needled by this fear, King Richard demanded that the king of France swear to preserve good faith towards him, and not knowingly or intentionally to break his word by attacking either his people or his land while he was still on pilgrimage. If King Richard seemed to be blameworthy in any matter, after he

77. Ambroise, lines 5305–32; also Roger of Howden, *Gesta*, 2 pp. 184–5; *Chronica*, 3 p. 125.

returned to his land he would reach agreement with the French within forty days on what measures should be taken to correct any offences which had occurred, before the king of France should be minded to seek redress from him.[78]

The king of France swore to King Richard that he would faithfully observe all this. He gave hostages to guarantee that he would keep his word: the duke of Burgundy, and Count Henry [of Champagne] and five or more others whose names are forgotten.[79] Everyone is well informed of how faithfully he stood by his oath and agreement! From the moment he returned to his homeland he shook the country and threw Normandy into confusion. To cut a long story short: taking his leave, the king of France left the army at Acre. Everyone wished him misfortune and gave him curses instead of blessings.

Chapter 23: The king of France goes with his hostages and the marquis to Tyre. The duke of Burgundy and many French remain with King Richard.[80]

On the day of St Peter in Chains [1 August 1191] the king of France went on board ship and sailed for Tyre, leaving the greater part of his army with King Richard. That unspeakable marquis went back to Tyre with him. He also took Caracois, already mentioned, and all the Saracen hostages who had fallen to the king of France by lot. The king of France reckoned that he should receive a 100,000 gold coins or more for their ransom, which would support his people in that country until Easter. Yet the agreed time period was passing and those whose responsibility it was to free the hostages seemed to have no concern about paying the ransom. In fact most of them died, and it is certain that not penny was paid for them, not even an egg. The hostages brought them nothing at all, and neither did they get their half share of the foodstuffs which had been found in the city when they took it over.

For this reason the French frequently remembered that they had not received any other payment from the king of France. This resulted in no

78. Ambroise says (lines 5317-21): when Richard returned home, the king of France should give him forty days' notice before attacking him.
79. 'Everyone is...into confusion' is not in Ambroise.
80. Ambroise, lines 5333-57.

little dispute and muttering among them, until King Richard, on the request of the duke of Burgundy, lent the duke on the security of his hostages 5000 marks of silver to pay his troops.

End of Book 3.

Book 4

Chapter 1: King Richard confers gifts on the knights and repairs the walls of Acre.[1]

Since King Richard saw that he now held chief responsibility for the entire enterprise, its progress, operations and costs, he cheerfully distributed great quantities of gold and silver to the French and foreigners of any nation so that they could more than recover their means and redeem the securities they had given for their debts.

While the king of France was prematurely hurrying back home, as stated above, King Richard was applying his attention to repairing the walls of the city so that they were higher and better than they had been before they were destroyed. He himself walked up and down constantly, encouraging the workers and giving instructions to the masons. He put every effort into the work, pressing on untiringly to conquer God's inheritance.

Chapter 2: Saladin does not keep the agreement regarding the return of the Lord's Cross and monetary payment; and he does not consider his hostages.[2]

King Richard was awaiting the expiry of the time limit agreed between himself and the Turks, as was explained above. Meanwhile he applied his efforts to packing up stonethrowers and mangonels for transportation. After the expiry of the time limit fixed by the Saracens for the return of the Holy Cross and the freeing of the hostages as stated in the agreement, he waited for another three weeks to see whether Saladin would stand by his word or whether the treaty-maker would infringe his own treaty. But Saladin seemed to have no concern about it. Perhaps this was through God's dispensation so that something more satisfactory should come about. Yet the Saracens were demanding a delay to give them time

1. Ambroise, lines 5358, 5384–92.
2. Ambroise, lines 5380–1; 5372–8; 5393–412.

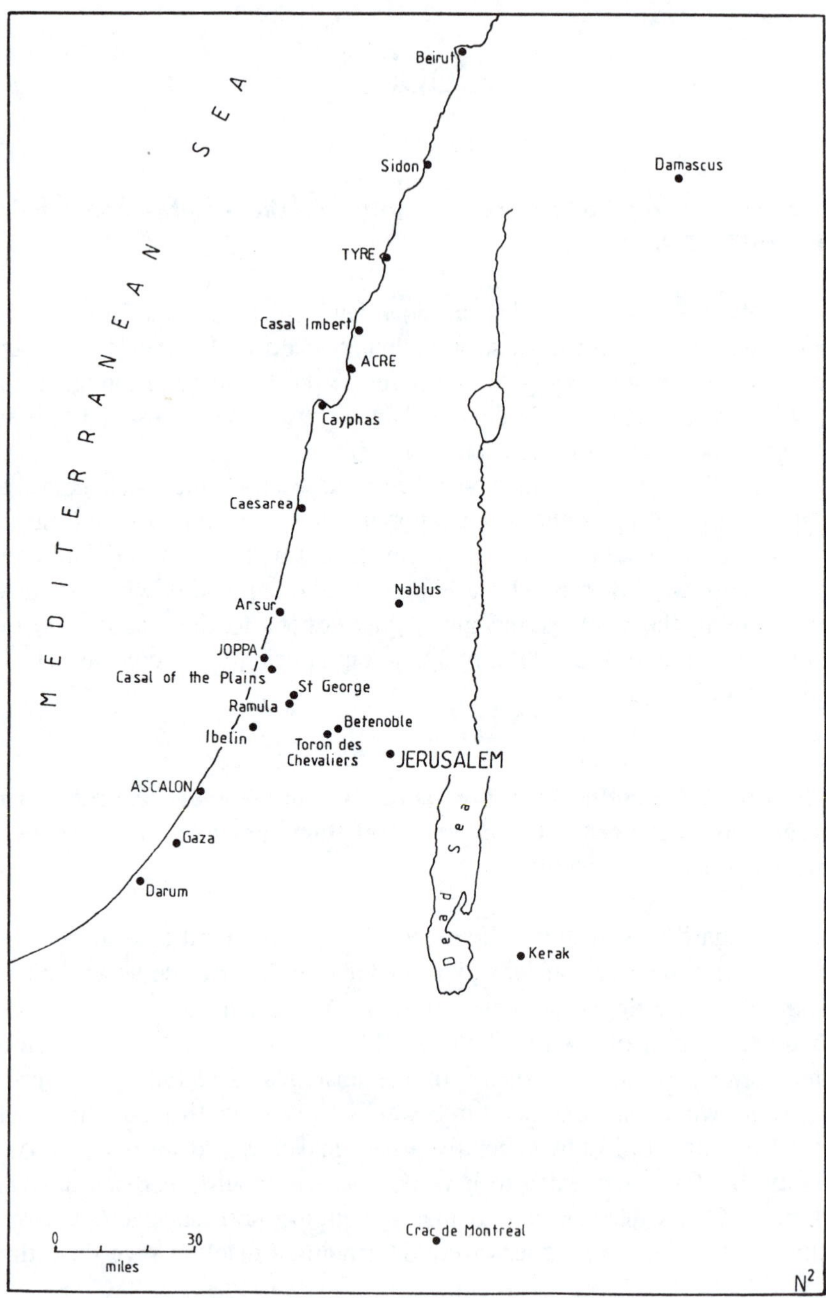

Map 4. Sites connected with the campaign of King Richard in the Holy Land, 1191–92.

to carry out their promises and make a search for the Cross.

You would frequently hear the Christians 'enquire for news of when the Holy Cross would come.' However, God did not wish the Cross to be given back in exchange for the liberation of those whose release had been promised, but preferred that they should perish. One person said: 'The Cross is coming now;' another said: 'It has been seen in the Saracen army,' but both of them were mistaken, for Saladin did not arrange for the Cross to be given back, and did not consider the hostages who had been promised in return. For he hoped to win better terms by using the Holy Cross as a negotiating tool.

Meanwhile Saladin sent the king frequent gifts and messengers, gaining time with deceitful and crafty words; but he never carried out any of his promises. He aimed at keeping the king hanging on for a long time through his myriad subtleties and ambiguities.[3]

Chapter 3: The king of England twice sent messengers to Tyre before our army could get Saladin's hostages back from the marquis. The marquis himself scornfully refused to return.[4]

Meanwhile ambassadors were sent to Tyre [5 August]. The marquis was commanded on our behalf to return to the army, bringing with him the king of France's hostages which had been entrusted to his keeping. He would then receive the share of the ransom which was due to the king of France, i.e. half the payment. Those sent on this embassy were the

---

3. This last paragraph is not in Ambroise. There seems to have been confusion over the terms agreed. Our author and Ambroise believe that the Cross was to be returned by the end of July. Roger of Howden states that the term was 40 days (*Gesta*, 2 p. 179, and *Chronica*, 3 pp. 121, 127), but that it was later extended (*Gesta*, 2 p. 187). Bahā' al-Dīn states, p. 271, that there were three terms of one month. At the end of the first Saladin was due to give up the Cross, 100,000 pieces of gold, and 600 captives. He had not yet made up the number of captives, but the Franks allowed negotiations to drag on until the end of the month. Saladin then offered to give captives and pledges for the hostages, so that they could be released; Richard refused and demanded the ransom. Saladin refused to pay it as he suspected that Richard would not release the hostages. Bahā' al-Dīn informs us that the Cross was in the sultan's camp, and that Saladin used it as a bargaining tool: pp. 270–1. 'Imād al-Dīn states that after King Richard broke the treaty by executing his hostages, the Cross was put into the sultan's treasury, to humiliate it: p. 330.
4. Ambroise, lines 5413–86; Roger of Howden, *Gesta*, 2 pp. 186–7 has the date and a different list of French messengers.

bishop of Salisbury, Earl Robert [of Leicester], and Peter des Préaux, an outstanding knight.

The marquis made an irate reply to these three ambassadors. In no way would he come - giving as his excuse that he feared the presence of King Richard. Besides, he boasted that if and when the True Cross was received he would take half of it on the king of France's behalf and he would not give up the hostages until this was done.

When they realised how stubborn the marquis was, the ambassadors tried to soothe him with flattery. They offered to leave one of their number as security for his safe journey to King Richard and his return. In no way would he consent; in fact he confirmed with an oath that he would not come. The ambassadors returned empty-handed, having achieved nothing, and informed the king of how the matter stood.

The king was extremely angry. On the king's request, a second embassy was sent to Tyre, consisting of the duke of Burgundy, Drogo d'Amiens and Robert de Quency [or Quincy]. They were to ask the aforesaid marquis to come with them. His presence certainly seemed essential for progress in these matters. He aspired to obtain the kingdom but he was running away from getting it, and those bringing foodstuffs in by sea needed free passage through Tyre, yet the marquis used to prevent their entering port.

The aforesaid messengers arrived in Tyre and explained the terms of their embassy. On King Richard's behalf they firmly requested the marquis to come to their aid in Syria - as he himself hoped to gain the lordship of that country. He replied rudely and arrogantly, asserting that in no way would he come, but would take care of his own city. So for some time each put forward opposing proposals, supporting the claims of their respective sides. At last the negotiations reached some sort of conclusion, whereby the three ambassadors were to take the Saracen hostages back with them to King Richard. Yet they had been unable either by reasoning or persuasion to prevail upon the marquis to abandon his obstinate inactivity.

Chapter 4: Our people kill Saladin's hostages.[5]

As the time limit had expired long before, King Richard was certain that Saladin had hardened his heart and had no concern about ransoming the hostages. He assembled a council of the greater people, which decided not to waste time waiting any longer for anything, but that the hostages should be beheaded. Only some of the greatest and most noble should be spared in case they could be ransomed or exchanged for some other Christian captives.[6]

King Richard always aspired to stamp out the Turks, to crush their shameless arrogance and to confound the law of Muḥammad, so as to vindicate Christianity. On the Friday immediately after the Assumption of the Blessed Virgin Mary [16 August] he ordered 2700 Turkish hostages to be led bound out of the city to be beheaded.[7] Men-at-arms leapt forward readily and fulfilled his orders without delay. They did this with glad mind and with the assent of divine grace, to take revenge for the deaths of the Christians whom the Turks had killed with shots from their bows and crossbows.

5. Ambroise, lines 5513-42.
6. Note that our author is anxious to point out that Richard did not act alone in executing the hostages; he had followed the proper procedure in taking the advice of the other leaders.
7. Roger of Howden, *Gesta*, 2 p. 189, and *Chronica*, 3 p. 127, states that the hostages were executed on 20 August. Bahā' al-Dīn could not understand why Richard executed the hostages: some said that it was to avenge the deaths of those slain by the Muslims, while others said that he did not want to leave so many prisoners in Acre while he marched on Ascalon. The Muslims regarded the executions as a terrible act of barbarism. The fact that our author keeps emphasising that the time limit had expired and insists that the decision to execute the hostages was taken jointly suggests that many in Europe also regarded it as a barbarous act. 'Ansbert', p. 99, certainly did; Bahā' al-Dīn, p. 281, indicates that many of the crusaders did not approve of Richard's action. Roger of Howden justifies it by saying that Saladin executed his Christian prisoners two days before Richard executed the Muslim hostages, and gives Duke Hugh of Burgundy and King Richard joint responsibility for the executions.

Chapter 5: King Richard makes advance arrangements for the army to move against Ascalon travelling both by sea and by land.[8]

As evening approached that day, a proclamation was made that the army would move on the following day. In the name of the Lord, giver of all good things, they would cross the river of Acre and advance towards Ascalon taking the coastal region as they went. Following this order they loaded enough food for ten days on to ships which would bring it to the army: biscuit, flour, meat and wine, and whatever food seemed necessary. The sailors were firmly instructed always to sail alongside the army as it advanced through the land, with their loaded barges and sneckas carrying food supplies and armed men. So it was arranged that they would advance with the army divided into two parts, half going by sea and half by land. It was not possible to acquire the land in any other way since it was occupied by the Turks.

Chapter 6: How many of our magnates died during a year and a half at the siege of Acre.[9]

It ought to be known that countless Christians had already died in the army. The army had remained at enormous loss and expense to capture the city of Acre for two winters plus a summer down to mid-autumn[10] when the Turks were beheaded as described above. In the eyes of God and humanity the Turks certainly deserved their fate because of their destruction of churches and slaying of people.

A recital of the enormous number of all those who died in the army in that short time would seem beyond belief. The total of the magnates alone, according to one writer, can be set out as follows, but that writer declared it was impossible to discover the losses among the masses.

In the army died:
six archbishops and the patriarch [Heraclius];
twelve bishops;
and besides these, forty counts died;

---

8. Ambroise, lines 5543–65.
9. Ambroise, lines 5567–611: more rhetorical than here.
10. Ambroise, line 5570, says '*le mi Aust*', i.e. mid-August, which is more accurate.

500 great nobles;
as well as a great crowd of priests, clergy and people whose number cannot be known.[11]

Chapter 7: King Richard forces the French to leave Acre, and pitches his tents outside the city.[12]

King Richard had now recovered his former good health. After the execution of the Turks he left Acre with his entire retinue and decided to pitch his tents on the plains outside the city.[13] He forced all his people to leave the city, even those who were unwilling to do so. So the army remained on the said plains outside our trenches, in order to make preparations for setting out on the march. He enticed some of the French out with flattery, some by prayer, others at a price and some he compelled to leave by force.

The king arranged for a great number of infantrymen to lodge around his pavilions in his tents and awnings to reinforce the guard because of the Turks' frequent raids. All day they kept approaching and suddenly shouting out a challenge, taking them by surprise. It was the royal custom to be always the first to go out armed against the Turks when they attacked, to punish them as far as divine providence allowed.

---

11. *LFWT*, p. 141, has similar but not identical figures to those here. Roger of Howden, *Gesta*, 2 pp. 147-50 gives a list of the names of those who died.
12. Ambroise, lines 5612-28, but not identical. Roger of Howden, *Gesta*, 2 p. 188, dates this to 14 August: before the executions.
13. 'He forced...by force' is not in Ambroise.

Chapter 8: An Hungarian count and the king's marshal who are pursuing Turks who charged down on our people are captured by them.[14]

It happened one day [18 August][15] that the Turks charged down suddenly on our people, making an commotion as was their wont. Our camp was in confusion as our people ran to arms. The king armed swiftly and advanced on horseback, and a certain armed count from Hungary and a great number of Hungarians went out with him against the Turks, who fled at once. They pursued them, but further than they should have done. Although they fought outstandingly some of our people were seized there and shamefully treated. That Hungarian count, a man of great prowess and renown, was seized and carried off by the Turks, as was a certain Poitevin knight named Hugh, who was King Richard's marshal. Forgetting his own safety the king put spur powerfully to horse and bore himself recklessly on, trying with all his strength to rescue his marshal Hugh, if he could; but the Turks fled more swiftly and Hugh was torn away from him and carried off.

O how uncertain is the lot of battle! 'Order is reversed, the victors are now vanquished; those who were conquered one moment often conquer the next.' So those knights routed the enemy only to perish themselves when they were seized by the pursued as they pursued them. What should by right have brought them glory was put down to stupidity, 'Thus their deed of valour was the cause of their danger.'

Now, the Turks were not weighed down with armour like our people, and because they were more lightly armed they were often able to inflict much greater damage and injury on our people. The Turks are almost unarmed, only carrying a bow and a club bristling with sharp teeth, and a sword; they also have a reedy spear with an iron tip and a light dagger. If they are hotly pursued a long way they flee on very fast horses. There are none nimbler in the world, with the swiftest gallop - like the flight of swallows.

It is the Turks' habit, when they realise that their pursuit has stopped following them, to stop running away themselves - like an infuriating fly

14. Ambroise, lines 5629-66.
15. Roger of Howden, *Gesta*, 2 p. 189; *Chronica*, 3 p. 127. Howden does not mention the losses our author gives. He records one death, that of Peter Mignot, a comrade of the king. Bahā' al-Dīn, p. 275, refers to a 'desperate encounter' in which one division of the enemy was cut off and severely beaten. Like the previous chapter, Howden places this episode before the executions.

which flies away if you drive it off and returns when you stop. As long as you chase it, it flees; as soon as you stop it is there again. The Turks are just like that. When you stop pursuing and turn back, then the Turk follows you; if you pursue, the Turk flees. So while the king pursued them with determination they fled, but when he decided to go back they threatened him from behind. Sometimes they did not escape unpunished, but sometimes they also damaged our people a great deal.[16]

Chapter 9: Our army can barely be forced to leave the city because it is addicted to pleasure. At last it crosses the river of Acre, while the Turks harass it on all sides.[17]

King Richard was still staying in his pavilions, waiting for the army to come out of the city. However, they came out slowly and rather unwillingly. The size of the army hardly grew, yet the city was filled with the greatest crowd. The whole army including those who had not yet come out of the city was reckoned to be 300,000 strong.

The people came out of the city in a trickle, because they were too addicted to idleness and easy living, and the city had too many pleasures, i.e. excellent wine and the most beautiful girls. Most of them led a dissolute life, resorting to women and wine, so that the city was polluted by their foolish pleasure-seeking and the gluttony of its inhabitants. Their shameless behaviour made wiser faces blush. After consultation it was arranged that in order to eradicate this unsightly blemish no woman should leave the city with the army; they should remain in the city. The only exception was laundresses on foot, who would not be a burden on the army nor a cause of sin.[18]

---

16. Bahā' al-Dīn agrees with this description of the Muslim tactics, but not as deliberate strategy. The Muslims were afraid and fled; then, when the enemy drew rein from fear of ambush, they recovered and attacked again (p. 291).
17. Ambroise, 5669–730; dates in Roger of Howden, *Gesta*, 2 p. 190.
18. Ambroise adds ungraciously, line 5698, that the washerwomen could also delouse the soldiers. The argument for leaving the women at Acre was that they would consume valuable stores and distract the men from the spiritual purpose of the pilgrimage. Casual sexual relations were outlawed for pilgrims (and so for crusaders); apparently even marital relations were out of bounds. However, Bahā' al-Dīn records a knight's daughter captured by Saladin during the march south from Acre (p. 281) and a non-noble woman in the army (p. 261). Probably Richard's main concern was to leave the prostitutes behind. Note that again he is depicted as only acting after consultation. The queens Joanna and Berengaria and Isaac Ducas Comnenus'

At last early in the morning on the preordained day the army armed itself and was arranged in suitable order. The king was in the rearguard so that the attacking Turks who were threatening them very closely could not disrupt the army.

That day's journey was short. When that unspeakable race saw our army move they poured down from the mountains in masses like rushing waves. They were scattered into groups, here perhaps twenty, there thirty, and so on; and spread out in this way they made every effort to oppress and damage our army as much as they could. They had suffered great grief over the deaths of their relatives, having seen their corpses cut to pieces, as described above. So they tormented our army more boldly than before, continually pursuing it and troubling it in any way they could.

Yet with the assistance of divine grace, the Turks got nothing that they wanted. Our army crossed the Acre river unharmed and pitched their tents again not far beyond the river, until the whole army could assemble. That was on Friday [23 August], which was the eve of St Bartholomew's day. On the following Monday it was two years since the Christians first besieged Acre.[19]

Chapter 10: Our army advances in marching order. They bravely repel the Turks who charge vigorously down on them. A description of the Standard.[20]

Early in the morning on the day after St Bartholomew's day - which was a Sunday - the army was drawn up in battalions in the Lord's name, in order to advance along the coast. If only you could have seen what a well prepared band of knights they were! It would be difficult to find such exceptional young warriors. You would have seen a chosen race, men-at-arms of much prowess and boldness, most becoming armour, so many pennants with fluttering flags and banners of many different shapes, so many white-tipped spears, gleaming mailshirts and helmets. It was an army terrible to the enemy, drawn up in battle-array.

King Richard led the vanguard and held supreme command. The

daughter remained at Acre, presumably for safety reasons. They rejoined the army later at Jaffa (Bk. 4 ch. 27, below). For women in the crusading army, see Nicholson, H. (forthcoming), 'Women on the Third Crusade'.

19. 104 weeks.
20. Ambroise, lines 5731-832; without the Standard.

Normans guarded the Standard. We have decided that it would not be irrelevant to describe the Standard, so that it may be better known.

It is a very long beam like a ship's mast placed on very solid planks on top of four wheels, held together by joints. It is covered with iron and appears invulnerable to sword, axe or fire. From the very top flutters the king's flag, which is commonly called the 'banner'. It is the custom to assign a force of elite knights to protect this implement, especially in the field of battle, so that it may not be broken down by hostile attack or knocked down by some injury; because if it happened to be knocked down by some accident then the army would be thrown into confusion and scattered because there would not be any rallying point. Their hearts tremble and they think that their commander has been overcome when they cannot see his emblem on display - and when the people are terrified that disaster has befallen their prince because his banner has been thrown down, they do not easily recover their strength and continue to resist their adversary. However, while the emblem remains erect the people have a sure refuge to which they can run; the infirm and wounded are brought here to be cared for and even those who happen to be killed in battle are brought here if they were renowned or illustrious men. So it stands, strongly contructed 'to rally the peoples' [Isaiah ch. 11 v. 10]. As it stands, it is called a 'Standard'.[21]

It is sensible to have it placed on wheels because it can be drawn forward as the enemy falls back or drawn back as they attack, according to the state of the battle. The Normans and English attended this Standard.

The duke of Burgundy and the French took the rearguard. As they did not follow quickly enough and lagged behind they almost incurred the greatest loss. The army was travelling next to the sea which was on their right, while on the left the Turkish race kept watch from the mountains on all our movements. Suddenly threatening clouds rushed in, and the sky grew overcast. The army had come to a narrow place in the road which was only wide enough for two pack horses carrying food to pass. On account of the narrow road the order of march became confused, and they proceeded spread out in a narrow line and in disorder. When they noticed this the Saracens suddenly rushed down on the carters and loaded carts, taking the people unawares, killing them and

21. Bahā' al-Dīn corroborates this description. 'In the centre of the army was a cart, on which was fixed a tower as high as a minaret, and from this floated the standard of the people,' (p. 283). Ambroise does not include this description.

their horses immediately and plundering a great deal of the baggage. They overran those who put up a stubborn resistance, scattered them and pursued them as far as the sea shore, slaughtering as they went.[22]

A very bitter conflict ensued, with everyone fighting manfully for their lives. A Turk cut off the right hand of one Everard - who was in the service of the bishop of Salisbury - with the drawn sword which he was holding in it. Without the slightest change in his expression he grabbed the sword in his left hand, brandished the sword in all directions, and closing in on the threatening Turks, defended himself courageously against all of them.

The rear of the army was in great confusion from this attack, absolutely bewildered by their misfortune. Then John fitz Luke put spurs to horse and informed King Richard, who was still ignorant of the situation, what had happened. At once he went back at a swift gallop to help the rearguard, surrounded by a detachment of his troops. With sword flashing like lightning he charged into the Turks, throwing them to the ground to the right and the left. In no time at all, just as the Philistines once fled before Maccabaeus,[23] so now the Turks were scattered and fled in all directions before King Richard into the mountains; although some of them remained with our people because they had lost their heads. One of the French whose name was William de Barres had previously been estranged from King Richard because of some enmity which had arisen between them, but through his magnificent prowess in that engagement he earned restoration to the king's friendship and grace.[24]

Saladin was not far from there with all the forces of his army. Yet the Turks gave up hope of gaining anything after this repulse, and held back

---

22. For this battle see Bahā' al-Dīn, p. 275.
23. Judas Maccabaeus, the liberator of the Jews from the rule of pagan kings in the second century BC, was regarded in the Middle Ages as the epitome of the knight of God.
24. Roger of Howden, *Gesta*, 2 pp. 155-6 and *Chronica*, 3 pp. 93-4 gives the details of the original quarrel, which occurred at Messina on 2 February 1191. King Richard and many of his household and some of the king of France's household assembled in their usual manner outside the walls of Messina to watch the city people's sports. As they were returning home through the city they met a peasant coming in from the country with an ass laden with canes. The king of England and the others each took one and charged each other as if the canes were lances. In this game William des Barres, one of the bravest knights of the king of France's household, unhorsed King Richard. Richard was unable to unhorse William and ordered him out of his sight. The king of France tried to negotiate on William's behalf but failed, and three days later William left Messina.

from assailing our people any further. Instead they watched us from a distance. Our army marched on with its order restored as far as a river which they happened to find [the Kishon] and cisterns which they tested and found to hold good water. They pitched their tents there and settled on the spacious plain, where they saw that Saladin had pitched his tents before them. They calculated from the wide extent of the trampled area that the Turkish army must be enormous.

God arranged for this to happen to our army on that first day, so that they would act more cautiously. So once and for all they learnt by experience to take what precautions they could as they travelled to guard against loss.

Chapter 11: From the Acre river our army reaches Cayphas.[25]

Saladin was always causing trouble for our army. He and the Turks laid ambushes in the mountain pass which our army was to pass through. As our people entered the pass in a narrow column they planned to attack and either kill, seize or scatter them.

Our people advanced from the aforementioned river cautiously and in order. Travelling in moderate stages they reached Cayphas [Haifa], where they pitched their tents while they waited for the common people who were following them.[26]

Our army stayed between the sea and the town of Cayphas, remaining there for two days. They turned over their baggage and examined it, throwing away what they thought they could do without and keeping the essentials. For the common people were travelling on foot and were heavily burdened with their bags of food and especially with their weapons. In the aforementioned battle a great many suffered with the effort of carrying these, while they were also destroyed by thirst.

---

25. Ambroise, lines 5833–60.
26. Bahā' al-Dīn, p. 283, states that the Christian army could never make long marches because of the infantry. Some of the noncombatants carried the baggage and tents because they had few baggage animals. He adds: 'One cannot help admiring the patience displayed by these people, who bore the most wearing fatigue without having any participation in the management of affairs, or deriving any personal advantage.' As these people were on pilgrimage they reckoned the hardship was part of the penance involved, while reaching the Holy Sepulchre would be their reward.

Chapter 12: From Cayphas our army goes along the coast, where they are wounded by thorns and find wild animals, and through Capharnaum. They reach the Casal of the Narrow Ways.[27]

One Tuesday, i.e. the third day after the halt at Cayphas, the army set out drawn up in battalions. That day the Templars formed the vanguard and the Hospitallers the rearguard. Both of them acted energetically and displayed an image of great valour. That day the army acted more cautiously than usual. A great deal of the road had not been made up, and they found it considerably obstructed by thorns and many luxuriant green plants which kept striking them in the face and were a particular problem for those on foot. In the most grassy and densely bushy areas of those coastal regions they found an enormous number of woodland animals, which kept leaping up from between their feet. So they caught plenty of game which they had not hunted but which was offered to them, so to speak.

The king came *en route* to the town of Capharnaum [Bir-el-Keneiseh?][28] which had been razed to the ground by the Saracens. He dismounted from his horse and ate, while the army waited, and those who wished also ate. Then they at once pressed on with their journey as far as the Casal[29] of the Narrow Ways [Casal Destroit, or 'Atlīt]; the path is certainly narrow here. They pitched their tents here and rested.

It was the custom in the army that each night before they went to bed someone who had been assigned to this duty would shout out loudly in the middle of the army the popular imprecation: 'Holy Sepulchre, help us!'[30] At this cry everyone would shout together, repeating the same words, and holding their hands towards Heaven begging with copious tears for God's mercy and aid. Then the public crier would repeat it, calling out the same as before: 'Holy Sepulchre, help us!' and they each repeated this the same; similarly he would shout a third time and everyone repeated the same words, with great remorse and shedding of tears. Who would not do the same in such a situation? Even simply recounting this action could move listeners to pious tears. The army seemed to refresh itself considerably by shouting like this.

27. Ambroise, lines 5861–904.
28. Stubbs (1864), p. 252.
29. Casal: a village.
30. Another example of this prayer in similar circumstances appears in one of the thirteenth century continuations of the prose *Merlin*: King Arthur's army is fighting the pagan Saxons. '...our men fell back and they cried out on all sides: "Help us, Holy Sepulchre"...' (*Le Livre d'Artus* (1979), p. 13 line 47.)

Chapter 13: About the tarantulas who damaged the people with their poisonous stings.[31]

As each night approached a sort of little vermin threatened them. They crawl in swarms along the ground giving the most horrible stabs and are popularly called 'tarantulas'. By day they did no harm; but as night came on they would make an assault armed with very irritating stings. Anyone they stung immediately swelled up with the raging poison and was in terrible agony, although the noblemen and the more wealthy eased the swelling and reduced the pain by immediately applying 'theriaca',[32] which was an effective antidote.

At last the more vigilant noticed that a loud noise would make the pestilential vermin run away. So when the tarantulas approached, they would begin to make an enormous bang and clatter, each of them banging and beating on shields and helmets, stools and boards, casks, flasks, basins, plates and cooking pots, and any appliance or item of furniture suitable for making a noise which came to hand, since the racket drove the vermin away.

As the place was large and very convenient for their camp the army stayed two days at the aforesaid casal, until the ships which they were waiting for arrived. These were barges and galleys loaded with food which they needed, i.e. the ships which were sailing alongside them carrying food as they travelled through the land.

Chapter 14: Our army goes from the Casal of the Narrow Ways to Merla and from there to Caesarea, and from there reaches the Dead River. The Turks attacked our people and our people triumphed.[33]

On their guard against the Turks who always remained on their flank, the army advanced as far as the town called Merla [al-Mallāha] where the king had spent one of the previous nights. There the king had already arranged that on the following day he would lead the vanguard in case of trouble, and the Templars would form the rearguard; for the Turks were constantly threatening and approaching from the flank.

---

31. Ambroise, lines 5905-42.
32. A classical Latin cure-all and antidote against poisonous snakebites.
33. Ambroise, lines 5943-6033.

That day when the king put spur to horse and charged into the Turks he would have won well-earned praise and glory for his deeds, if the idleness of certain people had not hindered and disgraced the whole proceeding. For while the king was driving the Turks far away, some of his people halted and stopped the pursuit. That evening they were reprimanded for this behaviour as they deserved. If they had accompanied the king as they should and pursued the fleeing Turks they would have finished off that extraordinary job magnificently. However, the king drove all the Turks before him.

The journey along the seashore was very difficult for the army because of the burning heat. Not only was it hot, but they marched a very long distance that day. A great many of them, sweltering and exhausted with the hunger and effort of the long journey, dropped down dead; they were buried where they fell. However because he was sorry for them the king had a great many who were tired from the journey or affected by ill-health or other problems transported in galleys and ships as far as that day's destination.

Having completed that day's journey with the greatest difficulty, the army reached Caesarea [Qesari]. The Turkish race had been there before them, partly demolished the walls and towers and destroyed as much of the town as possible. They fled on our people's approach. Our people pitched their tents there and passed the night next to the river very near to the city, which is called the River of Crocodiles [Nahr al-Zarqā'] because crocodiles had once eaten two knights who were bathing there.

Caesarea is a city of enormous extent and its buildings are of astonishing construction and workmanship. Christ used to frequent the place with His disciples, and made it famous with miracles.[34] The king instructed his ships to join the army there. Meanwhile he put out an edict in the city of Acre by public crier that the lazy people who were loitering there should by royal command get on board the ships which he had sent them and come to the army for the love of God and to exalt the religion of the Christian faith and to discharge their vows of pilgrimage more fully. At the king's command many came to Caesarea with the royal fleet, which was well laden with supplies of food. He arranged for

---

34. Our author is confused. The Caesarea visited by Christ was Caesarea Philippi, now Banyas, which is inland on the road between Tyre and Damascus. This Caesarea is a port, not mentioned in the Gospels but featuring in the Acts of the Apostles: ch. 8 v. 40, ch. 9 v. 30, ch. 10, ch. 21 vv. 8-16 and ch. 23 v. 23-ch. 26 v. 32.

the fleet to proceed alongside the army as it advanced.

A very great crowd of ships assembled and the army was armed and drawn up in troops. Then on a certain day [1 September][35] at around the third hour [9 am] they advanced from Caesarea. They went at a moderate pace because of the constant threat from the Turks: each day when they saw the army move on from its encampment they charged as close as they dared, inflicting what trouble and injury they could. That day they harassed the army more violently than usual, but with God's help we got out unharmed, and they left us one of their emirs whose head had been cut off. He was a very daring and extremely doughty man of renowned name. He was said to have been of such great strength that no one would ever be strong enough to throw him off his horse, in fact they would not even dare to attack him. He carried a lance which was thicker than two of ours.[36] His name was Aias Estoy [Ayāz al-Ṭawīl: 'the long man']. The Turks were so struck with grief and sorrow at his ruin that they cut off their horses' tails and would eagerly have carried off the corpse of their emir if it had been allowed.[37]

Our people proceeded from there to the river called the Dead River [Nahr al-Mafijr]. The Saracens had covered it over before our arrival so that it could not be seen and our people would be in danger of falling in unawares. Yet God also preserved us there: the river was uncovered and our people drank from it.[38] They remained there for two nights.

---

35. Bahā' al-Dīn, p. 282.
36. Ambroise says (line 6026): 'There were not two thicker in France,' which amounts to much the same. Contrast with Bk. 4 ch. 8 above, where the Turks are described as having thin spears.
37. Bahā' al-Dīn describes Ayāz al-Ṭawīl's burial, so clearly the Muslims recovered his body later. He was one of the sultan's mamluks (pp. 284-5). For cutting off a horse's tail (and ears) as a sign of grief, see the letter of Thierry, grand commander of the Temple, to King Henry II in *Conquest of Jerusalem*, p. 166.
38. In fact this appears to have been a dry river bed; the crusaders found water by digging down. As natives of northern Europe, Ambroise and Richard de Templo would not have been familiar with rivers which dry up in the summer.

Chapter 15: Our army goes from the Dead River. Before they reach the Salt River they suffer a great deal of trouble from the Turks who kill our horses and men.[39]

On the third day [3 September], the army proceeded slowly from the Dead River through an empty wasteland. That day the army was forced to advance through the mountains because they could not get through the road along the coast because it was blocked by luxuriant plant growth. As the army travelled the companies kept closer together than usual. The Templars were in command of the rearguard. They lost so many horses that day as the Turks charged them from behind that they almost despaired.

No less, the count of St Pol lost a great many horses there. Yet he himself was a man of such valour that he boldly exposed himself to the constantly threatening Turks. He untiringly opposed them as they each charged in turn, so that through his exertions the rest of the army could advance safely. So that day he earned supreme gratitude and acclaim from the whole people.

King Richard was wounded that day in the side by a dart, while he was driving away the Turks with slaughter. However, the wound was only a touch and actually incited him to attack the enemy as he was greedy to seek revenge for the pain of the wound. So he contended more strongly the whole day without stopping, charging the Turks continually in order to force them to withdraw.

On the other side the Turks raged in their stubborn wickedness, keeping alongside our army as it advanced, struggling to inflict what injury they could on us, firing darts and arrows which flew very densely, like rain. Alas! Many horses fell dead transfixed with darts, many were gravely wounded and died not much later! You would have seen such a great downpour of darts and arrows that where the army passed through you could not have found a space of four feet of ground free of fallen darts. All that day this unpleasant storm threatened them until as night came on the Turks withdrew to their tents and dwellings. Our people pitched their tents next to a certain watercourse called the Salt River [Nahr al-Qaṣab] and spent the night there. They came there on the Tuesday after the feast of St Giles and stayed there for two days [3–4 September].

A great crowd formed around the fat corpses of the dead horses who

39. Ambroise, lines 6034–90.

had died of their wounds. The common people made a great commotion as they struggled greedily to buy the meat, which was not cheap; even coming to blows. When the king heard this he decided to put out a proclamation by public crier that he would give a live horse to anyone who distributed their dead one among the most doughty men-at-arms who needed the meat. So they ate horsemeat as if it was game. Flavoured with hunger rather than sauce, they thought it was delicious.

Chapter 16: From the Salt River our army goes through the Arsur forest and reaches the River Rochetailie safely.[40]

On the third day [5 September] at the third hour, the army advanced from the Salt River. It was drawn up in battle order, for the rumour was that the Turks were lying in ambush for them in the forest of Arsur [Arsūf]. It was said that they were going to set fire to the wood to prevent the army from passing through. However, our people proceeded in order through the forest and passed unharmed through the place where the ambush was said to have been laid.[41]

Leaving the wood they found the welcome plain, where they pitched their tents and passed the night next to the river popularly called the Rochetailie [Split Rock: Nahr al-Fālik]. They sent scouts out to reconnoitre, who reported that the Turks' army was awaiting their arrival not far away. Their army covered the whole face of the earth all around and was beyond numbering, but they estimated it at 300,000 - whereas the number of Christians did not exceed 100,000.

The Christian army reached the River Rochetailie on the Thursday before the Nativity of the Blessed Mary [5 September 1191] and stayed there the following day.

40. Ambroise, lines 6091-121.
41. On 5 September King Richard and al-'Ādil, or 'Saphadin', had their first interview. Humfrey of Toron acted as interpreter (Bahā' al-Dīn, p. 288).

Chapter 17: Setting out from the River Rochetailie towards Arsur [Arsūf], our army is drawn up for battle against the Turks, as they had discovered that the Turks were going to attack them that day with all their strength.[42]

On the Saturday, i.e. the Eve of the Nativity of the Blessed Mary [7 September 1191], at the crack of dawn everyone put on their armour with great care, as if they expected the Turks to attack at once. They had already discovered that the Turks had seized control of their road ahead, and they could not get away from the Turks' brashness without a very difficult battle. They were already drawing up their battlelines to attack our people and were gradually approaching ever nearer. So all our people took careful precautions for their own safety and the whole army was most judiciously arranged in order. Of course King Richard, who was most experienced in the affairs of war, arranged the army into troops and decided who would be best appointed to command the vanguard and who to command the rear. He established twelve squadrons, which were divided proportionally into five battalions. These different units of extremely bellicose men were held together by military discipline. No warriors more effective in battle could be found under Heaven, as long as their hearts retained firm confidence in God, who advances the interests of all good people.

That day the Templars commanded the first battalion of the army. After them the Bretons and Angevins marched in order; after them in the third battalion King Guy with the Poitevins; in the fourth battalion the Normans and English who had been assigned to convey the royal Standard; the Hospitallers formed the last battalion. That rearguard was made up of an elite body of knights, divided into separate squadrons. The detachments kept themselves so closely together that an apple thrown into their midst would not fall to the ground without touching people or horses.

Our army stretched from the Saracen army as far as the sea shore. You would have seen very appropriate distinguishing symbols – flags of

42. Ambroise, lines 6122–210. See also Bahā' al-Dīn, pp. 289–93. Interpretations of this battle vary. Ambroise and the *Itinerarium* depict it as the most significant pitched battle of the crusade, but R. C. Smail (1955, 1995), pp. 163–5 argued that it was not a pitched battle as the Christian army continued marching on its route throughout. In a letter to the abbot of Clairvaux, Richard stated that the vanguard of the army was already setting up camp at Arsūf when Saladin attacked the rearguard: *Conquest of Jerusalem*, p. 180.

various designs, and emblems in myriad forms - and an extremely tough race which was courageous, vigorous and well-fitted for war. The earl of Leicester was there, Hugh de Gournay, William de Borris, Walkelin de Ferrers, Roger de Toony, James of Avesnes, Count Robert of Dreux and his brother the bishop of Beauvais, William des Barres, William de Garlande, Drogo de Merlo and a great many of his relations. Count Henry of Champagne kept guard on the side of the army towards the mountain, always keeping watch on the flank. There were also men-at-arms on foot. The archers and crossbowmen were drawn up in the last rank of all, bringing up the rear of the army. Carters and wagons carrying foodstuffs and baggage travelled between the army and the sea so that they would not be attacked by the enemy.

Drawn up in this way the army advanced very slowly so that it would not become separated, because when battle lines do not hold closely together they are less able to defend themselves. King Richard and the duke of Burgundy rode this way and that with a chosen company of knights, keeping a constant look out on all sides, to the right and to the left, carefully weighing up the Turks' position and behaviour so that they could advise the advancing army as they saw necessary. Their precautions were certainly absolutely essential.

Chapter 18: Our people suffered great evil from the Turks who were continually rushing down on them from all sides, especially from behind, wounding them and knocking them down. They would have weakened under the weight of battle and despaired; but they marched backwards and God's grace aided them.[43]

As the third hour [9 am] approached the huge Turkish multitude - around 10,000 of them - came charging down on our people at swift gallop! With a confusion of cries they eagerly threw darts and fired arrows, making a terrifying racket. After these ran a devilish race, very black in colour, who for this reason have a rather appropriate name: because they are black [*nigri*] they are called 'Negroes'. Also there were the Saracens who travel about in the desert, popularly called 'Bedouins': savage and darker than soot, the most redoubtable infantrymen, carrying bows and quivers and round shields. They are a very energetic and agile race.

43. Ambroise, lines 6211-353.

These threatened our army constantly without giving way.

Beyond these you would have seen the serried ranks of Turks approaching across open country. They were well drawn-up with so many emblems fixed to their lances, so many standards, so many banners with a variety of details, so many lines appropriately divided into troops and troops arranged in companies that there seemed at a guess to be more than 20,000 armed Turks approaching in order. They rushed down on our people in an inescapable charge on horses swifter than eagles, driven like lightning. Their swift gallop violently stirred up the dust which filled the sky like a dark cloud.

Certain people were assigned to go before the emirs sounding trumpets and clarions; others held horns, others flutes, tamborines, rattles or cymbals, others had other instruments for making a noise. They were assigned to the single task of raising shouts and horrible yells. The land all around resounded with the echo of their harsh cries and roaring noise. Even a thunder crash would not have been heard above the great uproar of trumpets and sounding horns. They had introduced this practice to arouse their courage and boldness: the louder the noise, the braver they became for the fight.

So the unspeakable Turks fell on our army from all sides, from the direction of the sea and from dry land. There was not a space for two miles around, not even a fistful, which was not covered with the hostile Turkish race. How relentlessly they attacked! As they kept up their persistent assaults they inflicted very grave losses on our people, for they shot our horses with darts and arrows, killing an enormous number of them.

How essential those valiant crossbowmen and archers were that day! Those absolutely inflexible men-at-arms who brought up the rear of the army drove back the relentless Turks as best as they could with a continuous volley of shots. But soon their adversaries threatened them so strongly, like water flooding over them, increasing their blows and raving like wild savages that a great many of the crossbowmen were unable to bear the weight of disaster and misery. Fearing that they would be surrounded and cut off by the enemy, they threw down their bows and crossbows and charged into the body of the army. Fear of death led them to give way in the face of unbearable injuries.

However, either because shame forbad them to give way or because their hope of winning a crown[44] gave them strength, those who were

44. The martyr's crown, for death in battle against non-Christians.

bolder and of more outstanding valour persevered in their agony. They struggled with great resolve and contended with untiring valour, turning to face the Turkish assault which threatened them from behind. So they walked backwards as if they were retreating, because otherwise they could not protect their backs adequately. In fact because of the Turkish threat from behind they advanced with their faces turned back towards them all that day, travelling back-to-front, fighting every step of the way.

O what great distress they suffered that day! What bitter tribulation! Anxious fears rushed on even the most resolute of them. There was no one there so confident or so exceptionally bold that at that moment they would not have much preferred to have completed their pilgrimage and gone back home rather than be awaiting the doubtful outcome of the battle with trembling heart. Such an excessively small number of people was under attack on all sides by an enormous number of Saracens that there was nowhere to flee even if they had attempted to do so. Nor did they appear to have sufficient forces to resist so many. No; they were surrounded, like a flock of sheep in the jaws of wolves, so that they could see nothing about them except the sky and their wicked enemies on every side.

Lord God! What was in the minds of those in that puny flock of Christ then? They were so bewildered and distressed; the enemy pressed relentlessly down on them with as much force as if they were trying to push them through a sieve. Whoever bore such barbarous exactors? Who was ever crushed by such destitution? There you would have seen our knights who had lost their warhorses walking on foot with the infantry. They were firing missiles from crossbows or arrows from bows at the enemy, returning blow for blow as far as means and strength allowed. Always eager to practise the art of the archer and crossbowman, the Turks for their part pressed on without a pause; bolts rained down, arrows flew, the air hummed. The sun's light was dimmed by the great number of missiles, as it does in winter in thick hail or snow. Horses were pierced by the points of darts and arrows. So many of these missiles covered the surface of the ground all around that anyone who wanted to collect them up could gather at least twenty in one grasp.

The Turks attacked so strongly that they had almost destroyed the Hospitallers' lines. They informed King Richard that they could not hold back the enemy's violent attack any longer unless the knights made a charge against them. 'But the king advises against this, and instructs them to be patient and continue to hold tightly together.' So they continue to endure, but the danger is so great that they can bear the miserable anguish only with difficulty. However, they advanced, fighting every step of the way. They groan continually, although they are hardly able to breathe. What was more, that day was extremely hot, so that they laboured under a double load: the boiling hot weather and the enemy's persecution. So Christ's proven martyrs sweated in agony. They were in dire straits: they had to endure both the heat of the day [Matthew's Gospel ch. 20 v. 12] and the pressure on them of that destructive and threatening race which was advancing relentlessly, each urging the other on to destroy the Christians. Anyone considering their position could reasonably doubt, despair, waver and foresee a sinister end for our little group of people who were surrounded like this by such an enormous crowd. Their opponents 'scored their backs with scorges' [Psalm 129 v. 3]. No longer did they employ arrows and darts from a distance; drawing even closer, they stabbed them with lances, crushed them with heavy clubs and assailed them with swords hand-to-hand. The echoes resounded of Turks beating on their hard armour like smiths on an anvil. They burned in torment, but were given no rest.

The battle was heaviest in the Hospitallers' final line, the more so because they were not permitted to fight back. When they were injured, they went on patiently; when they were crushed by clubs, they remained silent; when they were struck they did not strike back, but they gave way because they could not endure such great danger and feared threatening death. Giving way in confusion before the enemy's raging advance, they charged into the unit in front of them, fleeing the violent and unrestrained rage of the Turks who were threatening them from behind.

Certainly no one could sustain a constant and continual attack from such an enormous host of threatening enemies without fighting back. All the forces of Paganism had gathered together, from Damascus and Persia, from the Mediterranean Sea to the East. There was not a famous or powerful man or a people of valour or a bold race proven in the practice of war or anyone of action remaining even in the extreme corners of the earth whom Saladin had not summoned to aid him in crushing the Christian people; by prayer or price or because they were subject to his authority. He had hoped to wipe the Christians completely off the face of the earth, but all in vain, for through God's assistance they were not enough to bring about his desire. For the flower of Christendom's most exceptional young warriors and a doughty group of knights had flocked to that place together. Like grains separated from the chaff, they were assembled together there and then from the furthest ends of the earth. If anyone had routed them or crushed them to death, without doubt no one would have been left anywhere in the world who could have put up further resistance to the pagans.

Chapter 19: About the same battle, and the Christians' marvellous victory. [The battle of Arsūf, 7 September 1191].[45]

The sky was darkened with dust and the travellers were sweltering, especially because of the hot weather. As was said, a very fierce race of people threatened them from behind, proud and insolent, rendered unyielding by demonic instigation. Nevertheless that most doughty Christian people remained secure in the certain freedom of their faith and kept on advancing gradually. The enemy menaced them incessantly, cudgelling them from behind; however, the blows bounced off their protective armour.

Their lack of success made the Turks groan and mutter resentfully that their attacks were a waste of time. Then they raged with even worse barbarity, saying that our people were made of iron and could not be harmed. At last more than 20,000 Turks made a sudden massed charge, wielding clubs and swords in hand-to-hand combat. They redoubled their blows on the Hospitallers, crushing and striking them and piling on the pressure in various ways. Almost overcome by their barbarity, one of them named Brother Garnier de Nablus [master of the Hospital][46] cried out in a loud voice: 'St George, unique among knights, surely you aren't going to leave us to be defeated? Christianity is perishing because she is not fighting back against this unspeakable race!'

At this the master of the Hospital [Brother Garnier de Nablus] went to the king. 'Lord king,' he said, 'we are being violently attacked. We will be stained with eternal dishonour as if we did not dare to fight back. Each of us is losing his mount at no cost to the enemy. What more must we bear?'

'Good master,' the king replied, 'you must sustain their attack; no one

45. Bahā' al-Dīn's account of the battle (pp. 289–93) is close to this one, describing three charges by the Christians. Ambroise (6354–630) omits the final charge. He also states that the Christians marched on to Tyre after the battle (line 6615). This is presumably a copyist's error for Arsur.

46. Our writer is apparently unaware that Brother Garnier de Nablus was master of the Hospital at this time. This suggests that he was writing many years later. Ambroise makes the master's name clear (lines 6383–4).

can be everywhere.'

As the master returned to his troops, the Turks bore down on them again, hewing at them from behind. There was not a prince or count who did not blush scarlet with shame. They said to each other, 'Why don't we give rein to our horses and charge them? Alas! Alas! We shall deserve to be criticised forever for being idle cowards. Did anyone ever before have anything like this happen to them? Never before have unbelievers inflicted such shame and dishonour on such a great army. Unless we quickly defend ourselves and charge them, we will have eternal disgrace. In fact, the longer we delay before acting the greater it will be.'

O how blind is human fate! How it wavers about on slippery joints! How it spins on uncertain wheels, unrolling the course of human lives with such indeterminate results! If they had kept rank as they proceeded, as they had all decided beforehand, a countless crowd of Turks would have perished. However, it is believed that because of the exactions of their sins[47] when the potter's wheel sped, although a great wine jar was intended a small jug was produced [Horace, *de Arte Poetica*, v. 21]. For although our people discussed among themselves and came to a unanimous decision about how they were going to make their attack on the enemy, everything was thrown into confusion by two knights who could not bear to wait.

It was arranged by common consent that six trumpets should be blown in three different places in the army when they were going to engage the Turks, i.e. two trumpets at the front of the army, two at the rear and two in the middle of the army. This was so that the Christians' signal could be distinguished from the Saracens', and to mark the difference between them both during the engagement. If this had been observed all those Turks would have been intercepted and routed, but because the aforesaid knights were in too much of a hurry the general agreement was not observed, which marred the success of the common enterprise.

They burst out of line first; with horses at full gallop they charged at the Turks. Each of them pierced a Turk with his lance and laid him flat on the ground. One of these knights was the marshal of the Hospital. The other was named Baldwin de Carron, an excellent knight, confident as a lion.[48] He was a comrade of King Richard, who had brought him from his land in his retinue. The rest of the Christians heard these two

---

47. *Peccatis exigentibus*: a common reason given for failure in crusades.
48. *HGM*, lines 4571–4: a Flemish knight, skilled in arms. See also Bk. 5 ch. 52, below.

calling with loud voices for St George's aid as they charged boldly on the Turks. In the name of Christ the Saviour they spun their horses round and followed those two, charging as one into the relentlessly attacking enemy.

Despite being under great pressure, the Hospitallers and their detachments had kept ranks all that day as they rode; but now they immediately urged their horses to a gallop and charged manfully into the enemy. Likewise, each troop turned their horses around and charged the enemy, still keeping to their original order so that those who had been in the vanguard while they marched became the rearguard in the attack. So the Hospitallers, who had been placed at the rear of the army, became the first to attack.

The count of Champagne also sallied forth with his elite force; as did James of Avenses with his relatives, and Count Robert of Dreux and his brother the bishop of Beauvais. The earl of Leicester made a furious charge from the left flank towards the seashore. Why name everyone? All those who had originally been assigned to the rear line made a violent advance together. After these aforementioned, the Poitevins rushed forward very swiftly with the Bretons and Angevins, and all the others did the same with their troops. Brave and doughty as they were, every one of them gave each approaching Turk a bold reception, transfixing them with their lances and throwing them from their horses. The air grew black with dust stirred up in the confusion of their mutual encounter. The Turks who had deliberately dismounted from their horses to fire darts and arrows more easily at our people all lost their heads at once in that military engagement; the knights knocked them down and our foot-soldiers beheaded them.

When King Richard saw that the army had been thrown into confusion and was engaging with the Turks he put spur to horse and galloped swiftly back with his retinue to bring assistance to the Hospitallers, who had been the first to attack. He did not slow his charge until he had passed right through the Hospitallers' ranks, hurling himself swift as a thunderbolt from the right flank into the daunting crowd of Turkish infantry. Stunned by the strength of the blows he and his force inflicted on them, they fell back to the right and the left. You would have seen so many heaps of those who had suddenly been thrown to the ground and horses without their riders! – some groaning and bewailing their harsh fate while others, wallowing in their own blood, breathed their last. A very great number were but headless corpses trodden underfoot by friend and foe regardless.

How distant, how different is the life of contemplation and meditation among the columns of the cloister from that dreadful exercise of war![49] King Richard pursued the Turks with singular ferocity, fell upon them and scattered them across the ground. No one escaped when his sword made contact with them; wherever he went his brandished sword cleared a wide path on all sides. Continuing his advance with untiring sword strokes, he cut down that unspeakable race as if he were reaping the harvest with a sickle, so that the corpses of Turks he had killed covered the ground everywhere for the space of half a mile. The rest panicked at the sight of the dying and gave him a wider berth.

Turks were thrown down, riders left their saddles and the jumble of combatants threw up the dust. This was very dangerous to our people, because when they were tired with the slaughter they might withdraw from the thick of the battle to catch their breath, but they could not recognise each other because of the great cloud of dust hanging over their heads. So they struck out at random to left and to right because they could not identify their own people by sight, and they cut everyone to pieces as if they were enemies because the dust prevented them from recognising their friends.

Constantly slaying and hammering away with their swords, the Christians wore down the terrified Turks, but for a long time the battle was in the balance. Each struck each other, each struggled to overcome; one drew back stained with blood, the other fell slain. How many banners and multiform flags, pennants and innumerable standards you would have seen fall to the ground! So many good quality swords lay scattered about, so many cane lances tipped with iron, so many Turkish bows, so many cudgels bristling with sharp teeth. Twenty cartloads of quarrels and darts, arrows and missiles could have been collected from the fields, or more. You would have seen so many headless corpses of bearded Turks lying there! Growing more courageous from desperation, some of them struggled to resist for a while; but as our people grew stronger they scattered on horseback and concealed themselves among the bushes or hid in trees where they were shot and fell to the ground with a horrible dying groan. Others abandoned their horses and slipped away, fleeing on slippery twisting ways towards the sea where they threw themselves

49. This sentence is not in Ambroise, and must have been added by the compiler of IP2. Clearly he was a member of a religious order, writing for a cloistered audience. This is supporting evidence, if any were needed, for identifying him as the Augustinian canon Richard de Templo (see the Introduction, p. 7).

headlong down from the cliffs, which were perhaps eighty feet high.[50] The rout of the enemy was so complete that for two miles there was nothing to see except people running away, although they had previously been so persistent, swollen with pride and very fierce. Yet through God's aid their arrogance was so destroyed that they never ceased fleeing while our people never ceased their pursuit; for 'fear gave wings to the feet' [Virgil, *Aeneid*, Bk. 8 v. 224] of the fugitives.

Now, our whole army had rushed down on the Turks in its battalions. The Normans and English who had been selected to guard the Standard gradually came up at a slow pace to the place where the army was engaging the Turks. They took up a stand not far from the contest so that they would provide a fixed place of refuge for all, for it would have been very difficult for their force to be dispersed.

The slaughter was complete and the Turks were fleeing, so our people halted. However, when the Turks noticed that our people were going back they recovered their strength. Without delay, more than 20,000 of them set off in pursuit and rushed down on their rear as they went, brandishing very heavy cudgels in their hands in order to free those whom our people had thrown down. Then you would have seen our people being horribly thrashed! – they also fired darts and arrows at them as they fell back. They smashed the heads, arms and other parts of our cavalry so that they gave way under the heavy beating and bent down over their saddlebows, stunned. However, they swiftly recovered their spirit and resumed their strength. Thirsty for revenge, like a lioness whose cubs have been stolen from her, they charged even more vigorously into the enemy and passed through them as if they were breaking through a net.

Then you would have seen saddles twisted round and the Turks who had been fleeing coming back and pressing down so strongly on our people that they could not have safely travelled the distance of one bowshot if they had not remained in a tight, immoveable unit. An emir named Takieddin[51] commanded that Turkish horde. He was related to Saladin and had an astonishingly striking banner, cut into the shape of breeches, which acted as a very conspicuous standard for his forces.

---

50. *Quinque perticas*, five perches. At this time the perch could be anything between sixteen feet and twenty-five and a half feet; it was later set at five and a half yards (sixteen and a half feet). Perhaps a modern equivalent would be 'twenty-five metres high.'

51. This is Taqī al-Dīn's last appearance. He died 10 October 1191 while campaigning in what is now eastern Turkey. Bahā' al-Dīn gives a moving account of the sultan's reaction to his death: pp. 314–5.

This same Takieddin always persecuted Christians very savagely with an obstinate hatred. He had with him more than 700 elite and very tough Turks who had been assigned to him from Saladin's own household forces. A saffron-coloured banner, along with a pennant of a different colour, was carried before each of their troops as they advanced in line.

Approaching at a great charge and with much roaring and arrogance they fell on our people as they were retreating towards the Standard, hewing at them and stabbing them with their reedy spears, and injuring them so severely that the weight of their assault shook even our leaders' resolution. Yet our people remained unmoved, repulsing force with necessary force. They struggled very vigorously, redoubling their blows as the battle raged. One laboured to crush, the other to repulse; they exerted all their strength, each struggling with equal determination to win.

Yet our people were very few in number and facing a much greater number of adversaries; and because such a great number of the enemy was pressing heavily down on them the part of our army which was sweating in this contest was not easily able to get back to our Standard. Surrounded by their savageness, our people were beginning to totter and few of them dared to turn and face the enemy. Raging with violent fury, the Turks piled immeasurable pressure on our warriors, pounding them with cudgels and swords so that blood poured out of them from the battering. Noticing that they were staggering and about to fall, that extraordinary knight William des Barres burst out of line and charged the enemy headlong with his company. He struck them with such great force that those who did not fall prey to his sword at once fled before him in fear.

The king no less, mounted on a dun Cypriot horse which was without equal,[52] sprang forward towards the mountains with his elite troops and scattered any Turks he met. They fell back from him on all sides, with helmets ringing and sparks flying from the striking of iron on iron. He roused such great violence against the Turks that day and plied them with so many lethal blows that in a brief time the whole enemy turned from the unbearable conflict and gave way before our army's advance. So our people reached the Standard at last, somewhat wounded. The army was drawn up in its lines again and they advanced in due order as far as Arsur, where they pitched their tents outside the town.

---

52. Ambroise, line 6605, states that this is the horse which Richard had captured from the emperor of Cyprus.

While they were intent on pitching the tents,[53] an enormous detachment of Turks attacked the extreme rearguard of our army! Hearing the loud shouts of the combatants, King Richard urged his people to battle, turned back his reins and with only fifteen companions boldly approached the enemy at a fast gallop, shouting out in a loud voice: 'God and the Holy Sepulchre, help us!' He shouted the same a second and third time. When the rest of his people heard his voice they hastily followed him, attacked the Turks and immediately scattered them. The Turks fled away as far as Arsur Forest, out of which they had previously come. Our people pursued them, continually slaying and throwing them down. A very great number of the Turks also fell there.

At last the king and his people returned from the slaughter of fleeing Turks, back to the camp. They rested quietly that night, tired out after so many trials. Those who were greedy for gain and wished to gather the enemy's booty returned to the battlefield and returned well laden, carrying off whatever they wanted. Those who went back afterwards also reported that they had counted thirty-two of the Turks' emirs killed that day, who they judged from their noble armour and more costly equipment to have been men of the greatest authority and power. The Turks later came looking for their bodies to carry them away because they were reckoned to be their most worthy men. Besides these, according to estimate they also carried off the mutilated corpses of 7000 slain Turks; besides the wounded who had left the contest scatteredly and collapsed later, and whose dead bodies lay through the fields.

However, through God's protection our people's losses in the battle were less than a tenth of the Turks', even less than a tenth of a tenth.[54] O what a grievous day that was! How our knights were tested! For 'the misfortunes of one who is righteous are many' [Psalm 34 v. 19]. O what a mournful disaster, what bitter misery! How great must their sin have been, when they needed such a great fire of tribulation to purify them? But had they struggled to overcome their pressing necessity with pious longsuffering and without even a murmur of mental protest, they would have shown a more profound appreciation of their afflictions.

53. This paragraph is not in Ambroise. It is similar to King Richard's description of the whole battle in his letter to the abbot of Clairvaux: see *Conquest of Jerusalem*, p. 180.
54. From here to the end of the chapter is not in Ambroise.

Chapter 20: In the aforesaid fight James of Avesnes was killed, a wonderful knight.[55]

But the death of James of Avesnes was very regrettable. That great crowd of Turks had crushed him. While he was striving very bravely in that mournful engagement, by some most unfortunate accident his horse fell and he was thrown from the saddle to the ground. A crowd of Turks surrounded him and after much effort killed him. But according to those who were sent to seek and bring back his body, before his strength failed he had beheaded around fifteen Turks who were found lying dead around him. Three of his relatives were found dead with him. Some of our people there present had not given them due assistance but, shame to say, had deserted them as they struggled against the Turkish onrush. Afterwards the count of Dreux and those who had been there with him earned a mark of detestable dishonour for this, as they deserved. Alas for the unpredictable accidents of war!

What great groans and sighs there were in the army that night over the absence of that James of Avesnes, James the most outstanding knight, the renowned warrior;[56] for because they did not see him present with the rest they had a foreboding that he had been killed. When he did not appear with his companions the whole army was distraught and stunned; his loss was an irretrievable misfortune.

This battle which has been described was engaged on the Saturday just before the Nativity of the Blessed Mary. On the Sunday following, i.e. the Nativity of the Blessed Virgin [8 September 1191], it was decided that they must look for that most noble man's body so that it could be buried. So the Hospitallers and the Knights Templar armed themselves, taking with them a great many very strong Turcopoles [native auxiliaries]. Many others set out with them. When they came to the battlefield they searched carefully and at last found the body, with its face so smeared with congealed blood that they could hardly recognise it until it had been washed with water; it was all bloodied and swollen from wounds and very unlike what it was when he was alive. They wrapped up the body decently and, carrying it with them, returned to Arsur.

An enormous crowd of knights came out in procession to meet the

55. Ambroise, lines 6632–734; see Roger of Howden, *Gesta*, 2 p. 192; *Chronica*, 3 p. 129; 'Imād al-Dīn, p. 344.

56. James of Avesnes had been one of the leaders of the crusading army during the earlier part of the siege of Acre: Bk. 1 ch. 43, above.

body, and there was universal lamentation over the death of this great man. They recalled his prowess and generosity, and the many virtues with which he had been adorned. King Richard and King Guy assisted at his burial. Mass was solemnly celebrated for his soul in the church of the Queen of Heaven herself, Our Lady, whose Nativity it was that day; and much money was given during the offering. After the mass the funeral rites were duly celebrated. The nobles carried the corpse on their shoulders and placed it in the grave to be carefully covered with earth, while everyone there wailed and wept and lamented over him. When the burial was complete the clergy diligently performed the due services for the feast of the Blessed Mary.

Chapter 21: The Turks are in confusion. Previously they were swollen with pride, but now they are fleeing and leaving all their possessions behind them in the fields for our people to plunder.[57]

The emirs and most noble Saracens to whom Saladin had given lands and much wealth had been tickling Saladin's ears with their boastful tongues and pompous words. They had revived an empty hope in him, saying that without doubt with Muḥammad's help the Christians would be wiped off the face of the earth on the day of that battle.

Yet their prediction about Muḥammad was completely mistaken and their insolent bragging was stifled. According to eyewitnesses, you could pick out the tracks of the Turks as they fled through the mountains on the day of the battle by the plunder they threw away and the dead camels and horses lying about who had fallen by the wayside; hundreds and thousands of them, laden with very heavy baggage. For the Turks, 'bowmen all and marksmen, turned tail in the hour of battle' [Psalm 78 v. 9], and retreated with everything which they had. The more desperately they hurried to flee, the quicker they fell dead, throwing away an incredible amount of equipment. For in the last attack our people had charged the Turks with such great violence that if they had pressed on with a little more persistence and pursued them a little further none of those Turks would have ever renewed the war. No, the Turks would have been swept off the face of the earth, leaving it free for the Christians to inhabit.

57. Ambroise, lines 6735–68.

Chapter 22: Saladin rebukes and mocks the defeated. Yet they praise King Richard and his army above all other knights.[58]

When the sultan heard that his elite people in whom he had placed great confidence had been routed and overcome by ours like this he was beside himself with fury. He summoned his emirs, and said to them: 'So! What magnificent exploits and extraordinary achievements by my most trusted warriors! They used to be so full of boasting and unbearable arrogance; I had bestowed such great gifts on them so often; and now, look! the Christians travel through the land of Syria just as they like without meeting any opposition or resistance. Where are my soldiers' great boasts and brilliant exploits now? Where are their threats and extraordinary lance-thrusts now, and the sword-play their great boasts promised? Where are the brilliant opening battle manœuvres? Where are the indescribable armies that they boasted they were going to muster against the Christians to destroy them? See! the battle which they sought is now here, but where is the victory they boasted of? How the people of today have degenerated from our noble ancestors who gained so many brilliant and justly memorable victories against the Christians, victories which are retold to us daily and whose memory will endure forever! Things are going differently and shamefully for us. What a disgrace when our people have become the scum of the earth in warfare! We are nothing in comparison to our ancestors. We are not even worth an egg.'

The emirs stood in silence with heads bowed as Saladin mocked them with these and similar words. One of them, however, named Sanscun of Aleppo,[59] replied to him like this: 'Most sacred sultan, saving your majesty's grace, you have blamed us unjustly, for we attacked the Franks with all our effort and kept up a strong attack with the aim of destroying them, but we also sustained a very severe counterattack from them. Nothing can stand in their way, nothing can affect them or throw them into disorder. Their armour is not like ours; it is incalculable, inpenetrable; it will not yield to any sort of missile or dart or sword, so that we expended our efforts on them with absolutely no effect, as if they were made of flint.

'Besides, there is something especially amazing about one of them. He threw our people into disorder and destroyed them. We have never seen his like nor known anyone similar. He was always at the head of the

58. Ambroise, lines 6769–834.
59. Mayer (1962), p. 378, suggests that this is Sonqor al-Ḥalabī.

others; in every engagement he was first and foremost as an elite and most doughty knight should be. It is he who mutilates our people. No one can stand against him, and when he seizes anyone, no one can rescue them from his hands. They call him in their language "*Melech* Richard" [King Richard]. A king like this who is endowed with such great valour and powerfully conquers lands for himself certainly deserves to govern. And what can be done against such a strong and invincible man?'

Chapter 23: Saladin has all the fortifications destroyed except Jerusalem and Crac and Darum.[60]

In the heat of his anger, Saladin called his brother Saphadin [al-'Ādil] to him and said: 'I should inform you that I now wish to discover how much reliance I can place in my people in the present crisis. Go without delay and have the walls and towers of Ascalon razed to the ground; also the city of Gaza; but entrust Darum [al-Dārūm, Deir el Belah] to a garrison to defend it so that my people can pass through that way. Have Galatia [Qaratayyā] and Blanchegarde [Tell al-Ṣāfiya], Joppa, and the Casal of the Plains [Yāzūr] and Casal Maen [Bait Dajan], St George [Lydda] and Ramula [Ramla] and Belmont [Suba], Toron [des Chevaliers: al-Naṭrūn, now Latrun], Castle Ernald [Yalu], Beauvoir [Kaukab] and Mirabel [Majdal Yābā] destroyed.[61] Also, smash down all the mountain fortresses. May your eye spare neither city, castle or casal. Destroy everything, throw everything down, except for Crac and Jerusalem.'

So Saphadin set out and carried out all Saladin's orders without delay.

60. Ambroise, lines 6835–69. 'Imād al-Dīn, pp. 345–6, and Bahā' al-Dīn, pp. 295–304, agree in general with this, except that Saladin destroyed the castles while al-'Ādil remained with the main body of the army. It is unclear whether our author's 'Crac' is Kerak or Crac de Montréal. Ambroise says 'le Crac', i.e. Kerak – but ch. 31, p. 274 below, suggests that Crac de Montréal is meant.

61. Ambroise has an identical list but also includes 'Le Fier', Le Figuier, the Casal of the Figs (lines 6848–50).

Chapter 24: With 15,000 armed warriors the Turks attack our people across the River Arsur; but without success.[62]

Meanwhile, one of the best-known and powerful Saracens, named Caysac ['Alam al-Dīn Qaiṣar] spoke out. He began urging Saladin to send spies down into the plain of Ramula to reconnoitre the Franks' movements.

'For I hope,' he said, 'if I have doughty companions, to destroy most of the Franks if they intend to cross that way. We shall give them so little space to pass that few of them will escape from our hands in that tight squeeze.'

So on his instigation Saladin sent thirty renowned and powerful emirs to seize control of the River Arsur [Nahr al-'Aujā']. Each of them was accompanied by almost 500 of the strongest Turkish warriors. They kept watch on the river so that the Franks would not be able to cross without losses.

On the third day after the battle which has just been described, i.e. on the Monday after the Nativity of the Blessed Mary, King Richard set out from Arsur with the army [9 September 1191].[63] That day the Templars formed the rearguard of the army. They advanced in order and on their guard against sudden attacks by the enemy, yet when they had reached the aforesaid River Arsur they found nothing in their way. The Turks, who were waiting in ambush hoping to crush the Franks when they arrived, tried to attack them as they approached, throwing darts and arrows. However as they achieved little or nothing they retreated, remembering the earlier battle. Our people then pitched their tents next to the River Arsur and spent the night there.

In the morning [10 September] the common people and the infantry, who had hardly been able to keep up the effort required for the journey, went ahead of the army to Joppa. The quarter masters went with them. The city had been so completely destroyed by the Saracens that the army could not find anywhere to lodge except on the lefthand side. So they pitched their tents in a most beautiful olive grove and remained there awaiting the arrival of the army. What more shall I say? It was now three weeks since the army had first left Acre.

---

62. Ambroise, lines 6870–940.

63. Bahā' al-Dīn agrees the date (p. 294). The Turks attacked but the Franks refused to charge them.

Chapter 25: Our ships carry provisions to us from Acre to Joppa.[64]

So the army remained encamped outside Joppa in the gardens and was refreshed with a great variety of different fruits. The branches of the trees around them were completely loaded with quantities of grapes and figs, pomegranates and enormous almonds. Then King Richard's fleet and others' ships came to Joppa, following the army! Ships came and went freely from Joppa to Acre and back, carrying provisions and the other things which an army needs. The Turks were very much distressed because they could not prevent their sailing.

Chapter 26: King Richard takes advice as to whether he should rescue Ascalon from its destroyers and rebuild it. But the bad advice of the French prevails and they repair Joppa instead, where they indulge in vices and luxury.[65]

Meanwhile, Saladin had had the walls and towers of Ascalon destroyed. Some common people fled from there by night and came to our army to report that the Saracens were pressing on rapidly with the destruction of the towers.[66] Our people found it incredible that Saladin should have ordered this to be done out of desperation because he could not or did not dare defend the towers; for they believed that he was very strong and powerful. So on his magnates' advice King Richard sent Geoffrey de Lusignan, William de l'Étang,[67] and many others with them in one very strong galley to look into the truth of the matter. They sailed to Ascalon, hove-to before the city and reconnoitred the situation. When they had learnt exactly what was happening they rowed back swiftly and reported that what they had previously heard was true.

Then King Richard called the princes and magistrates of the people together. By common agreement, they decided to discuss whether it would be more beneficial for everyone to advance to Ascalon and drive the Turks away so that the city would not be completely destroyed, or to

64. Ambroise, lines 6941–56.
65. Ambroise, lines 6957–7050.
66. 13 September: Bahā' al-Dīn, pp. 296–300.
67. *HGM*, lines 10137–52.

advance towards Jerusalem.[68] Many arguments were put forward and many differing opinions expressed according to what seemed best to the speakers. At last King Richard put forward his own opinion in the presence of the duke of Burgundy and the most important of the people.

'It seems to me,' he said, 'to be unfitting and pointless for us each to hold different opinions, and it could result in no little disaster for us – may God avert it! The Turks who are destroying Ascalon do not dare to meet us in battle. I must tell you that I feel the soundest advice would be to chase off the Turks from Ascalon and preserve the city undamaged, because it is known to be essential for pilgrims who pass through from all over the world. You should all realise that this seems to me to be what we should do.'

Yet the French spoke stubbornly against this, claiming that it would be better to rebuild Joppa itself. It would be more appropriate to repair it because the work could be completed more conveniently and so their pilgrimage to Jerusalem would be shorter. What more can I say? The voice of the multitude was strongly in favour of following this advice. O blind counsel of the lazy! O destructive stubbornness of the idle! The more they seemed to be taking wise precautions for themselves and conveniently avoiding labour and expense, the more they would repent later! For if they had driven the Turks out of Ascalon then, the whole land could have been cleared of them.

However, the loud voice of the people prevailed and it was decided to make a collection towards rebuilding Joppa itself.

They pressed on with this with every care, making ditches and repairing towers. The army remained encamped there for a long time, free to relax and amuse themselves. As each day passed many different sins increased among the army, i.e. drunkenness and lust. For the women[69] were returning to the army from Acre, fomenters of sin and the seed of misdeeds; so that the people were greatly contaminated and their attention was distracted from their pilgrimage and they neglected the religious devotion they should have had.

---

68. To go to Ascalon would mean going further south than the direct road to Jerusalem; but control of Ascalon was essential to control the coastal road to Egypt.
69. i.e. women of ill repute.

Chapter 27: King Richard brings back to Joppa the people who had gone back to Acre and were loitering in the taverns there. The army remained at Joppa for seven weeks.[70]

It was now the end of September, and the city of Joppa was partly repaired. Then the army left their camp just outside the city walls and pitched their tents around Casal St Habbakuk! [Kafr Jinnis.] The size of the army had greatly reduced because no small part had gone back to Acre by sea and was loitering in the taverns. King Richard, noticing how idle the people were and how extremely lax the pilgrims had become, sent King Guy as his representative to Acre to urge and command the pilgrims to return to the expeditionary force at Joppa. Only a very few of them came. Then King Richard himself sailed to Acre and urged them with much careful insistence, making a very effective speech to the people about faith and the hope which we have in God and the remission of sins they would obtain provided that they were not fake pilgrims; so that he brought a good number who had been stirred by his speech back with him to Joppa.[71] He also instructed that the queens and their maids should come to Joppa.

They thought it best for the army to remain for almost seven weeks at Joppa [10 September–30 October], in order to muster the people who had by now been largely dispersed. Our people gathered together from this place and that, and when they had finally assembled in one body the army was much larger than it had been before.

---

70. Ambroise, lines 7051–82.
71. Bahā' al-Dīn states, p. 304, that Richard had gone to Acre by 10 October. He returned on the 15th (p. 306). He states that Richard went to try to win over the marquis, who was negotiating with Saladin. On 11 October, while he was at Acre, Richard wrote to the archbishop, podestà, consuls and people of Genoa, asking for them to bring their ships to assist him in an invasion of Egypt the following summer. See *Conquest of Jerusalem*, pp. 181–2.

Chapter 28: Having gone out unwarily with a few companions, King Richard would have been seized by the Turks if it had not been for William des Préaux, who pretended to be the king and gave himself up to the Turks in the king's place.[72]

At that time it happened that King Richard set out one day[73] almost unaccompanied with only a few of his household with him, for a hawking expedition and to reconnoitre the Turks' position and seize them unawares if he saw any of them. Tired and weary from the labours of the journey, he happened to fall asleep. The Turks discovered this and suddenly came charging at great speed to seize him! The king was awakened by the noise of their approach but barely had time to mount his dun Cypriot horse[74] – his companions at the same time mounting theirs – before the Turks rushed up and tried to seize him.

The king fell on them with drawn sword, and at once they all pretended to flee. He pursued them as far as the place where the rest of their forces were lying in ambush. Suddenly a great number of Turks burst out of their hiding place and immediately surrounded the king and his very few companions, in order to capture him.

He, however, brandishing his sword courageously, defended himself against them as they rushed down on him. Each stretched out a hand to take hold of him, but they quickly drew them back, fearing the blows of his sword. As he happened to be completely without human aid just then they would have captured him if the Turks had known who he was. But then, as they were struggling in the confused contest, one of the king's companions named William des Préaux shouted out loudly in the Saracen language that he was the *melech*! – which means king. The Turks believed William, seized him immediately and led him away as a prisoner to their army.

The king's companions who were killed in this engagement were

---

72. Ambroise, lines 7083–175; also Roger of Howden, *Chronica*, 3 p. 133.
73. Stubbs (1864), p. 286, dates this incident to 29 September, referring to Bahā' al-Dīn. The latter talks (p. 302) of a foraging expedition on 29 September, during which a Muslim aimed a blow at the king which would have killed him if a Frank had not thrown himself in the way of the blow. The Frank was killed while Richard escaped with a wound. However, there is no mention of a knight being captured in Richard's place. 'Imād al-Dīn (p. 347) relates an incident when one of Richard's knights sacrificed himself for the king and was taken prisoner; but he was captured because he had beautiful clothing, not because he shouted out.
74. 'Fauvel': Ambroise, line 7115.

Renier de Marun, an outstanding knight but almost unarmed, and his nephew, named Walter, and besides these Alan and Luke de l'Estable were also killed there.

The news of what had happened spread, and the whole army was thrown into panic. Hastily taking up their arms, they put spur to horse and set out to seek the king; but they met him as he was on his way back and were extremely glad to find him safe. He then faced about and they all advanced together at full gallop in pursuit of the Turks. Yet as the Turks had already gone a long distance they laboured in vain and were unable to catch up with them. The Turks fled swiftly away with the aforesaid William as their prisoner, rejoicing together exuberantly in the belief that they had captured the king. Yet God had made arrangements for the king's safety so that he could pursue more important and essential business.

As the Turks were departing rather swiftly, our people went back to the army, rejoicing exuberantly in the Lord over the fact that they had received the king back safe and sound. Their relief was greater because he had almost perished through wandering about so dangerously. Yet they felt great sorrow for William des Préaux, who had freely given himself to the enemy with such loyal generosity, redeeming his lord the king with his own body. What commendable loyalty! What rare devotion! - that anyone should voluntarily undergo danger in order to spare another!

Some of the king's household, while preserving the depth of their affection for the king, scolded him over his frequent recklessness and cautioned him against such behaviour. They requested him not to wander about in such a solitary manner in future in case he ever fell into hostile ambushes. For, as they said, the survival of all depended on his safety. He should remember that his life was with good reason more valuable than those of any of his forces, and the Turks wanted his life more than the lives of the rest.

'Whenever you think about arranging a trip like this,' they said, 'you ought to take brave auxiliaries and tough warriors, for your party does not always comprise of many individuals.'

With the boldness of familiarity his dear friends reprimanded the king with these and similar words. Nevertheless, in every engagement he still rejoiced to be first to attack and last to retire after it was over. For who can completely renounce their own nature, even under pressure? In fact, either through his valour or certainly through divine grace, he almost always succeeded in his undertakings, bringing many Turks back with him as prisoners and crushing and beheading those who resisted him.

Chapter 29: King Richard and his army rebuild the Casals of the Plains and Maen, and often slaughter the Turks when they attack.[75]

After the army had been refreshed by rest and seemed to have recovered its former vigour, a royal edict went out instructing everyone to arm for an expedition in the Lord's name! They would set out to restore the Casal of the Plains, for it was thought that this was absolutely essential for the safety of the pilgrim traffic, which passed through at that point. So the king appointed those who would watch over Joppa and complete its walls and keep a very strict guard on its gates so that none of the people could leave except for merchants carrying food. The bishop of Evreux, the count of Chalons and Hugh Ribol were assigned to watch over these things, with some others who would remain in Joppa.

On the Wednesday before the feast of All Saints [30 October 1191] when the king was wandering on the plains of Ramula, he happened to catch sight of some Saracen spies and boldly fell on them. Swift as a wild boar, he fell on them like lightning, scattering them at once and cutting some of them to pieces. Among these he dismembered a very noble emir, leaving him headless. The Turks fled.[76]

On the following day, All Hallows Eve [31 October], the king and the army advanced not far from there; cutting their day's march short, they pitched their tents and encamped between the Casal of the Plains and Casal Maen.[77] The Turkish army was then at Ramula,[78] from where they often launched sudden raids, harassing us. Our army remained for fifteen days or more between the two aforesaid casals, while the king repaired Casal Maen to perfection. What was more, the Templars rebuilt the Casal of the Plains; while the Turks constantly threatened them and harassed them however they could.

One day an enormous crowd of them with almost 1000 cavalry was on the point of charging down on our army. The king and his people hastily mounted and set out to meet them in battle. Our army was thrown into confusion, and while everyone was running to arms the Turks turned and fled. Twenty-six of them were killed and sixteen were

75. Ambroise, lines 7177–94.
76. 'On the Wednesday...Turks fled' is not in Ambroise. Bahā' al-Dīn records a raid on this date, p. 313.
77. At Yāzūr: Bahā' al-Dīn, p. 313.
78. Bahā' al-Dīn states that their headquarters were at al-Naṭrūn: pp. 303, 325.

taken alive. However no others were captured on that occasion as they were fleeing on the nimblest horses, although the king pursued them with great persistence until he was in clear view of Ramula, where the Turks' army was encamped. So all our people turned back from there and returned to the army.

Chapter 30: King Richard and his people win an incredible victory defending their squires against the Turks while they are foraging.[79]

Six days after the feast of All Saints, i.e. St Leonard's day [6 November] men-at-arms and squires went out into the area to look for grass and fodder for their horses and baggage animals. The Templars were responsible for protecting the squires as they dispersed and wandered through the valleys to look for grassy places. They spread out as they roamed, as was their wont when they went looking for grass; and some of them paid for it with their blood when they acted without due caution.

The Templars, as was said, were watching over the squires. Then almost 4000 Turkish cavalry, well ordered in four troops, sprang out from the direction of Bombrac and charged arrogantly down on the Templars! At once they had them shut in and surrounded and were pressing down on them relentlessly, intending to crush or capture them. The crowd of Turks grew continually as more flocked to join them. As the threatening enemy compressed them, the Templars realized that they must exercise their valour. They quickly dismounted from their horses, and standing with backs firmly against their comrades' backs and faces to the enemy they began to defend themselves manfully. But the Turks charged and immediately killed three Templars.

Then the bitterest fight ensued. There were powerful blows, helmets rang and sparks flew as striking swords collided; armour jangled, and there was a great noise of shouts and yells from the combatants. The Turks hurled themselves forward manfully, the Templars resolutely threw them back; those on one side threaten while the others beat them back; the Turks make an excellent assault, while the Templars defend themselves strenuously. At last the crowd of Turks broke in and each reached out a hand to seize the Templars, who were all but crushed and shattered by the persistence of their many attackers. Then Andrew de Chavigny

79. Ambroise, lines 7233–366; see also 'Imād al-Dīn, pp. 352–3; Bahā' al-Dīn, pp. 318–20.

discovered what was happening and came riding to their aid at full gallop with fifteen of his household knights! – and freed the hard-pressed Templars from the hands of their enemies.

The same Andrew was outstanding in that engagement, as were his companions. They charged the mob of Turks and put them to flight. However, the crowd of Turks was always increasing in size; one moment they fled, the next they pursued, and as both sides met battle was joined afresh. Meanwhile King Richard was giving his painstaking attention to the work of repairing Casal Maen. Hearing the loud shouting coming from the rowdy combatants, he ordered the count of St Pol and the earl of Leicester to ride rapidly to the Templars and take them timely assistance. He also sent William de Cageu[80] and Otto de Trasinges with them.

As they were setting out cries were heard: the aforementioned squires calling for help. Then the king urged the count and earl to hurry, ran to arm himself as quickly as he could, and followed the said count and earl at a very fast gallop. The count and earl were riding swiftly, when almost 4000 of the enemy, divided into two detachments, suddenly leapt out of ambush next to a river! 2000 attacked the aforesaid Templars, and 2000 wheeled towards the count and earl and those who were with them. When they saw them they marshalled their troops appropriately and arranged their lines for battle.

Then the count of St Pol made an uncommendable suggestion to the noble earl of Leicester, i.e. that the count of St Pol should engage the enemy while the earl of Leicester observed the outcome from the sidelines, ready to bring help if he thought it necessary; or else the earl of Leicester should fight with the Turks while the count of St Pol kept watch from the sidelines. So he could either stand at leisure on the outside or could take responsibility for fighting. The earl of Leicester chose to attack the enemy, because he would find it quite unbearable to watch the battle and do nothing. So he separated himself and his forces from the count's and charged with great force into the Turkish mob at the point where he saw it was densest. He manfully tore from the enemy's hands two of our knights whom they had captured and were treating cruelly.

80. In *HGM* William de Cageu is praised as an outstanding knight, lines 4547–50. Paul Meyer states that he was a Flemish knight, one of Richard's companions on the crusade. He fought against Philip II, king of France, at Bouvines in 1214 and was taken prisoner, but was soon ransomed and released (*HGM*, 3 p. 54, note.) William and Otto appear again in Bk. 5 ch. 24, below, taking the news to the marquis that he has been elected king.

He contended with such great valour and persistence, throwing down these, beheading those, that from that day on his glory and renown were greatly increased on account of his merits as a warrior.

The conflict was growing very heated on both sides with everyone mixed up together in confusion, when King Richard arrived, roaring. Since his little retinue reckoned that his efforts would be unequal to such a huge number of the enemy, some said to him:

'Lord king, we reckon that it would not be suitable to begin what cannot easily be completed. We do not judge that it would be safe at present to engage such a large, strong enemy force with a few. For even though you perhaps think that you should risk it, you will not be able to sustain the enemy's attack. Even though you believe that it is necessary to aid those who are in need of rescue, you will not achieve your desired end because our forces are insufficient against so many. No – we believe it would be less damaging if those who are surrounded by the enemy perish alone, rather than allow the Turks to swallow you up with them, for then the hope of Christendom would perish and its confidence be destroyed. We judge that you would be better advised to remain in safety while it is possible to avoid danger.'

The king changed colour as his blood boiled, and replied to their persuasions: 'When I have requested my beloved companions to go ahead to battle on the solemn promise that aid would follow, if I fail to do as I said and am not there to defend those who trust me so that they meet their deaths – which God forbid – because I am absent and idle, then may I never again usurp the name of king!' And without another word he put spur to horse and with indescribable rage – I might almost say madness – he charged the Turks, scattered their close-knit ranks with his powerful impact, passing through them like lightning and throwing down a great many with a single blow. Then, returning into them, brandishing his sword, he routed them all at once, charging back and forth this way and that, fearing none, just like a lion. Wherever he turned they fell back from him on all sides, as he cut off a hand here, there arms or head.

Among others he struck through and killed a certain emir whom he chanced to meet, very powerful and renowned, named Aralchais.[81] Why give details? All were overcome, some put to flight, others slain or captured. They pursued the fugitives for quite some time and returned to their people with a great many prisoners. Such were their deeds that

81. 'Imād al-Dīn, p. 353, mentions three leading mamluks martyred in this battle: Ayāz al-Miḥrānī, Jāwalī al-Ghaydī, and Ṣāru.

day, with no help at all from the French.[82]

That same day, perhaps from fear of death, three Turkish apostates who despised their empty superstition converted to the Christian faith and submitted to King Richard.[83]

Chapter 31: Saladin deceives King Richard with tricks and promises, detaining him for quite some time. He makes the king stop the war in the hope that Saladin will return the Holy Land to him, so that Saladin can destroy certain castles in the meantime.[84]

By now the two previously mentioned casals had been partly repaired. King Richard realized that his army loathed the Turks' arrogance and hated them with perfect hatred, and also feared them less after encountering them in frequent engagements and either routing them or, with God's help, at least inflicting greater losses on the enemy than they received. So he sent conscientious noblemen to Saladin and his brother Saphadin [al-'Ādil], demanding the whole kingdom of Syria with all that belonged to it, as the leprous king [Baldwin IV] had lately held it. In addition, he demanded tribute from Babylonia [Egypt] as his ancestors the kings had sometime received it. For he demanded back everything which had ever belonged to the kingdom of the land of Jerusalem, as was due to him by hereditary right because he was related to those who had acquired and held these things.[85]

The messengers charged with ambassadorial duties sought out and found Saladin and laid out clearly the whole of the royal demands. Saladin did not acquiesce. 'Your king demands what is not due to him,' he said. 'We cannot assent to this without prejudicing the honour of Paganism. But however, I will send word to your king through my brother Saphadin that I will give him the whole land of Jerusalem unconditionally, i.e. from the River Jordan to the western sea [Mediterranean] with-

82. 'The French' here must mean only those who were serving under the duke of Burgundy.
83. 'That same day...Richard' is not in Ambroise.
84. Ambroise, lines 7367–446: some additions in IP2.
85. Richard's great-grandfather, Count Fulk of Anjou, had married twice. By his first marriage he was ancestor of the Plantagenet kings of England. By his second marriage he had been king of Jerusalem and thus grandfather of Queen Sybil. As the queen had died at the siege of Acre and her half-sister Isabel's marriage to the marquis Conrad was canonically invalid, Richard could claim to be next in line to the throne.

out any exactions or restrictions, on the one condition that the city of Ascalon is never rebuilt by the Christians or the Saracens.'

So Saphadin came to announce this to King Richard [7 November].[86] The king did not wish to talk to him that day, because he had just been bled.[87] However, on the king's order Stephen de Turnham served the same Saphadin with many different delicious dishes at dinner. He dined that day on the plain between the Casal of the Temple [Yāzūr] and the Casal of Josaphat [as-Safiriya].

The following day, Saphadin sent King Richard seven valuable camels and an excellent tent. Then Saphadin came to the king and delivered Saladin's message to him. The king thought over their confused situation, reflecting that the outcome of the war hung in the balance, and judged that for the time being he ought to wait and see what came of it and be on his guard.[88] Alas! he was imprudent; he had no premonition of their fraud. He did not foresee that they would draw him on with prevarications with the intention of winning more time to destroy cities, castles and the fortifications of the country. Saphadin entrapped the overly credulous king with his shrewdness and deceived him with smooth words, so that at last they seemed to develop a sort of mutual friendship.[89] The king was happy to receive gifts from Saphadin and messengers kept running back and forth between them bearing little presents from Saphadin to King Richard. His people felt that the king was open to considerable criticism for this, and it was said to be sinful to contract friendship with Gentiles.[90] However, Saphadin claimed that he

---

86. 'The king did...an excellent tent' is not in Ambroise. The Muslim historians broadly agree with this account of negotiations. Bahā' al-Dīn, p. 320: Richard had sent a message to al-'Ādil after the ambush in ch. 28 above, complaining and asking for an interview. Bahā' al-Dīn was personally involved in the negotiations ('Imād al-Dīn, pp. 350–1). According to the Muslims, Richard suggested that al-'Ādil should marry Queen Joanna; but this fell through when Joanna turned against the plan (Bahā' al-Dīn, pp. 310, 324–6; 'Imād al-Dīn, pp. 350–1). Bahā' al-Dīn (p. 323) and 'Imād al-Dīn (p. 354) give similar reasons to our author for the breakdown of negotiations, but reversed: Saladin did not trust Richard. At the same time as Saladin was negotiating with Richard, he was also negotiating with the marquis: see Bk. 5 ch. 24, below.
87. This operation could be carried out routinely as a means of improving general health rather than for a specific ailment.
88. This sentence is not in Ambroise.
89. 'So that...friendship', is not in Ambroise.
90. In fact gifts had been exchanged since Richard's first arrival in Palestine: see Bahā' al-Dīn, pp. 256–7.

was anxious to make a true peace and firm concord between them. The king was kept hanging on for this reason. It seemed to him that it would be sound counsel to make an honourable peace which would increase Christendom and extend its frontiers. He was all the more anxious for peace because the king of France had already departed and he feared his unreliability and dishonesty - indeed, he had often discovered that his friendship was feigned and uncertain.

As was said, Saphadin seemed to be cultivating King Richard with gifts through his messengers, but at last the king realised that their assurances were nothing but words, and the negotiations were not proceeding to the hoped-for result. In particular, they stalled over Crac of Montréal [Shaubak] because the king demanded its destruction as one of the peace conditions, and they would not agree.[91] Then he would have nothing more to do with them.

So when it was known that peace and concord had not come about, you would have seen the Turks launching frequent raids from the right and left. King Richard often hurried to engage them in battle. To remove the stain of disgrace which he had incurred he brought back countless enemy heads to display in proof that he had been falsely accused and that the gifts had not encouraged him to be slow in attacking the enemy. However, there were some who had obstructed and defamed him who were often eager to take his money; indeed it is very rare to find someone who is not attracted by the sweet smell of profit.

Chapter 32: The discomforts our people endured from the rain and the enemy while they were staying between St George and Ramula, or in Ramula itself.[92]

When the two casals were repaired and guards had been set, the king moved the army towards Ramula, arrayed in due order.[93] When Saladin heard this, because he did not dare to risk battle he ordered the town of Ramula to be razed to the ground. But first of all he left that area and

91. This castle controlled the approach to the Palestine from the southern desert; it was captured by Saladin in May 1189 (Bk. 1 ch. 15). Richard was anxious to prevent the sultan from garrisoning it and threatening the kingdom's southern frontier.
92. Ambroise, lines 7447-78: first paragraph only.
93. 'Imād al-Dīn, p. 354: the Franks set out for Ramla on 22 November.

went towards Darum [al-Naṭrūn],[94] because he felt more secure in the mountains. Our army pitched camp between St George and Ramula where it remained for twenty-two days awaiting the arrival of people and grain. There we also suffered the most dangerous raids from the enemy, as well as pouring rain which drove us from our campsite, so that the king of Jerusalem and our people went to lodge in St George and Ramula instead. The count of St Pol, however, went to the Casal of the Baths [Yāzūr].[95]

We stayed at Ramula for around six weeks, but not in luxury! - although a sweet ending compensated for the difficult start. While we were staying there we suffered frequent Turkish raids. Begrudging us any rest, they often charged down to annoy us or threw darts to disturb us. On the Eve of the feast of the Blessed Apostle Thomas [20 December], King Richard went out of the camp with a small retinue towards a casal called Blanchegarde in order to lay ambushes for the Turks. However, feeling some premonition of danger, he abandoned his plan and returned to camp. It is believed that he did this by divine inspiration, because that very same hour he was informed by two Saracens who had then taken refuge with him that a short time before Saladin had sent 300 elite armed Turks to Blanchegarde, where the king had intended to go!

That same day King Guy set out for Acre. Stephen de Turnham also set out for Acre three days later.[96] In the middle of the night of Holy Innocents [28 December 1191] the Hospitallers and Templars went out of camp and returned to Ramula at dawn with their spoils: 200 cattle which they had herded together and driven away from the mountains near to Jerusalem.

---

94. Not Darum! Bahā' al-Dīn, p. 303, and 'Imād al-Dīn, p. 354, say al-Naṭrūn; Ambroise (line 7462) says Toron aux Chevaliers, i.e. al-Naṭrūn. IP2 confuses Toron des Chevaliers and Darum in Bk. 4 ch. 34 below, telling us that Darum was destroyed although it is still standing in Bk. 5 ch. 7; Ambroise tells us that Toron was destroyed.

95. This sentence, and all the material to the end of the chapter, is not in Ambroise.

96. Meanwhile, Roger of Howden, *Chronica* 3 p. 179, tells us that Richard spent Christmas at Toron (al-Naṭrūn). Saladin had gone to Jerusalem on 12 December: see ch. 34, below.

Chapter 33: The earl of Leicester's wonderful battle against the Turks, and his eventual victory when our people came to help him.[97]

It happened one day that the noble earl of Leicester, with just a few people, attacked and attempted to drive away many companies of Turks which were approaching with enormous arrogance. They fled rapidly and three knights, companions of the earl who were swifter than the rest, pursued them. However, when they unwisely hurled themselves at the Turks to kill them, the Turks seized them and led them away.

When the earl discovered what had happened he determined to hold back no longer, put spur to horse and threw himself at more than 100 Turks so as to rescue his companions. But as he pursued the Turks across a river, around 400 Turkish cavalry came up from the flank, each holding a reedy lance[98] and a bow! With a great charge from behind they cut off the earl and his few companions from the army so that they could not go back, surrounded them and strove determinedly to capture them.

They soon unhorsed Warin fitz Gerald and cruelly pounded him with iron clubs. There was a very bitter conflict; lances shattered loudly, swords rang on helmets, blows resounded on both sides. Not much later Drogo de la Fontenele 'de Putrell'[99] and Robert Neal were unhorsed! Such an enormous number of Turks and Persians came charging up to besiege and capture the earl himself that at last they succeeded with difficulty in throwing him from his horse, severely beaten. In the commotion they almost drowned him in the river.[100] Seeing that needs must, he brandished his sword and dealt out blows to right and left on the Turks who were threatening him. In that crisis the earl had the aid of Henry fitz Nicholas and one who deserves to be remembered, Robert de Newburgh, whose immortal generosity won him eternal renown. Seeing the earl was sweltering, cruelly cudgelled and labouring in the hazardous

---

97. Ambroise, 7479-604. On Ambroise and the earl of Leicester, see the Introduction, p. 14.
98. Ambroise describes their weapons as 'canes and turkish bows': line 7502.
99. Our writer's version of this name is odd - it is far too long. Ambroise reads (lines 7513-5): '*Dreu de Fontenil deu poutril/rabatirent il...*' (they knocked Drogo de Fontenil off his colt). Because of the way Ambroise has spilt the sentence over two lines, the surname could easily become 'de Fontenil de Poutril' in the eyes of a careless reader. This indicates that our writer was translating Ambroise's text and made a mistake here.
100. Ambroise says that the Turks almost submerged the earl beneath them; he does not mention the river here (lines 7516-9).

contest among so many enemy hands, he dismounted from his horse and offered it to the earl for him to mount; for he reckoned that the earl's safety was worth more than his own. I fear that very few would follow him in performing such a deed - certainly not, although every wicked deed is rich in imitators! Thus that noble man Robert saved both himself and the earl by his honourable deed.

Besides these, Ralph de Ste-Marie, Arnald de Bois, Henry de Mailoc and William and Saul de Bruil were with the earl, but what were these among so many? They defended themselves outstandingly for a long time, but the valour of a few was not enough against countless enemies. The battle continued for a long time; fresh Turks replaced those who were tired, inflicting a continual flogging on the earl and his few companions, shattering them with their enormous persistence. When they were unable to stand the unbearable weight of battle any longer they clung on to their horses' necks and endured the hammerers' blows without moving. When at last they were almost senseless and resisted no longer, the Turks led them away towards Darum,[101] prisoners.

Oh, how good it is to hope in the Lord! For 'the Guardian of Israel never slumbers' [Psalm 121 v. 4], nor does He test anyone beyond what they can bear [1 Corinthians ch. 10 v. 13]. When our army heard about these events, the knights set out armed, pursued the Turks with fervour, attacked them, scattered them and tore them to pieces. These belonged to our country: Andrew de Chavigny, Henry de Gray, Peter des Préaux and many other men most renowned for their valour. Each of ours killed the Turk they encountered in the first charge. The Turk whom Peter des Préaux attacked was so valiant and strong that neither Peter himself nor a great many of his companions were strong enough to capture that Turk in one piece or take him alive; they overcame him only with great difficulty and finally killed him. Andrew of Chavigny transfixed an emir whom he happened to encounter and threw him from his horse mortally wounded, never to cause trouble again. The same Turk, however, pierced and broke Andrew's arm with his reedy spear. As the emir fell the Turks flocked together and struggled fiercely to rescue their emir; but he was finished.

Nevertheless the Turks pressed our people violently, repeated their blows and drove them back with iron-tipped canes. They would have been reckoned the victors, but our numbers increased as the valour of

101. Ambroise, line 7613, says Toron (al-Naṭrūn) which is more likely to be correct.

the tired firstcomers was strengthened by the arrival of reinforcements. Then a relentless battle was joined. The earl charged and was charged, threw down Turks and was cudgelled, and shaved the necks of many who threatened him. He received a great many blows from many, dealing each a single blow in return without need to add a second. Two horses were killed under him. It was said of him that never did such a young man or one so small perform such magnificent exploits.

Such an enormous crowd of elite knights flocked to his assistance from our army that even in that great confusion not one of them was killed. Instead, the Turks were routed and scattered in all directions. Our people pursued the fugitives for a long time until they were weary, and then returned to the army in peace.

Chapter 34: The discomforts our people experienced from rains and storms and enemy raids while passing through Betenoble towards Jerusalem.[102]

Meanwhile, Saladin was informed that our people were ready to march on the holy city of Jerusalem and were already only two miles away from his army. As he did not think that it would be safe to fight the Christians, he ordered that the towers and walls of Darum [al-Naṭrūn][103] should be razed to the ground and fled from there to Jerusalem [12 December].[104] The Turks also left the plains and went into the mountains.

When the enemy had withdrawn, a public crier announced to our army that they were to advance to the foothills. So when things had been arranged and the army had been divided into battalions, they set out in due order as far as the casal called Betenoble [Bait-Nūbā]. Then very heavy rain poured down on us, and extremely violent storms broke out in which an enormous number of our pack animals died. In that terrible storm roaring rain, hail and winds attacked so furiously that they tore up tent-pegs and hurled them a great distance. Horses died because it was so cold and wet, and much of the food was ruined – biscuit crumbled away in the damp while pig meat, commonly called 'bacon', rotted. Most of the mailshirts and armour were covered in rust, and could only be returned to their previous brightness with a great deal of polishing; clothes disintegrated. Many people wilted and wasted away under this

102. Ambroise, lines 7605–72.
103. See note 94 on ch. 32, above.
104. 'Imād al-Dīn, p. 355.

epidemic of misery, because the environmental conditions disagreed with their natural constitution. Only one comfort was left: they hoped that they were very soon going to visit the Lord's Sepulchre, for they had an indescribable yearning to see the city of Jerusalem and complete their pilgrimage.

Each person contributed the food which would be needed for the duration of the siege. If only you could have seen the people streaming in from everywhere, happy and willing to undertake anything! Those who had fallen sick at Joppa were carried to the army on pallets and litters, hoping to advance to Jerusalem. In this way an absolutely enormous horde flocked together from all over the place so that they could visit the Lord's Sepulchre with the army. This hope alone overcame all their other discomforts.

However, while the sick were being carried along like this the Turks rushed down on them, killing the bearers with the sick because they did not believe that any of their enemies should be spared. What can we say? If 'the good man, even if he dies an untimely death, will be at rest' [Wisdom of Solomon ch. 4 v. 7], then those who have the merit of suffering martyrdom in such a glorious cause should be especially regarded as martyrs. Although their enemies inflicted death on them with bad intentions it turned out to be their gain, for 'in a short time they came to the perfection of a full span of years' [Wisdom of Solomon ch. 4 v. 13].

Chapter 35: The people get their weapons ready, rejoicing about the pilgrimage to Jerusalem. The Templars and the wiser ones advise against it, but the people do not listen to their advice.[105]

So the whole army was extremely joyful because they hoped that they would soon reach the long-desired Lord's Sepulchre. They polished their mailshirts to prevent them becoming rusty; they handled their helmets with cloths, so that their shine would not become dim with moisture; they wiped the sharp edges of swords dry with rags, so that no harmful dampness should mar their brightness. Why list everything? Everybody hurried to set out on the journey and no obstacle or hostile encounter could delay them. They made great boasts and looked forward to completing their pilgrimage as they had previously vowed, whether the Saracens liked it or not.

105. Ambroise, lines 7673–716.

Yet the wiser people were not of the opinion that they should acquiesce in the common people's rash desires. For the Templars and Hospitallers and also the Poulains,[106] natives of that country, who could see more clearly what needed to be done for the future, advised King Richard not to go towards Jerusalem at that juncture. Their reasons were, firstly: suppose they besieged the city and put all their efforts into attacking Saladin and those who were shut up with him? The Turkish army on the outer side which was stationed not far away in the mountains would launch sudden raids on the besiegers and they would be risking a rather dangerous battle, threatened on one side by the outer forces and on the other by the besieged breaking out of the city.

Secondly, suppose everything went as they wished, and they captured the city of Jerusalem? Even this did not seem to be an advantage unless they at once assigned the toughest men to guard the city, and they asserted that this would not be easy to do, especially because they realized that the common people were very eager to complete their pilgrimage so that they could go back home without delay, because they were absolutely worn out with the stress of the journey.

Considering all these things, they strongly recommended that the advance should be deliberately postponed in order to retain their military strength and the common people's forces. These would only remain together for as long as the pilgrimage was not complete, for as soon as their vow was discharged the army would break up.

However, full attention was not paid to their advice.[107]

Chapter 36: During the aforesaid journey towards Jerusalem, King Richard and his people lay in wait for some Turks at the Casal of the Baths and killed them.[108]

The new year had now begun, i.e. the year of Our Lord 1192. This was also a leap-year and had the Sunday letter D after the leap-day.

On the third day after the Lord's Circumcision [3 January] our army was making careful preparations for the advance. The previous night a horde of misshapen Turks had hidden among the bushes next to the Casal of the Plains to watch over the road along which our army was

106. The 'Poulains' were natives of Syria and Palestine but were of European descent.
107. This sentence is not in Ambroise.
108. Ambroise, 7717–60, but without calendar details.

about to come. Then at the break of dawn they leapt out, attacked the first two of our men-at-arms whom they had seen setting out that morning, and killed them at once! However, God had already arranged for them to be avenged. King Richard had been informed earlier about the Turkish ambush and for that reason had also been waiting in ambush that night at the Casal of the Baths,[109] i.e. to ambush the ambushers. In the morning when he became aware of the Turkish raid he advanced and charged towards them at great speed, hoping to rescue the said men-at-arms alive from their hands; but they had already been beheaded.

When the Turks recognised the king from his approaching banner they fled at once. There were almost 100 Turks. The king pursued some of them who fled before him into the mountains, and killed or captured seven of them. Eighty of the Turks fled towards Mirabel. The king, mounted on his bay Cypriot horse, spurred swiftly and caught up with them. In the engagement which followed he immediately beheaded two Turks who were thrown from their horses, before any of his companions were able to catch up with him. There was certainly nothing like that bay horse for speed. Geoffrey de Lusignan was there then with some others. They also killed or captured alive twenty of those Turks, but if they had pursued the fugitives further and with more effort they would certainly have seized far more.

End of Book 4. Start of Book 5.

---

109. Ambroise (line 7731) says 'Casal of the Plains'. In fact these are two names for Yāzūr, which was also called the 'Casal of the Temple'. See Pringle, D. (forthcoming), 'Templar castles between Jaffa and Jerusalem'.

Book 5

Chapter 1: On the advice of the Templars and people already mentioned and contrary to what the common people wanted, our people at last break off the pilgrimage to Jerusalem and concentrate on rebuilding Ascalon first.[1]

So in the year of Our Lord 1192, not many days after the Lord's Epiphany [6 January], a council was convened. The wiser people decided that they and the more discerning inhabitants of the country must have another discussion as to whether it would be more advantageous to advance and attack the city of Jerusalem or to turn elsewhere, as was explained above. The Templars, Hospitallers and Poulains, who were mentioned above, made a very strong case with various supporting arguments for completely abandoning the advance and instead pressing on with rebuilding the city of Ascalon. From there they could look out for Turks coming from Babylonia [Egypt] to Jerusalem, carrying foodstuffs. The leaders in general eventually gave their approval to this advice, believing that at that time the most advantageous course of action was to rescue Ascalon from the Turks, rebuild it and keep watch so that the Turks would no longer enjoy unhindered passage there.

However, when the army was actually informed about the decision to retreat, the common people pined away with indescribable grief. All sighed and groaned because their heartfelt hope of visiting the Lord's Sepulchre had suddenly been ended. Sadness hung over them, completely swallowing up their previous joy over the advance. Despair at what they now heard wiped out their earlier hope. In their distress they called down every evil on those who had published this decree, cursing the delay in carrying out their vow and those who had caused things to go against them.

Yet if these people had been more fully informed about the poor state of those who were in Jerusalem, they would perhaps have been less troubled by anxiety and taken some comfort from their enemies' adversities. The Turks who had shut themselves in Jerusalem were indeed in the

1. Ambroise, lines 7761–810.

direst straits. First they were crushed by heavy falls of snow and hail and then, when this melted, floods of water washed down from the mountains and swept away masses of their horses and pack animals while the rest died in the bitter cold. They suffered such extreme shortages and their strength was so much reduced that if our people had known about the Turks' true state and how badly they had been affected by the stormy weather, they could have taken them with little expense and labour. Without doubt, the long-desired city of Jerusalem could have been easily captured. Yet it could not have been held by our people for long, because when the pilgrimage was completed the people would have gone home and there would not have been anyone left who could defend it.[2]

Chapter 2: The people are indescribably distressed and suffer extreme grief because the pilgrimage to Jerusalem has been abandoned and they are returning to Ramula.[3]

The feast of St Hilary was now approaching [13 January]. Our people were so weighed down with anxiety and overwhelmed with grief at going back that an enormous number almost abandoned the Christian faith. They cursed the day they were born, regretting that they had survived only to suffer such despair. Also many were so weakened by debilitating sickness and poverty that they were hardly able to carry on even with great toil and effort, and could not manage to carry their own food. Their horses and pack animals were so weakened by the bitter cold and icy downpours that often their knees tottered, their strength failed, and they fell to the ground. In muddy places they often overturned under their loads because they were so weak from lack of food. If only you could have heard their drivers groan and wring their hands; or striking themselves in the face, and hurling words somewhat redolent of blasphemy in their bitterness and distress! It is reckoned that no one ever suffered a harsher plight or even anything like it, not even criminals or the wicked being punished. No one was ever worn down by such oppressive circumstances or was tortured as they were, almost to death! Alas for those young warriors renowned with the glory of so many brilliant deeds! Alas for those knights proven in so many crises! Now they were

2. The final sentence, which reveals an appreciation of the realities of the situation, is not in Ambroise.
3. Ambroise, lines 7811–42.

wasting away with sorrow and growing weak with despair. That countless horde of people were doubly worn down: for besides their physical weakness, their hearts were plagued by anxiety – which is worse than anything.

An enormous number of the sick would have died if it had not been for King Richard, because they could not take care of themselves and had no one to look after them. Prompted by his regard for divine mercy, he took care of everyone, sending messengers out all around to seek out those who were ill. In his goodness he gathered together those who were dying, and when he had assembled them all he arranged for them to be brought with him to Ramula. The whole army retreated there in order, after having left it only a little while before.

Chapter 3: The great trials and indescribable grief which beset the army between Ramula and Ascalon, due to the dangers of the road, the stormy weather and the departure of the French from the army.[4]

While the army was stationed in great sadness at Ramula an enormous number of people began to leave the army, either to escape the hardships of the journey or out of defiance and contempt for their commanders. As a result the army became a great deal smaller. For most of the French left because they were angry at how things were going, and remained at leisure at Joppa for quite some time. Also, some went back to Acre, where there was no shortage of food. Some even went to Tyre to join the marquis, who had been strongly urging them to do this. Also, in anger and contempt for the rest of the army, some went away with the duke of Burgundy to the Casal of the Plains where they stayed for eight days.

King Richard was considerably exasperated at the situation, but he set out towards Ibelin [Yibnā] with his nephew Henry, count of Champagne, and the rest of the army – now somewhat diminished in size. They found the roads so filthy with mud that when the time came for billeting they were so exhausted that all they needed was rest. The army stayed at Ibelin that night, as much troubled by grief as worn out by effort. Pen cannot describe nor tongue tell their great adversities and misery. At daybreak those who were assigned to pitch the tents went on in front and

4. Ambroise, lines 7843–96.

the army advanced under arms and in order. As for the misfortunes of that day's journey, it is impossible to describe how far the distress of the previous day had increased. As they marched, absolutely exhausted, icy snow rained down on their faces, thick hail beat on them, torrential rain enveloped them as if the whole sky had been assigned to beat them to death. But the muddy ground also gave way beneath their marching feet, so that carters, horses and people fell in the mire. As they struggled frantically, making every effort to get out, they got into even more desperate danger and a great many were unable to escape.

Who could describe the bitterness of that day? Who could tell the weight of its distress, or weigh up the unhappiness of those miserable people and their groans and sighs? Even the most resolute face was wet with as many tears as rain. Numbed by their fearful sufferings, they tired of life. On all sides their pack animals collapsed and died, and the food they were carrying was either washed away in the torrential waters or sank into the mud.

So crushed, tested, exhausted, often cursing the day on which they were born and frequently beating themselves, they at last reached the city of Ascalon. They found that it had been so completely razed to the ground by the Saracens that it was only with great effort that they were able to get in through the gates over the heaps of stones. That was 20 January. That night each person was free to do what they liked, according to their own means.

Chapter 4: Again, the discomfort suffered by the army at Ascalon from the stormy weather and lack of food.[5]

The city of Ascalon is situated next to the Greek sea [Mediterranean]. It would have the most suitable location, most defensible site and finest suburbs of any city; if only it had a harbour fit for landing ships. It does indeed have a harbour, but it is a dangerous one in which ships are often broken up by the constant tossing of the ever-raging sea. The army arrived there in bad weather, and for eight days because of the threat of storms no ship dared to go to Ascalon carrying food, so that the army experienced a great shortage. For the space of eight days neither humans nor pack animals tasted anything except the little that they had brought with them, and it was not safe to go out to look for food because of

5. Ambroise, lines 7897–932.

Turkish ambushes in the area.

At last in a long period of calm weather some ships came laden with foodstuffs; but immediately afterwards the storms returned and the army again began to run short. Ships called 'barges' and 'galleys' which had been sent for food were broken up and sunk by the force of the gale and almost all who were in them drowned. The king's sneckas and those which belonged to others were also smashed. Out of their materials the king constructed his longships, in which he intended to cross the sea,[6] but this was not to be.

Chapter 5: Saladin hears that our army has turned back and dispersed, so he dismisses his princes and army to their homes until May.[7]

When he heard that our people had dispersed along the coast and that our army had partly broken up, Saladin allowed all the princes of his army to return to their homes with their forces so that they could all attend to their domestic affairs. They would be free until the month of May, i.e. a season suitable for campaigning. Meanwhile the Turks who had by now been fighting under Saladin continuously and most laboriously for four years willingly departed to their fortresses to see their longed-for families again.

If only you could have heard so many emirs, princes and magnates of the army recollecting that disastrous campaign! They were stunned by their misfortunes, because in the past they had been used to coming out victorious from almost every engagement, crushing their opponents and carrying off plunder; but now not only had they won nothing for a long time but on many occasions they had lost a large number of their relations in battle and suffered great personal expense. What was more, they were inconsolable over the loss of those princes, emirs and others whom Saladin had failed to ransom and whose execution King Richard had ordered at Acre, as was described earlier. As a result of this they developed a relentless hatred and contempt for Saladin.

So with wailing and weeping Saladin's army withdrew for the time being.

---

6. Presumably to invade Egypt, as he was intending to do in the summer of 1192: see his letter in *Conquest of Jerusalem*, pp. 181-2.
7. Ambroise, lines 7933-66.

Chapter 6: King Richard entices back as many of the French who had left the army as he can. By common consent they rebuild Ascalon.[8]

By now it was the end of January and better weather was approaching. The king, upset at the dispersal of the army, sent messengers to persuade the French to return to the camp at Ascalon. Then the whole army would be strengthened in united fellowship and all could decide what their best move would be.

'For it is best,' he said, 'if the whole army is present so that we can discuss these things with proper deliberation. Otherwise - God forbid - there may be disagreements and we may be left dangerously lacking in mutual aid, reduced to desperate straits and overcome by our treacherous enemies.'

The French informed the king that they were certainly ready to obey his instructions but only until Easter and on condition that if they preferred to leave before Easter they would be allowed to depart freely without any obstruction or interference, and he would give them leave to depart and an escort.[9] Realising that circumstances forced him to put up with their behaviour for the time being, the king approved all this. So the French returned and the army was united.

The common decision was that they should repair the walls of Ascalon and rebuild the city, although the chiefs and greater people were already so impoverished that they hardly had enough to do anything. Nevertheless they began the work, each according to their own means. They threw out a heap of broken stone and dug down deeply, searching for the foundations of one of the greater gates, until they hit solid masonry. You would have seen everyone working together, chiefs, nobles, knights, squires, and men-at-arms passing stones and rocks from hand to hand. There was no distinction between clergy and laity, noble and commoner, servants and princes. All laboured equally together at equal work, and so in a short time they made so much progress that even the workers themselves were impressed.

When masons had been found and contracted 'the work seethed' [Virgil, *Aeneid*, Bk. 1 v. 436] and the walls rose rapidly. The city of Ascalon has a great many towers which had been completely levelled to the ground: fifty-three which are taller and very strong as well as lesser

8. Ambroise, lines 7967-8096. For the rebuilding of the city and Richard's role see Pringle, D. (1984), 'King Richard I and the Walls of Ascalon'.
9. They left just before Easter: below, ch. 14.

ones which are not so high. The names of five of these towers are derived from their founders.

According to the ancient witness and general tradition, the first and most powerful of the sons of the famous Noah was Cham [Ham]. He fathered thirty-two sons, who reigned after him and constructed the city of Ascalon. Tradition says that in order to complete the city which they had begun they took on helpers from all over their domains. It is said that Girls' Tower was built by girls who wanted to win their favour and eternal fame. In a similar way, Shields' Tower was built by knights. Bloody Tower is said to have been built by some criminals as punishment for their crime: it is called Bloody Tower because they are said to have ransomed their lifeblood from the punishment due for their crime by undertaking this service. The fourth, called Emirs' Tower, is supposed to have been built by emirs. The fifth, called Bedouins' Tower, was built by Bedouins. Thus these five towers are said to have been built by these people and drew their respective names from them.

When they had brought in skilled masons the work grew more rapidly. The king played a prominent part in the work as he did in all his operations. By building with his own hands, urging others on and distributing money he helped the work to advance more effectively. On his encouragement, each of the chiefs and magnates took on responsibility for completing a part of the building, each according to their means. If any of them abandoned the work because of their lack of money, the noble-minded king, whose heart was greater than his rank, would bestow on them whatever they needed from his own resources. So the work advanced so much at his nod, with his persuasion, through his efforts and expense that it was said that he was responsible for completing the rebuilding of three quarters of the city.

Chapter 7: King Richard rescues from the Turks at Darum 1200 Christian captives who were being taken to Babylonia.[10]

Meanwhile Saladin had arranged for 1200 Christian captives, i.e. French and natives of that country, to be taken to Babylonia [Egypt]. Saladin's own servants brought them as far as the castle called Darum where they spent the night, intending to proceed on the following day. However, by the dispensation of God, or so it is believed, it came about that King

10. Ambroise, lines 8090–136.

Richard rescued them from slavery.

As it happened, the king had gone out that day with a force of elite knights to see how the castle of Darum could be captured, because the Turks had a convenient route there for carrying provisions and food between Babylonia and Jerusalem. The Turks had reached Darum just before sunset. When they realised from his approaching banner that the king was coming they were terrified. Fearing for their lives, they rushed into the main tower of the castle, leaving their captives outside. The latter quickly took refuge in a church which they spotted nearby. When the king came up he released them and let them all go unharmed. He then cut a great number of the Turks to pieces; all those who happened to fall into his and his people's hands. There the king gained a great many valuable horses. He took twenty of the more important Turks alive, besides those he killed.

Who can doubt that God brought about the king's arrival, which was so essential to the captives? If he and his people had not arrived then, all those he rescued from the enemy's hands would without doubt have been condemned to perpetual slavery.

Chapter 8: King Richard sends for the marquis, but he refuses to come.[11]

After these exploits, King Richard sent ambassadors to that oft-mentioned marquis, as he had done many times before. He instructed him to come to the army at Ascalon and be earnest in executing his duties on behalf of the kingdom to which he aspired, commanding him to do this on the basis of the oath of loyalty which he had previously made to the king of France. That degenerate marquis made a perverse and mocking response to this mandate. He claimed that he would in no way come unless he could first hold a conference with King Richard; otherwise he would not lift a foot to go to the army, nor would a foot lift him.

So they agreed to meet later at Casal Imbert for a conference.[12]

11. Ambroise, lines 8143-55.
12. See ch. 11, below.

Chapter 9: The duke of Burgundy, who has been recalled to Ascalon by King Richard, leaves for Acre because the king is unwilling to lend him money.[13]

So while the king and the rest were concentrating all their efforts on restoring the walls of Ascalon, disagreement arose between the king and the duke of Burgundy, caused by rivalry. Most of the foodstuffs had been consumed, and each person's resources were almost stripped bare. Then the French began to demand from the duke the wages that they were owed, claiming that they would not be able to serve in the camp any longer without them. They were putting the duke under some pressure over this and he himself did not have enough to pay. However, it seemed to him that King Richard would agree to lend him more money because at Acre he had provided the French with cash on the duke's request, as was described above. This was to have been repaid out of the ransoms for the Turks captured in Acre. Yet this first loan came to nothing because nothing was paid for the prisoners' ransom except their own heads; hence King Richard would not agree to the duke's request.

For this reason, and because some other seeds of disagreement arose on the duke's side, the duke departed in an agitated state. Despite his failure to pay them the French set out with him and hurried towards Acre.

Chapter 10: At Acre the Pisans, who support King Guy, are fighting with the Genoese, who support the marquis and the French. The Pisans throw the duke of Burgundy from his horse, and he flees with the marquis to Tyre. They send for King Richard, who makes peace.[14]

Coming to Acre, they found the Genoese in bitter conflict with the Pisans. The Pisans, out of sheer magnanimity and regard for the juster cause, supported King Guy, while the Genoese favoured the marquis' side, particularly because of the oath of loyalty which the marquis had sworn to the king of France. For this reason disagreement arose, blood was shed and they launched attacks on each other, so that there was civil war and general disturbances in Acre and the whole city was

13. Ambroise, lines 8155–77.
14. Ambroise, lines 8177–234.

thrown into confusion.[15]

As the French were approaching the city they heard a great uproar, the noise of people shouting and urging each other to the fight. The duke and French quickly put on their armour and proceeded under arms, wishing to bring help to the Genoese. Their arrival raised the Genoese to even greater stubborn arrogance; but when the Pisans realised that they were under attack they grew angry. They set out to meet them and since they appeared to want a fight, they greeted them boldly with battle. Focusing their attack on the duke of Burgundy, who appeared to be the leader, they made a great charge, encircled him and immediately threw him from his horse to the ground, transfixed with a lance. Then they retreated into the city and firmly shut and barricaded the gates against further attack. For the Pisans had already found out that the Genoese had informed the marquis that he should come as soon as he could to seize the city of Acre because they promised to hand the city over to him. So the Pisans were on their guard against tricks of this sort, in order to protect themselves and the city.

The marquis came at once in his galleys with a large armed force, hoping to seize the city unexpectedly. The Pisans kept up a constant resistance to his arrival, using stonethrowers and mangonels. They resisted their attackers like this for three days, trusting to their valour and better cause. So they strove manfully, measuring each other's strength, until the Pisans informed King Richard of what was happening and asked him to come quickly.

At that time the king was at Caesarea, on his way to the conference which he was to have with the marquis. The said messengers came to the king and explained how the matter stood, and on behalf of the Pisans begged him to come quickly to save Acre. Then they returned to Acre under cover of darkness. However, when the marquis learnt that King Richard was about to come he hurried back to Tyre without delay, as if he was uneasy about the king's arrival because he was aware he had done wrong. Likewise, the duke of Burgundy had already gone to Tyre with the French.

The king arrived in Acre the day after Ash Wednesday [20 February 1192] and was made aware of the disorder. On the following day he took on himself responsibility for all affairs,[16] as he was now almost the

15. The merchant cities of Genoa, Pisa and Venice were constant rivals. See Schein, S. (1986), 'From "*Milites Christi*" to "*Mali Christiani*"'.

16. What follows, to the end of Richard's speech, is not in Ambroise.

only person left in the country who could do so. Calling the people together, he made a persuasive speech, in which he set out very incisive arguments:

'Between partners, nothing is more honourable than friendship, nothing more delightful than fellowship, nothing sweeter than agreement and harmony. On the other hand, nothing is more destructive than rivalry. There is nothing that is more dangerous in destroying unity and peace and also pollutes the alliance of affection. Whatever is created by the bond of mutual love and strengthened by the grace of friendship is dissolved by the ferment of envy.'

With such assertions the king restored the Genoese to the unity of peace and harmony with the Pisans. Their former companionship was restored with the kiss of peace.

Chapter 11: King Richard holds a conference with the marquis at Casal Imbert, and instructs him to return to the united forces of the army. Since he is unwilling to do this, he is judged to have forfeited the lands and revenues which had been promised to him.[17]

When peace had been made King Richard sent instructions to the marquis to come to a conference at Casal Imbert. If through divine grace they came to some agreement, they could proceed more efficiently in their affairs and the whole kingdom could be administered more effectively by their combined authority.

So they met and had long discussions, but achieved little because the marquis endeavoured to excuse himself from any involvement with the army, resorting to specious quibbling and pointing out that the duke of Burgundy and the French had departed. Abandoning the military camp, he returned to Tyre and devoted himself to the marriage bed, claiming the absence of the French as his justification.

King Richard decided that the duke of Burgundy, the marquis and the French had absented themselves from the army of their own free will, and was now convinced that the terms of their peace agreement had been broken. Yet for a long time he was uncertain as to what should best be done in such a crisis. He held a secret council with the greater and wiser people to discover what they regarded as the most appropriate

17. Ambroise, lines 8238–70.

further course of action, and when they had carefully weighed up the merits of the case they issued their judgement. They considered that because he had violated his duty the marquis should be deprived of the revenues which, as was said above [Bk. 3 ch. 20], had been legally assigned to him long before from revenues of the kingdom of Jerusalem.

This was the source of persistent disagreement between the magnates of France and King Richard, especially between him and the marquis. The marquis then as often before urged all the French to come to him from Ascalon to Tyre. The whole kingdom and country was thrown into such confusion that King Richard, who was not unaware of the marquis' tricks, did not leave the city of Acre from the day after Ash Wednesday to the Tuesday before Easter [20 February 1192–31 March]. For it is prudent to guard against even a humble foe.

Chapter 12: While King Richard is at Acre, our people go out from Joppa and Ascalon and return with an infinite amount of booty. At Acre, the king makes Saphadin's son a knight.[18]

On the third day before Palm Sunday [27 March 1192] a crowd of young warriors went out from Joppa to Mirabel and carried off an enormous number of animals as booty. They massacred thirty Turks and led fifty back alive to Joppa with an infinite quantity of booty. They gave half of it to the count who guarded the city; the other half was sold for 8000 Saracen bezants in good coin.[19]

Again, on the following day, that is the Saturday before Palm Sunday [28 March] everyone who had horses went out of Ascalon and rode through the whole region. According to those who were with them, they went four miles beyond Darum towards Egypt. They gathered together a great quantity of animals as booty, stallions and mares, twenty asses, thirty camels and 700 sheep and other livestock. They also took back with them almost 200 Saracens with women and children, and returned briskly to Ascalon.

18. Ambroise, lines 8271–304, except the last paragraph.

19. In 1248 the Saracen bezant was worth seven *sous tournois*; in 1250 there were seventy-nine *sous* six *deniers tournois* to the pound sterling (Spufford, P. (1986), pp. 298, 209). So the Saracen bezant was worth just under 2 shillings sterling. To work out a rough modern equivalent, note that a loaf of bread cost a penny sterling (see note 73 on Bk. 2 ch. 18, p. 165 above): there were twelve pence to the shilling or *sous*. In Bk. 4 ch. 29 above, the count guarding Jaffa was the count of Chalons.

On Palm Sunday at Acre, King Richard magnificently honoured Saphadin's son with the belt of knighthood. He had been sent to King Richard for this purpose.

Chapter 13: Envious of King Richard's successes, the duke of Burgundy and the marquis send for the French who were with the king at Ascalon and Joppa.[20]

Meanwhile the duke of Burgundy and the marquis were burning with jealousy, which always tries to undermine the virtues of a superior. They sent ambassadors from Tyre to Ascalon, instructing the remaining French who were there to hurry to them at Tyre as quickly as they could and submit to their advice. Then they could all follow a common purpose, in accordance with the oath they had previously given to the king of France.

It then became clear that the marquis had been forming his deceitful schemes when he had made his agreement with the king of France and the French, i.e. because after the king's departure the French would support him, so that he could achieve the things he had planned more efficiently. Since the French were obliged to obey him alone, he intended to withdraw them from the campaign so that King Richard would be left less able to carry on the business of the kingdom.

Chapter 14: King Richard returns to Ascalon. The French, i.e. 700 knights, leave the king for Tyre as they have been recalled by the duke of Burgundy and the marquis.[21]

On the Tuesday before Easter [31 March 1192] the king returned from Acre to the army at Ascalon, extremely sad and disturbed. On the following day, which was a Wednesday [1 April], the leaders of the French approached the king and requested him to provide them with an escort and safe conduct, as provided by the terms of their agreement. The king agreed at once and assigned a great number of companions to escort them on their journey, i.e. Templars and Hospitallers, Count Henry of Champagne and many others. He also, omitting none of the necessary

20. Ambroise, lines 8305–26.
21. Ambroise, lines 8327–52.

formalities, accompanied them as they set off, freely imploring and begging them with tears and flattery to stay with him a little longer at his own expense so that they could aid the desolate country as far as possible. They absolutely refused.

So he dismissed them and returned to Ascalon, from where he immediately sent a messenger at full speed to Acre, instructing the commanders of the city not to allow the French into the city to lodge.[22] On the other hand, they were not to cause them any offence or annoyance from which scandal or any grounds for contention could arise. Thus, when the French arrived they stationed themselves outside the city.

Chapter 15: Hearing that the French have withdrawn, Saladin sends for his army. It comes.[23]

On Good Friday the army was absolutely devastated because the departure of the French had greatly reduced its strength. Almost 700 French knights had withdrawn, who were doughty in arms, efficient and renowned for their brilliant deeds. The people grieved and lamented over their departure and the reduction of the army. They wept and pined away with sorrow.[24]

However, the Turks were full of joy when they heard what had happened, and informed Saladin of what they had heard. Saladin immediately sent out ambassadors and couriers bearing his letters with an edict ordering all his subjects and emirs to put aside every grounds for delay and return quickly to the land of Jerusalem.

'For,' he said, 'rivalry has arisen among the Franks and they have withdrawn. The country is left almost without defence since the strength and valour of the Christian army has fallen. Hence we have no doubt that the whole country and its principal cities, Acre and Tyre, can be

22. From here to the end of the chapter is not in Ambroise.
23. Ambroise, lines 8353–80. Bahā' al-Dīn states that Saladin did not recall his army until after 1 June (p. 339).
24. Not only had 700 knights departed, but also all the personnel who accompanied each knight: squires (knights' assistants and trainee knights) mounted men-at-arms and men-at-arms on foot, archers and crossbowmen and other servants and craftsmen, plus all their horses and supplies of weapons, other equipment and food. In ch. 28, below, there are almost 10,000 French encamped outside Tyre; presumably many of these had left with the duke of Burgundy in ch. 9, but our author and Ambroise suggest that these 700 knights and their entourages comprised the bulk of the French forces.

quickly and easily captured.'

The Turks returned at the sultan's command, but not very willingly, for they had not forgotten the past. Their army was smaller than before, although in comparison to our small force their number was excessive.

Chapter 16: At the Lord's Sepulchre, as is the custom, fire from Heaven lights a lamp. Seeing this, Saladin three times orders it to be extinguished, but three times it is relit.[25]

On Easter Eve [4 April 1192], Saladin, surrounded by his retinue, went to the venerable Lord's Sepulchre in Jerusalem. He went in order to discover the truth about the heavenly fire which customarily comes down by divine power on that day each year and lights a lamp. For some time Saladin and other Turks attentively watched the devotion of many Christian captives in shackles, as they beseeched God's mercy with tears. Suddenly, before their very eyes, the divine fire came and lit the lamp! At once it began to burn brightly.

When they all saw this the people were immensely moved. The Christians rejoiced and praised the greatness of God in loud voices, while the Saracens were stunned by such an obvious miracle, denying what they had seen and claiming that the fire was a crafty illusion contrived to fool them. Wishing to be certain on the matter, Saladin ordered the lamp which had been divinely lit to be put out. When it was put out, it was relit at once by divine action. The infidel ordered it to be put out a second time: again, a second time it was relit; a third time put out, a third time relighted.

O great power of God! What can resist the invincible? 'No counsel avails against the Lord' [Proverbs ch. 21 v. 30]; no one can resist His Will.

The sultan was astonished and painfully moved by the sight of this miracle and the faith and devotion of the Christians. Inspired by a prophetic spirit, he declared firmly: 'Without doubt, either I will soon leave this life, or I will lose possession of this city.' The augury did not deceive him, for Saladin died during the following Lent.[26]

---

25. Ambroise, lines 8381–428.
26. 4 March 1193: Lyons and Jackson (1982), p. 363.

Chapter 17: King Richard celebrates the solemnities of Easter Day at Ascalon.[27]

King Richard passed the solemn festival of Easter, which fell on 5 April, at Ascalon, providing plenty of food and drink for all who wanted it. He had had his pavilions pitched in the fields outside Ascalon, and arranged for everything appropriate to be provided for his people in great quantities so that they could celebrate the festival more magnificently. There was nothing more glorious to see, however, than his own willing generosity, in which noble deeds were complemented by goodness of heart.

'Since distinguished heart and brilliant deeds go together,
It is not appropriate for a mean heart to hold the open hands back,
No; may the hand follow a bounteous heart in giving.'

Chapter 18: The rebuilding of Ascalon is completed at royal expense.[28]

On the Monday of Easter week [6 April], the king diligently and enthusiastically returned to his project of completing the walls of the city, and in a friendly way urging the rest to work. Through his organisation and collaboration the project was completed soon afterwards at his labour and expense. Everything was completed without any trouble to the French, who had withdrawn but who ought by right to have taken on an equal share of the toil.

Chapter 19: King Richard sets out to reconnoitre Gaza and Darum.[29]

On the Tuesday of Easter week [7 April] the king set out with a few companions to reconnoitre Gaza. On the Wednesday he set out to Darum in the same way. He walked all round it, carefully examining it to see which part seemed most suitable for an assault. The Turks who had shut themselves up inside Darum fired many missiles from bows and cross-

---

27. Ambroise, lines 8429–34, with less elaborate description.
28. Ambroise, lines 8435–42.
29. Not in Ambroise.

bows at the king and his people, together with insults, although these were incomprehensible. When the king had considered everything he returned to Ascalon.

Chapter 20: After being recalled from Ascalon to Tyre, the French idle their time away in luxury and taverns.[30]

The French departed, as was said. While those who had accompanied them on the king's order as far as Acre were on their way back to the army at Ascalon, the French arrived in Tyre. It would not be irrelevant to describe the occupations and activities with which they idled away their time there. For although it was thought that their devotion had led them to come to the Holy Land on a true pilgrimage,[31] they had left the military life and indulged in the amatory life, with songs about women and bawdy feasting. According to eye-witness reports, they also delighted in dancing-girls. Their luxurious dress was further evidence of the effeminate life they were leading: the seams of their sleeves were held closed with intricate lacing;[32] their wanton flanks were bound by intricate belts; and to reveal the fitting of their pleated garment more clearly to onlookers, they wore their cloaks back-to-front, twisted round to the front of their body and compressed between their arms. So things which were originally designed to cover the rear parts were forced to serve other parts of the body: their cloaks covered their stomachs, not their backs.

Around their necks, necklaces 'flashed, star-studded with glittering jewels.' They placed garlands on their heads, woven from many flowers. Their hands carried dishes instead of swords. They passed sleepless nights in drinking parties, and then, inflamed by wine with desire for girls, they used to frequent the brothels. However, if others had already been admitted on the same business and they found the doors closed, they would tear down the doors, hurling bombastic words and oaths - as is the well-known French custom - and horrifying sober listeners.

What more should I say? Their behaviour proved that they did not take their pilgrimage seriously. However, we must assure you that they

30. Ambroise, lines 8443-78; with much less detail.
31. From here to 'glittering jewels', is not in Ambroise. Richard de Templo claims his own eyewitness reports for these events.
32. Sleeves were wrist-length and tight-fitting. They were open elbow to wrist and laced or sewn up each time they were worn.

should not all be charged with this foolish behaviour; there were certainly some who were greatly upset by their dissolute lifestyle and who were saddened by the disagreement between them and the king.[33]

Chapter 21: Examples prove that the disagreement which now came between our Christians in the Holy Land never occurred among those of old.[34]

The magnificent King Charlemagne, renowned in name and deed, conquered many lands and subdued many kingdoms to his authority. Yet it is never said that contention divided his army when he set out to subjugate Spain,[35] nor even when the same king went on campaign to seize Saxony, where he did many remarkable deeds, and where he destroyed that notorious Witedin.[36] Again, there was no disagreement between comrades when he advanced through Rome to encounter the most powerful Aguland and meet him in battle - Aguland had landed near Reggio, a city in Calabria, with a very strong force of Saracens which was almost invincible to human strength except with God's aid.[37]

Also, when the land of Jerusalem was so often shaken by wars in which so many massacres were inflicted on the unbelieving enemy and so many battles brought to a happy conclusion - or when famous wars are described in any country, under any of the princes of old, no army fighting under a single general was ever broken up by disagreement; those from different regions were never torn apart by contentious rivalry. Those acting under the authority of one prince were never divided by envy; there was never abuse or taunts between them. No: each showed the others mutual honour and friendship, and they were called one people because they were of one mind and no disagreement could endure

33. Ambroise says (line 8478), 'the king of France', but this must be the king of England.
34. Ambroise, lines 8479-518; but the second paragraph is different from the corresponding part of Ambroise.
35. This is legend; in fact Charlemagne went to assist Muslim allies in Spain. See Riché, P. (1993), *The Carolingians*, pp. 92-3, 115-6.
36. Widukind, a Saxon chieftain. In the 770s he emerged as leader of the Saxons. Charlemagne invaded Saxony in 775 and 782. From 783 the Saxons revolted and a three-year war followed. Eventually Charlemagne offered Widukind terms and peace was made, under which Widukind became a Christian. See Riché (1993), pp. 104-5.
37. See Bk. 2 ch. 11, above.

among them. Hence the Franks once vanquished all other peoples. It would have been advantageous for our modern French to have imitated the example of those of old.

Chapter 22: The prior of Hereford is sent as an ambassador from England to the Holy Land. He instructs the king to return to his country because of the unrest which is affecting his kingdom.[38]

When Easter was over and the weather became suitable for crossing the sea, there came to King Richard a messenger who was to throw the whole army into confusion. He was a prior, of a certain priory in Hereford in England. This prior came carrying a letter to the king on behalf of Bishop William of Ely [William Longchamp], the king's chancellor, informing him that he and others whom the king had appointed to govern the kingdom of England while he was absent had already been expelled from the fortresses of the country, and some of those who supported him had been killed in the unrest, which the prior testified that he had seen himself. Through the actions of the king's brother John, who was then a count [of Mortain], the king's chancellor had been expelled from England, and no money remained in the royal treasury or anywhere except only a little which was kept hidden with difficulty in the churches.

The prior added that after many troubles and injuries the same chancellor, priest, bishop and prefect of the whole kingdom had fled to Normandy; and the aforesaid count was firmly demanding from the earls and nobles of the kingdom oaths of loyalty and submission and the custody of the castles. He had also reached out his hand to usurp the annual payments into the royal treasury, which are called 'Exchequer payments'.[39]

'And because of this,' said the prior, 'unless you can get speedy agreement to your returning home as quickly as possible to avenge yourself for these injuries which are arising against you, worse may follow, and you will not be able to recover your rights again without the peril of war.'

The king was so violently stunned by what he had heard that for a

38. Ambroise, lines 8519–79. A few lines are missing in Ambroise.
39. For all this see Appleby, J. (1965), pp. 56–106. The account in IP2 is basically correct although Count John had not in fact gained control of the kingdom.

long time he said little, turning over many things in his mind. He found the news almost incredible; such great crimes seemed to surpass belief. Yet, who can patiently bear the sight of his possessions being plundered? Who can suffer injury with equanimity? Besides, when bad news comes, even when it is uncertain, anxious fear tends to feel intuitively that it is true.

When others were informed of the crisis they were also distraught, their minds wavering in agitation as they considered how confused matters had become and how relentless the disputes between the princes. They realised that if the king left they would not be able to find anyone to remain in the country, since there was jealousy and wrangling between the people of Ascalon and of Tyre. So without a doubt the empty country would fall into Turkish hands forever.

Chapter 23: Having heard the secret news that the king has received from the ambassador and his intention of returning home, the army decide to appoint a king for themselves. They prefer the marquis to Guy.[40]

The following day King Richard called together the leaders of the army and laid out the problem as he had heard it, explaining the prior's words and stating that it was necessary for him to return home. However, he pledged that if he left he would provide the campaign in that country with 300 knights and 2000 elite infantry at his own expense. So he enquired which of them wished to return home with him at once, and who wished to remain in that country. He would force no one to do either, he was leaving it to their own choice. They could freely choose whichever they preferred.

When they had discussed this for some time, the wiser of them returned this reply to the royal enquiry: because the country had been devastated by disputes and disagreements, and the eventual outcome was still uncertain because King Guy had so far been unsuccessful in the business of winning the kingdom,[41] they thought the most essential thing was to create a new king whom everyone would obey, to whom the country could be entrusted, who would wage the people's wars and

40. Ambroise, lines 8580–640.
41. Ambroise makes more of the rivalry between the marquis and King Guy and depicts the two as having equal influence.

whom the whole army would follow. If this did not happen before King Richard's departure, they declared that they would all leave since they were unable to guard the country by themselves.

The king replied to this immediately, asking which of the two they would prefer to elect, King Guy or the marquis. At once all the people, small and great, went down on their knees and begged and implored him to raise the marquis to be their prince and defender, as they considered him to be of more use to the kingdom because he was the more powerful. The king respected the universal petition, but he was somewhat critical of their fickleness because in the past they had often slandered the marquis.

Chapter 24: In order to satisfy the people, the king sends for the marquis, even though he is subversive and in league with Saladin.[42]

Having considered the petition which the whole people had presented to him in support of the marquis, King Richard gave it his consent and arranged for noblemen to be sent to Tyre to bring the marquis back with due honour. It was generally decided, with the king's consent, that the following well-learned and most noble men should be sent to inform the marquis that he had been elected by all: Henry, count of Champagne, Otto de Transinges, and William de Cayeu. They put on their helmets and set off with their retinue for Tyre, hurrying to bear the marquis the excellent news he had desired so long.

But, as the proverb says, 'There's many a slip 'twixt cup and lip!' Perhaps God had rejected the marquis as unworthy of the kingdom.[43] The following evidence can be adduced for this assessment: after the departure of the French King Richard had asked him many times, as he had before, for his assistance in the conquest of the kingdom – as we have said already – but he always insolently refused, and for this he deserved blame. And besides all this, he was now involved in a plot against the honour of the royal crown and against the army at Ascalon. He had made a peace treaty with Saladin on these terms: he would go to Saladin and swear that he would observe peace between them from then on, and in return he would receive half of the city of Jerusalem, which

42. Ambroise, lines 8641–714.
43. Ambroise omits the proverb and differs in what follows.

he would hold from Saladin, and the castles of Beirut and Sidon, and half of all the country on this side of the River [Jordan]. Saladin was happy enough with these conditions, although his brother Saphadin consistently opposed them. We heard afterwards that he kept trying to dissuade Saladin from conceding any peace terms to any Christian without King Richard's consent.

'You will find no better Christian than him,' he said, 'not even anyone as good as him. I will not advise or agree to any peace terms whatsoever without his knowledge and agreement.'

As a result the wicked plan was destroyed, and this treachery did not come to fruition.[44]

This scheme was later revealed by the clearest evidence. While ambassadors were busily hurrying back and forth between Saladin and the marquis, carrying their words to each other, negotiating this unspeakable business, Stephen de Turnham happened to meet them coming away from Saladin in Jerusalem. Their names at that time were of notoriously ill repute: one of them was called Balian of Ibelin, the other Reginald of Sidon.[45] But we shall not dwell on them. All their work and anxious zeal justifiably came to nothing, like dust thrown into the wind.[46]

Chapter 25: When the marquis hears that he has been elected king, he and all his people are filled with joy. They prepare their weapons and other things necessary for his coronation.[47]

The messengers who had been sent to bring the marquis back reached Tyre and discharged their mission, fully explaining to the marquis that he had been elected unanimously by everyone to be king, with King Richard's assent. The crown of the kingdom had been conceded to him

44. Bahā' al-Dīn describes negotiations as beginning late September/early October 1191 (pp. 302-3). Saladin's council opposed a treaty with the marquis (p. 324), but a treaty was made on 24 April (p. 332), four days before the marquis' death.
45. Leading barons of the kingdom of Jerusalem, allies of the marquis: in Bk. 1 ch. 63, above, they supported the marquis' marriage to Lady Isabel. Bahā' al-Dīn confirms that Reginald of Sidon was the marquis' ambassador to Saladin on many occasions: pp. 317, 321-2, 323-5, 329-30, 332.
46. Ambroise, lines 8712-4, is less philosophical: 'They came to seek and purchase the filthy and unclean peace; they should be hunted down with hounds.'
47. Ambroise, lines 8715-71.

on condition that he come with his army to take on manfully the responsibilities of the kingdom, exact vengeance from the Turks, and apply himself henceforth to the government of the kingdom of Jerusalem, as it would belong to him.

When the marquis heard this, he is said to have stretched out his hands to heaven in his great exultation of heart, and prayed like this:

'Lord God, who created me and placed a soul in my body, who is the True and Benign King, grant me, I beg, Lord, that if You judge me worthy to govern Your kingdom, I will live to see myself crowned. But if You think differently about me, Lord, may You never consent to my being promoted to it.'

When it became known in Tyre that the marquis was going to be crowned, there was great joy in the people. Each person made their own preparations and busily worked at preparing whatever seemed appropriate for celebrating a coronation. They borrowed money for putting towards either clothes or armour, so that their finer appearance would reflect the dignity conferred on him whom they served and his increased importance. They busied themselves with their weapons, removing rust, sharpening swords, polishing mailshirts. Knights and youths engaged in sham battles, imitating fierce conflicts and boasting that they were going to crush the Turks. And indeed they were a people of great valour, if only they had not lacked divine aid. So they were destroyed by their joy, which was as inappropriate as it was excessive. As the proverb says, 'Do not rejoice overmuch, do not grieve overmuch,[48] - for all excess may be censured.'

Chapter 26: The marquis is stabbed by two young Assassins who had been sent by the Old Man of the Mountain.[49]

Their mission completed, Count Henry and the other messengers and their comrades went off to the city of Acre to equip themselves more suitably. They were about to return to the army at Ascalon when death unexpectedly overtook the marquis at Tyre.

One day he had been given a friendly invitation to dine with the bish-

48. Old French proverb, 'Nul dul sordoleir ne nule joye sorjoyr': Morawski (ed.) (1925), *Proverbes*, no. 1403.

49. Ambroise, lines 8772-878.

op of Beauvais,[50] and was returning peacefully from the feast, absolutely cheerful and good-humoured. He had reached the Toll-house[51] when two young Assassins, unencumbered by cloaks, rushed up to him at great speed, stretched out the two knives which they held in their hands and stabbed him this way and that in the stomach, mortally wounding him, before running off at full speed!

The marquis at once fell dying from his horse. One of the homicides was at once beheaded. The other at once took refuge in a church, but he was pulled out of it and condemned to be dragged through the middle of the city until he died, giving up the spirit which was guilty of such great treachery.

However, before he expired, he was closely questioned and asked by whose instigation or for what reason he had done this. He confessed that they had been sent there a long time before to carry it out, and had ventured to do it because their superior commanded it and because they would win salvation through their obedience. This was clearly shown to be true. Those young men had been in the marquis' service for a long time, awaiting a suitable moment to carry out the deed. They claimed that they had been sent by the Old Man of the Mountain [Rashīd al-Dīn Sinān], who judged that the marquis ought to die and had instructed that he should be slaughtered within a certain time. In the same way the Old Man of the Mountain brought about the deaths of all whom he reckoned unworthy to live.

It is the hereditary practice of the Old Man of the Mountain to bring up a great many noble boys in his palace, to serve him. He has them taught all wisdom and knowledge and various languages, so that they know that they can deal on familiar terms with every race and in any land without an interpreter. Their creed is extremely cruel and obscure. The disciples are instructed to follow it with great care and persistence. When the Old Man sees that they have reached adult age he admits them to stand in his presence. He enjoins on them that in return for remission of all their sins any powerful man or prince whom he mentions to

50. One of his leading supporters, who had performed his marriage to Lady Isabel (Bk. 1 ch. 63). E-B (p. 289) and the Lyon *Eracles* (*Conquest of Jerusalem*, pp. 114–5) give a different account of events. Lady Isabel was at the baths and the marquis was waiting for her to come back so that they could have dinner together. When she did not return he went to have dinner with the bishop, but found that he had already eaten. So he set out home, and encountered the Assassins.

51. Lat.: *teloneum civitatis*. Ambroise calls it *le change*, 'The Exchange', (line 8785).

them by name should die, and he gives each of them a horribly long sharp knife in order to carry out this service. They set out without delay, pressing on in devoted obedience to his command until they reach the named prince, whoever he is. They remain in his service for a while, until they find an opportunity for carrying out their business, hoping that they will merit heavenly glory in return for this service. Those who heinously killed the marquis certainly belonged to this sect.[52]

The marquis was already drawing his last breath. Surrounding him, his entourage lifted him gently in their arms and carried him to the palace, grieving and weeping inconsolably because the joy they had been given shortly before had ended so soon. He received the salutary sacraments of the faithful, and firmly enjoined his wife [Isabel] to concentrate on vigilantly guarding the city of Tyre and not to surrender it to any person except King Richard or someone to whom the kingdom belonged to by hereditary right. Then almost at once he died, and was buried with great mourning at the Hospital [of St John of Jerusalem].

And so their overflowing exultant joy was cut short. The supreme power which he had long desired and had not yet foretasted, vanished completely. So the solace which had been destined for the desolate land was snatched away, and their earlier joy was replaced by an abundance of new troubles![53]

Chapter 27: Out of jealousy, some of the French defamed King Richard over the murder of the marquis.[54]

In the great confusion which now arose among the people it was as if the Enemy had sown discord, which was now springing up like tares and spoiling the wheat [Matthew's Gospel ch. 13 vv. 24–30]. For a murmuring was put about by certain French who were hoping to hide the French villainy by this fiction. Fabricated by a poisonous tongue, a hateful hissing in the people's ears, it accused King Richard of villainously bringing

52. The members of the sect were called 'Assassins' because the Old Man was believed to control his followers by supplying them with hashish.
53. Our author gives no date for the assassination. Roger of Howden says 27 April 1192 (*Chronica*, 3 p. 181) Ralph of Diceto says 28 April (2 p. 104). Bahā' al-Dīn (pp. 332–3) agrees with Diceto, and also states that the assassination was prompted by King Richard. Ibn al-Athīr, 2 p. 58, says that Saladin bribed the leader of the Assassins to assassinate the marquis.
54. Ambroise, lines 8879–909; William of Newburgh, pp. 365–6; Roger of Howden, *Chronica* 3 p. 181; Richard of Devizes, p. 80.

about the marquis' death. He had hired Assassins with money and sent those two homicides to do the deed.

O infamous spite! Always slandering and gnawing at better things, jealous of good, and when it cannot extinguish brilliant exploits it tries to denigrate them. And the envious were not content with defaming King Richard in that part of the world! No: they sent word to the king of France to beware of the Assassins, the attendants of the Old Man of the Mountain, because the marquis had been killed by them and King Richard had sent four servants of this cult to France to kill the king of France.

What punishment should the authors of this invention be reckoned to deserve? – through them so many 'nations were thrown into tumult' [Psalm 46 v. 6] and provinces violently shaken! These disreputable people thought that they could increase their strength and cloak their wicked deceit with their malicious fiction.[55]

Chapter 28: At Tyre, Count Henry is elected king by the French. Messengers are sent to inform King Richard of this and of the murder of the marquis.[56]

When the marquis had been buried, the French who had encamped outside the city assembled, almost 10,000 of them. After discussing the situation for some time, they commanded the marquis' wife [Isabel] to give up the city to them without delay or refusal, so that it could be kept safe for the use of the king of France. She replied that when King Richard came to see her she would instead give the city up to him, but she would give it to no other, as her dying lord had instructed her.

'There is no one else,' she said, 'who has laboured so much to tear the country from the Turks' hands and restore it to its original liberty. He has the strongest right to dispose of the kingdom as seems best to him.'[57]

The French were extremely angry and indignant at this reply.

While they were struggling like this over control of the city, Count Henry came to Tyre, astounded at hearing what had happened. As soon as the people saw him among them, as if he had been sent by God, they immediately elected him their prince and lord. Coming to him, they

55. Ambroise adds that later King Richard was put in prison because of the assassination (lines 8905–6): see Bk. 6 ch. 37, pp. 384–5.

56. Ambroise, lines 8909–50.

57. Stronger words than her corresponding speech in Ambroise.

began diligently to entreat him to submit to receiving the royal crown, and not to refuse it or make excuses. They also begged him to marry the marquis' widow, to whom the kingdom belonged by hereditary right. The count immediately replied that he would follow the advice of his uncle the king in deciding how he should settle this matter to which God called him. Ambassadors were sent without delay to inform King Richard that the count had been solemnly elected by all the people and that the marquis had been heinously murdered.

Chapter 29: King Richard's persistence in daily attacking, killing and capturing Turks.[58]

Meanwhile, before the said messengers came from Tyre to King Richard, as clearer weather was approaching after the savage wintry months, King Richard kept up untiring activity, pursuing the Turks tirelessly and persistently. There never was his like in that country, or anyone whom the Turks feared so much: he attacked them so often, wearing them down without a break, frequently charging almost alone against many. Almost every day that he happened to run into the Turks he would carry back perhaps ten, or twelve, or twenty, or thirty heads of his enemies. He also brought back captives alive, whatever seemed best to him. Never in Christian times were so many Saracens destroyed by one person.

Chapter 30: Mestoch is ransomed and departs. Some squires from our side who were out foraging are captured by the Turks.[59]

On the Thursday before the feast of St Alphege [16 April 1192], the Mestoch, who had been captured with the others in the city of Acre, as was said above [Bk. 3 ch. 18], was ransomed. He was allowed to depart freely.

Not long after, our squires and servants went out to look for fodder for the pack animals and unwarily went too far. Saracens leapt out from ambush, killed some of them and led others away prisoner, along with a great many horses.

---

58. Ambroise, lines 8951–71.
59. Not in Ambroise.

Chapter 31: A fight between King Richard and a wild boar which he encountered, which almost endangered the king.[60]

On the Wednesday before the Feast of St Mark the Evangelist [22 April] the king set out with his army towards Blanchegarde, but found no one there because the enemy had already fled at his approach. While he was going back he came upon a very fierce wild boar, armed with very long tusks. At the king's shout it retreated a little way at a moderate pace and stopped to face its pursuer. Foaming at the tusks, inflamed with wrath, with its raised hairs bristling and ears erect, it seemed to be rousing itself to anger and working itself up to a fury so as to be stronger to meet its attacker or to attack.

The king shouted, but it did not move. Instead it held its ground, spinning round to face the admiring king as he rode around it. The king attacked, thrusting a lance into it as if it were a hunting spear, while the boar came forward a little to meet the king as he attacked its flank, wishing to strike back. It had a monstrous body, and appeared horrendous to the timid. The lance was strongly fixed in its broad chest but could not bear the impact of the two as they charged into each other, and broke in half.

The boar was maddened by the wound, and made a powerful charge against the king. He, having only the briefest time and space for manœuvre, put spurs to the horse on which he sat, and leapt straight across the boar, escaping unharmed. The boar only damaged the horse's rear trappings, for the horse's swift leap had frustrated its blow, and the lance fragment which stuck out a little from its chest prevented it approaching nearer.

They each attacked each other again. The boar launched a charge against the king; the king brandished his sword as it came and struck the back of its neck, cutting into it. While the boar was stunned by the blow the king moved quickly, spun his horse around again and cut the boar's throat. Then he assigned the conquered animal to the care of his huntsmen.

60. Not in Ambroise. Our author included this episode in order to demonstrate the king's prowess. A strikingly similar episode occurs in the thirteenth century Latin prose romance *De Ortu Waluuanii*, ed. Bruce, J. D. (1898), p. 401. Its English author may have taken it from the *Itinerarium*, as much of the central part of the story resembles King Richard's voyage to the Holy Land.

Chapter 32: The capture of some Turks by our people.[61]

On the Tuesday before the feast of the Holy Apostles Philip and James [28 April 1192], Roger de Glanville set out with his comrades from Blanchegarde and passed powerfully before the gates of Jerusalem. He forced some Saracens whom he intercepted into chains and took them back with him as captives. On the Wednesday following [29 April] King Richard found some Saracens between Blanchegarde and Gaza. He killed three of them and captured five, and sent them to Ascalon.

Chapter 33: Again, Turks are captured by the king at Furbia and by the Templars at Darum.[62]

On the day of the Blessed Apostles Philip and James [1 May] and the following night, the king was spending the night at Furbia [La Forbie] with a few people. At the break of dawn Turks charged on them, thinking that they would capture or crush our people completely unawares. The king was the first to leap out from under his blanket. Seizing only a shield and sword, he advanced to meet the attackers, captured seven Turks and killed four. The rest fled before him.

Afterwards when the king sent out the Templars and Turcopoles to reconnoitre the country around the castle called Darum, they found twenty Saracens who had come out of the castle and were reaping barley. They captured them and sent them to Ascalon.

Chapter 34: The aforementioned messengers come from Tyre and inform the king of the marquis' death and the election of Henry. The king is glad about the election, and gives the count all he asked for. He also sends for the French.[63]

While King Richard harassed the Turks on the plains of Ramula and pursued them as they fled, there appeared the aforementioned messengers who had been sent to him from Tyre. They informed him of the situation, the marquis' death and the election of Count Henry to the kingdom, but added that the count did not venture to take it without his consent

61. Not in Ambroise.
62. Not in Ambroise.
63. Ambroise, lines 8972–9016.

and advice.

When the king heard of the marquis' death he was silent for a long time, stunned at such an unusual and unexpected death. However, he was extremely pleased that his nephew had been elected and the regal honour solemnly conferred to him, for he knew that his people had hoped for this very much.

'Since you tell me that the marquis has met his inevitable fate,' he said, 'what comfort will excessive grief bring to the living? How can mourning benefit the soul of the dead? I am delighted at the election of Count Henry, and if it is God's will it is my entire desire that he should be appointed to govern the kingdom, after the country has been completely conquered. I do not advise him to marry the marquis' widow, since the marquis snatched her unjustly while her husband was still alive and committed adultery.[64] However, the count should receive the kingdom. I give him the lordship of the city of Acre, to hold forever with all that goes with it, also Tyre and Joppa and all the land which is to be won if God approves.[65] Tell him on my behalf that he should return to us as quickly as he can for an expedition, bringing the French with him. For I intend to capture Darum,[66] if there are any Turks who dare to resist.'

Then the king returned to Ascalon.

Chapter 35: The aforesaid ambassadors return from the king to Tyre and announce his wishes. The marchioness marries the count, to universal rejoicing. Tyre and other castles are handed over to him.[67]

When they had heard the king the ambassadors returned to Tyre to the count, the king-to-be, and reported the king's words. Then joy revived, and everyone exulted. The count's entourage urged him to marry the heir to the kingdom, but the count refused, not wishing to offend King Richard. The French and the magnates of the kingdom claimed that the marriage would strengthen his position and urged him to do it. While they were endeavouring to bring this about, the marchioness [Isabel] came to the count of her own accord and offered him the keys of the

64. Isabel's first husband was still alive, so if the marquis' marriage to her had been invalid so too would be her marriage to Henry.
65. For King Richard's own claim to the kingdom, see p. 272 note 85, above.
66. This fortress controlled the coast road to Egypt, south of Ascalon.
67. Ambroise, lines 9017–62.

city.

The French now anxiously hurried matters along. At their insistence solemn matrimony was contracted immediately between Count Henry and the marchioness, in the presence of the Church and with a great many clergy and laity present [5 May].[68] I don't think that those who persuaded the count to do this had much to do, for it is no effort to force the willing!

The wedding was celebrated with regal magnificence, and everyone rejoiced that matters had been completed as they desired. The French exulted, the Normans rejoiced. Both were equally content because the count was the nephew of both the king of France and the king of England. They hoped that happier times would result from this bond between them and that disagreements would return to harmony.

When the wedding celebrations were over, the count sent out people to take custody of the cities of Acre and Joppa, and the other cities and castle of the country in his name and put them under his control, so that he would have lordship over everything and from now on they would answer to him as their lord. After this he put out an edict: everyone should be prepared to set out without delay on an expedition to capture the castle of Darum.

Chapter 36: As Count Henry heads towards Ascalon with the duke of Burgundy and his army to aid King Richard, he is received at Acre with great joy.[69]

When he had appointed faithful guards to watch over the city of Tyre and the country's fortresses, Count Henry and the duke of Burgundy moved the army towards Acre so that they could make arrangements for the campaign and obtain the necessary supplies. The count took his wife

68. The date is in Ralph of Diceto, 2. p. 104, eight days after the marquis' death. 'Imād al-Dīn depicts Count Henry forcing his way into Isabel's house at night and compelling her to marry him. 'Imād al-Dīn was scandalised because she was remarried while pregnant with her dead husband's child, and he declared the marriage worse than concubinage. 'I asked one of their messengers: "To whom is the child to be attributed?" He replied, "It's the princess' child." See the permissiveness of this band of miscreants!' (p. 377). The child, Marie, became queen of Jerusalem on the death of Isabel's fourth husband, Aimery de Lusignan. Isabel and Count Henry had a daughter, Alice, who married Hugh I, king of Cyprus, son of Aimery de Lusignan by his first wife.

69. Ambroise, lines 9063-102.

with him, as he could not yet bear to be parted from her. When those staying at Acre were informed that the count was approaching they went out to meet him as he came. They received their new lord with reverence and honour, cheering and dancing in the greatest delight.

Surrounding him, they led him into the city. You would have seen it decorated like a temple, with hangings on all sides and silk cloths stretched out and the streets and squares infused with the sweet smell of incense. Women led dances, and the crowd was wild with joy and exultation. Why give details? An infinite number of armed people, perhaps 60,000, went out to meet him, in recognition that he was their new lord - attesting in this way that they were receiving him with willing hearts.

The clergy led him by the hand before the altar of the church and showed him the Holy Cross[70] and the other relics to kiss. There he and others offered many precious gifts. Then he was escorted to the royal palace where he arranged for a magnificent banquet to be prepared. Each person strove to honour the future king according to their means.

Chapter 37: Prompted by compassion, King Richard confers the island of Cyprus on King Guy in recognition of his prowess and to compensate him for the loss of his kingdom.[71]

Yet when one rises another almost invariably falls - in other words, one man's loss is another's gain. Count Henry prided himself in gaining the kingdom which had been taken from King Guy, for which the latter had fought so many battles and which he had recovered and defended with such labour and sweat. Now he went about as a private citizen - not because he was not worthy of a kingdom, because no king was of nobler character than he - but because he was a straightforward man, and not cunning enough. Hence the attributes which by rights should have won him more respect earned him only contempt.

He was a very doughty knight. When Acre was first seized by the Saracens he besieged it with tremendous energy.[72] But although he attacked it for a long time, the number of Turks was continually increasing and he lacked the forces to capture it from the sea. In fact, as has

70. A fragment of the 'True Cross'; not the fragment lost at the Battle of Hattin, Bk. 1 ch. 5, above.
71. Ambroise, lines 9103-26; shorter than the *Itinerarium*.
72. From here to 'without a kingdom', is not in Ambroise.

already been noted, even two kings had difficulty in taking it.

Surely having a straightforward character should not have hindered him from gaining what was his by right? The world's values have certainly turned upside down when the more horrible people's deeds are, the more honour they receive! While the wisdom of this world rules, cunning is reverenced while straightforward honesty is sunk in ignominy. This is Guy, the king without a kingdom!

However, King Richard, prompted by compassion and by King Guy's good reputation, conferred on him for nothing the government of the island of Cyprus, although the Templars had previously bought it from the king. So the terms of the Templars' purchase were exchanged and King Guy became emperor of the island of Cyprus.[73]

Chapter 38: Messengers often come from England with differing messages for the king which make the king uncertain as to what he should do.[74]

At the time when the marquis was killed at Tyre, as was described above, messengers frequently came to King Richard appealing to him to return home. Some of them claimed that all was well, others that the kingdom of England was about to be conquered, some tried to persuade him to come home, others to concentrate on completing his pilgrimage in the country where he was. They confused him so much with their various claims that he was completely baffled as to whom he should believe. Besides, his earlier experience had given him an adequate estimate of the king of France's character.[75] As the proverb says: 'He who has a bad neighbour will have a bad morning.'[76]

---

73. For a discussion of this, see Edbury (1994), 'The Templars in Cyprus', p. 190. Two versions of the French continuations of William of Tyre give different accounts of these transactions. The Templars had bought Cyprus from King Richard to ease his financial problems and increase their own landholdings and revenues. They were unable to control the island and returned it to Richard. Far from obtaining the island for nothing, Guy apparently reimbursed the Templars 40,000 dinars which they had paid Richard for it and took on an outstanding balance of 60,000 dinars, which he never paid. Guy became lord of Cyprus, not emperor; but our author seems to imply that he was the successor of Isaac Comnenus.
74. Ambroise, lines 9128-50.
75. By May 1192, King Philip of France had tried to make an alliance with Count John, and had attempted to persuade the French magnates to join him in attacking Normandy. However, Queen Eleanor and the justiciars had suc-

Chapter 39: How King Richard with only his own forces and without any help from the French took the castle of Darum by storm within four days and captured 300 Turks in it.[77]

While Count Henry and the French were making careful preparations at Acre for the attack on Darum, King Richard, who could not bear waiting around, set out with his forces from Ascalon and placed his stonethrowers in detached sections in ships, for transporting towards Darum. He appointed people to guard Ascalon and spent a great deal of money hiring the most doughty men-at-arms whom he sent to garrison the neighbouring castles. Their task was to watch over all the thoroughfares by day and also set watches by night so that the Turks would not be able to go freely towards Darum as they could before. Nor would they be able to carry provisions, weapons or anything else the Turks had arranged to transport to their army in Jerusalem, nor any longer have the safe refuge they used to have at Darum when they were passing through, from which they frequently used to launch ambushes against our people.

When the king had arranged these things he set out under arms with only his own retinue for the castle of Darum. They arrived on a Sunday and his tents and those of his comrades were pitched not far away. However, because there were only a few of our people they were uncertain as to which side of the castle they should attack, as so few people could not besiege it from all sides. If they split up and stationed themselves on all sides, they would not be able to withstand a Turkish assault, nor storm the enemy. So they stayed together near the town, on the plain.

Disdainful of an attack by so few, the Turks came out of the castle. For quite a while they harassed our people as if trying to provoke them to battle - as if they were sizing them up. At last they retreated into the castle, barred the gates firmly and prepared to defend themselves.

Almost at once the king's stonethrowers arrived! - the ones which had been brought by ship. We[78] then saw the king and the other chiefs and nobles carrying them on their shoulders in sections from the shore for the distance of almost a mile, going on foot with much sweat. Then, when the stonethrowers had been fitted together and stood upright, guards

---

ceeded in keeping the peace in the kingdom. See Appleby, J. (1965), p. 101.

76. 'Qui a mal voisin si a mal matin', Morawski (ed.) (1925), *Proverbes*, no. 1809.

77. Ambroise, lines 9151-373; 'Imād al-Dīn, p. 378.

78. Ambroise claims to be an eyewitness here; this time our author also claims to be an eyewitness.

were assigned to them and the king himself undertook the operation of one of them, which would attack the main tower. The Normans had another and the Poitevins a third. All three kept up a bombardment, to smash down the castle.

When the Turks saw that their end was about to come they were devastated, but concentrated on trying to defend themselves like men. The king kept the stonethrowers hurling by day and night, without a pause.

Seventeen very strong and well-built towers project above the castle of Darum. One of them is taller and stronger than the rest and is surrounded by a deeper ditch on the outer side. On one side this ditch is reinforced with a layer of paving while the other is cut out of natural rock. The king ordered sappers to dig skilfully under the ground, break through the paving and undermine the wall. Then that perfidious race became so immobilised by fear that they could not defend themselves effectively or even run away. The stonethrowers kept hurling, and their repeated blows broke up one of the Turks' mangonels which stood on the main tower. The Turks were absolutely devastated at this.

At first they drove our people back with stones and darts from bows and crossbows, and missiles flew very densely. However, our crossbowmen were always watching out for an opportunity to destroy their adversaries, and whenever they happened to catch sight of them exposed on the battlements they would shoot missiles at them. They wounded and killed so many of them that the rest were almost too frightened to move.

Their position was weak. The castle gate was burned up by fire, smashed by the king's stonethrower and destroyed! Driven to desperation by their continual trials, the Turks were not strong enough to continue their defence, for a great many had been killed and others were lying wounded. What is more, they realised that King Richard was absolutely resolute in everything he began and could not be defeated now, for he never rested from undermining towers or firing stonethrowers. Then three of the Saracens came out and went to the king, seeking peace. They offered to surrender the castle on condition that every soul could depart in freedom, leaving behind everything which they possessed. The king did not agree. He told them to defend themselves as best they could.[79]

79. If the garrison had surrendered as soon as Richard arrived, he would probably have let them depart in peace, according to the custom of war. However, after giving him the trouble and expense of storming the castle, he was not going to let them get away free. This was Friday: (Ambroise, line 9167).

When they had returned to the castle the king's stonethrower was worked more strongly than ever. It was never quiet. Almost at once one of the towers which had been shaken by repeated blows fell with a horrible crash. It had already been weakened by the underground tunnelling of the king's sappers. Our people pursued the Turks as they fled from the ruins, killing those who were not able to resist. The Turks took refuge in the main tower, having first hamstrung all their horses so that they could not be used by anyone else – as is their wicked customary practice.

While they fled, our people manfully entered the castle. The first was Seguin Barrez with his squire, named Ospiard. The third was Peter de Gascony,[80] and a great many others followed after whose names have been forgotten. The banner of Stephen Longchamp[81] was the first one raised above the wall. The second was the earl of Leicester's, the third Andrew de Chavigny's, the fourth Raymond fitz Prince's.[82] Then the Genoese and Pisans raised their various emblems above the walls. So our banners were raised and the Turks' thrown down.

You would have seen the Turks running swiftly towards the tower, or being struck by swords and falling to the ground or shot by darts and dying before they could reach the tower. Our people found some still on the ramparts and threw them out into the void to be smashed to pieces on the ground. Sixty Turks were killed in various parts of the castle.

Those who had fled into the tower saw that they were already lost. The castle had been captured and the tower was about to be destroyed, for on the king's order valiant men had already set to work demolishing it. They realised that there was no chance of survival in resisting the king. As their situation was hopeless, on the Friday before Pentecost [22 May 1192] they threw themselves on the royal mercy and surrendered themselves into perpetual slavery. They were forced to do this mainly because a very powerful emir named Caysac[83] who had been entrusted with the protection of the castle had failed to bring them help.

When Darum Castle had been seized almost forty Christian captives were found in chains. They were released and restored to freedom. On

80. MSS A and B and Ambroise, line 9308, agree that Peter was from Gascony, not 'de Garston', as in MS C.

81. *HGM*, line 12712: Richard later made him seneschal of Normandy.

82. Paris, G. (1897), p. 558, reckoned that this was the eldest son of Prince Bohemond III of Antioch.

83. Qaişar: last seen in Bk. 4 ch. 24 persuading Saladin to send him out to ambush the Christian army; and see below, ch. 41, p. 320.

the following night, the king made his people stand guard over the Turks who were still in the tower until Saturday morning. Then on Pentecost Eve the Turks came down out of the tower on the king's order and their hands were bound behind their backs with thongs, so tightly that the bonds bit into the skin. There were 300 of them, as well as children and women.

So King Richard took Darum neatly by storm in four days, with the aid of his own retinue alone, before the arrival of the French. Our people certainly worked very hard to do this without the French, so that they would gain greater glory.

Chapter 40: When Count Henry arrived at Darum King Richard gave the castle to him, and then left and went to Furbia.[84]

When Darum had been seized, Count Henry came at a great hurry with the French and the duke of Burgundy, so that they would be present when the castle was captured. But it was all over already. The king went out to meet the count as he approached and received him with particular rejoicing. Escorting him into the castle, he conceded to him and gave him in the presence of many[85] that castle with all its appurtenances – those which had been acquired and those which were still to be acquired. This gift represented the firstfruits of the kingdom which they were to conquer.

Everyone[86] remained at Darum Castle on the day of the great feast of Pentecost [24 May].[87] On the Monday the count left a garrison in the castle and then they set out towards Ascalon, passing through the middle of Gaza as far as Furbia where the king stayed for three days. The rest however went on to Ascalon, where the French celebrated the solemn Feast of Pentecost.

84. Ambroise, lines 9374–89.
85. Legal jargon, as if copied from a charter of donation. The details of what King Richard gave Count Henry are given in more detail in the *Itinerarium* than by Ambroise.
86. Ambroise says 'we' (line 9385).
87. Bahā' al-Dīn (p. 337), and 'Imād al-Dīn (p. 378), state that this is when the siege of Darum began, and that the castle fell 28 May.

Chapter 41: Hearing that Emir Caysac and 1000 Turks are fortifying the Castle of Figs, King Richard goes there and storms it, but everyone in it runs away.[88]

At Furbia a certain spy of the king's returned from the region of the Castle of Figs[89] and told the king that 1000 Saracens or more were staying in the Castle of Figs with Emir Caysac, and that they were busily occupied in fortifying the castle against the Christians, in case they happened to come that way. When the king heard this he at once set out in that direction, and the army followed him. They spent the first night at a casal called Arundinetum or the Canebrake of Starlings.[90] At dawn they set out for the aforementioned Castle of the Figs, as they had intended, which the Turks were said to be fortifying against them. But they found no one there except two Turks whom they took away with them as prisoners. The Turks had demolished the castle gates to the ground when they withdrew. They had fled at great speed when they were informed that King Richard and the army were coming, because they had been absolutely terrified by the capture of Castle Darum. Remembering the loss of all of those who had been found in it, they took precautions for their own safety so that they would not end up in a similar predicament.

So when the army found the castle deserted, they climbed up to the highest ramparts and looked all around to see whether there was any enemy in sight whom they could attack. As they did not find anyone to fight, they went back and spent the night at the Casal of the Starlings.

Chapter 42: When he is informed of the disturbances his brother Count John is causing in his lands he is extremely shaken and claims that he wishes to return home.[91]

At the Canebrake of Starlings a messenger who had been sent from England came to the king, a clerk named John d'Alençon.[92] He reported that England had been thrown into disorder by Count John, the king's bro-

88. Ambroise, lines 9395–9432.
89. South-west of Hebron: Pringle (1986), *The Red Tower*, p. 18.
90. Possibly 'Uyūn al-Qaṣṣāba: Lyons and Jackson (1982), p. 124.
91. Ambroise, lines 9433–80.
92. Archdeacon of Lisieux and vicechancellor of England. According to *HGM*, line 10376, he was the host of Count John in Lisieux while the count was in hiding from King Richard after Richard had returned to England.

ther, who would not be persuaded by his mother the queen nor anyone else but was acting according to his own whims. He was being encouraged by the king of France, and messengers kept running back and forth between them. He asserted that matters had already gone so far that unless something restrained this abominable treachery there was a danger that very soon England would be taken from King Richard's authority.

The king was disturbed to hear this news, and afterwards he sat for a long time in silence, turning things over in his mind and weighing up what should be done. At last he admitted that he would really have to go home, so that he would not be unjustly banished like an exile from the soil of his native land and the kingdom of his forefathers. However, as the king's wish had not yet been made widely known, some people were saying that: 'The king will certainly go,' but others said: 'No, he will carry on. Uncertain reports will not call him away from completing such a pious undertaking. This would prevent him from conquering this country, and it would not win him honour.'

Chapter 43: All the army agrees as one to go and besiege Jerusalem, whether King Richard returns home or not.[93]

While different people held different opinions over King Richard's departure, the leaders and masters of the army assembled together: French, Normans, English, Poitevins, people of Maine and Angevins. With one voice they promised each other that whether the king went or stayed, nothing would stop them advancing to besiege Jerusalem. When this was known to the army, the people were filled with an indescribable delight. Everyone rejoiced together, rich and poor, small and great, and there was not a soul in the army who did not in their own way exhibit exterior signs of the inner joy of their hearts. They lit masses of lights, and led dances and sang various songs together until the middle of the night, 'wakefully passing the livelong night with applause.'

Only the king's mind was troubled by cares. Deep in thought over what he had heard, he considered one thing after another until, exhausted by the weight of his problems, he threw himself angrily into bed.

Yet now as the month of June began, with one accord the whole army was eager to advance.

93. Ambroise, lines 9481–508.

Chapter 44: At Ibelin flies called cincenelles ravage the faces of the army with their stings, so that they look like lepers.[94]

The king and army advanced, setting out from Arundinetum of the Starlings and going briskly down the plain towards Ibelin of the Hospitallers [Bait Jibrīn] next to Hebron, near the valley where the Blessed Anna was born, mother of Mary the Mother of God. The army made a halt there. They were extremely happy, because of their hope of advancing towards Jerusalem. There certain tiny flies attacked the army. They were like flying sparks, and they[95] called them 'cincenelles'. The whole region around was full of them. They swarmed around the pilgrims incessantly, stinging their hands, necks, throats, foreheads, faces or wherever their bare skin lay exposed. A burning swelling immediately followed the sting, so that everyone they stung looked like lepers. They barely succeeded in getting some protection from their troublesome attacks by folding cloths around their heads and necks.

Nevertheless, they were full of hope and exhilaration and thought that they should bear their adversities bravely. All were allied together and had plighted their faith to each other that they would advance to besiege Jerusalem. Only the king was anxious and uneasy at what he had heard.

Chapter 45: One of the king's chaplains addresses the king with a powerfully persuasive speech. The king is moved and defers his return home.[96]

One day King Richard was sitting in his tent in solitary meditation, his eyes fixed on the ground. A certain Poitevin chaplain, named William, was deeply grieved to see him, but since he knew that the king was irritated by the messengers' reports he did not dare to join him to relieve his mind from the things which were troubling him. So he regarded the king with sympathetic eyes, crying bitterly, but saying nothing. When the king realised from his eager movements that he was burning to speak, he said to him: 'Lord chaplain, I entreat you by the loyalty you owe me not to hesitate or prevaricate. Tell me why you are crying, if the reason for your sadness has anything to do with me.'

---

94. Ambroise, lines 9511-52.
95. Ambroise, line 9532, says 'we'.
96. Ambroise, lines 9553-680.

His eyes full of tears, the chaplain replied in a weak voice: 'I will not speak until your excellency has assured me that you will not be exasperated with me because of what I say.' The king promised with an oath that he would not be punished.

Now confident, the chaplain began like this. 'Lord king, because you are hurrying to return home everyone in the army maligns you, especially those who are closest to you and most desire your honour. God forbid that uncertain rumours should divert you from conquering this desolate country. We believe that this would bring you eternal disgrace. Having begun so brilliantly, do not allow a swift retreat to obscure the glory you have won so far; let it not be said against you in the future that you made a cowardly retreat leaving unfinished business.[97] How very different the end will be from what was expected, if it fails to live up to the beginning! I beg you, take care that the glorious value of what you began is not blackened in the eyes of posterity because your valour withered away.

'Lord king, remember how much God has done for you. He has prospered your actions, so that they will be remembered for ever and ever. Never did a king of your age accomplish more glorious deeds than you have done. O king, recall how, when you were count of Poitou, you never had any neighbour of valour, any aggressive adversary, who was not subdued by your strength and surrendered to you. O king, remember the great struggles and disturbances caused by the Brabaçons,[98] whom you routed and scattered so many times with a small force. O king, remember how gloriously you triumphed when you raised the siege at Hautefort, which the count of St Gilles[99] was besieging; and you drove him away, putting him shamefully to flight. O king, remember your kingdom, which you acquired free and undisputed without shield or helmet, without anyone's opposition. O king, remember your great deeds of valour, how many great nations you have subdued, how you manfully seized the city of Messina, how you showed your prowess there when you restrained the Greek people who had dared to provoke and attack you. Divine clemency freed you from their hands and they were routed and destroyed. Recall, O king, the marks of virtue with which God

97. From here to 'withered away' is not in Ambroise.
98. See Roger of Howden, *Gesta*, 1 p. 120–1 and Gillingham (1984), 'Richard I and the Science of War', p. 81. In May 1176, Richard defeated a force of Brabaçon mercenaries employed by a coalition of rebel barons from the Angoumois and Limousin.
99. Raymond V, the count of Toulouse.

endowed you, 'in the richness of His Grace' [Ephesians ch. 1 v. 7], when you subjugated the island of Cyprus, which no one before you ever dared to do, but which through God's help you were able to conquer in fifteen days, and you also captured the emperor. Then you met that extraordinary ship which was not able to enter the port of Acre because of contrary winds, and with your galleys you overwhelmed it and 800 armed Turks, when the snakes were swallowed up in the waves of the sea.

'Remember, lord king, the siege of Acre, and how you arrived at the ideal time to capture it, and when you attacked it, it surrendered. You had been very ill with the sickness they call Arnaldia, but by the mercy of God you recovered, while a great many other princes died of the same illness. Remember, O king, this land which God has committed to your protection; it is your responsibility alone, because the king of France went away like a coward. O king, remember the Christian captives whom you freed from their chains at Darum, whom the Turks had put in fetters to lead them into captivity, but God sent you there to help them. Pray consider deeply in your heart how God has honoured and magnified you with countless triumphs and successes, so that now there is no longer a king or prince who may resist you. Surely it hasn't slipped out of your memory how the castle of Darum was recently subdued by your valour and persistence in four days? And what should we think about that time when you were rashly lying asleep and were almost seized by the wicked infidels, when God quickly tore you unharmed from their hands?

'Need I say more? Need I mention any other adversaries from any country which your strong hand has subdued at last, or cities you have crushed, when you prevail happily in every business you undertake? Remember that since you set out from the western world until now you have been victorious everywhere. Your enemies fell at your feet to be put in chains, and before you "Antaeus gained nothing by falling, nor the Hydra by growing."[100] The sultan quakes before you. Babylon is stunned to the heart. The violent Turks tremble. What more shall I say? Everyone agrees in saying that you are the father of all, the patron and

100. In Greek mythology Antaeus was a powerful giant, ruler of Libya, who forced all strangers to wrestle with him. Each time he fell to the ground he gained new strength. Hercules (Heracles) killed him by holding him up in the air. The Hydra appears in another of the labours of Hercules: it was a many-headed watersnake which lived in the Lernaean Lake. Whenever a head was cut off, two new ones grew from the wound. Hercules killed it by cauterizing each neck as he cut off its heads.

defender of Christendom. If you desert it, it will be the same as if you left it to be destroyed by its enemies.[101]

'O mighty king, as you began
endure longer!
Bring help to this people
Who hope attentively in you
as their protector! And with Christ's help
Go on and prosper.'

Chapter 46: The king has a public announcement made to the army to the effect that he will not return home until next Easter [1193].[102]

The king hung on the chaplain's words, silently turning many things over in his mind and weighing up the value of his words. While the chaplain talked, the king remained silent and those who were sitting with them in the tent 'held their gaze fixed on him' [Virgil, *Aeneid*, Bk. 2 v. 1].

The king's heart was completely changed by that speech. It confirmed his ideas and strengthened and clarified his convictions. So, the following day at the ninth hour [3 pm] the king and the whole army returned and stopped in the orchards outside Ascalon. Each person was thinking that the king really was going to depart and that already he was hurrying his departure. In fact he had changed his mind through the inspiration of God's grace and the chaplain's speech, and he told his nephew Count Henry and the duke of Burgundy and the other chiefs that he would not leave the country before Easter [1193], no matter what appeals, rumours or complaints messengers brought him.

So on 4 June, which was in Holy Trinity week, he summoned his herald, Philip, and ordered him to proclaim throughout the army that without any doubt King Richard would remain in the country until next Easter, and that each person should equip themselves according to their means and prepare to besiege Jerusalem.

101. Except for 'What more...its enemies', the last paragraph is not in Ambroise. Neither are the verses which follow.

102. Ambroise, lines 9681–720.

Chapter 47: When they hear the king's wish the army is delighted and they prepare themselves to attack Jerusalem.[103]

When they heard the herald's voice, everyone gave thanks like a bird does when day dawns. Then without delay they all equipped themselves and packed up their baggage, ready for the journey. Stretching up their hands to heaven, they said:

'We adore You, Almighty God, and we give thanks, because now we shall see Your city, in which the Turks have dwelt too long. How happy has our long delay been! What blessed expectation! How well-deserved have been the trials and sufferings we have each experienced! - since the result is that now we shall see the city we have longed for so long.' Each person declared these and similar things.

Their only anxiety was to set out on the advance. More cheerful now from hope, the crowd of humble common people carried bags of foodstuffs on their own backs, each claiming that they were sure that they were carrying enough food for a month, for they wanted so much to advance towards Jerusalem. There is nothing that a willing mind cannot overcome, and in God's service difficult things become easier.

Chapter 48: Heading from Ascalon towards Jerusalem, the king and the army come to Blanchegarde, where two of our people die from snake bites.[104]

So, as was said before, they each equipped themselves for the campaign. In their unanimous goodwill it seemed to them that everything was going right. The king and army were encamped outside Ascalon. Everything was prepared for the march, and on the first Sunday after Trinity [7 June 1192] they left Ascalon very early in the morning and set out towards Jerusalem. That excellently equipped and elite race of people advanced slowly because of the heat. The more powerful, sympathising with the weaker, decided to give them free assistance and charitable service. With liberal humility, they provided those on foot with transport. Those who had horses or any kind of pack animals supplied them to the poorer pilgrims to carry both them and their baggage, while they - the agile young warriors, strong enough to march - voluntarily

103. Ambroise, lines 9721-47.

104. Ambroise, lines 9748-97.

walked after them on foot.

You would have seen countless renowned banners tossing in the wind, many sorts of pennants, so many mothers' sons from so many regions, so many different sorts of weapons, crowns of helmets covered with jewels, glittering mailshirts, shields emblazoned with fiery lions *passants* or golden flying dragons. There were high horses eager to gallop, full of indignant ardour at being restrained and foaming at the bit; so many mules, so many sharp-pointing glittering lances. The air was bright with flashing swords. There were so many doughty and elite knights that I think they would have been enough and more than enough to crush or at least withstand the Turkish horde.

So they advanced so far on their journey that after crossing a river of sweet water they arrived at Blanchegarde. They briskly pitched their tents on the plains outside it and spent the night there.

That first night, within a small stretch of ground a knight and his squire died from the bites of two snakes. May God absolve their souls, for they were taken in His service! The army[105] remained there for two days.

Chapter 49: In three days the king and the army come to Betenoble from Blanchegarde. The king is there for a month, waiting for people, and meanwhile he does many remarkable things.[106]

On the third day, 9 June, the army went forth *en masse* and arrived at Turon des Chevaliers [al-Naṭrūn] without meeting any obstacle or opposition. That night our people captured fourteen Parthians, who had come down from the mountains to plunder.[107]

On the following day after breakfast the army moved on from there. The king went in front with his household retinue, towards [Castle] Arnald. He ordered his tents pitched on the higher, righthand side of the castle. On the following day [10 June] the French came and the whole army advanced towards Betenopolis [Bait Nūbā].[108]

The army stayed here for quite some time in order to wait for Count Henry whom the king had sent to Acre to bring back the people who

105. Ambroise, line 9797, says 'we'.
106. Ambroise, lines 9798-864.
107. 'That night...to plunder' is not in Ambroise.
108. 'Imād al-Dīn agrees the date: p. 379. Bait Nūbā was a day's march from Jerusalem.

were staying there, doing nothing, to take part in the campaign. For this reason the whole army had to remain there for a month or more, next to the foot of the mountain which pilgrims used to cross on their way to and from the Holy City.

While the army remained in the valley where it had camped we saw many things happen which we don't think should be passed over in silence.[109]

On the day after the feast of St Barnabas [12 June] which was a Friday, the king's scout reported that Turks were in the mountains, lying in ambush for passers-by. Very early in the morning the king set out for the mountains, looking for the Turks. He went as far as the Spring of Emaus[110] and as the sun rose he caught them unawares and charged down on them, killing twenty and routing the others. He also captured Saladin's herald, who used to proclaim his edicts. Him alone he spared. He also seized three camels and horses and mules, and beautiful turcomans.[111] In addition, he gained two excellent she-mules loaded with the most costly silken clothes and many kinds of spices, aloe and so on.

He also went through the mountains in hot pursuit of the Saracens, slaying them as they fled. Catching up with one of them in a valley, he ran him through and threw him dying from his horse. Having killed him, the king looked round - and saw in the distance the city of Jerusalem.[112]

---

109. The account now leaves the direct course of the crusade until the beginning of Book 6. Our author now again uses the first person, which Ambroise has been using for the whole journey from Darum. It seems odd that our author should sometimes deliberately use 'they' when Ambroise has 'we', yet sometimes repeat Ambroise's 'we', unless he himself was present for some events and not others.
110. 'Amwas, or possibly Abu Ghosh: see Pringle (forthcoming), 'Templar castles'.
111. A type of horse.
112. According to our author and Ambroise, this is the only time that Richard saw Jerusalem. He did not join the pilgrims who visited it in September 1192 after the Treaty of Jaffa.

Chapter 50: Hearing that the king is coming, the Turks in Jerusalem flee in fright and Saladin himself prepares for flight.[113]

When those in Jerusalem were informed by the fleeing Turks that King Richard was coming they were so terrified that if the king had advanced with the whole army at that point, when they were in a panic, the Turks would have abandoned the city of Jerusalem completely and left it for free and undisputed Christian habitation. All the Saracens quickly left the city and fled, so that there was no one to defend the city or who dared to live in it. The sultan's threats could not deter them nor his money tempt them to stay. Even Saladin demanded his best horse, ordering a swift warhorse to be provided for him so that he could flee from King Richard, because he did not dare to wait for his arrival.[114]

Chapter 51: Again, while they are staying at Betenoble, the French fight 200 Turks and would have been routed if the bishop of Salisbury had not come to their assistance.[115]

On the same day [12 June] while the king was concentrating on such pursuits and had time for such business, 200 Saracens came down from the mountains on to the plain and headed for the French tents. The whole army was thrown into confusion before they were chased away. They had already killed two of our men-at-arms who had gone out too far in search of fodder for the pack animals, and when they heard these two cry out, the French, the Templars and the Hospitallers leapt up and charged into the Turks. The Turks manfully resisted our people at the foot of the mountain and boldly threw them back. Yes, when the Turks engage our people on the plains they run away very fast, but on the mountain slope they resisted and suddenly knocked down one of our knights. The French won no little disgrace for this.

There was a certain knight whose valour would have won him renown if he had not infringed the rule of his order. Yet he seems to have presumed that his action would be excused on the grounds of his bold prow-

113. Ambroise, lines 9865–80.

114. Bahā' al-Dīn states that there was no panic in Jerusalem, but steps were taken to defend the city (p. 341). Ambroise gives our author's details and then says that Saladin found out from a spy that the great army was not coming, as God did not wish it at that time (lines 9881–4).

115. Ambroise, lines 9885–946.

ess. This man was a Hospitaller named Robert of Bruges. He passed the royal standard and came up to the king. Then, out of eagerness to engage the enemy and contrary to discipline, he strongly spurred the excellent horse on which he sat, abandoned the ranks of his comrades and before the others could advance in military order he charged alone into the enemy.

Catching sight of a very finely armed Turk he approached him at a swift gallop. The Turk's firm protective armour was useless before the strong lance he carried; he impaled him through the middle of his body so that the lance came out of his back. The Turk fell to the ground, but his body was not left lying there. At once all our people sent their horses charging into the enemy.

Then the master of the Hospital, Garnier [of Nablus][116] told the aforenamed Robert of Bruges to get off his horse and await the discipline of the order. The brother obeyed him and returned on foot from the field of conflict to the tents. He waited there patiently until powerful and noble men went down on their knees before Master Garnier and won pardon for Brother Robert for his offence, but on condition that he took care not to act like this in future.

For a long time the contest was in doubt, and on both sides they sweated, each side attacking their opponents with equal determination. The heavens rang with the battle; the soil was wet with blood. Swords rang as they struck, shields clattered. This side was full of anger, that side of fury. Our people were already exhausted by the weight of battle and beginning to waver, when, by God's providence, the count of Perche arrived, after hearing the uproar of the engagement! However, he acted timidly and if the bishop of Salisbury and his troop had not come quickly to their help the French would have been routed that day.[117]

---

116. Last seen Bk. 4 ch. 19, p. 251.
117. This last paragraph is not in Ambroise.

Chapter 52: Again, while they are staying there, our most doughty knights who have been assigned to escort our caravan coming from Joppa to the army receive disgusting treatment from the Turks and are very heavily beaten with clubs. They would have completely perished if the earl of Leicester had not come to their assistance.[118]

On 17 June, that is St Botolph's day, which was a Wednesday, our caravan left Joppa and set out for the army, loaded with foodstuffs and other necessary baggage. The task of escorting the caravan had been assigned that day to Ferric de Vienne. He was acting in place of Count Henry, who ought to have guarded its rear but had been sent to Acre. Ferric had asked Baldwin Carron and Clarembald de Mont-Chablon to guard the caravan for him that day, and to keep our people together on their march and not allow them to become separated. Nevertheless, they wandered along incautiously that day and paid for their carelessness and negligence.

There was Manessier de l'Isle, and Richard d'Orques, and Thierry, Philip and some comrades of Baldwin Carron, Otto and a great many of their squires, relations and friends, whose friendship was proven in necessity. Those in front travelled along quickly, while the rear followed more slowly, dawdling along. Then, suddenly! not far from Ramula, Turkish horsemen leapt out of hidden ambush and came rushing down on our rearguard at great speed, each struggling to go in front of the others. Those with the swiftest horses broke into our last detachment and passed through them. Baldwin Carron was thrown from his horse, and drawing his sword at once he brandished it at his attackers, striking so many blows in continuous succession that they could not touch him. In that engagement Richard d'Orques and Thierry were also thrown from their horses. Baldwin struggled on bravely until his men provided him with a horse that they had found and remounted him.

You would have seen a very bitter conflict: very fine encounters, well-aimed blows, glittering swordthrusts, untiring attacks meeting inflexible resistance. Countless horses wandered around riderless, the Turks charged, our people kept struggling persistently. Whenever the Turks knocked someone down others bore into the thick of the battle, lifted him up and remounted him. They gave each other much doughty

118. Ambroise, lines 9947–10088. 'Imād al-Dīn, p. 380, and Bahā' al-Dīn, p. 342, describe an ambush of a caravan on 16 June, which is probably this incident.

mutual assistance.

However, our people were fighting at a great disadvantage. As our few fought with the enemy troops they were widely separated from each other, so that they were effectively hidden from each other among the great number of the enemy. With such a great number of Turks surrounding our people it was not very surprising if even the most immoveable of them was thrown down, overpowered by the impact of so many enemies. Turkish darts flew very densely, wounding the horses and greatly weakening them. What was more, Baldwin was knocked off his horse again! At once he ordered one of his squires to get off the horse he was riding and give it to him. The squire had displayed great prowess while he was mounted on horseback, but as soon as Baldwin mounted he saw his squire's head cut off.

Our people stood their ground, defending themselves. Baldwin's comrade Philip was captured – he had been the most distinguished warrior on the field. The Turks also led away a most outstanding squire with Philip, and killed Richard's brother. Another engagement like that would be horrendous to the timid. With all their strength Baldwin and his comrades strove and struggled with their swords. Clarembald de Mont-Chablon had already deserted them: he fled away at speed as he saw the number of Turks increasing.

As that bitter conflict began again, Baldwin was thrown from a third horse, and they pounded him so heavily with clubs that he was rendered almost helpless. Blood poured from his nose and mouth, and the edge of his sword was blunted and useless from dealing constant blows. As the hostile masses pressed in on him, he cried out in a loud voice to Manessier de l'Isle, an outstanding knight who was crushing all the Turks: 'O Manessier, have you deserted me?'

When Manessier heard this he flew quickly to rescue Baldwin from the enormous pressure of the Turks, but there were too many Turks for the two of them to defeat. For some time the two of them struggled against the countless hordes pouring down on them. Manessier was also thrown from his horse, and they beat him cruelly with iron-toothed clubs as he lay on the ground, standing over him, lacerating him, crushing him and so mercilessly shattering his body that they broke the bone of one of his legs. So Baldwin and Manessier sank under the hostile mob, while their own people had lost sight of them and had no idea what had happened to them.

Then God sent them a liberator and defender! – the most outstanding earl of Leicester, who had not been aware of their position. The earl came up with a great charge and immediately threw the first Turk he met off his horse. Anscon, Stephen Longchamp's comrade, cut off the Turk's head and hurled it away. Stephen himself also acquitted himself manfully in every situation. Our people's forces grew, and the Turks' courage faded, and they turned and fled towards the mountains at a fast gallop! - except for those our people caught up with. Then they gently laid our wounded and fallen on horses and took them back to the army.

So I think that what was done that day ought to be remembered: how the earl of Leicester routed the Turks, killed some and captured others.

Chapter 53: Again, while they are staying there the Syrian bishop of St George brings a piece of the Lord's Cross to King Richard and gives it to him.[119]

When the Saracens first came to the region around Jerusalem and destroyed it, the Syrian bishop of St George had paid tribute to Saladin on behalf of himself and his people. Now he came with a great crowd of his people, men and women, to King Richard with a fragment of the Holy Cross, and gave that piece of cross to the king.[120]

Chapter 54: Again, while they are staying there a certain abbot tells the king that he has hidden a fragment of the Holy Cross in a certain place. The king goes with the abbot, finds it and brings it back, and he and the army adore it.[121]

Again, three days before the feast of St John the Baptist, St Alban's day [22 June] the whole army was comforted by some news that came to the king at the place where the army was then staying. For a certain devout abbot came to the king. His face showed his saintliness: he had a long

119. Not in Ambroise.

120. Presumably, thereby showing that he recognised Richard as his lord rather than Saladin. The Syrian Orthodox Church operated in the Latin East alongside the Latin Church, each with their own clergy and bishops.

121. Ambroise, lines 10089-136. Roger of Howden, *Chronica*, p. 182, describes this in the context of a raid by Richard up to Jerusalem. He came to the chapel of St. Elijah and found a cross called 'the Syrians' Cross', made from the wood of the Lord's Cross. He took it away with him. Ralph of Coggeshall, pp. 40-41, says that a hermit gave the cross to the king. Chs. 53 and 54 may in fact be different versions of the same incident.

beard, snowy-white hair and a venerable appearance, and he was the abbot of St Elijah.

He told the king that he had for a long time kept a fragment of the Holy Cross hidden, waiting for a time when, by God's aid, the Holy Land would be freed from the Turks and all things restored to their former state. He claimed that he alone knew of this buried treasure. He said that Saladin had often pressed and coerced him with very persistent questions to produce this piece of the Cross, but he had always left his interrogator uncertain with his ambiguous answers and deluded him with dishonest replies. Saladin had ordered him to be tied up tightly so that he could interrogate him, but the abbot consistently claimed that he had lost that piece of the Cross when the city of Jerusalem was captured. So he misled all his careful interrogations.

When the king heard this he and a great many people at once set out in due order with the abbot to the place of which the abbot had spoken. They lifted that piece of the Holy Cross from its place; then, quickly and with fitting reverence, they brought it back to the army. There the people adored it with the greatest devotion, eagerly kissing it and weeping many pious tears.

The end of Book 5; the start of Book 6.

Book 6

Chapter 1: The French wish to go to Jerusalem, but for many reasons King Richard will not consent to this unless the Templars, Hospitallers and natives of the country agree.[1]

So for some time the army rejoiced over the Holy Cross and adored it. Then the ordinary common people began to complain. 'Lord God, what shall we do now? Surely we don't still have to go to Jerusalem? What more is left for us to do? Do we have to go on until the pilgrimage is complete?' There was much murmuring and complaining among the masses.

The king and the leaders of the people assembled to discuss whether or not it would be advantageous to go forward to besiege Jerusalem. The French kept begging and urging the king insistently to advance to a siege, since this seemed to them to be the most appropriate thing to do. However, the king replied that this could not be done. 'And you will not see me leading the people in this undertaking,' he said, 'for it will bring me blame and disgrace. You are rash in urging me into this venture. However, if you wish to head for Jerusalem now, I will not desert you. I will be your comrade, not your leader. I will follow you, but not precede. You know that Saladin finds out everything that goes on in this army. He knows our strength and what we are capable of. We are a long way from the coast.[2] Supposing Saladin and his people come down into the plain of Ramula, and keep watch on the thoroughfares and blockade the usual routes, so that no supplies can reach us; don't you think that this will be absolutely disastrous for the besiegers? And it would be much too late to repent of having begun.

'Besides, we understand that this city of Jerusalem which we would be besieging covers a very large area. If our tiny force were to besiege it equally from all sides there would be insufficient personnel both for the siege and to rescue those bringing our food supplies, if they happen to be attacked by the Turks. No: everyone could easily be completely anni-

1. Ambroise, lines 10137–211.
2. And hence from their supply base.

hilated, for there would be no one to help them.

'If I were the author of this rash venture and anything unfortunate were to happen to the army while I was leader, which God forbid, I alone would be accused of stupidity. If I were now to lead the army to besiege Jerusalem I would be to blame for endangering everyone. Besides, I am absolutely certain that there are some here present, and others in France, whom I know have wished for a long time and still wish and very much desire that I should expend my efforts in rash enterprises like this and carry out operations which are open to criticism, so that I will win terrible disgrace. For this reason, I do not judge that we ought to rush rashly headlong into such difficult enterprises when the outcome is so uncertain.

'Besides, we and our people are foreigners and know absolutely nothing about this region, its thoroughfares or its passes. If we knew them we could advance more safely and carefully, and so we would be able to win our desired success. In my opinion, it would be safer to act with the advice of the natives of the country, who wish to recover their former territories and inheritances, and do what seems most appropriate to them, because they have better knowledge of the terrain. It seems to me that we ought to follow whatever course of action the Templars and the Hospitallers honestly judge and decide that we should undertake: whether we should advance to besiege Jerusalem; whether we go to seize Babylonia [Egypt]; or to Beirut,[3] or to Damascus. If we act in accordance with their decision our army will no longer be torn into factions by our disagreements, as it is now.'

Chapter 2: By common assent, twenty wise men are chosen and everyone is to abide by their advice. Having been sworn in, they advise a campaign to Babylonia rather than Jerusalem. The king approves this but the French oppose it.[4]

So on the king's encouragement everyone agreed that twenty honest jurors should decide on the course of action and all would give their unanimous consent to this without opposition. Therefore the following were chosen to make the decision: five Templars, five Hospitallers, five

---

3. They did attack Beirut later: see ch. 14, p. 352 below. Richard had been planning an attack on Egypt: see note 71 on Bk. 4 ch. 27.
4. Ambroise, lines 10212–66.

natives of the land of Syria[5] and five French chiefs. These twenty assembled together and after discussing the aforesaid matters together for some time replied that without doubt the most advantageous course of action would be to go to besiege Babylonia [Egypt]. When the French heard this they resolutely opposed it, protesting that they would not move on anywhere except to besiege Jerusalem.

When the king became aware that the French were being rude and rebellious, he was disturbed. 'If the French would accept my advice,' he said, 'keep their oath and agree to proceed to besiege Babylonia, look, I would provide them with my fleet at Acre, which is well fitted out and which could carry supplies of food and all their necessities, and the army could then proceed confidently along the coast. I will also lead 700 knights and 2000 men-at-arms at my own expense, in God's name. Besides, if anyone is in need of my labour or money or anything which I have, it will certainly be generously provided according to their need.

'However, because they think we ought to do something else, I will not refuse to go with them, but only with my own retinue. I will not lead strangers.'

Then he immediately ordered that his people should assemble in the Hospitallers' tents and find out what each person would contribute towards the siege and how many people they would provide. So they came, and there, as was said before, the magnates and the rest promised to provide great things for the siege, even those who had very little in their purses. But it would appear to have been extremely unwise and audacious to desire this course of action at such a doubtful and uncertain juncture, let alone to begin a siege of Jerusalem after the jurors had advised so much against it.

5. i.e. descendants of the European settlers in Palestine and Syria.

Chapter 3: Again, while they are staying there, Bernard the king's spy reports that enormous caravans are coming from Babylonia. The king and the French leap out to seize them, while on the other side Saladin sends knights to protect them.[6]

So while they were busily setting down what each person ought to contribute to the siege, along came Bernard, the king's spy, with two others. They were all natives of the country and wore Saracen clothes. They had come from Babylonia [Egypt] and were no different from Saracens in their appearance, and their sole occupation was to keep King Richard fully informed of the Saracens' movements. They spoke the Saracen language better than anyone. In return for their service, each of these three had previously received from King Richard 100 silver marks. So these three informed the king that he and his people should come without delay to intercept caravans which were coming from Babylonia, and they promised to lead them to them.

The king was absolutely delighted at what he heard and instructed the duke of Burgundy to come quickly with him on this undertaking and bring the French with him. He did so, but the French only promised to come with him on condition that they receive a third of the booty. The king agreed.

So without delay around 500 well-armed knights set out. The king also led 1000 very agile hired men-at-arms. Evening was already drawing on as they set out, the king in advance of the others. They marched all night, travelling by moonlight, as far as Galatia [Qaratayyā]. They rested a little there and sent to Ascalon for food. Meanwhile they took the precaution of carefully donning their armour until the servants who had been sent for the food returned.

It is said that when our people first set out to seize the caravans, a certain spy at once informed Saladin in Jerusalem that he had seen King Richard hurrying towards the caravans with his people; and so our 'secret intentions were revealed.'[7] Saladin, therefore, immediately sent 500 elite Turks hurrying to guard the caravans. They were armed with bows and arrows. When they had all assembled together with those who had originally been assigned to escort the caravans there were reckoned to be 2000 horse besides a great number of infantry.

---

6. Ambroise, lines 10267–328. Bahā' al-Dīn, pp. 343–4; 'Imād al-Dīn, pp. 380–1. There were three caravans; Richard captured the last one.
7. According to Stubbs (1864), p. 385, the Latin is from the Book of Judith, ch. 2 v. 2.

Chapter 4: King Richard and his forces manfully struggle with the Turks and capture one caravan of very precious things of incalculable value, and countless camels, dromedaries, horses, mules and asses.[8]

While King Richard and his people were halted at Galatia, along came a spy who informed him that one of the aforesaid caravans was passing by the Round Cistern [nr. Tell-Khuwailifa][9] and advised him to advance quickly to capture it. In the meantime, the army should remain together. 'Whoever captures this caravan will make a great profit,' he said. However, since that spy was a native of that country, the king did not consider that complete trust could be placed in his word alone. So he at once sent a Bedouin and two very prudent native Turcopoles to look into the matter and investigate the truth, and he made them swathe themselves up like Bedouins, so that they would look like Saracens.

They set out by night, crossed hills covered with watchtowers and descended on the other side, until they caught sight of some Saracens above them. They were also scouts, lying in wait for passers-by. When our Bedouin cautiously approached them to reconnoitre, the Saracens made careful inquiries into where he was coming from and where he was going. Giving a sign to his two companions to keep quiet so that they would not be recognised from their accent, the Bedouin replied that they were returning from the Ascalon region, where they had gone to pillage.

'No, you have come to ambush us, you wretch,' said one of the Saracens, 'for you are with the king of the English.'

'You're lying,' said the Bedouin, and with that advanced hastily towards the caravans.

The Turks pursued them for a while with bows and arrows and harassed them quite energetically until, growing bored, they left off the pursuit, strongly suspecting that they were on their side rather than being strangers. So when our spies had ascertained the truth about the said caravans, they returned without delay to King Richard and said that without doubt he would be able to capture the caravans provided he advanced quickly.

When the king realised this, he had the horses refreshed with a quick feed of grain and then set out hastily with his people. They marched the

8. Ambroise, lines 10329–508. The caravan was captured on Tuesday 23 June: Roger of Howden, *Chronica*, 3 p. 182.
9. 'Imād al-Dīn, p. 381.

whole of that night[10] until they came near to the place where the caravan had halted while its guards rested. The king and his companions stopped not far from there, armed themselves without delay and drew up their battle lines troop by troop, the king in the first rank and the French in the last. Through a herald's proclamation, the king forbad all looting; everyone should instead press on manfully to break through and crush the Turks' battle lines.

It was already daylight and they were pressing on busily with drawing up the detachments when along came another spy at full gallop. He informed the king that since the crack of dawn the caravan had been preparing to move swiftly on from there as the guards had been informed that the king and his forces were about to attack. When the king heard this he at once ordered lightly armed crossbowmen and archers to make the Turks delay their journey and detain them by appearing to challenge them to battle, so that their progress would be slowed and our people could catch up with them more quickly.

While the Turks were delayed by the frequent attacks our ordered battle lines approached speedily. When the Turks saw them coming, they took refuge on a certain mound on a nearby mountain, assembled together as if they regarded the higher ground as more secure, and drew up their army in troops; but their arrogance was less in evidence than usual. So as our battle lines charged, the Turks fired arrows and darts at them very densely, falling like dew on the surface of the ground; while the caravan waited in one place. The king had divided the army in two. He now rushed suddenly down on the Turks, and he and his followers burst powerfully through the Turkish front line and routed it. He had charged them so violently that he knocked them flat, and even those whom he had not struck through fell back from him on all sides. They crushed those who fled, so that already there was no one left to resist, except perhaps those who fired a dart or an arrow behind them as they fled. Everyone fled swiftly like hares escaping dogs, and scattered in various directions before their pursuers.

The caravan was left abandoned. Our people went on untiringly, continually slaying to the right and the left. They did not cease the pursuit, and the Turks fell everywhere and died of thirst in the arid desert. All those whom our knights pursued and threw from their horses were killed

10. MSS A and B say 'the following night'. Stubbs (1864), pp. 384, note, and 386, suggests that the spies returned on 22 June and the army marched during the night of 22–3 June.

by the squires. There saddles were seen overturned, and the conquered miserably destroyed.[11]

The king's people fought exceptionally well, and the French extremely energetically, since they were experienced in battle. Yet King Richard was beyond compare. He outshone all the rest magnificently with glorious privilege. Borne on a high horse, he charged alone into the enemy – until his couched ashwood spear became weakened from piercing the enemy too many times with savage blows and shattered into many bloodstained splinters. Then he immediately brandished his drawn sword and bore down on the fugitives, seized them, threw them down, mowed down the hindmost and shaved off the last. He was the tamer of the slowfooted common people; he shone out as he advanced, he tore the fugitives to pieces. He struck anyone he caught, armour of any type notwithstanding, with the edge of his drawn sword from the crown of the head to the teeth. He tossed and hunted down the scattered like a wolf pursues fleeing sheep.

However, while the king was tirelessly tossing the Turks like this, everyone who was left had scattered in various directions. Riding at a swifter gallop, the king had already seized the foremost as they fled through the mountains.[12] Some of them, despairing of escaping the king's hands by direct flight, eluded him by taking a curving route and turned back towards our rearguard along a narrow path from the flank. They hoped that they would be better able to achieve something against some of the others in the king's absence; for whenever they saw him, their valour faded away. They were scared to death of the king, with good reason, for the enemy's death was in his hands.

So around thirty Turks turned round as they fled and made a great charge against Roger de Toony, immediately killing his horse under him. They had almost seized him when one of Roger's companions, Jokelin of Maine, came to rescue him from their hands. He was also thrown at once from his horse, but Roger de Toony, who was resolutely defending himself on foot, came up and freed him. Meanwhile our people ran up: the earl of Leicester threw them down to the right and the left; Gilbert Malmain also came with four companions; and Alexander Arsic[13] came and around twenty other knights. Also Stephen Longchamp did Roger de Toony generous service, providing him with a horse to raise himself out of the midst of the warlike Turks.

11. From here until 'bloodstained splinters' is not in Ambroise.
12. From here until 'in his hands' is not in Ambroise.
13. *HGM*, lines 4719–22 praises his prowess and good looks.

Then the slaughter began again, the sky rang with battle, the air was bright with the flash of swords, the soil flowed with blood, weapons rang as they struck together, corpses were torn limb from limb. Everywhere lay scattered arms, hands, feet and heads which had been cut off. Some of the heads had been split to the eyes or mouth or throat by the blow which had struck them: the force of the delivery depended on fate or the heat of the engagement. The corpses of dead Turks lay so densely through the countryside that they impeded our people as they marched, and the bodies which they had just beheaded obstructed them and tripped them up. The Poitevins, French, Normans and Angevins were outstanding; but King Richard, the flower of virtue and the crown of knighthood, 'took all the applause' [Horace, *de Arte Poetica*, v. 343], from everyone, and won the most distinction.

If only you could have seen that enormous slaughter of Turks, greater than any of our ancestors ever saw before! They melted away in such great confusion and were so overcome that even a weak boy could have killed ten of them, or every one he hit. The Turks' pride was completely frustrated; their arrogance was destroyed, and their audacity checked; and our people powerfully took possession of the caravan.

The Turks who guarded the carters and laden pack animals which made up the caravan spontaneously gave themselves up to our knights and squires as prisoners. Stretching out their hands in supplication they begged for mercy and compassion, reckoning that nothing else mattered if only their lives would be spared. They offered them yoked horses and laden camels which they led by their halters, and he-mules and she-mules carrying various sorts of precious spices, enormous quantities of gold and silver, silken cloth, purple cloth, robes, and purple dye, and many sorts of clothes, besides various sorts of weapons, embroidered mailshirts commonly called 'casigans' [*kesagenda*: Saracen mailshirts] woven in many layers, quilts variously embroidered with much workmanship, pavilions and very valuable tents, biscuit, wheat, barley and flour, a great many cordials and medicines, basins, bottles and chess boards, silver pots and candlesticks, pepper, cinnamon, sugar, and wax and other choice spices of various types, a countless quantity of money, and incalculable supplies of other things. There were so many different sorts of things and such great variety that it was said that never at any time from any battle had such great booty or anything like it been acquired all at once.

Chapter 5: How many camels and dromedaries were captured and how many Turks were killed.[14]

When the slaughter of the infidels was complete and the caravan had been captured, our people had a new task to perplex them: herding together the racing camels and dromedaries. This threw the whole army into confusion. When our horsemen chased them, trying to catch them, they ran away so fast that you never saw an animal with such a great turn of speed. A stag or doe or any other animal of the chase would seem sluggish and slow in comparison, and they needed only a very short distance to reach a gallop.[15]

When they had eventually been gathered together by one means or another there were reckoned to be round about 4700 camels and dromedaries. They had also captured so many he- and she-mules and baggage donkeys they could not be counted, so that they seemed somewhat burdened with such great plenty. Moreover, more than 1700 Turkish horsemen were killed in various places that day, in addition to a considerable number of infantry crushed to death.

Chapter 6: The king returns with the booty to Betenopolis, from where he started. Count Henry comes to meet him from Acre, with the army which he was sent for.[16]

When these things had been done the baggage was packed away for the return march and the king and the army went back at a gentle pace with much booty. They returned by prearranged stages to Bethaven, which is four miles distant from Joppa. There they divided up their booty and plunder. From there on the following day they went on to Ramula [26 June].

Meanwhile, Count Henry arrived at Ramula from Acre with the forces he had brought from there for the army. From Ramula they all went to Betenopolis [Bait-Nūbā] from where they had originally set out.

So joy was renewed and everyone rejoiced together and admired the great numbers of baggage animals which filled the army. There the munificent king distributed his camels, which were the best ever seen, to

14. Ambroise, lines 10539-64.
15. Ambroise says that a stag, doe, buck or gazelle could not have caught them if they had a short start.
16. Ambroise, lines 10565-92.

his knights. Those who stayed behind to guard the army received the same share as those who accompanied the expedition. In this he was neatly imitating the mighty warrior King David, in that those who stayed with the stores were to have the same share as those who went into battle [1 Samuel ch. 30 v. 24]. He also divided all the donkeys among the men-at-arms. The army was so full of camels and donkeys and other pack animals that they could hardly be controlled. The troops happily ate the meat of the younger camels fried in lard; the flesh was white and quite palatable.

Chapter 7: The people grieve because sound reasoning and wise advice prevent them from going towards Jerusalem.[17]

The people soon became disgusted with the distribution of so many pack animals and began to complain that they were eating too much wheat and barley. For this reason the price of grain had risen. They also began wailing and complaining again because no preparations were in train to advance to besiege Jerusalem, as they wished. This was because - as was said above - the twenty jurors appointed to make a decision on this had been opposed to it. They had argued that it would be very difficult to do, if not impossible, because of the lack of water, which humans and pack animals cannot do without; especially because the feast of St John [24 June] was now fast approaching,[18] when everything naturally becomes dry as the summer heat increases, particularly around Jerusalem, which is in the mountains. Besides, the Turks had blocked all the cisterns on every side of the city[19] so that there was no drinking water to be found for two miles, so that the army would be in very great difficulties. Once the siege had begun it would not be safe to go too far looking for water. The tiny rivulet which runs down the foot of the Mount of Olives would not be enough for such a large army - this is the water of Siloam [see John's Gospel, ch. 9 v. 7]. For these reasons they advised against besieging Jerusalem at that time.[20]

17. Ambroise, lines 10593-638.
18. As Stubbs (1864), points out, p. 393 note 6, this is incorrect; it was now Friday 26 June.
19. Bahā' al-Dīn, p. 346, confirms this.
20. Bahā' al-Dīn, pp. 351-2, states that this discussion took place on a Friday. Richard opposed the advance for the reasons given here. The matter was referred to a council who decided against the advance. The retreat began on Saturday 4 July 1192. Bahā' al-Dīn attributes the retreat to the prayers of the

When it became known to the army that they were not going to advance to Jerusalem and that in fact the army was going to turn back they were devastated. In their terrible sorrow they began to curse their delay in advancing and the hopes they had conceived. They said that they had only wished to live until the Christians gained Jerusalem and to ensure that holy things were not given into the hands of strangers. However, God the Just Judge [2 Timothy ch. 4 v. 8] directs times and seasons for the human emotions with inscrutable dispensation. It is believed that through His clemency and mercy He punishes the vices of those who err, 'taking vengeance on all their inventions' [Psalm 99 v. 8].

Chapter 8: Because of their jealousy the French lacerate and slander each other and separate themselves from our people. Henry [Hugh] duke of Burgundy composes an abusive song about King Richard.[21]

It is not surprising that the pilgrims were so annoyed and frustrated or that they were grieving that things had not gone as they wished, since great disagreement had grown between them. The aimless and fickle character of the French and their unreliable behaviour had cut them off from the rest. For when the army was advancing anywhere and dusk was falling the French gathered together in a group for the night, often moving away from the rest of the army and camping in another place at a distance, as if they scorned the others' company. Not content with just this separation, they also disagreed among themselves, hurling derisive words loaded with loathing and bitingly witty abuse. Sometimes obscene

---

sultan on the Friday and God's support for the Muslims (pp. 11-14). Roger of Howden records that Richard was determined to besiege Jerusalem as long as he still had one nag to eat, but the French refused (*Chronica*, 3 p. 183) as the king of France had ordered them to return to France. Ralph of Coggeshall, pp. 38-9, states that Richard was being kept informed by a religious woman in Jerusalem of events there, and the army was about to advance; but the duke of Burgundy, Templars and French refused to advance because the king of France would be angry if King Richard took the city with their help. King Richard discovered (pp. 39-40) that the duke of Burgundy was secretly in league with Saladin. The duke was ashamed and returned to Acre. This alternative version of events seems to have been put about by Richard's supporters to defend him for having failed to besiege Jerusalem. *LFWT*, pp. 146-8, gives reasons for the retreat similar to those in IP2.

21. Ambroise, lines 10639-82.

insults were exchanged, each boasting of their own superiority and disparaging the other's cowardice.

On top of all this, Henry [Hugh III] duke of Burgundy, prompted by a spirit of worthless arrogance or perhaps led on by the most unbecoming malicious envy, composed the words of a song to be sung in public. Such shameful words should never have been made public if its composers[22] had retained any sense of propriety, for they were revealed not so much as men but as men beyond raping women.[23]

Those who applied their efforts to such shocking and silly activities certainly made themselves conspicuous and revealed the hidden intentions of their hearts, for streams must be like their spring, cloudy or clear. This invidious composition was sung all through the army. The king was extremely annoyed about it,[24] and thought that he should punish them by paying them back in their own coin. So he also sang something about them, and it was little trouble to compose because there was plenty of material to hand. So what if he responded to so many fictions and taunts with some truths? The reputation of King Richard's exceptional exploits remained undoubted; but since his rivals despaired of equalling his valour, they attacked it freely with all the hatred they could.[25]

These were not like the pilgrims who were once on the expedition to Antioch, which our people powerfully captured in a famous victory which is still related in the deeds of Bohemond and Tancred and Godfrey de Bouillon and the other most outstanding chiefs, who triumphed in so many glorious victories, whose feats even now are like food in the mouth of the narrator.[26] Because they performed their service freely and wholeheartedly for God, God 'rewarded their labours' [Wisdom of Solomon ch. 10 v. 17], and exalted their magnificent feats so that they would be remembered forever and all their descendants would also be praised with ample reverence.

---

22. 'If its composers...cloudy or clear' is not in Ambroise.
23. Unclear passage; this makes best sense but assumes the Latin is corrupt. I have assumed *viros* must be *viris*.
24. From here to 'material to hand' is not in Ambroise.
25. This last sentence is not in Ambroise.
26. The siege of Antioch, which took place during the First Crusade in 1098–9, was recounted in the popular epic poem *La Chanson d'Antioche*.

Chapter 9: The Christians return from Betenopolis to their homeland.[27]

After the capture of the caravan, the army remained sadly for some days at Betenopolis. They were absolutely devastated, because they had been advised against advancing to Jerusalem to visit the Lord's Sepulchre, which was now only four miles away.[28] So it was with the greatest sadness that they turned back. Never was an elite force worn down with such weariness.

When they had drawn up their detachments and the army was setting out on its journey in order, the Turks rushed down from the mountains and attacked the rearguard, killing some of our men-at-arms in their charge. However the cavalry, which had swift horses, firmly withstood them and drove them away.

Proceeding on their way, they reached a point between St George and Ramula where the army spent the night. The French took up a position on the left, while the king and his people were on the right. On the following day they travelled in the same divisions. On the next night, that is 6 July, they rested at Casal Medium [Casal Maen?].[29] Some people left the army there and continued to Joppa, because of the disgusting conditions and the scarcity which they had endured during the campaign.

Chapter 10: Saladin learns that the Christians are in disagreement and are withdrawing from their attack, and summons an infinite number of Turks.[30]

When Saladin was informed of the state of our army and that our council had taken the decision to withdraw, his hope revived and he relaxed into delighted joy. He immediately sent fast messengers with letters sealed with his seal to all his emirs, princes, satraps and prefects of regions under his authority, informing them that as the Christians had been scattered by disputes and had split up and left, anyone who wished to serve under his pay should come without delay to him in Jerusalem.

---

27. Ambroise, lines 10683–718.
28. Ambroise says (line 10691), four leagues, which is four hours' travel, or ten miles. Stubbs (1864), p. 396 note 5 points out that they were actually ten miles from Jerusalem.
29. Stubbs (1864), p. 396.
30. Ambroise, lines 10719–37.

Immediately an enormous number of Turks flocked together. There were reckoned to be 20,000 armed horsemen and so many infantry that they could not easily be counted.

Chapter 11: When King Richard sees that his forces are disappearing he requests the truce which had previously been offered, but is refused. So he destroys Darum, fortifies Ascalon, and goes via Joppa to Acre.[31]

Meanwhile our people were gradually slipping away; some of them withdrew to Joppa. When the king realised that he was unable to keep them together because they had no unity of purpose, he acted as he thought best in that situation. He instructed Saphadin to agree a truce with Saladin in accordance with the terms offered on the plains of Ramula, to keep things as they then were until such time as he could return from his own country. Saphadin should inform him of what would advance these negotiations more quickly. However, the full details of our army's state were not hidden from Saladin, who was aware that our strength was gradually weakening. Hence he would not consent unless Ascalon were razed to the ground.[32]

When messengers returned and informed the king of this he seemed unmoved and his expression remained completely unchanged. He at once commanded the Templars and Hospitallers and certain others with them to mount their horses, 300 knights in all, and ordered them to proceed to break down and destroy Darum Castle, and to strengthen Ascalon very strongly and set guards. Those thus commanded hurried to carry out the king's commands, and having razed Darum Castle to the ground, they returned to the army.

So the army returned to Joppa, distressed and with heavy heart. From there they at once set out for Acre, the king with the rest, although a great many stayed in Joppa, some healthy and some infirm. So the army returned to Acre, indescribably devastated and dismayed because so many things had been going against them. Obviously God still considered their merits unworthy of the gift of His benign grace.

---

31. Ambroise, lines 10743–86.
32. Bahā' al-Dīn, pp. 353–9, gives details of the negotiations, which lasted from 4 July to 20 July. He agrees with our writer on the outcome: war was renewed because Richard refused to allow the demolition of Ascalon.

Chapter 12: The army with which Saladin came to Joppa.[33]

Hearing that the Joppans were without the king's protection, Saladin made his army ready to advance towards it, hoping that he would be able to capture the city easily in King Richard's absence. So he moved his army, which was made up of a great number of assembled forces: there were 20,000 horsemen; the very powerful emir of Bila[34] was present and the son of the Assassin,[35] as well as around 107 emirs, and a countless horde of infantry from the mountains who covered the face of the earth like locusts. The army set out from Jerusalem and descended into the plain of Ramula with great pride and noise. They ran along in troops and cohorts as if they were driven by the Furies and they swore that the Christians should be completely destroyed.

Chapter 13: Saladin attacks Joppa with such strength that he would have captured it if the besieged had not sought a truce until the next day.[36]

On that same Sunday, the Sunday before St Peter in Chains [26 July 1192] when King Richard reached Acre with the army, Saladin and his army approached to besiege Joppa. They began to besiege the fortress on the Monday following. Those who were in the city leapt out into the suburban area outside the walls and resisted them all day so that the Turks could not approach the walls. Neither could they make any progress on Tuesday, when they convened the same contest, nor on the Wednesday. Making a virtue of necessity, they defended themselves strongly and withstood the advance.

By the Thursday the Turks were grieved that they had been repelled by so few and had achieved nothing. Their fury increased and the siege was strengthened. On Saladin's order, four very heavy and effective stonethrowers were set up, as well as two easily-operated mangonels. What great complaining you would have heard from the besieged! –

33. Ambroise, lines 10787–806.
34. Presumably the emir of Byla of Bk. 1 ch. 5, whom Mayer (1962) identified as the emir of al-Bīra.
35. Here Arcissus, but Assasisus in ch. 14, p. 353 below. Ambroise says (line 10799) 'the son of the Hausasis', i.e. 'the son of the Assassin'.
36. Ambroise, lines 10807–934; see also Ralph of Coggeshall, pp. 42–3; 'Imād al-Dīn, pp. 384–8; Bahā' al-Dīn, pp. 361–71.

more than 5000 of them including those who were infirm, lamenting and saying: 'Lord God of Hosts, what refuge is left for us? Alas, king of England, our leader and protector, what took you to Acre? Christians, you are growing weak, you are already perishing!'

Meanwhile the Turks pressed on fiercely, attacking the city with great strength. The besieged resisted manfully. It would have moved anyone to tears of deep pity to see them so bewildered, running up to the battlements and down again, and dashing in different directions to the various tasks which had to be done.

The stonethrowers hurled without a pause and the mangonels never stopped. Those inside the city certainly had stonethrowers but they were not skilled enough to use them. At last on Friday, due to the Turks' continual persistence in constantly firing the stonethrowers, the gate which faced Jerusalem was broken and the wall on the righthand side was shattered for the length of two perches [11 yards, or 10 metres].

How bitter that conflict was! The besieged resisted the Turks and drove them back as they entered. However as the Turkish force grew and strengthened the Christians were driven back from the entrance and the Turks entered and pursued our people into the citadel of the fortress.

Alas for the pitiful slaughter of the sick! They lay weakly on couches everywhere in the houses of the city; the Turks tortured them to death in horrible ways. A countless number of them were killed and should certainly be reckoned as martyrs. Some of our people fled from the harsh ferocity of the approaching Turks on to the seashore. Meanwhile the Turks continued their merciless invasion by thoroughly searching the houses, plundering wheat but smashing the wine barrels and pouring away all the wine. A part of the enemy army attacked the main citadel of the fortress, while part pursued those who were fleeing to the ships to save themselves. A great many of those in the rear were killed. Aubrey de Reims, whose duty it was to guard the fortress, took refuge on a ship intending to flee in it and escape death. For shame! His extreme fear revealed him as a disgrace to his race. His comrades who had remained behind criticised his cowardice, stirred him to firm courage, told him to act like a man and forced him somewhat violently into the citadel. Seeing nothing but danger around him, he said, 'We must die here for God, then, since there is nothing else to be done.'

On all sides the Turks were still pressing on with demolishing the citadel. Darts and arrows flew like hail; the air was thick with them. The besieged did not know on which side to defend themselves.

The assault continued all day without a pause. The besieged might have been overcome by its force and given way before it, had it not been that by God's dispensation the newly created patriarch[37] was present, who was not daunted by fear of death and did not go to pieces in the face of great danger. Necessity made him a skilful negotiator; he sent a message to Saladin and appealed to his brother Saphadin to obtain a generous truce for them in the attack on the citadel until the next day, on the condition that if no help had come to the besieged from anywhere before the ninth hour[38] each of those who were left in the citadel would pay Saladin ten gold besants, each women would pay five besants and each boy three, to compensate him for giving them such a long truce. The patriarch offered himself as a hostage to guarantee that these terms would be faithfully kept, along with other noblemen. They would be bound in chains until the ninth hour the following day.

Saladin approved. When they had given security, according to their rites, that the terms of the delay would be observed, hostages were given: the patriarch, Aubrey de Reims, Theobald de Troyes, Augustine de London and Osbert Waldin, and Henry de St John, as well as some others whose names we do not have.[39] These were later all taken as captives to Damascus. The besieged had already conceived some hope that the king would come to relieve them, as they had sent to Acre for him when Saladin had first arrived.[40]

---

37. Ralph, bishop of Bethlehem: see Hamilton (1980), p. 131.
38. *hora nona*, i.e. 3 pm. But here it may mean noon: Stubbs (1864), p. 403.
39. Ambroise gives only two people: Aubrey and Theobald de Troyes, a sergeant of Count Henry of Champagne who had brought up the count's father (lines 10929–32).
40. The last two sentences are not in Ambroise. Bahā' al-Dīn gives a slightly different account of the negotiation of the truce, in which he was involved. The Christians had been trying to negotiate a truce since before the fall of the city. The truce was made on Saladin's terms: it would expire on Saturday, but no precise time was set (pp. 363, 365). Aubrey de Reims and the patriarch are not mentioned at this point; they negotiated a further truce the following day (see below).

Chapter 14: Although King Richard was about to embark for home, and although the French refused to help, when the Joppans' messengers recalled him he came hastily by galley and sent knights by land.[41]

Meanwhile, King Richard was hurrying to depart from Acre so that he could get home quickly. His ships were fully equipped and he was about to go on board. He had already taken his leave of the Templars and Hospitallers and received their blessing. As his route lay via Beirut he had sent seven of his galleys there with armed men with the intention of alarming those who were in the fortress, as if he were challenging them to an engagement; but they were terrified and fled the fortress.[42] While the king, as I said, was in his tent conferring with his people about the arrangements for his departure, the messengers sent by the besieged in Joppa came running up! They stood before the king with their clothes torn and informed him that Joppa and everything in it had been taken by the Saracens and that the survivors were besieged in the citadel; and in accordance with the conditions of the agreement already mentioned[43] the besieged were all certainly condemned to perish, unless he speedily brought them help. The life and death of all depended on him alone.

When he heard that they were in danger of death, the king pitied the besieged and interrupted the messengers while they were still pressing their case. 'As the Lord lives,' he said, 'with God as my guide I will set out to do what I can.' Immediately an edict was proclaimed by public criers, summoning the army to set out on an expedition. However, the French did not deign to honour the king with a response. They only repeated haughtily that they would go no further with him. In fact they did indeed march no further with him nor with anyone else, for they all

---

41. Ambroise, lines 10935–11078.
42. Saladin had heard about this expedition on 23 July (Bahā' al-Dīn, p. 360). He took the opportunity of Richard being occupied in the north to attack Jaffa. Although our writer only mentions it in passing, the Muslim historians imply that the attack on Beirut was a large expedition: see also 'Imād al-Dīn, p. 386.
43. The order of events is confused: as Richard eventually reached Jaffa on the night of Friday 31 July after being becalmed below Haifa for three days, this conversation must have taken place before the agreement was actually negotiated. Ambroise, line 10967, does not refer to the agreement but says simply, 'As I have already told you'.

met a miserable death soon afterwards.[44]

However, those from other countries 'whose hearts God had moved' [1 Samuel ch. 10 v. 26] and who were moved to pity by their neighbours' tribulations hurried to set out with him. Templars and Hospitallers and many other very valiant knights hurriedly set out for Caesarea, taking the land route. However, the glorious king, taking 'his life in his hands' [1 Samuel ch. 19 v. 5] proceeded by sea in his galleys, which were very securely equipped. With him went his comrades, the earl of Leicester, Andrew de Chavigny, Roger de Sathy, Jordan de Hommet, Ralph de Mauleon, Auçon de Fay, the knights of the de Préaux family, and other renowned men, Genoese and Pisans.

Those who had proceeded to Caesarea remained there for a while as if they were under siege, because they had learnt that Saladin had arranged ambushes for anyone passing through on the road. There was no better way for them to proceed because the son of the Assassin was keeping watch over the coastal roads between Caesarea and Arsur. What was more, a contrary wind blew up from the area and the king's ships remained immobile for three days off Cayphas. The king found the untimely delay unbearable.

'Lord God!' he said, sighing deeply, 'why are You holding us back? Consider! – this is an emergency, and we are acting out of our devotion to You.'

Without delay, at God's assent a favourable wind sprang up behind them and brought the fleet safely into the port of Joppa in the depths of night on the following Friday. The deadline for paying the aforesaid ransom was at the ninth hour on the Saturday following, when all the people were going to be disposed of according to the conditions. Faithless good faith and treachery of the treacherous! Early on the Saturday, that is on the day of St Peter in Chains [1 August 1192] the besieged were compelled to pay the agreed ransom by the importunate insistence of the Turks.

So early in the morning they were forced to begin paying some of the bezants promised for the ninth hour. Then those despicable Turks who are more savage than beasts and lack all human feeling beheaded them

---

44. Ralph of Coggeshall, p. 42 and Roger of Howden, *Chronica*, 3 p. 184 describe the death of the duke of Burgundy, a few days later at Tyre; Howden adds that Lord Ralph of Coucy and the vidame of Picquigny also died. Richard of Devizes, pp. 79–80, states that the duke died at Acre while Richard was ill at Jaffa. Following the death of the duke, the bishop of Beauvais assumed overall command of the French forces.

as they were paying. They had already thrown seven headless bodies into a ditch when those who were still in the citadel discovered what was going on. Terrorstruck and horrified, they began to wail and utter tearful cries. How they all mourned when they saw inevitable death hanging over them! Each knelt in tears to pray, beating their breasts and confessing the sins that they had committed. As they believed that they were about to die, they despaired of saving their bodies and took care of their souls, seeing that these alone would survive.

Each fled as far away as they could to gain even a very short extension to their lives. Even the most resolute person would certainly be alarmed by fear of imminent death! So each of them eagerly threw themselves into the inner fortress of the citadel in order to defer their death, even if only a little, and there the warrior force waited for their lives to be completed with martyrdom. 'A trembling shakes the deepest marrow of their bones' [Claudian, *de Raptu Proserpine*, Bk. 3 v. 152], and bitter tears flowed copiously as if torn from their innermost guts.

So they won divine clemency, for Divine Mercy was quickly placated by these sacrifices and had already sent them a deliverer to liberate them. They saw the king's fleet was already in the port, and knights were being carefully armed ready to disembark![45]

Chapter 15: In a great battle the king seizes the shore and frees the citadel of Joppa and those shut up inside it.[46]

When the Turks saw the king's galleys and ships approaching masses of them ran on to the shore with bucklers and shields to resist them, raining down spears, javelins, darts and arrows densely so that they would have nowhere free to land. The shore was seething, so covered with crowds of the enemy that there was no empty space left. They did not wait to engage them as they disembarked, but hurled missiles at the ships and galleys themselves as they were far out at sea, while their cavalry rode

45. Bahā' al-Dīn (pp. 366–70) gives a different account of these events, in which he himself was involved. Richard arrived at daybreak. When he realised that reinforcements had arrived, Saladin sent Bahā' al-Dīn to insist that the citadel be evacuated. Forty-nine men, with their horses and wives, left safely, but when the defenders realised that Richard had brought thirty-five ships and that the city could be relieved, they decided to hold out. They made a sortie from the citadel, but were driven back, and sent the patriarch and the castellan (Aubrey de Reims) to treat for a truce.

46. Ambroise, lines 11079–202.

out into the water as far as they could, striving to fire their arrows to best effect to prevent them from seizing the shore.

The king drew his ships together and took counsel. 'Well then, my excellent fellow-knights who have shared everything with me, what should be done? Surely this cowardly rabble blockading the shore won't prevent us from landing? Or do we reckon that our lives are more valuable than the lives of those who are perishing in our absence? What is your opinion?'

Some of them replied that further attempts were useless as they did not believe that there was anyone left to be rescued, and a landing would be very difficult among so many thousands of the enemy. Then the king, whose wandering eye was carefully scrutinising everything, saw a priest throwing himself from the land into the sea to swim out to the king. Out of breath and with heart pounding, he was admitted to the royal galley.

'Glorious king,' he said, 'the remnant of our people are yearning for your arrival. With necks bared they now await the drawn swords of their executioners "like sheep for the slaughter" [Psalm 44 v. 22]. At this very moment they are on the point of certain death unless divine aid comes through you.'

'Surely no one is left alive?' asked the king. 'Where are they?'

'Even now, my lord,' the priest replied, 'they are shut up to die in that tower.'

When the king heard this, he said: 'If it so pleases God in whose service and with whose leadership we have come here that we should die here with our brothers, death only to those who do not advance!'[47]

So on the king's command the galleys were driven towards the shore. With no armour on his legs he threw himself into the sea first, up to his groin, and forced his way powerfully on to dry land. The first and next after the king were Geoffrey du Bois and Peter des Préaux. All the rest followed them, jumping into the sea and advancing on foot. They boldly attacked the Turks who obstinately opposed them on the shore; the whole shore was covered with them. The outstanding king shot them down indiscriminately with a crossbow he was carrying in his hand, and his elite companions pursued the Turks as they fled across the beach, cutting them down. At the sight of the king, they had no more spirit in them; they did not dare approach him.

47. Bahā' al-Dīn (pp. 370–1) confirms this account, and states that Saladin had been about to grant a truce to the patriarch and Aubrey de Reims, but when he heard that Richard had landed he had them arrested.

Brandishing his bared sword, the king followed in such hot pursuit that none of them had time to defend themselves. They fled from his weighty blows. In the same way the king's comrades constantly assailed the fugitives, driving them on, crushing, rending, beheading and tossing them about until all the Turks had been violently expelled from the shore and left it empty. Afterwards they brought logs and barrels, and driftwood and broad boards and suitable materials from old ships and galleys on the shore, and constructed a sort of fortification for themselves against enemy attacks. The king appointed knights, servants and crossbowmen to guard it and to keep the Turks away. As they retreated from the shore the Turks filled it with importunate wails and shouts, since they could not impede our people in any other way.

The king was the first to enter the city. He entered alone, by a spiral stairway that he had happened to spot in the Templars' houses. There he found more than 3000 Turks plundering everything, ransacking the interiors of the houses and carrying off spoils. The courage of the unconquered king! As soon as he had entered within the city walls, he raised his unfurled banners on a high point so that the Christians who were besieged in the citadel would see them. Delighted beyond words at the sight, they gained confidence, took up arms and came down from the citadel to meet the king.

When they discovered what was happening the Turkish army was thrown into confusion. The king fell on them with unsheathed sword, pursued them, beheaded and slew them. They fled before him, falling back in dense crowds to his right and left. Then the others who came in from the citadel inflicted a horrible slaughter on the Turks, so that the streets were filled with their headless corpses. Why should I delay over details? All of those who were in the fortress were cut to pieces without delay, except for those who were lucky enough to escape by running faster than the others. So the former victors received their just deserts in death. The king pursued them as they ran out of the town, smashing them as a strong wind smashes ships [see Psalm 48 v. 7]. He believed that he should press on in pursuit of success so that he could not be accused of sparing the enemies of Christ's cross whom God had given into his hand. Besides, no one ever hated idleness more than he did.

Chapter 16: Again, the king chases Saladin from the siege in a battle, and pitches his tents where Saladin's had been pitched.[48]

The king only had three horses at that point. What are three among so many? Never was another warrior of any creed so prominent for such unique courage, not even in the deeds of old, the traditions of story-tellers or historical writings from times long ago, as King Richard was that day. He was without precedent. As he came out from the city the Turks caught sight of his bright standards aloft, and a horrible howl went up from the right and the left as the king advanced into the enemy. Never was the air so dark with fog or raindrops as it was then with the Turks' darts flying through space. Although the sun was shining, 'with the firing of arrows the sky becomes night.'

Saladin heard that the king had arrived and of his fine combat with his Turks and how he had cut to pieces all he met without distinction. Sudden fears rushed on him, for he was a very timid creature, like a frightened hare. Hurriedly tearing up his tents from their pitches he put spur to horse and fled before King Richard, not wishing to be seen by him. The king and his fellow-knights steadfastly pursued him, continually slaying and unhorsing, while the king's crossbowmen inflicted such slaughter on the fugitives' horses that the Turks ran away swiftly for more than two miles.

So the king, unaware of the coincidence, ordered his pavilions to be pitched in the same place from which Saladin had torn up his tents with fear and fled a short time before.[49] Thus with God's help the Turkish army was repulsed by a few people.

Saladin called together the more noble of his emirs and addressed them. 'So who is troubling us?' he complained. 'Surely the Christian army returned from Acre can't be harassing, routing, and overcoming us? What sort of equipment have they got, whoever are they, to dare to attempt such things? Were they on horseback or on foot, these people whom our army was unable to resist?'

A certain person with a perverse turn of mind and who was aware of the state of our army replied: 'Lord, it is not like you think. They have no horses or any kind of pack animal except for only three horses which that wonderful man the glorious king found in Joppa. However, it is my opinion that it would be an easy task to seize him because he is lying

48. Ambroise, lines 11203–66.

49. Bahā' al-Dīn states that the Turks fled to Yāzūr, and mentions that Richard's tent was pitched where Saladin's had been (p. 371).

exhausted almost alone in his tent. The person who could capture him would end our problems and wrap everything up.'

'The saying became current' among the Turkish army [John's Gospel ch. 21 v. 23] that the rout by a few people of a great army of so many thousands of Turks and the violent capture of Joppa would bring them eternal disgrace and disrepute. So they murmured and grumbled among themselves in a confused way about what the Christians had accomplished.

Chapter 17: What was done about the Christians, Turks and pigs who were killed in the city.[50]

When the Turkish people - curse them! - had seized Joppa, they had slaughtered countless numbers of the infirm and also no few pigs, all that they found. It is part of the Muḥammadan superstition not to eat pigs: they naturally detest pigs as unclean, because pigs are said to have devoured Muḥammad.[51] So to insult the Christians the Turks collected together the corpses of the pigs with the bodies of the people they had killed. At last the bodies of the Christians were buried in peace by the Christians, but they threw out the Turks' corpses to rot with those of the pigs.

Chapter 18: The repair of the walls of Joppa.[52]

The following day, on Sunday, the king carefully made arrangements for the demolished walls to be repaired. In the same way on the Monday and Tuesday the breaches in the walls were repaired so that they would have some sort of fortification. The repairs were made without lime or cement, but were necessary because an immense army of Turks threatened them from the close vicinity.

---

50. Ambroise, lines 11274-93.
51. A reference to the medieval Christian legend about Muḥammad: Muḥammad was drunk one night and lay down on a dung hill to sleep, whereupon sows ate him.
52. Ambroise, lines 11294-302.

Chapter 19: Some Turks called Mamluks and Kurds[53] boast that they will capture the king unawares while he is asleep in his tent.[54]

Meanwhile, a crooked type of Saracen people called 'Mamluks' of Aleppo and 'Kurds', who were lively young warriors, assembled together to discuss what should be done in the present situation. They claimed that it was a disgrace for such a great horde to have abandoned Joppa before a few people who had no horses. They condemned themselves for cowardice and said that they ought to be ashamed of their own idleness. So they made a mutual pact between themselves, boasting arrogantly that they would seize King Richard in his tent and present him to Saladin, who would give them a very grateful reward.[55]

Chapter 20: The arrival of Count Henry in Joppa from Caesarea; and his numbers.[56]

Meanwhile Count Henry and his comrades came in a galley from Caesarea. As the rest of our army was still detained there against its will because of the Turkish ambushes lying in wait on the thoroughfares and the bridges, the king could not have any of his army with him at that juncture except around fifty-five knights and up to 2000 very tough infantry, crossbowmen and men at arms, Genoese and Pisans and others. He had also acquired from various places barely fifteen horses, good and bad.

---

53. *Menelones et Cordini*.
54. Ambroise, lines 11303–17.
55. Bahā' al-Dīn, p. 364, depicts the attempt to capture King Richard in his tent as Saladin's own plan.
56. Ambroise, lines 11318–44.

Chapter 21: The aforesaid Mamluks and Kurds would have seized the king in his tent as they had boasted if a certain Genoese had not detected them and woken him.[57]

Meanwhile, the enemy were preparing to carry the king off unawares and unarmed. At midnight the aforesaid Mamluks and Kurds set out under arms, travelling by the light of the moon, discussing between themselves the best way of carrying out the deed. Unforeseen approach of the faithless! The enemy carefully debated the capture of Christ's dutiful knight, while he slept. Many armed men rush to seize one who is unarmed and unaware of the danger. They were already not far from the royal tent, and were arranging themselves to seize him unawares. But the God of Mercies, who works in marvellous ways even with those who do not know Him and does not neglect those who hope in Him, sent a spirit of contention into the aforesaid Kurds and Mamluks!

The Kurds said: 'You go in on foot to seize the king and his people, and we will keep watch on horseback so they cannot escape to the fortress.'

'You should go on foot,' the Mamluks replied, 'because we are of higher rank. Knighthood is our duty, while this footwork is more appropriate for you.'

So their advance was delayed for some time while they exchanged words, each obstinately striving over 'which of them should be considered the greatest' [Luke's Gospel ch. 22 v. 24]. At last with difficulty they came to an agreement over how they would undertake their treachery. As they were running headlong forwards dawn appeared, the forerunner of day. It was the Wednesday next after the feast of St Peter in Chains [5 August].

Now, God had made provisions to prevent these degenerate unbelievers from surprising His great champion, devoted to His service, while he was sleeping. He inspired a certain Genoese to go out into the neighbouring countryside at daybreak. As this person hurried to return he was amazed to hear the noise of travellers and clattering of horses walking. Keeping his head down, he saw at a distance against the sky the glittering tops of helmets. As soon as he saw this he ran quickly back to the camp shouting all the time in a loud voice again and again that everyone should arm themselves at once! Hearing the noise, the king was roused

57. Ambroise, lines 11345–95.

and leapt in great alarm from his bed. Putting on his mailshirt of unbreakable mesh he ordered his fellow knights to get up without delay.[58]

Chapter 22: The king's astonishing fight, which will amaze for all time.[59]

Lord God of Hosts! Who could remain unmoved by such sudden commotion and alarm? The enemy rushed in on them unexpectedly, the armed on the unarmed, countless hordes on a few. They did not have enough time to arm, or even to dress. As a result the king himself and a great many others in the confusion and urgency of the moment advanced barelegged to battle, some even without underpants.[60] All day they would remain fighting in whatever way they had armed themselves hurriedly then.

So our people were anxiously arming themselves, but the Turks were already upon them. The king mounted a horse for the advance. Only ten of his comrades had horses: these are their names: Count Henry, the earl of Leicester, Bartholomew de Mortimer, Ralph de Mauleon, Andrew de Chavigny, Gerard de Furnival, Roger de Sacy [or Sathy], William de l'Étang, Hugh de Neville, a most doughty man-at-arms, and Henry Teuton, the king's standard-bearer. Only these had horses, and some of them were certainly bad quality, weak ones, not used to arms.

The battalions and detachments were drawn up, wisely arranged into ranks and troops, and commanders were assigned to control each. The knights were sent nearer to the sea shore, not far from the church of St Nicholas and on its left side, since the more closely packed detachment of Turks was hurling itself in that direction. Again, the Pisans and Genoese were assigned to the area outside the suburban gardens with a collection of various peoples.

---

58. Bahā' al-Dīn, p. 375, describes a surprise attack by Saladin and his army on the night of Tuesday 4th and the morning of Wednesday 5th August. The Muslims were beaten off and refused to attack again. He states that the Christians had no more than seventeen horsemen - some say nine - and at the largest estimate 1000 infantry; some say 300. The English chronicler Ralph of Coggeshall obtained his account of this battle (pp. 44-51) from Hugh of Neville, who was present (see below). He records that Richard had only six horses and one mule (p. 46). Smail (1956, 1995), gives an analysis of this battle, pp. 188-9.
59. Ambroise, lines 11396-592.
60. *feminalibus*.

Who could fully describe the infidels' weighty attacks? First the Turks rushed in with horrible shouts and then began to howl and fire javelins, darts and arrows very densely. Our people arranged themselves as best as they could to receive their terrible assaults. So that they could hold together more firmly and remain steady they each placed their right knee on the ground and fixed the toes of their right foot in the soil and held the left foot forward with the left knee bent. They held a buckler in front of them in their left hand, or a targe or some other type of shield. In their right hand they held a lance, with the blunt end fixed into the ground, and the sharp end with its iron head pointing forward threateningly towards the attacking enemy.[61]

The king, who was very skilled in warfare, placed a crossbowman between each two who were protecting themselves with their shields like this, and another person next to him who could keep pulling back the crossbow quickly. So one person had the job of loading crossbows while the other kept firing bolts.[62] This was no little help to our people and did great harm to the enemy.

When each person was arranged like this, as far as the lack of time and the small numbers allowed, the king ran up and down between them, like the active encourager he was.[63] He urged them to be steadfast, condemning as unworthy of their race those whose spirits weakened from fear or cowardice.

'Oppose the adversary with a firm and fearless mind,' he said. 'Let courage grow in your breasts to resist the fierce enemy and escape the storms of fortune. Learn to endure adversities, since everything is bearable to those of manly character. Adversities reveal virtues, just as prosperity hides them. Besides, there is nowhere to run. The enemy has already occupied everything, so any attempt to flee means certain death. So you must stand firm. Let urgent necessity become the material for courage. True men should either triumph courageously or die gloriously. We should receive our approaching martyrdom with a grateful heart. But before we die, while life is with us, we should avenge our death, giving thanks to God that we have found in martyrdom the sort of death we were striving for. This is the wages for our labours, and the end of our life and our battles.'

---

61. Ralph of Coggeshall has a similar description of the setting up of a wall of lances, p. 47.
62. Presumably each pair had two crossbows; while one was being loaded the other was being fired.
63. Ambroise, line 11473, says that John des Préaux was with him.

Scarcely was his sermon over when the enemy army came charging headlong in all their arrogance down on them! It was arranged into seven battle lines and troops, each of which contained around 1000 cavalry. Our people prepared themselves to meet their impact, bracing themselves against them by fixing their right feet into the sand so that they remained solidly unmoveable against the onrush, with the heads of their lances held forwards. If our people had given way at all at that moment the Turks would certainly have broken through them. The first Turkish line approached and was about to charge into them, but because our people waited without moving, they suddenly recoiled and turned aside. As the Turks retreated our crossbowmen pursued them with a dense volley of missiles, which transfixed a great many people and horses.[64]

Immediately the next battle line followed, and realising that it could not break through our people because they were immobile, it turned aside as the first had done. Turks kept coming up in the same way like a driving whirlwind, intending that our people would scatter of their own accord before the imagined attack and could be brought to battle. Yet, just as it seemed that they were about to engage hand-to-hand combat, with dextrous cunning they pulled the reins and turned their horses round in another direction.[65]

The king and his people realised that they were not going to do anything else. When they were unable to bear this half-hearted and evasive strategy any longer, the king and those who had horses put spur to horse and with lances couched charged powerfully into the thick of the enemy, throwing them down to right and to left, emptying saddles of their riders and transfixing some of them. Their initial impact was so great that their violent spirit carried them through all the Turkish lines as far as the last. Then the king looked back a little and saw at a distance the noble earl of Leicester, who had been thrown from his horse! When the unconquered king caught sight of him defending himself with outstanding skill, he vigorously rescued him from the hands of his wicked oppressors and performed him the service of helping him mount a horse.

---

64. Ralph of Coggeshall, p. 47, agrees: the Christians did not move, and the Turks retreated. He praises the skill and courage of the crossbowmen that day.
65. Ralph of Coggeshall, p. 48, states that the Turks kept charging and retreating, but the Christians did not move and the Turks could not break through. After 3 pm Richard ordered the crossbowmen to advance in front of the knights and fire at the enemy.

What harsh battle was joined there! A great swarm of Turks streamed together and pressed on with all their efforts to crush so few. Grieved by our people's successes, they kept charging up to the royal standard with the lion on it,[66] seeking the king's life alone in preference to 1000 others.

Immediately afterwards the king saw Ralph de Mauleon fall in the conflict, and the Turks dragging him off as a prisoner. With his horse at a gallop the king flew swiftly to tear him from their hands. Driving the Turks away with great force he recovered Ralph. He was like a giant in battle, renowned for his unique courage. Among so many thousands of the enemy he turned himself so vigorously in so many different directions, and bore himself so finely as he rode, almost unaccompanied. He was one on his own, without any example to follow. Even a man of great superiority, a courageous or powerful prince, would reasonably be regarded as much inferior to him.

That day he bore himself manfully into the mass of roaring Turks and cut to pieces countless numbers with his flashing sword, cleaving them from the crown of the head to the teeth and cutting off their head or arms or any other part of their body until the skin of his right hand tore because it was so damaged by the continual effort of brandishing his sword. Then as the king was expending such unbelievable labour in the struggle a certain Turk rode towards him at a rapid gallop, carried on a high foaming horse. He came on behalf of Saphadin of Archadia [al-'Ādil], Saladin's brother, a very noble and munificent man, who would have been worthy to be compared with the best of men if he had not rejected the creed and faith of the Christian religion. This Saphadin sent two very noble Arab horses to the king in recognition of his noted prowess. He particularly requested the king to be so gracious as to accept the horses and to mount, as he seemed to be short of horses at that time. If divine grace should bring him safe and sound from danger, he could repay him in whatever way he pleased at such time as he should remember his service. The king accepted the horses and later repaid him magnificently.[67]

Courage is praiseworthy, even in an enemy! So a Turk and an enemy

---

66. This was Richard's first badge, a single lion. In 1198 he changed his seal to show the three lions or leopards which still appear on the English royal coat-of-arms.

67. *Eracles* tells another version of this story where the gift was a trick to capture King Richard: *Conquest of Jerusalem*, pp. 117-8. Bahā' al-Dīn implies that al-'Ādil was actually absent from the battle, because he was ill: p. 376.

judged that the king should be honoured in this way because of his exceptional courage. The king did not refuse the offer, especially in such a moment of crisis. He declared that at that moment he would have accepted many more horses like that even from a worse enemy, because they are so essential in battle.

Then battle was joined more seriously. Countless swarmed against a few; the whole earth was covered with the infidels' darts and arrows so that enough darts to fill a bag could be gathered at a single grasp. Countless people were hurt by them. As the weight of battle became unbearable for our people the oarsmen fled and fell back on the galleys in which they had come. For shame! They alone fled to gain safety; they alone lost their steadfast courage.

Meanwhile a great shout went up from the Turks who were struggling to occupy the town. They were entering the town on all sides, hoping to find our people and crush them. When the king heard this he ran up quickly, accompanied by only two knights but bringing some crossbowmen with him. Coming upon three very nobly equipped Turks in a street of the town, he charged impressively down on them in the regal manner, cut the riders to pieces and made a profit of two [*sic*] horses. Brandishing his sword, he drove out all the rest of the Turkish resistance which he found in the town. Terrified, they scattered in different directions, looking for a way out even where there was none. The king ordered that the breaches in the walls be blocked up at once, and set guards to guard the city against Turkish incursions.

Chapter 23: Again, the king's astonishing fight which will amaze for all time, in which he threw down myriads of the enemy with divine help and returned unharmed from their midst to his people.[68]

When he had arranged these things the king rode hurriedly to the seashore, where with trembling hearts a great many were attempting to escape in the galleys. The king called them back and used very effective reasonings to stir them up to fight and to stand by their comrades while life was with them. With his encouragement they all returned to the struggle ready to accept willingly whatever fate God might send. The king set only five guards on each galley and hurried back with the rest

68. Ambroise, lines 11593-652.

to the fight, in order to assist his little hardpressed army.

When he arrived he bore himself into the mass of struggling Turks with such a violent spirit and such a fierce charge that he went through scattering everything. Even people at a distance from him whom he had never touched were thrown to the ground, pushed over as others fell. Never was such a celebrated assault related of a single knight.

Bearing himself like a renowned warrior, he reached the middle of the enemy army and at once the Turks surrounded him, enclosed him and tried to crush him. Meanwhile our people realised that they could not see the king anywhere. Their hearts quaked and they feared the worst, for when they did not see him they were afraid he was dead. Some of them judged that they ought to go looking for him. Our battle lines were barely holding together; but if our ordered ranks had been broken or our line had opened up then all our people would without doubt have perished.[69]

What of the king, one man surrounded by many thousands? The fingers stiffen to write it and the mind is amazed to think of it. Who has heard of anyone like him? His courage was always firm, he 'could not be overwhelmed by the hostile waves of life' [Horace, *Epistolae*, Bk. 1 no. 2 v. 22],[70] he was always full of courage and, to sum up in a few words, always vigorous and untiring in war. What more is there to say? The story goes that the strength of the fabulous Antaeus was restored when he fell and he was invincible while in contact with the earth; but this Antaeus died when he was lifted up and held above the earth during a long struggle.[71] The body of Achilles, who defeated Hector, is said to have been impenetrable to weapons because it had been dipped in the River Styx; but a lance head hit him in his heel, which was the only part of him which was vulnerable.[72] The ambition of Alexander of Macedon armed his headlong pride to subjugate the entire globe. He certainly undertook difficult ventures and won countless battles with a force of elite knights; however, all his strength was in his vast forces. All peoples tell of the battles of the mighty Judas Maccabaeus. He fought many remarkable battles which should be admired forever; but when his people

69. From here to 'a means of expression' is not in Ambroise.
70. Also quoted in Bk. 2 ch. 5, p. 146 above.
71. See note 100 on Bk. 5 ch. 45, p. 324 above.
72. In classical legend, Achilles' mother held her son in the River Styx (over which the spirits of the dead pass to reach the underworld) so that he would be invulnerable where the water touched him. But she held on to his heel, which remained dry. During the siege of Troy, Paris shot him in that heel from the walls of Troy.

had deserted him in battle, he engaged many thousands of foreigners in battle with a small company and he fell nearby with his brothers and died [1 Maccabees ch. 9 vv. 1–22].

However, King Richard had been hardened to battle from his tender years. In comparison to his strength, Roland would be reckoned weak.[73] I do not know how he remained invincible and invulnerable among all enemies; perhaps by divine protection. His body was like brass, unyielding to any sort of weapon. His right hand brandished his sword with rapid strokes, slicing through the charging enemy, cutting them in two as he encountered them, now on this side, now on that. He bore himself with indescribable vigour and superhuman courage into the mass of Turks, not turning tail for anyone [Proverbs ch. 30 v. 30] scattering and crushing all he met. 'He mows the enemy with a sword as if he were harvesting them with a sickle.' It could justly be said of his memorable blows that whoever encountered one of them had no need of a second! As he raged it seemed as if his resolute courage was rejoicing that it had found a means of expression. Driven by his powerful right hand, his sword devoured flesh [Deuteronomy ch. 32 v. 42] wherever he turned. He sliced riders in two from the top of their heads downwards and horses too, without distinction.[74] The further he found himself separated from his comrades, the more hotly he urged himself to fight. The more bitterly the enemy tried to crush him by firing darts, the more his courage was stirred up and its ardent impulses took control of him.

Among many other distinguished exploits which he happened to perform on that occasion, he killed a certain emir with a single amazing wound. This emir was more eminent than the others and was adorned with more notable equipment, and his bearing had seemed to boast great things and criticise the others for being idle cowards. He had put spurs to horse and come at a rapid gallop from the opposite direction to meet the king and throw him down. However the king held out his sword in his way as he charged and cut off his heavily-armoured head along with his shoulder and right arm.

When they saw this there was no spirit left in the rest of the Turks. They gave the king a wide berth on all sides and hardly even tried to fire arrows at him from a distance. So he returned safe and sound from the enemy's midst and rode swiftly to encourage his people. How their

73. According to the *Chanson de Roland*, as Roland lay dying he killed a man with a blow from his horn and split a stone with his sword (lines 2273–354).

74. 'The further...control of him' is not in Ambroise. The two paragraphs which follow are different in Ambroise.

spirits rose out of the deep abyss of despair when they saw the king emerge from among the enemy! They had been in doubt and had not known what to do, for if he were dead all the Christians' efforts would be completely for nothing.

The king's body was completely covered with darts, which stuck out like the spines of a hedgehog. His horse was also bristling with the countless arrows which were stuck in its trappings. Thus this extraordinary knight returned from the contest.

The battle lasted from early in the morning until dusk, and I would say that it was a very cruel and very weighty contest. So it will be thought amazing and perhaps unbelievable that they were able to keep up the unequal fight so long. There is no doubt that this was achieved through the assistance of the God of Mercy. Only one or two of our people fell on that deadly day, but it is said that there were more than 1500 dead Turkish horses lying scattered everywhere through the fields, while more than 700 Turks were killed. Yet they did not fulfill their boast and hand the king over to Saladin! Instead the king himself and his comrades - his fellow knights who were so brilliantly skilled in battle - performed so many great exploits before their very eyes that the enemy's hair stood on end as they watched.

Chapter 24: Saladin jeers at his people for boasting about capturing King Richard. They defend their overconfidence by replying that they had never seen such an energetic knight.[75]

So divine clemency preserved our people unharmed, and the Turkish army withdrew.

Saladin is said to have taunted the cowardice of those who had been making boastful promises by asking: 'So where are those who are bringing *Melech* Richard as a prisoner? Who got him first? Where is he, I say? Aren't you going to produce him?'

One of the Turks, a man from the furthest ends of the earth, replied. 'Truly, lord, this *melech* of whom you ask is not like the rest of humanity. Such a knight has been "unheard of since time began" [John's Gospel ch. 9 v. 32] - so steadfast, so doughty, so skilled in arms. He is the first in each exchange. He is unique in every undertaking. He heads the advance and is the last to retreat. We tried as best we could to capture

75. Ambroise, lines 11653-75.

him but without success. No one can withstand his sword or his terrible charge unharmed. It is death to encounter him. His exploits are superhuman.'

Chapter 25: The king is ill from the effort and exhaustion of battle.[76]

King Richard and our people were absolutely worn out by the pressures of the day and the weight of the battle. The king fell ill from the exhaustion of the battle and the stink of the corpses, which polluted the area so much that everyone almost died.

Chapter 26: Saladin informs the sick king that he is coming to capture him. The king sends to Caesarea for the French, who refuse to come.[77]

Meanwhile, Saladin informed the king that he would come down with his Turks and capture him, if he dared to await his arrival. The king immediately replied that he would certainly wait for him there. In no way would he run even a footstep away from him while he lived and had the means to resist him on his feet, or at least on his knees. The royal courage could not be broken by adversity. Yet the king realised that he was burdened with sickness and as he considered the present crisis and how things stood, knowing that he could not relax while the serpent was near, he sent Count Henry to Caesarea to command the French who had gone there earlier to come to him and assist him in defending the country. He also notified them that he was extremely sick and informed them of Saladin's message.

However, the French refused to give him any aid at all, not even a little. If it had been left to them he would have been left deserted and exposed to the enemy hordes and destroyed if he had not obtained a truce, even if it was criticised by some of them. What can we say? What safety was there for so few, not to mention sick, people among so many swarms of Turks? At that point in time it seemed more advisable that Ascalon should be destroyed than to be at the mercy of uncertainty.

76. Ambroise, lines 11680–90.
77. Ambroise, lines 11691–726; see also Bahā' al-Dīn, pp. 376–80 for negotiations between Richard and Saladin.

For if the enemy had captured the sick king without any resistance as he lay on his bed they could have overrun Ascalon without opposition and consequently Tyre and Acre would have been threatened.

Chapter 27: The king wishes to return to Acre to get well, but his people manfully oppose him. So the king seeks and obtains a three-year truce.[78]

The king was particularly concerned at his untimely ill-health at a moment when matters were so finely balanced. He ordered his relative Count Henry and the Templars and Hospitallers to come to him in person, explained his indisposition to them and declared that because the area was polluted and not securely fortified he would leave it. He appointed some of them to go and watch over Ascalon, and others to remain there and take charge of guarding Joppa. He would return to Acre to take medicines and get well. He said that there was nothing else to be done. With one mind and identical voice, all of them opposed him. They claimed that under no circumstances would they watch over any fortification in his absence, and they persisted firmly in this decision, refusing to guard any castles at all. Having said this they 'drew back and no longer went about with him' [John's Gospel ch. 6 v. 67].

The king was exasperated and distressed by this reply.[79] Their refusal grieved him bitterly, because he could no longer find anyone who would agree with his plans and wishes. So for some time he wavered over what he should do, wondering what would be the best course of action. Yet after applying his thoughts in many directions he came back to the fact that he could find no one who 'spared a thought' for him [1 Samuel ch. 22 v. 8]. At last because he was aware that everyone was drifting away and no one had even the slightest concern for the common interest, he ordered an edict to be issued stating that anyone who wished to be hired and paid by the king should assemble to give him their help. 200 infantry and fifty knights flocked together without delay.

However, the king's illness had now become so extremely serious that he despaired of ever recovering his health. He was very anxious about this, as much for others as for himself. His astute mind considered many options but his preferred choice, the least disagreeable, was to demand a

78. Ambroise, lines 11727-800; Ralph of Coggeshall, p. 52.
79. From here to 'for others as for himself' is not in Ambroise.

truce. The alternative would be to depart leaving the campaign unfinished and abandon the country altogether to depopulation, as all the others had done who were already leaving in hordes by ship.

So, perplexed and not knowing what else he could do, the king sent a message to Saladin's brother Saphadin, asking for him to mediate and obtain a truce between them on the most honourable conditions that he could. Saphadin was a man of exceptional liberality who had also frequently demonstrated that he thought the king worthy of much honour because of his unique prowess. He now took care to obtain a truce of the sort requested.[80] The terms were:

> Ascalon, which had always been a threat to Saladin's authority while it remained intact, was to be destroyed. It should not be repaired by anyone within a period of three years beginning from next Easter. But after three years Ascalon would be ceded to whoever was occupying it, irrespective of who had the greatest power.[81]
>
> Saladin also conceded that Joppa should be restored to the Christians. They could inhabit it freely and peacefully, along with all the region around, the coast and the mountains.
>
> He sanctioned an inviolable peace between the Christians and Saracens. Both should have safe and free passage everywhere, and access to the Lord's Holy Sepulchre without any exactions, and free passage through the whole country for those carrying any sort of goods for sale. Commerce was to be exercised freely.

These terms were recorded in writing and read out to King Richard, who approved them [2 September 1192].[82] He certainly could not hope for anything better since he was sick and had so little assistance, and had gone no further than two miles from the enemy's position. Anyone who

80. Bahā' al-Dīn, pp. 383, 387, points out that Saladin also wanted a truce, because his troops were worn out and could not continue the war. 'Imād al-Dīn, pp. 391, 393, states that a general truce by sea and land was made for three years and eight months from 1 September 1192; the Franks held the land from Jaffa to Caesarea, and from Acre to Tyre; and Richard gave Ascalon up to Saladin. Bahā' al-Dīn, p. 381, generally agrees the terms as our author states them.

81. Ambroise, lines 11779–80, says that after three years, whoever could take Ascalon could have it and repair it. In fact it was left deserted until it was rebuilt by Earl Richard of Cornwall during his crusade of 1240–1.

82. Bahā' al-Dīn, pp. 384–5.

wishes to put forward a different opinion of this peace agreement is liable to be labelled a perverse liar.

Chapter 28: King Richard and Saladin converse amicably through messengers.[83]

So this was done in the moment of necessity. The king, whose great spirit was always aiming higher, undertaking difficulty, striving for the top, sent ambassadors to Saladin. While many of Saladin's satraps listened, they said that the king had only sought a truce like that for three years because he intended to return to see his country and to get more people and money. Then he would return and tear the whole country of Jerusalem from his dominion – if indeed Saladin reckoned that he could resist him with any confidence.

Saladin sent messengers with a reply to this. He called to witness his holy law and all-powerful God that he thought so highly of King Richard's prowess, noble mind and superiority that if he had to lose the country during his lifetime he would prefer that King Richard capture it through the means of his virtues than any other prince whom he had ever seen. What deep blindness obscures human eyes! They make plans for a long time ahead, but they do not know what the next 'day may bring forth' [Proverbs ch. 27 v. 1]. So the king's sharp mind reached far ahead, making mental arrangements for the future, hoping that he would recover the Lord's Sepulchre sometime, but completely unaware that 'all human affairs hang by a slender thread' [Ovid, *Epistolae ex Ponto* Bk. 4 no. 3 v. 35].

Chapter 29: The king goes to Cayphas to get well.[84]

When the truce had been confirmed in writing and by oaths, the king arranged for himself to be taken to Cayphas as best as he could, to take health-giving medicines and be restored to health.[85]

---

83. Ambroise, lines 11801–30.
84. Ambroise, lines 11831–8.
85. Richard left Jaffa on 9 September. Bahā' al-Dīn states that he was so ill that a notice was circulated of his death (p. 389).

Chapter 30: The king arranges for the French to be prohibited from visiting the Lord's Sepulchre, because of their malicious behaviour. The others are permitted to visit it.[86]

Meanwhile the French were taking their ease in Acre and were already making careful preparations to return home. Although they had bitterly criticised the said truce they agreed to complete their pilgrimage more fully before returning home by going to the Lord's Sepulchre. King Richard remembered how idle they had been and unwilling to bring him aid in the recovery of Joppa, as was said above, and in many other previous necessities, yet they were now demanding an escort to go to the Holy Sepulchre! So he sent zealous messengers to instruct Saladin and his brother Saphadin that no one should be allowed to go to the Holy Sepulchre in Jerusalem unless they had a letter from him or from Count Henry - whichever they preferred. This would ensure that the said agreement between them was kept.

The French were extremely shocked and embittered at this. Realising that there was nothing to be gained, they returned bewildered to their homeland soon afterwards, taking nothing back with them except ungrateful quibbles. When the king heard that the greater part of the French who were his detractors had returned home, and the 'mouths of liars were stopped' [Psalm 63 v. 11] - as it is written, 'Banish the insolent, and strife goes too' [Proverbs ch. 22 v. 10] - he forebore from 'spreading over all his reproach against a few' [Ovid, *Ars Amatoria* Bk. 3 v. 9] of those pestilential people. He decided that it should be announced by public crier that the people who wished could now visit the Lord's Sepulchre and that they should bring their offerings to Joppa to help rebuild the walls.

86. Ambroise, lines 11839-71. See also Bahā' al-Dīn, p. 388 and 'Imād al-Dīn, p. 394, who both say that the sultan allowed all the Christians to visit Jerusalem, but Richard tried to prevent the Christians from going. 'Imād al-Dīn states that Richard tried to restrict access to those who had a letter or escort from him, but the sultan refused to agree to this.

Chapter 31: The pilgrimage of the first party to Jerusalem. Andrew de Chavigny was in charge. Their fear which resulted from a rash advance.[87]

The people were organised for the advance, and divided into three parties. Each party was placed under the control of an individual commander: the first to Andrew of Chavigny, the second to Ralph Taissun, the third to Hubert, bishop of Salisbury. The first, which was under Andrew, set out in order with the royal letter, but they almost fell into very severe trials, perhaps through the exactions of their sins.

As they travelled along, they reached the plain of Ramula. There, by common agreement, they sent messengers to inform Saladin that they were coming to Jerusalem with a letter from King Richard and asking him to arrange for them to have safe passage proceeding and returning. Those engaged in this embassy were certainly noble and active men, but on this occasion their renown was almost destroyed through their idleness. One of them was William des Roches, another was Gerard de Furnival, the third Peter des Préaux. When these three envoys reached Turon des Chevaliers, they stopped there, waiting for the protection of an escort from Saphadin before proceeding further on their journey. While they were waiting there, slumber seized them and 'they all dozed off to sleep' [Matthew's Gospel ch. 25 v. 5].

At sunset all those who had appointed them as ambassadors passed by them as they were sleeping. The party proceeded in order, crossed the plain and was already approaching the mountains when Andrew de Chavigny and the rest looked back and saw their aforesaid messengers, who had been asleep, hurrying after them! When they recognised them they stopped, absolutely terrified. Some said: 'Lord God, help us, we are lost, we are like "sheep for slaughter" [Psalm 44 v. 22] if the Saracens notice our rash journey, for their army has not yet disbanded. Look - our messengers whom we hoped had already completed arrangements for our safe return are behind us! Dusk is falling, we are unarmed, we have been brought into the danger of imminent death.'

At last the messengers caught up with the party, and were criticised bitterly for their carelessness. They sent them on with repeated prayers, urging them to hurry. Travelling quickly, they reached Jerusalem and found that almost 2000 Turks or more were staying in tents outside the city. They sought Saphadin, found him at last and set out their case be-

87. Ambroise, lines 11872-970.

fore him. He reproved the leaders of their journey very harshly for their foolishness. He accused them of hanging their lives on a thread, because they had gone in among enemies without any escort or protection while night was falling.

While they were conversing like this at sunset the aforesaid party of pilgrims came, unarmed and inadvisedly. The Turks snarled at their arrival, watching them and grimacing with savage eyes as they went past. Their faces showed clearly the spiteful contempt which was going round in their thoughts; for attitude of mind is often revealed in facial expression. At this, even the more steadfast of our people were alarmed and full of uncertain trepidation, and at that moment they would have much preferred to be safely back at Tyre or have gone to Acre. The pilgrims spent the night in great fear not far away from there, next to a certain mountain.[88]

Chapter 32: The Turks seek revenge from our pilgrims. Saladin and the satraps do not allow it.[89]

On the following day the Turks came and knelt before Saladin, beseeching him to allow them to wreak revenge on the Christians who were staying nearby in return for the deaths of their fathers and brothers, sons and relatives, who had been killed - first at Acre and later all over the place. They claimed that now they had found their opportunity. Saladin ordered that the Turkish leaders be summoned to advise him on their petition.

Mestoc, Saphadin, and Bedredin Dordern [Badr al-Dīn Dildirim al-Yārūqī ibn Bahā' al-Daula, lord of Tell Bāshir] were present. After discussing the proposal between themselves, they at last came to the unanimous decision that the Christians should come and go freely and without any impediment or injury. 'Because,' they said to Saladin, 'it would detract greatly from our prestige if the treaty which has been made between you and the king of England was broken because we violated it. The Turks ought to keep good faith with people of any nation, no matter what their beliefs. Our word would forever be regarded as worthless, and with justification.'

As the satraps repeated these and similar words, Saladin without delay

88. Ambroise, line 11969, says a certain wall; presumably it should be the city wall.

89. Ambroise, lines 11971-12013.

ordered his attendants to take responsibility for escorting the Christians into the city without their being harassed and escorting them back in peace. Saphadin was assigned to fulfill this duty reliably, and he undertook it willingly. He arranged for the pilgrims to visit the long-desired Lord's Sepulchre freely and peacefully and took splendid care of them with gracious liberality. When they had completed their pilgrimage as they wished they returned briskly to Acre.

Chapter 33: The pilgrimage of the second party to Jerusalem. Ralph Teissun was in charge.[90]

While these people were returning, between Castle Arnald and Ramula they met the second party of pilgrims, which was under Ralph Teissun. Saladin, as was said above, had arranged for his people to watch carefully over the thoroughfares and paths when any pilgrims were travelling towards Jerusalem. So we passed through freely and without obstruction.[91] Coming over the mountains, we reached Mount Joy, from where we saw the city of Jerusalem at a distance. With exceptional joy, we knelt on the ground and humbly rendered thanks to God, as is the custom. From there we could also see the Mount of Olives.

Afterwards everyone proceeded briskly. Those who had horses went on quickly in front, so that they could kiss the Lord's Sepulchre more freely as they desired. What is more, those with horses who had gone on in front told us that Saladin had the Lord's True Cross, which used to be taken into battle, shown to them so that they could kiss and adore it. However, those of us who were at the back on foot saw what we could, to whit, the Lord's monument. Some offerings were placed there, but because the Saracens carried them off we did not leave many offerings there but instead divided them between the French and Syrian prisoners we saw there labouring in chains at their allotted servitude.

From there we proceeded to the right to Mount Calvary, where the Lord was crucified, where the stone on which the Lord's cross was fixed in Golgotha cracked open.[92] When we had kissed this place, we pro-

90. Ambroise, lines 12014–100.
91. Both our author and Ambroise use the first person in this chapter. The whirlwind tour of the sights of Jerusalem is rather like a late-20th century guided tour! – except that the pilgrims kiss each site rather than taking a photograph.
92. Latin: *increpuit*, 'made a noise'. Ambroise says *se depesca e fendi*, 'split open'.

ceeded to the Church sited on Mount Sion. On the left side is the place from which Mary the Blessed Mother of God passed from this world to the Father.[93] Having kissed this place with tears, we hurried on and went to see the sacrosanct table on which Christ deigned to eat bread. Having hastily kissed this, we left in groups without delay. For it was not safe to go about except in groups, because of the ambushes of the godless people. Where pilgrims were wandering about dispersed, the Turks dragged them, now three, then four, into the entrances of cellars and secretly strangled them.

We hurried on from there as far as the Sepulchre of Mary the Blessed Mother of God in the middle of the vale of Josaphat [Jehoshaphat], next to the pool of Siloam, which we kissed devotedly and with contrite heart. From there, not altogether safely, we went up into that vaulted room in which it is said that our Lord and Redeemer was held for the night, awaiting his crucifixion on the morrow. We poured out pious tears there and placed affectionate kisses on the place. Then as the Turks were throwing us out we left quickly. We felt great pain at the pollution profaning the holy places because of the horses which the infidel Turks had irreverently stabled there.[94] Leaving Jerusalem, we reached Acre.

Chapter 34: The pilgrimage of the third party to Jerusalem. Hubert Walter, bishop of Salisbury, was in charge. Saladin showed him much honour and fulfilled all his requests.[95]

In the morning the third party was already not far from Jerusalem. The bishop of Salisbury was in charge of it. Saladin sent his people to give the bishop an honourable reception and escort him around the holy places as he wished. Because Saladin had already been informed of his commendable character, reputation for prudence, and famous merits he offered to receive him within his own mansion, to be entertained at his

---

93. The legend of the Assumption of the Blessed Virgin Mary. However, the Hospitallers of St John claimed that the Mother of God had ascended from their Hospital in Jerusalem: see Borchardt, K. (1994), 'Two forged alms-collecting letters'.
94. On the other hand, the Templars had stabled horses under the al-Aqsa mosque while it was their headquarters: *Theoderich's description of the Holy Places* (1891), pp. 30–1.
95. Ambroise, lines 12101–94; William of Newburgh, p. 378, says that Hubert Walter went on King Richard's behalf because there were fears for his safety if he went to Jerusalem in person.

own expense.[96] The bishop refused. 'Impossible,' he said, 'for I am a pilgrim.'

Saladin enjoined his servants to show the bishop and his people every kindness. He also sent him a great many carefully prepared gifts and later invited him to an interview so that he could see his manner and appearance. He also showed him the Holy Cross and then they sat down together and talked to each other for some time in a friendly way.

Saladin enquired into the character of the king of England, and what the Christians said about his Saracens. 'What I can say truly about my lord the king,' the bishop replied, 'and what can be said with justification, is that there is no knight in the world who is his equal in military matters, nor equal to him in outstanding courage, nor in generous giving. He is certainly remarkable in having a character full of all commendable graces. What more shall I say? Putting your sins aside, if anyone, in my opinion, could combine your virtues with those of King Richard, and share them out between you so that both of you were furnished with the abilities of both, two such princes would not be found in the whole globe.'

Saladin listened patiently to the bishop, and at last said: 'It is well known to us that the king has the greatest prowess and boldness, but he frequently hurls himself into danger imprudently – I do not say foolishly. He is too extravagant with his life. Wherever and in whatever kinds of countries I may be the distinguished prince, I would much prefer to be enriched with an abundance of wisdom and moderation together, rather than with boldness and lack of self control.'

After they had a wide and friendly discussion through interpreters, Saladin said that the bishop should ask for whatever gift he most desired and it would be given to him. When the bishop had rendered him copious thanks for this, he asked for time to deliberate, until the following day. So on the following day the bishop asked that two Latin priests and the same number of Latin deacons should be allowed to celebrate the divine service honourably at the Lord's Sepulchre, which he had visited. In accordance with the barbarous Syrian custom, divine service was hardly ever celebrated there. The Latin priests and deacons, together with the aforesaid Syrians, would be provided from the offerings of the pilgrims. He also asked for the same number at Bethlehem for the same purpose, and the same at Nazareth. It was indeed a great request, and

96. Bahā' al-Dīn states (pp. 388–9) that Saladin used to give honourable entertainment to any of the pilgrims he thought fit and talk with them, in order to annoy Richard, who did not want the Christians to go to Jerusalem.

very welcome to God, it is believed. The sultan approved what he asked. Then the bishop found priests as he had obtained permission to do, and installed them in each of the aforesaid places with deacons, offering service to God where there was none before.

And so, having taken their leave, they left Jerusalem and returned to Acre.

Chapter 35: Those going home after completing their pilgrimage suffer many shipwrecks and other dangers.[97]

As the people had discharged their vow of pilgrimage,[98] they prepared ships to go home. With favourable winds they set the sails and each committed themselves to their planned voyages. At once they were separated by a variety of winds and carried in different directions. The pilgrims were thrown far away through the tracts of the sea. Some of them were thrown out into various harbours, and escaped unharmed; others were scattered and endangered by shipwreck; others died in the sea on the voyage, and their allotted cemetery was the vastness of the sea. Others were infected by incurable disease and never regained their health, even in their homeland. Others, although they survived unharmed, are believed to have borne a bitter enough martyrdom from the loss of fathers and brothers, relatives and friends who were either killed by weapons or died of sickness. Their hearts were pierced by swords of sorrows from different sorts of suffering. Each of them should be acknowledged to have borne a sufficiently horrible martyrdom, although they did so in various ways. With straightforward heart and devotion they all exposed themselves to this pilgrimage for love of God.

Furthermore, afterwards some people used to taunt them and go foolishly on and on saying how little the pilgrims had achieved in the country of Jerusalem since they had not yet recovered Jerusalem. They did not know what they were saying, because they were criticising things which they had not experienced and knew nothing about. We think that we ought to be believed, because we saw and experienced the trials and difficulties which they bore. And we boldly declare, in the hearing of those who were present, that 100,000 Christians died on that pilgrimage, only because in the hope of divine reward alone they kept themselves

97. Ambroise, lines 12195–256.
98. The vow was to go to the Holy Sepulchre. The battles on the way there were necessary in order to discharge the vow.

from women, reckoning that it was wicked to gain bodily health by sacrificing their purity. They endured patiently even to the extent of allowing their bodies to deteriorate, so that the chastity of their minds would remain unpolluted.[99]

Again, we know that 300,000 pilgrims and more died from infection and from hunger, both during the siege of Acre and afterwards within the city.

Besides, who could be doubtful about the salvation of the souls of noble, good men who heard divine service daily from their own chaplains? It is certainly believed that these must have been saved.[100]

Chapter 36: Before he is prepared to go home the king ransoms William des Préaux, who was captured in the king's place when he said in battle that he was the king. He gives ten most noble Turks in exchange for him.[101]

Meanwhile, King Richard's voyage was being arranged and all necessary provisions and arms were being prepared and put in order for his return. Then the king, on an impulse of sheer magnanimity and in virtue of his illustrious noble mind, ransomed William des Préaux, setting ten noble Turks free in exchange for him. As was said above [Bk. 4 ch. 28], William was earlier captured in the king's place. The Turks would willingly have spent an infinite sum of money to keep the said William,[102] but the king's brilliant and lofty spirit would not condescend to be denigrated in any respect.

---

99. Ambroise goes further: he states (lines 12237–42) that 100,000 men died because they did not lie with women, yet they would not have died then were it not for their abstinences. He appears to mean that sex is essential for men's survival! This passage would make sense if our author meant that these men were so determined to retain their physical purity that they refused medical assistance from women. In the same way, the Rule of the military order of the Hospital of St John forbad the brothers to allow women to touch them, even to wash their hair: Delaville le Roulx (ed.) (1894–1906), *Cartulaire Général de l'ordre des Hospitaliers*, vol. 1 no. 70.
100. i.e. their souls are now in Heaven.
101. Ambroise, lines 12257–70.
102. Ambroise states (lines 12266–70) that the Turks Richard released would have been worth a large amount of money in ransom, but Richard gave up this opportunity in order to recover William.

Chapter 37: King Richard returns home. His voyage and misfortunes.[103]

When everything was done and the king was standing ready to go on board ship he decided to ensure that not even a trace should remain of anything which could detract from the perfection of his great exploits. So he gave orders through a public crier that all his creditors should come and all his debts would be paid to the full and beyond. This would ensure that there would be no grounds for slander or complaint to arise later over things which had been taken or requisitioned by royal authority.

On the day of the feast of St Michael [29 September 1192] the two queens - that is, Berengaria, queen of England, King Richard's wife, and Joanna, dowager queen of Sicily, King Richard's sister - went on board ship at Acre.[104] On St Denys' day [9 October] King Richard went on ship to return to England. When the royal fleet weighed anchor, how many sighs were wrenched from affectionate breasts, while tears flowed copiously from the eyes! They wished blessings on the king and prosperity in his affairs. They remembered his prowess, and the mass of virtues collected in this one man. Lamentations were broken with weeping; many voices were heard bewailing and saying, 'O land of Jerusalem, now abandoned by all aid! What a great defender you have lost! Who will protect you from your attackers if the truce is broken, now that King Richard is going away?' They each kept tearfully repeating these and similar words.

---

103. Ambroise, lines 12271-305, but increasingly divergent. From here onwards MSS A and B also differ in many details from C. The first sentence of the chapter is not in Ambroise; the material in the second paragraph on the dates of the departure of the queens and of Richard is only in MS C and is not in Ambroise. 'So he ordered...royal authority' is not in MS C but is in MSS A and B and Ambroise. Only C has the long description of Richard's character and reforms at the end of the chapter.

104. Roger of Howden, *Chronica*, 3 pp. 228-9, describes the journey of the queens and the daughter of the emperor of Cyprus, who accompanied them. They sailed to Italy and arrived in Rome in 1193, escorted by Stephen de Thornham. They remained there for six months, and were then escorted to Pisa and on to Genoa and Marseilles, where the king of Aragon, who also ruled Provence, met them and escorted them to his frontier. Count Raymond V of Toulouse then escorted them through his lands and they eventually reached Poitou. In 1196 Queen Joanna married Count Raymond VI of Toulouse (*Chronica*, 4 p. 13).

The king had not yet fully recovered his health, but he had everyone's prayers for his recovery. The sails were raised, and he set out on his prepared voyage.

They sailed all night, navigating by the stars. As day broke on the following day, the king looked back with affectionate eyes at the land he had left. For a long time he stood meditating, and prayed, 'O Holy Land, I commend you to God. In His loving grace may He grant me such length of life that I may give you help as He wills. I certainly hope some time in the future to bring you the aid that I intend.' Many people heard him say this.

When he had spoken these words, he urged the sailors to spread the sails fully to the wind so that they could pass over the seething seas more swiftly. He did not know that many trials and difficulties still awaited him, and that he would experience much adversity through the treachery[105] which had been devised in France, where his despicable capture in a hostile ambush was originally planned. He expected nothing of the sort while he was on God's service in the hardships of pilgrimage.

After a long tossing in the stormy sea, around the feast of St Martin [11 November] King Richard had had enough of the voyage, and headed for the first land he saw as quickly as he could. This country was part of the empire of Constantinople, a place called Corfu. However, he did not wish to be seen there since he had a well-justified suspicion of the cunning of the emperor and the Greeks, because of matters already mentioned [Bk. 1 chs. 21–2]. So he wisely came to an agreement with some pirates he happened to find there, and immediately gave them as much money as they demanded in return for their carrying him speedily to a more suitable country. So he abandoned the royal fleet, hid the fact that he was king, and entrusted himself undaunted to the cruel pirates. His appearance was altered but not his nature; for there was nothing beyond the daring of King Richard's noble soul: 'The noble man cannot conceal his inborn courage.'

Taking only four companions with him, he was carried across into

105. After this, Ambroise's text is quite different from MS C (line 12305–end). He summarises the material which follows, down to Richard's return to England. The details in MS C of Richard's voyage and capture are like those in Ralph of Diceto, p. 106. For more detailed descriptions of Richard's journey and capture and the negotiations for his release, see Ralph of Coggeshall, pp. 53–7, and Roger of Howden, *Chronica*, 3 pp. 185–6.

Slavonia. From there he passed through Aquileia and entered the land of Duke Leopold [V] of Austria, where he was captured in the city of Vienna on 20 December.[106]

How unfairly his merits were repaid! He had laboured heart and soul on behalf of the common cause, yet already his inheritance had been seized through an abominable attack made on his castles in Normandy.[107] His rivals advanced against him mercilessly and without cause, and he was not released from the unjust imprisonment until he was ransomed; the duke of Austria and Henry, emperor of Germany, shared the sum of money. In order to bring in the required sum for the ransom a great many levies were raised from all his people and various things were requisitioned. The chalices were taken from the churches, and the gold and silver plate which had been consecrated for ecclesiastical use [MSS A and B add: and the monasteries had to do without them]. Yet this was not illegal according to the decrees of our forebears, since it was a necessity at a time of desperate crisis.

After winning so many renowned and glorious triumphs over the Turks, King Richard was trapped by his brothers in faith, seized by those who were believed to share his Christian profession – if only it were true![108] It is true that hidden treachery should be much more feared than open disputes; as it is written, 'it is easier to escape dispute than to avoid deceit.' What a shocking thing to happen! Although all his adversaries had not been able to withstand him, he was shut up by obscure people. Although the combined forces of the whole of Saladin's empire were not strong enough to overcome him, he was held prisoner in Germany.[109]

---

106. 'After a long...December' is not in MSS A or B. Our author has completely omitted the incident which led to the duke's hatred of Richard: Richard of Devizes, pp. 46–7, and see p. 221 note 68, above. 'Ansbert' gives two further reasons for Richard's arrest, although the banner incident was the most important. Richard had captured the Emperor Isaac of Cyprus and his wife, who were related to Duke Leopold; and the duke suspected that Richard was behind the assassination of Marquis Conrad, who was the duke's first cousin. 'Ansbert' also gives a letter from King Philip of France to Leopold, dated early 1193, just after Richard's arrest, accusing Richard of bringing about the marquis' death. Our author rejects this accusation below.
107. By King Philip of France: Appleby (1965), p. 111.
108. MSS A and B state in place of this exclamation, 'in name only.'
109. Here MSS A and B add: 'How difficult it is for those brought up in liberty to be at the beck and call of others.' What follows is only in MS C, until it joins A and B again at: 'the king was released from captivity'.

What a treacherous turn of events! The renowned king was shamefully treated, and even though he was not in chains he had inappropriate guards. There is certainly nothing more annoying for royal blood than to be subject to the authority of unworthy people and be at the beck and call of enemies. The freeborn are anxious to avoid anything disagreeable or disordered. In any case, experiences are more damaging when they have not been encountered before.

Some of his accusers may claim that King Richard deserved his maltreatment because he was guilty of the marquis' death; but there is in fact greater authority for his innocence, and this defence comes from a foreigner, rather than being envious slander whispered by someone or other. While Duke Leopold of Austria was holding the king in prison – perhaps on the sole grounds of that suspicion or perhaps on the request of certain crooked people[110] – he received a letter sent to him on the subject of the marquis' death. It went as follows:[111]

> The Old Man of the Mountain to Leopold, duke of Austria, greeting.
>
> Since a great many kings and princes overseas accuse Richard, king and lord of England, of the death of the marquis, I swear by God, who reigns eternally, and by the law that we hold, that he had no blame in his death. In fact the cause of the marquis' death was this. One of our brothers was coming in a ship from Saltheya [Antalya] to our region and a storm happened to drive him into Tyre. The marquis had him captured and killed, and seized much money from him. We sent our messengers to the marquis and instructed him to give back our brother's money to us, and make his peace with us for our brother's death. He did not wish to do this, rejected our messengers, and blamed the death of our brother on Lord Reginald of Sidon. But through our friends we discovered the truth: that he had him killed and seized his money.
>
> We sent another messenger to him, named Edrisus, whom he

110. King Philip of France and Count John of Mortain.
111. This is also in Ralph of Diceto, pp. 127–8; presumably our author took it from there. William Longchamp, King Richard's chancellor, sent the letter to Ralph of Diceto in 1196 so that he could insert it into his chronicle. It is unlikely to be genuine, although the contents may be true, but the original source is unclear. It is written in a very simplistic Latin, quite unlike MS C's usual rhetorical style.

wanted to drown in the sea; but our friends quickly made him leave Tyre, and he came swiftly to us and informed us what had happened. From that hour we longed to kill the marquis. Then we sent two brothers to Tyre, who killed him openly and before almost all the people of Tyre.

This, then, was the cause of the marquis' death, and we assure you that Lord Richard, king of England, had no blame for this death of the marquis. If anyone should do harm to the lord king of England because of this, they act unjustly and without cause. You should know for certain that we never kill anyone in this world for reward or money, unless they have previously harmed us.

You should know that we wrote this letter in our house at our castle of Messiac in the middle of September, in the presence of our brothers, and we have sealed it with our seal, in the year 1505 from Alexander.[112]

This establishes without a doubt that the king was innocent, because voluntary confession is rightly preferable to a falsely conceived presumption of guilt. Yet there seems to be no space for reason when headlong willfulness is controlled by its own random impulses; and 'it is no crime if it has good reason.'

At last by God's clemency, his own efforts and the management of those faithful to him, the king was released from captivity - although money played a large part in the negotiations, because it was known that he could pay much - and he was set free.[113] After a successful journey he reached England at Sandwich on [[114]]. Four days later he reached

112. i.e. September 1193. The leader of the Assassins is dating by the Seleucid era, which was named after Seleucus I Nicator (c.358-281 BC). He accompanied Alexander the Great in his campaigns in Asia and after Alexander's death became Satrap of Babylon (in what is now Iraq). In 316 BC he lost Babylon and fled to Egypt, but regained the city 1 September 312 BC. The Seleucid era dates from his recovery of Babylon.

113. MSS A and B then state: 'Restored at last to his native soil and the kingdom of his fathers, in a short time he pacified the dissent in the kingdom as he wished.' The rest of this paragraph is only in MS C and most of it has been taken almost verbatim from Ralph of Diceto, 2 p. 114. For this, see also Roger of Howden, *Chronica*, 3 pp. 238-40; Ralph of Coggeshall, pp. 62-4.

114. MS C has no date here. Diceto (2 p. 114) states 20 March, 1194; Roger of Howden, *Chronica*, 3 p. 235, and Ralph of Coggeshall, p. 62, state 13 March. The compiler of MS C obviously decided to leave a blank until the point could be settled, intending to fill it in later: Stubbs (1864), p. 446.

London. The city was crowned with great exultation, and he was solemnly received in the church of St Paul by a procession of the clergy and laity. Afterwards he remained for three days in his palace at Westminster. From there he went on a pilgrimage to Bury St Edmund's, where he gave that precious banner which belonged to the emperor of Cyprus as an offering.[115] Turning towards Nottingham next, within three days he received the surrender of the defenders.[116] He kept Easter at Northampton. On the Sunday after Easter he was crowned at Winchester.[117] Hubert, archbishop of Canterbury,[118] performed the divine service, and King William of Scotland was present. In a short time he pacified the dissent in the kingdom as he wished.

Afterwards [12 May 1194][119] he crossed over to Normandy, and prepared himself to drive back the unjustified and unrestrained incursions of his rival, i.e. the king of France. He threw back his invasion with repeated repulses, powerfully recovering his alienated rights and more by spear and sword.[120]

[Postscript: MS C only]

King Richard displayed three astonishing and remarkable virtues, which are very seldom found together in one person. He was extremely active in arms, showed foresight in giving advice, and was effective with words. Each of these certainly glorify a person, but he was endowed with all of them. He employed each of them according to circumstances,

---

115. See Bk. 2 ch. 33, p. 187 above. This sentence is not in Diceto's work.
116. Nottingham castle was being held by the supporters of Count John, who was in France with King Philip.
117. This could be a ceremonial crownwearing, but Appleby argues that it was a ceremonial recrowning: Appleby (1965), p. 135.
118. Previously bishop of Salisbury.
119. Roger of Howden, *Chronica*, 3 p. 251.
120. MSS A and B end here. The Norman Pipe Rolls indicate that during these campaigns Richard employed Saracens at Domfront, Maine in autumn 1193 or 1194, apparently during a siege of the castle. One hundred and nine pounds, nine shillings was paid, and Reginald Cruiete, who brought the Saracens, was paid four pounds four shillings each day for fifty-seven days. One Gibelin Saracen received 50 shillings in part payment for his horse, while eight pounds, eighteen shillings and nine pence was paid for the Saracens' clothing: see Stapleton, T. (ed.) (1842), *Magnus Rotulus Scaccarii Normanniae*, 1 p. 221. I am grateful to Dr Vince Moss for drawing this reference to my attention.

using arms against his enemies, advice for his friends, and words for everyone.[121]

No other prince was ever more ready than he to show favour and respect towards the clergy and ecclesiastics. What is more, no one was ever more acute at detecting the character of individuals at sight, so that no unworthy person or anyone of base character or whose conscience accused them of cowardice could ever bear the king's presence. He had learnt that exterior appearance often reveals the interior state and that human expression is formed by the cast of the mind within. Hence he only considered those who were recommended by their fine character or marked out by their singular prowess as worthy of his friendship and companionship. Indeed, what could unite the minds of equals more effectively than similarity of character? He only took pleasure in the companionship of knights who were such as he knew himself to be.

On this subject, it is said of Caesar Augustus that he admitted two people to his friendship and favour principally because of the particular virtues he had found in each of them: Maecenas because of his modest silence and Agrippa because of his patient hard work.[122] No one ruled at a more fortunate time than this Caesar, when the Author of Time deigned to be born![123] In having comrades and friends whose outstanding characters commended them, King Richard was not unlike this Caesar. At no time could his noble soul bear to be inactive; and although those jealous of Success may frequently strive after her rewards, they cannot deprive their stepmother of her glorious renown.[124]

When he had been released from prison and returned to England, he was concerned about[125] royal prestige. Therefore he endeavoured with care to profit posterity as much as he preceded it. He believed that in this way he would both be serving God and benefitting his people and

---

121. Gerald of Wales, *Liber de Principis Instructione*, p. 248, gave a similar assessment of Richard, describing him as active in arms, generous, and steadfast in mind and soul.

122. Our author, here the compiler of MS C, seems to be showing off his classical education by referring to Suetonius, *Vitae XII Caesarum*, Divus Augustus LXVI; but has confused the reference. Suetonius states that Augustus wished that his friend M. Agrippa had more patience and Maecenus could hold his tongue.

123. See Luke's Gospel ch. 2 v. 1.

124. i.e. simply being jealous is not enough to win the renown that the source of their jealousy has won; another side-swipe at King Richard's detractors.

125. *Mesciens*, which Stubbs (1864), p. 447 amended to *metiens* 'weighing up'. *Mesciens* seems to mean 'misknowing', i.e. 'doubting', 'unsure about'.

kingdom, as the wise man wrote: 'A prudent king is the anchor of his people' [Wisdom of Solomon ch. 6 v. 24]. So he wanted competent persons to be legitimately appointed without delay to the vacant bishoprics and abbacies.

Again, as soon as he arrived in the country he issued a precept ordering that the sea ports were to be guarded so that no foreign or even native ships could carry grain or any other type of food to foreign kingdoms, as they had seen in the past. His intention was that England would not be deprived of plentiful supplies of her own produce.

Again, he established that the quarter and bushel measures and other measures used for selling grain, which at that time varied greatly from place to place, should be uniform throughout the whole kingdom.[126] So that no one could make them smaller or damage them in any way, he arranged for iron rings to be fixed around the top edges of these containers. Similarly, he ordered the common gallon to be made a legal measure for tubs and buckets and casks.[127] Royal measures of this sort were to be kept by the officials of each shire and the provosts of each city to approve the correct measures and detect the false ones.

Again, all woven cloth was to be throughout its length two ells in width between the edges commonly called the 'lists' [90 inches or 230cm between the selvages]. Furthermore, cloth was to be woven consistently throughout without anything fraudulent being introduced into it. If anything defective was found, either a different material introduced into the cloth or a fault in the weaving, whether it was woven in this country or brought in from somewhere else it would be publicly burned by the royal officials, notwithstanding anybody's authority or influence. Thus no one could hope to gain anything through fraud. In vendors' stalls previous to this cloths of the best colour had been hung against each other so that with the reflection of adjoining colours even a faked colour could not be seen properly and seemed better than it was. As there was only the reflection of forged colours to light that shadowy place, by this means sellers outwitted the shrewdness of their customers.

The king commanded that all this deceitful covering was to be removed, so that the material and form of the cloths could be judged as they should be, in the open light of day. He also ordered iron ells to be made, which no one could shorten.

---

126. These regulations and those on the sale of cloth were in Richard's assize of weights and measures: see Roger of Howden, *Chronica*, 4 pp. 33–4.
127. The gallon remained a legal measure in England until 1996.

Again, he set up proctors for the Jews, who enforced justice between the Jews and could determine a case between Christian and Jew if any dispute should arise. Also, detecting from frequent complaints that the Jews were craftily forging charters, he laid down that no secret contracts were to be made between Catholics and Jews. Contracts should be solemnly made with the knowledge of and witnessed by certain people who were appointed to do this, and records should be produced in triplicate. One of these would be kept by the fiscal officers, the next in the reliable custody of a worthy man, and the third by the Jewish creditor. In this way nothing could be contrived as it used to be, because it would be disproved when the copies of the contract held by the others were brought out.

Again, so that no Christian would be apprehended for usury, there was to be no agreement to repay more than had been lent. If anyone had taken from another as security for a loan rent or lands or anything else which produced an annual income and had received the principal of the debt, the pledged property should return to the original owner even if the agreed term of the agreement was not yet complete. If anyone was convicted of acting against this statute they would be punished in the penury of prison for a year and a day, and afterwards be subject to the royal mercy.

These things and others like them which were very necessary to the people of the country were established by the king out of his zeal for justice and were observed in their entirety for all his time.

Again, as soon as he landed in Normandy he met his brother John, who was then a count. The latter threw himself at the king's feet, seeking mercy for his crimes. The king immediately pardoned him. His excellence of mind did not deign to punish an inferior, thinking it sufficient that he had the power to avenge himself.

Again, he happened to notice that some of the churches in the countryside did not have silver chalices.[128] When he learnt that they had previously been taken because of his ransom, he seemed to blame himself for the divine offices being unsuitably celebrated in this respect. He ordered a great many chalices to be made in various places and distributed all over the place to the needy churches. However, his premature death prevented this and the restitution was not completed. The state of affairs is always altered by a change in personnel, and after the death of whoever issued a mandate, the mandate also expires.

128. On this, see Roger of Howden, *Chronica*, 3 p. 290.

Therefore, as there is no more material worthy of eloquence, we have decided to suspend our pen from further writing until it is judged that this work should be resumed in order to tell more of the magnificent deeds thought worthy of praiseworthy memory, in which his name resounds by the grace of God.

Here ends the Itinerary of the Pilgrims and the deeds of King Richard. May the loving-kindness of Him who wishes that none may perish have mercy on his soul: the Saviour of the World, Jesus Christ our Lord, to Whom be praise, power, and authority. Amen.

Bibliography

This is a list of the sources used in the preparation of this translation and the footnotes.

Unprinted source

Guy of Bazoches, *Cronosgraphia*, BN lat. 4998.

Primary Sources

Chronicles are listed under author where author is known, and under the first word of the title (excluding the article) where they are anonymous. Collections of sources by different authors are listed under the editor's name; translations and editions of the *Itinerarium* are listed under the name of the editor or translator.

Ambroise (1897), *Estoire de Guerre Sainte: Histoire en vers de la troisième croisade,* ed. G. Paris, Paris: Imprimerie Nationale. [There is a translation by Hubert, M. J., and La Monte, J. L. (1976): see secondary sources, below. A new translation is being prepared by M. Ailes.]

Ansbert: see *Historia de Expeditione Friderici Imperatoris.*

Archer, T. A. (1889, 1978), *The Crusade of Richard I*, New York: G. P. Putnam's Sons; AMS Print.

Bahā' al-Dīn ibn Shaddād (1897), *The Life of Saladin,* trans. C. W. Wilson and C. R. Conder, London: Palestinian Pilgrims Text Society.

Bohn, H. (ed.) (1848, 1900), *Chronicles of the Crusades: contemporary narratives of the crusade of Richard Coeur de Lion by Richard of Devizes and Geoffrey de Vinsauf and of the crusade of Saint Louis by the Lord John de Joinville,* London: H. G. Bohn, George Bell and Sons.

Brundage, J. (1962), *The Crusades: a documentary survey,* Milwaukee, Wisconsin: Marquette University Press.

Le Charroi de Nîmes (1931), ed. J.-L. Perrier, CFMA, Paris: Champion Editeur.

La Chanson d'Aspremont (1923), ed. L. Brandin, 2 vols., CFMA 19, Paris: Champion Editeur.

La Chanson de Roland (1942), ed. F. Whitehead, Oxford: Basil Blackwell. [Translated as 'The Song of Roland', trans. G. Burgess, Penguin Books.]

Chrétien de Troyes (1981), *Le Conte du Graal (Perceval),* ed. F. Lecoy, 2 vols., *Le romans de Chrétien de Troyes éditées d'après la copie de Guiot*, 5-6, CFMA 100, 103, Paris: Champion Editeur.

Chronique d'Ernoul et de Bernard le Trésorier (1871), ed. L de Mas Latrie, SHF, Paris: Jules Renouard.

Chroust, A. (ed.) (1928), *Quellen zur Geschichte des Kreuzzuges Kaiser Fried-*

richs I. Monumenta Germaniae Historica: Scriptores rerum Germanicarum nova series 5, Berlin: Weidmannsche Verlagsbuchhandlung.

The Conquest of Jerusalem and the Third Crusade; Sources in Translation (1996) trans. P. W. Edbury, Aldershot: Scolar Press.

La continuation de Guillaume de Tyr (1184–97), (1982), ed. M. R. Morgan, Paris: Paul Geuthner. [Translated in *Conquest of Jerusalem*, above.]

Delaville le Roulx, J. (ed.) (1894–1906), *Cartulaire Général de l'ordre de S. Jean de Jérusalem, 1100–1310*, 4 vols., Paris: E. Leroux.

De Ortu Waluuanii (1898), in Bruce, J. D., '*De Ortu Waluuanii*: an Arthurian romance now first edited from the Cottonian MS Faustina B VI of the British Museum', *Proceedings of the Modern Language Association of America*, 13. [There is a translation by Day, M. L. (1984), *The Rise of Gawain, Nephew of Arthur*, New York: Garland.]

Epistola de Morte Friderici Imperatoris, in Chroust, A. (1928).

Eracles: Estoire de Eracles Empereur et la Conqueste de la Terre d'Outremer in *RHC Occ* 2.

Gerald of Wales (1891), *Liber de Principis Instructione*, ed. G. F. Werner, in *Giraldi Cambriensis Opera*, 8, RS 21, London: Eyre and Spottiswode.

Gerald of Wales (1867), *Expugnatio Hibernica*, ed. J. F. Dimock, in *Giraldi Cambriensis Opera* 5, RS 21, London: Eyre and Spottiswode.

Hallam, E. (ed.) (1989), *Chronicles of the Crusades – Eyewitness Accounts of the Wars between Christianity and Islam*, London: Weidenfeld and Nicolson.

Historia de Expeditione Friderici Imperatoris, der so-genannte Ansbert, in Chroust, A. (1928).

Historia Peregrinorum, in Chroust, A. (1928).

L'Histoire de Guillaume le Maréchal (1891–1901), ed. P. Meyer, 3 vols., SHF, Paris: Librarie Renouard.

Ibn al-Athīr (1872), *El-Kāmel Altevarykh*, in *RHC Or* 1–2.

'Imād al-Dīn al-Iṣfahānī (1972), *Conquête de la Syrie et de la Palestine par Saladin (al-Fath al qwsī fī l-fath al qudsī)*, trans. H. Massé, Paris: Librarie orientaliste Paul Geuthner.

Die lateinische Fortsetzung Wilhelms von Tyrus (1934), ed. M. Salloch, Leipzig: Kommission-Verlag Hermann Eichblatt.

Libellus de Expugnatione Terrae Sanctae per Saladinum (1875), in Ralph of Coggeshall (1875).

Le Livre d'Artus (1916, 1979), 7 of Sommer, H. O. (ed.) (1908–16, 1979), *The Vulgate Version of the Arthurian Romances*, 7 vols., Washington: Carnegie Institution and New York: AMS Print.

Mayer, H. (1962), *Das Itinerarium Peregrinorum. Eine zeitgenössische englishe Chronik zum dritten Kreuzzug in ursprünglicher Gestalt*, Stuttgart: Anton Hersemann.

Michael the Syrian (1899–1910), in *Le Chronique de Michel le Syrien, Patriarche Jacobite d'Antioche (1166–99)*, trans. J. B. Chabot, 4 vols., Paris: E. Leroux.

Monachi Florentini Acconensis Episcopi de recuperatione Ptolemaidae Liber (1870), ed. W. Stubbs, in Roger of Howden (1868–71), *Chronica*, vol. 3.

Morawski, J. (ed.) (1925), *Proverbes français antérieurs au XV siècle*, CFMA 47, Paris: Champion.

Narratio Itineris Navalis ad Terram Sanctam, in Chroust, A. (1928).

Neophytus, 'De calamitibus Cypri', in Stubbs, W. (1864), *Chronicles and Memorials* 1.

Ralph of Coggeshall (1875), *Chronicon Anglicanum,* ed. J. Stevenson, RS 66, London: Longman.

Ralph of Diceto (1876), *Ymagines Historiarum,* 2 in Stubbs, W., ed., *The Historical Works of Master Ralph of Diceto,* 2 vols., RS 68, London: Longman.

Recueil des Historiens des Croisades (1841-1906), L'Academie des Inscriptions de Belles-Lettres, 16 vols., Paris: Imprimerie Nationale.

Recueil des Historiens des Croisades: Historiens Occidentaux (1841-95), L'Academie des Inscriptions de Belles-Lettres, 5 vols., Paris: Imprimerie Nationale.

Recueil des Historiens des Croisades: Historiens Orientaux (1872-1906), L'Academie des Inscriptions de Belles-Lettres, 5 vols., Paris: Imprimerie Nationale.

Röhricht, R. (ed.) (1893, 1904), *Regesta Regni Hierosolymitani,* 2 vols., Innsbrück: Libraria Academica Wagneriana.

Richard of Devizes (1963), *The Chronicle of Richard of Devizes of the Time of King Richard the First,* ed. and trans. J. Appleby, London and Edinburgh: Nelson.

Rigord (1882), *Chronique,* 1 in Delaborde, H. F. *Oeuvres de Rigord et de Guillaume le Breton, historiens de Philippe Auguste,* 2 vols., Paris: Librarie Renouard.

Roger of Howden (1867), *Gesta Regis Henrici Secundi,* ed. W. Stubbs, 2 vols., RS 49, London: Longman.

Roger of Howden (1868-71), *Chronica,* ed. W. Stubbs, 4 vols., RS 51, London: Longman. [Translated by H. T. Riley (1853), as *The Annals of Roger of Hoveden.*]

Roger of Wendover (1886-9), ed. H. R. Hewlett, 3 vols., RS 84, London: Longman.

Saladin, chanson de geste du Deuxième cycle de la Croisade (1972), ed. L. S. Crist, Geneva: Librarie Droz.

Stapleton, T. (ed.) (1842-4), *Magnus Rotulus Scaccarii Normanniae sub regibus Angliae (1180-1201),* 2 vols., London: London Society of Antiquaries.

Stubbs, W. (1864), *Chronicles and Memorials of the Reign of Richard I,* 1: *Itinerarium Peregrinorum et gesta regis Ricardi, auctore, ut videtur, Ricardo canonico Sanctae Trinitatis Londoniensis,* RS 38, London: Longman.

Theoderich's description of the Holy Places (1891), trans. A. Stewart, London: Palestine Pilgrims Text Society.

Walter Map (1983), *De Nugis Curialium,* ed. and trans. M. R. James, C. N. L. Brooke and R. A. D. Mynors, Oxford: Oxford University Press.

William of Newburgh (1884), *Historia Rerum Anglicanum,* 1-2 in Howlett, R. (ed), (1884-9), *Chronicles of the Reigns of Stephen, Henry II and Richard I,* 4 vols., RS 82, London: Longman. [There is a translation by J. Stevenson, 1856.]

'Ein zeitgenössisches Gedict auf die Belagerung Accons' (1881), ed. H. Prutz, *Forschungen zur Deutschen Geschichte,* 21, 449-94.

Secondary sources

Appleby, J. (1965), *England Without Richard, 1189-99,* London: G. Bell and Sons.

Barber, M. (1993), *The New Knighthood: A History of the Order of the Temple,* Cambridge: Cambridge University Press.

Borchardt, K. (1994), 'Two forged alms-collecting letters used by the Hospitallers in Franconia', in Barber, M. (ed.), *The Military Orders: Fighting for the Faith and Caring for the Sick,* Aldershot: Variorum.

Brand, C. M. (1968), *Byzantium Confronts the West, 1180-1204*, Cambridge, Mass.: Harvard University Press.

Brewer, J. (1861), introduction to *Giraldi Cambrensis Opera*, 1, RS 21, London: Longmans.

Brundage, J. (1971), 'A Transformed Angel: The Problem of the Crusading Monk', in *Studies in Medieval Cistercian History presented to Jeremiah F. Sullivan*, introduction by J. F. O'Callaghan, Cistercian Studies Series no.13, Spenser, Mass.: Cistercian Publications. Reprinted in Brundage, J. (1991), *The Crusades, Holy War and Canon Law*, Aldershot: Variorum.

Bulst-Thiele, M. L. (1964), review of H. Mayer, *Das Itinerarium Peregrinorum,* in *Historische Zeitscrift* 168.

Bulst-Thiele, M. L. (1965), 'Noch einmal das *Itinerarium Peregrinorum*', *Deutsches Archiv für Erforschung des Mittelalters,* 21.

Casson, L. (1971), *Ships and Seamanship in the Ancient World,* Princeton: Princeton University Press.

Demurger, A. (1993), *Vie et Mort de l'Ordre du Temple,* Paris, Éditions du Seuil.

Duparc-Quioc, S. (1955), *Le Cycle de la Croisade*, Paris: H. Champion.

Edbury, P. W. (1994), 'The Templars in Cyprus', in M. Barber, ed., *The Military Orders: Fighting for the Faith and Caring for the Sick*, Aldershot: Variorum.

Edbury, P. W. (1997), 'The Lyon *Eracles* and the Old French Continuations of William of Tyre', in Riley-Smith, J., Kedar, B. Z., and Hiestand, R. (eds), *Montjoie: Studies in Crusade History in honour of Hans Eberhard Mayer*, Aldershot: Ashgate.

Forey, A. (1992), *The Military Orders: From the Twelfth to the Early Fourteenth Centuries*, Basingstoke: Macmillan.

Gabrieli, F. (1969), *Arab Historians of the Crusades*, London: Routledge.

Galyon, A. (1978), '*De Ortu Walwanii* and the theory of Illumination', *Neophilologus*, 62.

Gibb, H. A. R. (1950), 'The Arabic sources for the life of Saladin', *Speculum,* 25.

Gillingham, J. (1982), 'Roger of Howden on Crusade', in Morgan, D. O. (ed.), *Medieval Historical Writing in the Christian and Islamic Worlds*, London: School of Oriental and African Studies.

Gillingham, J. (1984), 'Richard I and the Science of War in the Middle Ages', in Gillingham, J. and Holt, J. C. (eds), *War and Government in the Middle Ages: Essays in honour of J. O. Prestwich,* Cambridge: D. S. Brewer.

Hamilton, B. (1978), 'The Elephant of Christ: Reynald of Châtillon', in Baker, D. (ed.), *Religious Motivation: Biographical and Sociological Problems for the Church Historian, Studies in Church History,* 15.

Hamilton, B. (1980), *The Latin Church in the Crusader States: The secular Church,* London: Variorum.

Haywood, J. (1991), *Dark Age Naval Power: A reassessment of Frankish and Anglo-Saxon activity*, London and New York: Routledge.

Holt, P. M. (1986), *The Age of the Crusades: the Near East from the eleventh century to 1517*, London and New York: Longman.

Hubert, M. J. and La Monte, J. L. (ed. and trans.) (1976), *The crusade of Richard Lion-Heart by Ambroise*, reprint, New York: Octagon Books.

Jacoby, D. (1993), 'Conrad, marquis of Montferrat, and the kingdom of Jerusalem

(1187–92), in Baletto, L. (ed.), *Atti del Congresso internazionle 'Dai feudi monferrine e dal Piemonte ai nuovi mondi oltre gli Oceani' Alessandria, 2–6 aprile 1990,* Biblioteca della Società di storia arte e archeologia per le province di Alessandria e Asti, no. 27, Alexandria: Accademica degli Immobili.

Lyons, M. and Jackson, D. (1982), *Saladin: the Politics of the Holy War,* Cambridge: CUP.

Mayer, H. (1972), 'Studies in the History of Queen Melisende of Jerusalem', *Dumbarton Oaks Papers,* 26.

Mayer, H. (1982), 'Henry II of England and the Holy Land', *English Historical Review,* 97.

Möhring, H. (1982), 'Eine Chronik aus der Zeit des dritten Kreuzzugs: das sogennante *Itinerarium Peregrinorum* 1', *Innsbrucker Historische Studien,* 5.

Nicholson, H. (forthcoming), 'Women on the Third Crusade', *Journal of Medieval History.*

The Oxford Classical Dictionary (1970), ed. N. G. L. Hammond, N. G. Leonprière et al., 2nd edn., Oxford: Oxford University Press.

The Oxford Dictionary of the Christian Church (1983), ed. F. L. Cross et al., 2nd edn., Oxford: Oxford University Press.

Paris, G. (1897): see Ambroise (1897), *Estoire.*

Pringle, D. (1984), 'King Richard I and the Walls of Ascalon', *Palestinian Exploration Quarterly,* 116.

Pringle, D. (1986), *The Red Tower (al-Burj al-Ahmar): settlement in the Plain of Sharon at the time of the Crusaders and Mamluks,* AD *1099–1516*, London: British School of Archaeology in Jerusalem.

Pringle, D. (forthcoming), 'Templar castles between Jaffa and Jerusalem', in Nicholson, H. (ed.), *The Military Orders: Welfare and Warfare,* Aldershot: Ashgate.

Radice, B. (1973), *Who's Who in the Ancient World,* Harmondsworth: Penguin.

Richards, D. (1993), "Imād al-Dīn al-Iṣfahānī: Administrator, Littérateur and Historian', in Shatzmiller, M. (ed.), *Crusaders and Muslims in twelfth century Syria,* Leiden: E. Brill.

Riché, P. (1993), *The Carolingians: A Family who Forged Europe,* Philadelphia: University of Pennsylvania Press.

Riley-Smith, J. (1973), *The Feudal Nobility of the Kingdom of Jerusalem,* London: Macmillan.

Riley-Smith, J. (1991), 'Family Tradition and Participation in the Second Crusade', in Gervers, M. (ed.), *The Second Crusade and the Cistercians,* New York: St Martin's Press.

Rogers, R. (1992), *Latin Siege Warfare in the Twelfth Century,* Oxford: Oxford University Press.

Schein, S. (1986), 'From "*Milites Christi*" to "*Mali Christiani*" – the Italian communes in western European literature', in Airaldi, G., and Kedar, B. (eds), *I comuni Italiani nel regno crociato di Geruslemme: atti del Colloquio 'The Italian Communes in the Crusading Kingdom of Jerusalem',* Geneva: Brigati Carucci.

Smail, R. C. (1956, 1995), *Crusading Warfare, 1097–1193*, 2nd edn. with introduction by C. Marshall, Cambridge: CUP.

Spufford, P. with Williamson, W. and Tolley, S. (1986), *Handbook of Medieval Exchange,* London: Royal Historical Society.

Tyerman, C. (1988), *England and the Crusades, 1095–1588*, Chicago and London: Chicago University Press.

Further reading

The bibliography above includes many scholarly studies of aspects of the Third Crusade, and translations of primary sources. At the time of writing there is no full-length study of the Third Crusade, but accounts of the Third Crusade are included in Holt (1986), and Lyons and Jackson (1982). For King Richard's role in the Third Crusade, see:

Gillingham, J. (1978), *Richard the Lionheart*, London: Weidenfeld and Nicolson.

Index